Creating Social Trust in Post-Socialist Transition

Political Evolution and Institutional Change
Bo Rothstein and Sven Steinmo, editors

Exploring the dynamic relationships among political institutions, attitudes, behaviors, and outcomes, this series is problem-driven and pluralistic in methodology. It examines the evolution of governance, public policy, and political economy in different national and historical contexts.

It will explore social dilemmas, such as collective action problems, and enhance understanding of how political outcomes result from the interaction among political ideas—including values, beliefs, or social norms—institutions, and interests. It will promote cutting-edge work in historical institutionalism, rational choice and game theory, and the processes of institutional change and/or evolutionary models of political history.

Also in the series

Restructuring the Welfare State: Political Institutions and Policy Change
Edited by Bo Rothstein and Sven Steinmo

The Problem of Forming Social Capital: Why Trust?
By Francisco Herreros

The Personal and the Political: How Personal Welfare State Experiences Affect Political Trust and Ideology
By Staffan Kumlin

Building a Trustworthy State in Post-Socialist Transition
Edited by János Kornai and Susan Rose-Ackerman

Creating Social Trust in Post-Socialist Transition
Edited by János Kornai, Bo Rothstein, and Susan Rose-Ackerman

Creating Social Trust in Post-Socialist Transition

Edited by
János Kornai,
Bo Rothstein,
and
Susan Rose-Ackerman

© János Kornai, Bo Rothstein, and Susan Rose-Ackerman, 2004

All rights reserved. No part of this book may be used or reproduced in any manner whatsoever without written permission except in the case of brief quotations embodied in critical articles or reviews.

First published 2004 by
PALGRAVE MACMILLAN™
175 Fifth Avenue, New York, N.Y. 10010 and
Houndmills, Basingstoke, Hampshire, England RG21 6XS
Companies and representatives throughout the world

PALGRAVE MACMILLAN is the global academic imprint of the Palgrave Macmillan division of St. Martin's Press, LLC and of Palgrave Macmillan Ltd. Macmillan® is a registered trademark in the United States, United Kingdom and other countries. Palgrave is a registered trademark in the European Union and other countries.

ISBN 1–4039–6449–1

Library of Congress Cataloging-in-Publication Data
    Creating social trust in post-socialist transition / edited by János Kornai, Bo Rothstein, and Susan Rose-Ackerman.
      p. cm.—(Political evolution and institutional change)
   A project of the Collegium Budapest.
   Includes bibliographical references and index.
   ISBN 1–4039–6449–1
    1. Social capital (Sociology) 2. Democracy. 3. Post-communism. 4. Economic development. I. Kornai, János. II. Rothstein, Bo, 1954-III. Rose-Ackerman, Susan. IV. Collegium Budapest. V. Series.

HM708.C73 2004
303.3'72—dc22   2003066426

A catalogue record for this book is available from the British Library.

Design by Newgen Imaging Systems (P) Ltd., Chennai, India.

First edition: June, 2004

10 9 8 7 6 5 4 3 2 1

Printed in the United States of America.

CONTENTS

List of Tables and Figures	vii
Notes on Contributors	ix
Preface *János Kornai and Susan Rose-Ackerman*	xiv
Participants in the Project	xviii
Introduction Bo Rothstein	1
Part I Social Capital and Democratic Transition	**11**
One Social Trust and Honesty in Government: A Causal Mechanisms Approach Bo Rothstein	13
Two Honesty, Trust, and Legal Norms in the Transition to Democracy: Why Bo Rothstein is Better Able to Explain Sweden than Romania Eric M. Uslaner and Gabriel Badescu	31
Part II Trust and the Business Environment	**53**
Three Measuring Trust in Transition: Preliminary Findings from 26 Transition Economies Martin Raiser, Alan Rousso, and Franklin Steves	55
Four Underground Financing in Russia Alena V. Ledeneva	71
Five How Trust is Established in Economic Relationships when Institutions and Individuals Are Not Trustworthy: The Case of Russia Vadim Radaev	91

Six	Establishing Confidence in Business Partners: Courts, Networks, and Relationships as Pillars of Support *Christopher Woodruff*	111
Seven	The Selective Use of State Capacity in Russia's Economy: Property Disputes and Enterprise Takeovers, 1998–2002 *Vadim Volkov*	126
Eight	Mafia Transplantation *Federico Varese*	148
Nine	Beyond Law Enforcement: Governing Financial Markets in China and Russia *Katharina Pistor and Chenggang Xu*	167
Part III	**Trust, Cooperation, and Success**	191
Ten	The Emergence of Trust Networks under Uncertainty: The Case of Transitional Economies—Insights from Social Psychological Research *Karen S. Cook, Eric R. W. Rice, and Alexandra Gerbasi*	193
Eleven	Blindness to Success: Social Psychological Objectives Along the Way to a Market Economy in Eastern Europe *György Csepeli, Antal Örkény, Mária Székelyi, and Ildikó Barna*	213
Author Index		241
Subject Index		246

LIST OF TABLES AND FIGURES

Tables

2.1	Trust and corruption across nations	40
2.2	Trust in other people and perceptions of corruption in Romania, 1995 World Values Survey	44
3.1	The quality of the courts in transition, 2002	64
3.2	Determinants of prepayment in transition countries, 2002: with characteristics of courts; simple correlations	65
3.3	Determinants of prepayment in transition countries, 2002: social and business networks	66
4.1	Types of extra-legal enforcement in Russia	85
5.1	Basic parameters of the sample of Russian firm owners and managers, 1997–98	92
5.2	Trust in institutions in Russia, 2000–01	95
5.3	Contract infringement in Russia (percent)	98
5.4	The most important personal features of business partners in Russia	98
6.1	Percentage of bill paid with delay (trade credit)	121
7.1	Bankruptcy statistics: Russian arbitration courts, 1995–2001	132
11.1	Attributions of success and wealth in 1991 by regions (percentages of "often" and "very often" responses)	222
11.2	Attributions of success and wealth in 1991 and 1996 in Eastern Europe (percentages of "often" and "very often" responses)	226

Figures

1.1	Universal and selective benefits and generalized trust, Sweden, 2000	24
2.1	Trust and corruption across nations	32
2.2	Correlation between trust and perceptions of corruption (WVS) and TI estimates of corruption, 1998	41

2.3	Correlation between confidence in legal system and perceptions of corruption (WVS) and TI estimates of corruption, 1998	42
3.1	Prepayment and trade credit, transition countries, 2002	59
3.2	Prepayment and GDP per capita, transition countries, 2002	60
3.3	Prepayment and governance, transition countries, 2002	60
3.4	Prepayment and economic reform, transition countries, 2002	61
4.1	The diversion of payment	77
6.1	Trade-off of reliability of customers and effectiveness of courts	115
7.1	The logic of enterprise takeovers	130
8.1	Factors that facilitate successful Mafia transplantation	153
8.2	Factors present in the unsuccessful Mafia transplantation in Rome	162
8.3	Factors present in the successful Mafia transplantation in Hungary	162
11.1	Attributions of success and wealth in 1991 (aggregated variables—means of five-degree scales)	223
11.2	Suspicion of success and wealth (aggregated variables—means of scales)	223
11.3	Attitudes toward the market economy based on positive internal attribution patterns for success and wealth	224
11.4	Percentages displaying attitude types toward the market economy in 1991, by regions	225
11.5	Attributions of success and wealth in 1991 and 1996 in Eastern Europe (aggregated variables—means of five-degree scales)	226
11.6	Suspicion of success and wealth in 1991 and 1996 in Eastern Europe (aggregated variables—means of five-degree scales)	227
11.7	Percentages showing attitude types toward the market economy in 1991 and 1996	227
11.8	Regional embeddedness and lack of confidence in the market economy, 1991	230
11.9	Regional embeddedness and special envy	232
11.10	Five years of transition and lack of confidence in the market economy	233
11.11	Five years of transition and special envy	234
11.12	Five years of transition and forced egalitarianism	235

NOTES ON CONTRIBUTORS

Gabriel Badescu is Associate Professor of Political Science at the Babes-Bolyai University, Cluj-Napoca, where he has taught since 1996. His publications include *Social Capital and Political Participation in Romania* (2001) and *Roma Population in the 2000 Romanian Local Elections* (2000). Badescu's edited books include *Social Capital and the Transition to Democracy*.

Ildikó Barna has an M.A. in Sociology from the Eötvös Loránd University, Budapest, where she now serves as a research assistant. At present she is doing her Ph.D. course at the Institute of Sociology. Her publications include *Survival Kit to SPSS* (2002), "The Interpretation of Trust in Empirical Research" (2001), and "Trends and Delusions" (2000), each coauthored.

Karen S. Cook, Ph.D., is currently the Ray Lyman Wilbur Professor of Sociology and the Cognizant Dean of the Social Sciences at Stanford University. She is the recent editor of *Trust in Society* (2001) and *Social Capital* (2001). She has published on social exchange networks, distributive justice, trust and physician–patient relationships. She is the coeditor of the *Annual Review of Sociology* and a member of the American Academy of Arts and Sciences.

György Csepeli is Professor of Sociology at the Eötvös Loránd University in Budapest. He holds a Doctor of Sciences degree from the Hungarian Academy of Sciences. He spent several years as visiting professor at various universities in the United States. He is a member of the Hungarian Sociological Association which he chaired in 1993. His research has focused on empirical studies of national identity in Hungary and Central Europe and on the sociological and sociopsychological problems of the Information Society. At present he serves as the Political State Secretary at the Ministry of Informatics and Communications, Hungary.

Alexandra M. Gerbasi received an M.A. from Stanford University in 2001 where now she is a Ph.D. candidate. Her research interests include social exchange theory, the emergence of trust under uncertainty, and the role of obligation in exchange.

János Kornai is Professor Emeritus at Harvard University and Emeritus Fellow at Collegium Budapest. He is the author of many books including *Anti-Equilibrium* (1972), *Economics of Shortage* (1980), and the *Socialist System: The Political Economy of Communism* (1992). He is an honorary doctor of several universities and has been a visiting professor at the Yale, Princeton, Stanford, and Stockholm universities and the London School of Economics. He is an honorary member of the American Academy of Arts and Sciences and the American Economic Association, and foreign member of numerous academies and other scholarly institutions. Currently, he serves as the President of the International Economic Association.

Alena V. Ledeneva is Reader in Russian Politics and Society at the School of Slavonic and East European Studies, University College, London. She studied economics at the Novosibirsk State University and social and political theory at the University of Cambridge (Newnham College, M.Phil. 1992; Ph.D. 1996). She is author of *Russia's Economy of Favours* (1998) and *Unwritten Rules: How Russia Really Works* (2001), coeditor of *Bribery and Blat in Russia* (2000) and *Economic Crime in Russia* (2000).

Antal Örkény is Professor of Sociology at the Institute of Sociology at the Eötvös Loránd University, Budapest. He holds the chair of the ELTE-UNESCO Minority Studies Department and is the director of the Minority Research Institute. His major research fields are cross-national surveys on social justice, national identity and national stereotypes, interethnic relations in the Carpathian Basin, attitudes, negative stereotypes, and prejudice against Gypsies. He has published eight monographs including the coauthored *Ideology and Political Beliefs in Hungary. The Twilight of State Socialism* and *Grappling with National Identity. How Nations See Each Other in Central Europe*.

Katharina Pistor is Associate Professor of Law at Columbia Law School. She has also taught at the Kennedy School of Government and worked at the Max Planck Institute for Foreign and International Private Law, Hamburg. Her main research interests are comparative law, comparative corporate governance, and the development of legal institutions with special emphasis on the evolution of law in transitional and emerging economies. Recent publications include the coauthored "The Evolution of Corporate Law" (2002) and the also coauthored "Economic Development, Legality, and the Transplant Effect" (2003).

Vadim Radaev received his Ph.D. in Economics at the Moscow State University and another Doctoral Degree in Economics and Sociology from the Institute of Economics, Russian Academy of Sciences. He is professor of the Higher School of Economics, Moscow, where he chairs the economic sociology department and also serves as the First Vice-Rector. He is editor-in-chief of the web journal *Economic Sociology*. He has published six books, including *Economic Sociology* (1997, in Russian), *Formation of New*

Rusian Markets (1998, in Russian), *Sociology of Markets* (2003, in Russian), and numerous articles in journals and edited volumes.

Martin Raiser is the Country Manager for Uzbekistan at the World Bank. Formerly he was Director for Country Strategy and Analysis at the EBRD. He joined the EBRD in 1996, coming from the Institute of World Economics in Kiel, where he was a research fellow and from where he holds a Ph.D. in Economics. He was an editor and contributor to the EBRD's Transition Report between 1997 and 2003 and was the lead economist for Central Asia. His research at the EBRD focused on corporate governance, the determinants of institutional change, the impact of reforms on transition outcomes, and the role of social capital in transition.

Eric R. W. Rice is sociologist at the University of California, Los Angeles, where he is a postdoctoral fellow. He took Ph.D. in Sociology from Stanford University in 2002. He is interested in how social uncertainty affects commitment formation and the use of power in social networks. He is also interested in utilizing theoretical work on social network processes to explain the development of risk-behaviors among populations vulnerable to HIV/AIDS.

Susan Rose-Ackerman is the Henry R. Luce Professor of Jurisprudence (Law and Political Science) at Yale University. She holds a Ph.D. in Economics from Yale and has held Guggenheim and Fulbright Fellowships. She has been a fellow at the Center for Advanced Study in the Behavioral Sciences and Collegium Budapest and was a visiting research fellow at the World Bank. Her most recent book is *Corruption and Government: Causes, Consequences and Reform* (Cambridge 1999). She has written widely on corruption, law and development, administrative law and regulatory policy, the nonprofit sector, and federalism and urban economics.

Bo Rothstein is August Röhss Professor in Political Science at Göteborg University in Sweden. He received his Ph.D. from the University of Lund in 1986. He was a visiting scholar at the Russell Sage Foundation, Cornell University, Harvard University, and the University of Washington in Seattle. Among his publications in English are *The Social Democratic State: The Swedish Model and the Bureaucratic Problems of Social Reforms; Just Institutions Matters: The Moral and Political Logic of the Universal Welfare State*. Recent publications in English are "Trust, Social Dilemmas and Collective Memory" (2000), "Social Capital in the Social Democratic State" (2001), and "The Universal Welfare State as a Social Dilemma" (2001).

Alan Rousso is currently Senior Political Counsellor at the European Bank for Reconstruction and Development, where he covers governance and anticorruption issues as well as political developments in Russia and the Western CIS states. Prior to joining the bank in 2001, he was Director of the Carnegie Endowment's Moscow center, was project manager at the East West Institute in New York, and taught on the political science faculties at

Dartmouth College, Cornell University, and Columbia University. He holds an M.A., M.Phil., and Ph.D. in Political Science from Columbia University.

Franklin Steves is a political analyst at the European Bank for Reconstruction and Development and a doctoral candidate in the Department of Government at the University of Essex. He holds an M.A. in international relations from the London School of Economics. His current research focuses on the international dimension and political economy of post-socialist regime change, particularly the role of international agencies in promoting democratic consolidation and the impact of regime change on transitional states' foreign relations. He has published articles and book chapters on the international dimension of regime change in Eastern Europe, the former Soviet Union, South America, and the Horn of Africa.

Mária Székelyi is Professor of Sociology at the Institute of Sociology of Eötvös Loránd University, Budapest and vice-director of the ELTE Institute of Sociology. Her major research fields are cross-national surveys on social justice, national identity and national stereotypes, interethnic relations in the Carpathian Basin, attitudes, negative stereotypes, prejudice against Gypsies, anti-Gypsy attitudes and discriminatory behavior among Hungarian police toward Gypsies and research methodology. She has published several articles and four monographs including: *Survival Kit to SPSS* (coauthored), and *Grappling with National Identity. How Nations See Each Other in Central Europe* (also coauthored).

Eric M. Uslaner is Professor of Government and Politics at the University of Maryland, College Park. He is the author of *The Moral Foundations of Trust* and coeditor of *Social Capital and Participation in Everyday Life* and *Social Capital and the Democratic Transition*, as well as eight other books and numerous articles in journals and edited volumes. His work focuses on social capital, legislative politics, democratization, and the Internet with an emphasis on the United States, Canada, Romania, Israel, and cross-national analyses.

Federico Varese is University Lecturer in Criminology at the University of Oxford and Fellow of Linacre College, Oxford. He obtained a D.Phil. in Sociology from the University of Oxford and has published papers in *Archives Européenes de Sociologie, Low Intensity Conflict and Law Enforcement, Political Studies, Cahiers du Monde Russe*, and *Rationality and Society*. His 2001 book, *The Russian Mafia*, was the recipient of the 2002 Ed Hewitt Book Prize in political economy.

Vadim Volkov is Chair of the Sociology Department of the High School of Economics, St. Petersburg Branch and Associate Professor of Sociology at the Department of Political Science and Sociology at the European University in St. Petersburg. In 1998, he was visiting professor at the University of Chicago. He received his Ph.D. in Sociology from the University of Cambridge in 1995. He is author of *Violent Entrepreneurs: The Use of Force in the Making of Russian Capitalism* (2002). His research interests include economic sociology, problems of state and violence, public and private security, comparative mafia, sociology of everyday life, and politics in the context of culture.

Christopher Woodruff is Associate Professor of Economics at the Graduate School of International Relations and Pacific Studies at UCSD. His primary research focus is on the development of markets in transition economies. Woodruff studies how firms do business with one another in environments in which inadequate legal systems make formal contracting difficult. Geographically, his research spans a broad area of the developing world: Mexico, Vietnam, and Eastern Europe. His research has been published in the *American Economic Review*, the *Quarterly Journal of Economics*, the *Journal of Law, Economics, and Organization*, the *Journal of Public Economics*, and other scholarly journals.

Chenggang Xu received his Ph.D. in Economics from Harvard University in 1991. He has taught in the Department of Economics, London School of Economics since then and is currently a lecturer (tenured in 1998). His publications, mainly concerned with institutions and transition, include "Incentives, Information, and Organizational Form" (2000), "Institutions, Innovations, and Growth" (1999), "Financial Institutions and the Financial Crisis in East Asia" (1999), "Why is China Different from Eastern Europe? Perspectives from Organization Theory" (1999), each coauthored.

PREFACE

The problems of dishonesty and distrust are ubiquitous in Eastern Europe and the Soviet successor states. These issues are aired daily in the press and on television and are discussed at home, at work, and among friends. Corruption, deception, lying, and abuse of trust are mentioned more often these days than they were before the change of system. Although distrust and dishonesty permeated social relations before the transition, these problems were concealed, or it was forbidden to talk about them.

Research on honesty and trust is wide ranging and covers many fields of inquiry. The Collegium Budapest project, Honesty and Trust: Theory and Experience in the Light of Post-Socialist Transformation, aimed to integrate that disparate activity and to draw some lessons for the transition countries. The project sought to foster integration in at least three senses: in research approaches, in international coverage, and in disciplinary reach.

The huge international literature on the subject centers around two major topics. One of these is *trust* and its relation to *social capital*. What is meant by these concepts? What helps or hinders their formation? What are the beneficial or detrimental effects of trust in its various guises, and how is it related to social capital and democratic consolidation? The second is concerned with the *institutional* roots of *dishonest behavior* and with the difficulty of promoting *honesty*. Many authors study various forms of dishonesty: corruption, conflicts of interest, deception of business partners or the state, or the theft of others' property.

In the world of science and scholarship, these two research themes have hardly been cognizant of each other. Exponents of one scarcely ever cite work of the other, let alone attend each other's conferences. The project set out to bring together some prominent representatives of each group and prompt them to exchange and integrate their ideas.

The group was *international*, with over 50 scholars recruited from 17 countries of the "East" and "West." Researchers came from Bulgaria, Canada, China, France, Germany, Hungary, Italy, Mexico, Norway, Poland, Romania, Russia, Sweden, Switzerland, Turkey, the United Kingdom, and the United States. (See the list of participants following the preface.) Some were experts on the post-socialist transition. Others were invited because they showed a willingness to learn and to cooperate with those who specialize in analyzing the post-socialist transition. Most importantly, the members of the group agreed to think seriously about what lessons could be drawn for the post-socialist region from research—both theoretical and empirical—dealing with other parts of the world.

The research was *interdisciplinary*. The disciplines represented were political science, economics, sociology, law, anthropology, and political philosophy. We hope that those who take the baton onward will be able to extend the cooperation further by including history and ethical philosophy.

If those doing research in neighboring topics hardly know each other's work, that was all the more so between different disciplines. The papers that participants submitted when they joined the project tended to cite works within their own discipline, mainly because that was almost exclusively what they had studied. This limitation relaxed somewhat in the course of the project. The personal conversations, seminars, and workshops helped to familiarize members of the group with each other's work and with the approaches, methodologies, methods of argument, and styles prevalent in "neighboring" disciplines.

Interdisciplinary work, apart from being thought-provoking and helping to enrich everyone's set of research tools, also exerts a disciplinary force in another sense. Every field becomes inured to its own, narrowly employed and narrowly understood jargon. Interdisciplinary discourse obliges people to talk and write in a way comprehensible to a wider intellectual circle. This also forces people to clarify their ideas.

Within each discipline, there is general acceptance of certain simplifying assumptions, abstract schemata, and accepted criteria for convincing argument or a valid defense of a statement. As one climbs out of one's disciplinary bunker, it immediately becomes clear that such "generally accepted" abstractions, simplified assumptions, or techniques of argument are by no means self-evident or convincing to exponents of another field. Interdisciplinary confrontation did indeed prompt the members of the group to explain themselves, revise lines of argument, and reappraise assumptions.

The purpose of the project was not to arrive at a uniform point of view. This was not a "task force" exercise designed to produce a joint report. On the contrary, it was designed to stimulate debate, and there were several important problems on which no agreement was reached. Respecting each other's points of view, the participants cooperated and differed in a friendly manner. That is natural enough in democracies with a long history behind them, but far from common in the post-socialist region of the world, where the academic world all too often reflects the impatience and antagonism of political divisions.

When a research group assembles to examine a big subject, there are a number of organizational principles to choose from. One possibility is to draw up in advance, plainly and accurately, a limited number of questions and designate clearly which members are expected to respond to which questions. If answers to one question are expected from several researchers, prior agreement is reached on methodological principles as well, so that the responses become comparable. The upshot of collective work organized in such a decisive, even strict, fashion will be a publication whose parts constitute a coherent, rigorously structured whole. Equally likely is a collection that is artificial and uninteresting.

The project directors were aware of this organizational strategy and its inherent advantages. Nonetheless, it was deliberately set aside in favor of a different course. Pursuing the integrating purpose outlined earlier meant drawing the members of the group from a very wide area. Recruiting leading researchers from different disciplines and countries meant allowing each to write on a subject of his or her own choice. The members could not be confined to a Procrustean bed of compulsory, previously formulated questions. The most important thing was to build on their individual initiatives and ideas to produce papers that spoke to the broad themes of our project.

Given the integrating objectives already described, it is hard to imagine a more favorable organizational setting than Collegium Budapest. This institution, founded in 1991 during the post-socialist transition's first great burst of organization and creation, belongs to a genus of scientific institutions usually referred to (after the original institute at Princeton) as "institutes for advanced study." Others include the Palo Alto Center for Advanced Study in the Behavioral Sciences, the Wissenschaftskolleg in Berlin (which initiated the foundation of Collegium Budapest), and similar bodies in the Netherlands, Norway, Romania, Sweden, and elsewhere. There is no teaching in such institutions, only research. Each operates with a small permanent staff, and most of the researchers are guest fellows invited for a year or less. Each institute is international and interdisciplinary in its makeup.

The fellows invited to Collegium Budapest pursue their research individually. But it has become a tradition to have one or two "focus groups" each year in which a number of scholars approach a specific theme. The project on Honesty and Trust was such a focus group, and it was the largest focus group in the Collegium's history.

Many of the authors of the studies in this book and its companion voulme, *Building a Trustworthy State in Post-Socialist Transition*, spent shorter or longer periods as fellows or visiting scholars at the Collegium. The interaction among them was not confined to a brief conference but lasted for weeks or months. The fellows had lunch together every day, and each author led an intensive seminar on his or her own research. Furthermore, there were many informal discussions that provided opportunities for exchanging views or debating about each others' ideas and writings. In addition, three workshops, each of two days, were organized at Collegium Budapest for fellows in residence along with invited experts. These larger gatherings were also attended by group members unable to spend an extended period at the Collegium. Results and findings were posted on the

Internet (http://www.colbud.hu/honesty-trust) as working documents while the research continued.

The most tangible products of this project were two volumes—*Building a Trustworthy State in Post-Socialist Transition* (edited by János Kornai and Susan Rose-Ackerman) and *Creating Social Trust in Post-Socialist Transition* (edited by János Kornai, Bo Rothstein, and Susan Rose-Ackerman). In addition, many members of the group will subsequently publish articles and books begun in Budapest. However, the success of the project should not be measured simply in terms of published pages. Another important product of the project was the discourse and the intellectual influence that members exerted on each other while at the Collegium Budapest, housed in a lovely Baroque building in the historic Castle District of the city. The spirit of that discourse, we hope, was valued by all participants who will disseminate it in their own environments.

We would like to express thanks on behalf of all group members for the intellectual inspiration contributed by the rector of Collegium Budapest, Professor Imre Kondor, the institution's permanent fellows, and the research fellows whose visits to the Collegium coincided with the project. We are especially grateful to Katalin Szabó, János Varga, and the Collegium staff for their manifold kind and attentive help and to Julianna Parti for her excellent editorial assistance in preparing the manuscript and the indices. Bo Rothstein, a member of the focus group, assisted us with the editorship of *Creating Social Trust in Post-Socialist Transition*, and we are very grateful for his contributions. David Pervin, the books' editor at Palgrave, has been a great help in shepparding the book through the production process.

We would also like to extend our sincere thanks to the Bank of Sweden Tercentenary Foundation and the William and Flora Hewlett Foundation for their generous financial support for the project. Without their support the project would not have been able to go forward.

September 2003

JÁNOS KORNAI
SUSAN ROSE-ACKERMAN
Project Directors

PARTICIPANTS IN THE PROJECT

Bruce Ackerman, Yale University, New Haven CT
Jens C. Andvig, Norsk Utenrikspolitisk Institutt, Oslo
Gabriel Badescu, Babes-Bolyai University, Cluj-Napoca
Ildikó Barna, Eötvös Loránd University, Budapest
Bernard Chavance, University of Paris 7, CEMI, EHESS
Karen S. Cook, Stanford University, Palo Alto CA
Bruno Frey, University of Zurich
Scott Gehlbach, University of Wisconsin, Madison
Russell Hardin, New York University
Joel. S. Hellman, World Bank Institute, Washington DC
Cynthia M. Horne, Seton Hall University, Newark NJ
Rasma Karklins, University of Illinois, Chicago
Daniel Kaufmann, World Bank Institute, Washington DC
János Kornai, Harvard University and Collegium Budapest
Ivan Krastev, Centre for Liberal Strategies, Sofia
Jana Kunicova, California Institute of Technology, Pasadena
Alena A. Ledeneva, SSEES, London
Natalia Letki, Nuffield College, Oxford
Margaret Levi, University of Washington, Seattle
Larissa Adler Lomnitz, Universidad Nacional Autonoma de Mexico
Marie Mendras, CERI, Paris
Julius Moravcsik, Stanford University, Palo Alto CA
John Mueller, Ohio State University
Helen Nissembaum, New York University
Claus Offe, Humboldt-Universitaet, Berlin
Annamária Orbán, Central European University, Budapest
Antal Örkény, Eötvös Loránd University, Budapest
Margit Osterloh, University of Zurich
Katharina Pistor, Columbia Law School, New York City
Vadim Radaev, State University, Moscow
Martin Raiser, World Bank, Washington DC

Participants in the Project

Susan Rose-Ackerman, Yale University, New Haven CT
Bo Rothstein, Göteborg University
András Sajó, Central European University, Budapest
David Shugarman, York University, North York, Canada
Mária Székelyi, Eötvös Loránd University, Budapest
Piotr Sztompka, Jagiellonian University, Krakow
Davide Torsello, Max Planck Institute for Social Anthropology, Halle/Saale
Eric M. Uslaner, University of Maryland
Alexandra Vacroux, Harvard University and Center for Economic and Financial Research, Moscow
Federico Varese, University of Oxford
Vadim Volkov, The European University at St. Petersburg
Christopher Woodruff, University of California, San Diego
Chenggang Xu, London School of Economics
Ekaterina Zhuravskaya, Center for Economic and Financial Research, Moscow
László Zsolnai, Budapest University of Economic Sciences

Introduction

BO ROTHSTEIN

Gradualism Versus Shock Therapy

After the fall of the Soviet system, an intense debate started about how the transformation to Western style democracy and market economy should be carried out. Many economists argued for radical and rapid reforms of massive privatization and deregulations. What was needed was a "shock therapy," which would once and for all defeat the old system of central control and planning. Others pointed at the many difficult problems such a massive and rapid privatization would bring about in societies lacking many of the most basic legal and administrative institutions needed for markets to prevail, especially institutions securing property rights. This so-called gradualist argument was that institutions had to be enacted before any large-scale privatization of the state-owned industries should take place (for overviews and comments on this debate see Kornai 2000; Roland 2000).

However, both sides in this debate agreed on one basic premise, namely that the rule of law must be established to make a market-based economy work (Pejovich 1997; Weingast 1993, 1997). Rule-of-law institutions must secure property rights through the enforcement of legally produced private contracts and must safeguard market agents against arbitrary actions by the various branches of the state apparatus. Such institutions can, following George Tsebelis, be labeled "efficient" because they are not enacted in order to redistribute resources to a special group or certain agents known beforehand. Contrary to "redistributive" institutions, efficient institutions are supposed to serve the collective interest of all market agents by lowering their transaction costs (Tsebelis 1990). This means that market agents can trust that other market agents will respect agreements they have entered into; they know that if they do not, the agent can turn to an impartial court for remedies. They also know that tax rules and other government regulations will be implemented in a way that does not give improper advantage to some agents. In any case, the disagreement between the "shock therapist" and the "gradualists" was not about the importance of such efficient institutions, but on how they would come about. The dominant view, especially among neoclassical economists, was that a swift and massive privatization would in itself create a demand for efficient institutions. A large majority of the agents in the markets would soon realize that they would be better off with impartial and uncorrupted institutions, and this self-interest would be transformed into political pressure for the creation of credible and efficient institutions. This reasoning was sometimes linked to a functional view of social causation—the needs of the market system would, by some hidden device and by its internal logic, create the necessary demand for functional institutions. And some kind of intrinsic "invisible hand" will create this functional devise (Åslund 1995).

The gradualists' argument against this view was that if the institutions for protecting property rights and democratic freedoms were not secured in the first place, the privatization reforms risked setting off the economic system in a negative direction, which by its own logic of operation would be difficult to change. A vicious circle could be set in motion if the right type of efficient institutions were not established early in the transition. Dysfunctional institutions would lead to the entrenchment of political, and thereby economic, corruption and result in a predatory capitalism (Hedlund 1999). The argument was that without due attention to the sequencing of institutional reforms and privatization, the political and economic system could develop in a very wrong direction that would be difficult to change later. This idea was built on the new institutional economics, where concepts such as increasing returns and path-dependency had become central. According to Douglass C. North, one of the most prominent scholars behind this theory, there was no reason to believe that the post-socialist societies would automatically create efficient institutions. On the contrary, history showed that most societies did not (1998b: 494).

According to North: "Neoclassical theory is simply an inappropriate tool to analyze and prescribe policies that will induce development. It is concerned with markets, not with how markets develop" (1998a: 247). He also says that institutions are not only important for creating market compatible incentives; the most important function of institutions is the role they have in the formation of "belief systems" that are, or are not, compatible with a market-based economy.

The Mystery of Institutions

This view has recently been stressed by the work of development economist, Hernando de Soto. As shown in his much-cited book *The Mystery of Capital* (2001), assets in the form of physical capital are a substantially more complex phenomenon than is generally believed in the Western world. According to de Soto, physical assets can be converted to capital only after the society has created a legal terminology to describe them. A piece of land, for instance, does not become physical capital until the society has instituted the legal term "real property" and created institutions in which the size, location, and ownership of the assets are recorded and acknowledged. Only when ownership of a piece of land (or a fishing boat, a firm, etc.) can be legally established can the asset be mortgaged or sold so that the owners can convert it to capital. According to de Soto, much of the poverty rife in the third world does not exist because those areas lack assets. Instead, the source of poverty is either the lack of any form of conceptualization of capital in the culture, or the lack of functioning legal institutions whereby the assets that people actually possess can be recorded in the form of legal concepts and thus converted to capital. As de Soto shows, it took centuries for the universal and impartial institutions upon which market economies are predicated to emerge in the industrialized countries. The jurisprudential regulations are complicated; the institutions required are many and comprehensive. It is not solely a matter of police and public courts, but also of institutions like registrar offices that establish ownership rights to real property, a working land survey office, receivers, official agencies for the collection of debts, taxation, inspection authorities, and so on. This problem has also been emphasized by the well-known economist Dani Rodrik in a report to the International Monetary Fund (IMF) about the relations between economics as a discipline and the reforms needed in developing societies. It is worth citing him in length:

> The encounter between neoclassical economics and developing societies served to reveal the institutional underpinnings of market economies. A clearly delineated system of property rights, a regulatory apparatus curbing the worst forms of fraud, anticompetitive behavior, and moral hazard, a moderately cohesive society exhibiting trust and social cooperation, social and political institutions that mitigate risk and manage social conflicts, the rule of law and clean government—these are social arrangements that economists usually take for granted, but which are conspicuous by their absence in poor countries. (1999: 6)

It is this "taken for granted" view about institutions that is a central focus in this volume. The argument is that what has been left out in the discussion between the shock therapists and the gradualists is that a precondition for the establishment of efficient institutions is social trust. If we accept that impartial rule-of-law institutions are vital for the market to be efficient, then how should such institutions be achieved? Neoclassical economic theory tells us it is a walk in the park: those in high places in the system simply create a bureaucratic incentive system by which the risks and costs entailed in the discovery of corruption, patronage, and other irregularities are greater than the potential gains to be made from participating in such activities (Weibull 1995). That is, society institutionalizes a system in which the fear of getting caught triumphs over the greed of individual market agents, politicians, and civil servants. The problem with this solution is partly theoretical: it raises the problem only to another level. Why should self-interested utility maximizing senior bureaucrats, who have the most to gain through bribery and corruption, be interested in implementing such a system? Moreover, why should their political bosses, who stand to profit even more by a corrupt system, be the slightest bit interested in such a change? This has been formulated as the question of "who will execute" the reforms needed to change a corrupt structure if top management is made up of self-interested utility maximizers (Shleifer and Vishny 1998: 5). As Hans Blomkvist has asserted, much of the advice emanating from organizations like the United Nations Development Program (UNDP), the IMF, and the World Bank on the importance of action against corruption and the establishment of working administrative bodies under the rule of law is based precisely on the presumption of access to the kind of administrative praxis that these countries lack; that is, they presume that the desired end already exists (Blomkvist 2001). One can define this problem as a social dilemma of the second order, meaning that the achievement of social norms of trust and confidence, without which universal institutions cannot be created, is in itself a social dilemma (Ostrom 1998). If political leaders successfully shape a state that is administratively strong enough to protect the rights of individuals from corruption and the abuse of power, they will also have access to an administrative machine that can violate those rights (North 1990: 59). If those in control of the state are the type of actors assumed by the utility maximizing model, they will also exploit that power to enrich themselves at the expense of the rights of market agents (Weingast 1993: 287). In so doing, they inevitably create distrust of the state as an institution, which will work as a barrier to willingness to invest in markets. This problem is, of course, prominent in the post-socialist countries where decades of authoritarian socialist rule seem to have destroyed trust in many social, economic, and political relations in the Eastern European countries (Rose-Ackerman 2001).

The problem can be summarized as follows: However cleverly designed, efficient institutions will only work properly if there is an initial amount of social trust in society. But social trust is to a large extent the result of the existence of efficient institutions (Putnam 1993: 167). From a policy perspective, this makes things very complicated. How should efficient institutions be established in societies with low social trust? Moreover, how can social trust be increased in a society with dysfunctional institutions? This is a case where simple models of explanation between the central variables will fail, because of strong feedback mechanisms and lock-in effects (Pierson 2000; Rothstein 1992). Some institutional devises may increase social trust, which in its turn can make it possible to establish more efficient institutions, that will strengthen social trust, and so on. Or the logic can work the other way round—a lack of social trust will corrupt the few efficient institutions that exist, which in its turn will decrease social trust, making it even more difficult to establish credibility in institutions (Hooghe and Stolle 2003). If there is one simple lesson to learn from the twentieth century, it is that history is not efficient. In economic terms, there are many equilibria, and there is no guarantee that a society, by its own internal logic or the rationality of its agents, will move from inefficient to efficient equilibria (Bendor and Swistak 2000).

Individual Chapters—A Short Introduction

This volume starts with two chapters that engage in a debate about the causal logic between social trust and the existence of corruption in political institutions. The Scandinavian countries have often been put forward as examples of societies with high levels of social trust and low levels of corruption. In contrast, countries like Romania have been portrayed as the opposite. In a critique of the idea that social trust is a result of the vitality of voluntary associations, Bo Rothstein puts forward a theory about how to understand the causal mechanisms between institutions and social trust. The argument is that the high levels of social trust in a country like Sweden has much to do with the existence of universal and impartial government institutions, especially those responsible for the implementation of public policies. A theory of causal mechanisms does not claim that institutions cause trust (or distrust). Instead, the idea is to specify more precisely what it is in individuals' experience of corrupt practices that will make them trust (or distrust) other citizens. In the following chapter, Gabriel Badescu and Eric Uslaner question the generality of this argument. According to them, the theory put forward by Rothstein does not travel beyond the Scandinavian countries. Instead, social trust is to be seen as an individual moral virtue that is not caused by the experience of corrupted political institutions. In a society where corruption is the rule, individuals will distinguish between public officials and ordinary citizens, and their view of the trustworthiness of officials will not influence their view of the trustworthiness of ordinary citizens. Instead, they argue that the causal link is more likely to go from trust in others to confidence in the law. The policy implication is that fighting corruption will not lead to more social trust. Instead, high levels of social trust are caused by economic equality (cf. Uslaner 2002). Then, the high level of economic equality in Scandinavia may be the product of universal and uncorrupted welfare state institutions (Rothstein and Stolle 2003). This debate about the sources of social trust is sure to continue (for a recent and excellent overview see Hooghe and Stolle 2003).

The following section contains seven chapters that all deal with the importance of legal institutions in promoting economic activity. Martin Raiser, Alan Rousso, and Franklin Steves present results from a large survey carried out by the European Bank for Reconstruction and Development (together with the World Bank) about firms in no less than 26 transitional societies. Their starting point is that while trust in general is a scarce commodity, the very existence of a transition period can make this asset even more rare especially because this is a period of what Schumpter called "creative destruction." The central question is how firms deal with the uncertainty of contract relations in a situation with low trust and dysfunctional institutions for solving disputes over contracts. The interests of firms in such a situation are unclear. On the one hand, they are likely to act in a trustworthy way if they have reason to believe that their counterparts will do the same. However, if not from a strictly economic point of view, it is better to cheat than to be cheated. The results of this are important for theories about the relation between efficient institutions, trust, and economic prosperity. For example, firms that believe that courts can be efficient in solving contract disputes are more likely to take economic risks with business partners. Another interesting result is that trust between firms in a society seems to be unrelated to trust between individuals. Social trust and economic trust may thus be two different things. The good news, from a policy perspective, is that reforming government regulations and courts increases trust and thus business opportunities between firms. This theme is taken up in Vadim Radaev's chapter that deals with how firms in Russia handle the problems of low interfirm trust and dysfunctional government institutions. Using both surveys and in-depth interviews with owners and top managers, Radaev shows how firms that operate in a society in which formal institutions cannot be trusted, invent compensatory strategies for overcoming the problem of mutual distrust. Two different levels or coping are found. One is the private contract enforcement that stands in opposition, and in the long run may undermine, the standard rule-of-law solution. This solution seems also to hinder the entry of newcomers into the market because they are treated with suspicion by established actors, which leads to fewer entrepreneurs and less competition. The other solution identified by Radaev is the establishment, through continuous interaction and negotiations, of conventions within specific segments of the market. Such "bottom-up" conventions are based on informal shared understandings between firms in a certain segment of the market organized within business organizations, but they may eventually be backed by government agencies and thus translate into formal government regulations. However, the path to this solution is not automatic as business communities and government agencies operate under different logics. As is known from the literature about neocorporatism, bureaucracies usually want more regulation than the market needs, and business associations want special regulations that serve their particular interests, for example, hindering entry into their market (for an overview see Cawson 1986; Lewin 1992; Olson 1982).

Radaev's theme about the relation between informal conventions and formal rules for the building of trust between market agents is taken up in Chistopher Woodruff's chapter. In addition to a valuable summary of the existing literature, Woodruff shows two important things. First, he highlights the importance of legal institutions in transferring information about the trustworthiness of firms. In light of the problems of asymmetric and imperfect information, this is an important finding. Second, Woodruff shows that not only legal institutions but also private institutions, such as credit bureaus and accountants, may fulfill the task of increasing trust between firms by providing accurate information about a firm's financial situation and its history of honoring contracts. The policy implication may be that governments may be able to increase the efficiency of markets by authorizing private firms that perform these kinds of functions.

The Russian economy is usually described as dysfunctional, plagued by lack of transparency, corruption, and predatory behavior. Without neglecting all these problems, Alena Ledeneva's approach is to look at what market agents do in order to operate under such conditions. What sort of norms and practices exist or are invented to compensate for the lack of trust in government institutions? Using an anthropological approach, Ledeneva explains how, out of necessity, agents use various illegal or semilegal strategies to survive. Among these are so called "monkey firms," double invoicing, and the use of blackmail files against competitors. The central concept in this chapter is necessity, that is, agents perceive that they have to engage in practices like these because of the lack of both social trust and efficient institutions. Such precise information about how the causal mechanisms in different schemes work to hide vital information from government agencies as well as other market agents is central for any reform initiative to be successful.

Ledeneva's rather grim view of the situation in the Russian economy is furthered in Vadim Volkov's chapter, which concerns the practice of "hostile takeovers" of firms. Volkov stresses the importance of the implementation problem—no matter the formal qualities of a law, it is the way it is applied in various contexts that counts. The description he gives for various takeovers of firms are in themselves troubling, but the theoretical implications are important as well. According to his analysis, the effects of laws are to a great extent determined by the existing "extra-legal" reality in which they are implemented. This means that the very same law that in a liberal Western society works to increase social trust may, because of differences in the extra-legal environment, have a fundamentally different impact in a country like Russia.

Following in this direction of "extra-legality" is Federico Varese's chapter about "Mafia transplantation." An important question in the post-socialist societies, with their weak legal institutions, is whether the cancer of organized crime would spread out of control. Varese gives an original and fascinating description of two cases in which the Russian Mafia has tried to export its activities, one successful (Hungary) and the other a failure (Italy). He shows that the different outcomes in these cases have to do with the way the legal institutions operate. The reason for the Mafia's success in Hungary was, according to Varese, that a market economy was established before the legal system had become effective in securing property rights. Thus, the demand for protection could be filled by organized crime. From our theoretical point of view, this underlines the importance of sequences in the relation between institutions and social trust. Creating a market economy without proper institutions for securing property rights may provide a fertile ground for organized crime, which in its turn will make the establishment of both efficient institutions as well as the creation of social trust more difficult, which will increase the demand for private protection, and so on.

The last chapter in this section is a comparison of the regulation of financial markets in China and Russia by Katharina Pistor and Chenggang Xu. As with Volkov's chapter, the starting point is that no written law can account for every possible situation that will arise. In other words, the law itself is always an incomplete source for explaining outcomes. It is therefore necessary to complement the study of the law itself with other social and political variables. The conclusion they draw is that laws that work well in Western countries may do so in transition countries because of the existence of other extra-legal conditions, such as the access to reliable systems of information. As shown by the many recent scandals in the U.S. financial markets, this information problem is not confined to transitional countries. Yet, their analysis underlines the observation that if these problems are difficult to handle in many Western countries, they are likely to be even more acute in transition economies. Pistor and Xu offer a suggestion that has important policy implications, namely that proactive enforcement by regulatory agencies may, because of the possibility to access more reliable information, be a better solution than relying on reactive courts. Yet, they emphasize that neither laws nor regulatory agencies can safeguard against the temptation to engage in opportunistic behavior that may result in the collapse of financial markets. The conclusion is that access to reliable information is a key problem. There are two ways of getting such information— one is through efficient government institutions, the other through the knowledge of trustworthy private agents.

The last section of this volume deals with the more psychological aspects of the institutions-and-trust nexus. Karen Cook, Eric Rice, and Alexandra Gerbasi give an overview of the vast and important experimental research on social trust. Although one should be wary of drawing general conclusions from single experiments, this research area has now produced so many results that point in the same direction that such conclusions can be drawn (Sally 1995). For example, many of the standard assumptions about self-interested behavior in neoclassical economics are not to be borne out in experimental research (Ostrom and Walker 2003). This chapter summarizes results concerning behavior under risk and uncertainty, which can be said to be the rule in most post-socialist societies. The conclusion they draw from the experimental research is that in such circumstances people tend to develop trust only toward people who are close to them, while they view people outside these closed networks with suspicion. This type of trust is what Eric Uslaner labeled "particularistic trust," that is, you trust only people of your own kind. This is very different from "generalized trust," which is the belief that most people in your society, even those you do not know personally and are different from you, can be trusted (Uslaner 2002). The problem is that most accounts of the relation between trust and democracy and between trust and economic growth show that generalized trust is crucial while particularized trust may be detrimental to these goals.

The last chapter by György Csepeli, Antal Örkény, Mária Székelyi, and Ildikó Barna has the title "Blindness to Success." The aim of this chapter is to analyze how the transition to a market-based economy has changed the way people in the post-socialist countries think about economic and social matters. The central concepts are confidence and suspicion, which are seen as opposites. Both have a central impact on the legitimacy of the new economic system. Confidence implies that people view the results of economic distribution as fair, that is, the result of hard work, marketable talents, or entrepreneurial skills. Suspicion, in contrast, means that people believe that others' economic success is due to corruption, patronage, and fraud. The empirical analysis in this chapter builds on survey data that are both comparable over time and between countries (both former socialist and Western). The results are, from a promarket normative perspective, quite disturbing. Over time and compared with people in Western Europe and the United States, people in the former socialist countries tend to believe that success in a market economy is mostly due to untrustworthiness, dishonesty, and fraud. In the East European countries, the market is seen as a Hobbesian place where people are engaged in a mean and bitter struggle with one another for small and finite resources. In the West, the market economy tends to be seen as a place where people are engaged in processes of mutual exchange that are, in the end, beneficial for all. However, this study also reveals important differences between Western Europe and the United States, especially when it comes to meritocratic values. The conclusion is that although the transition to a market economy has, in absolute terms, been a tremendous success, this is not reflected in a corresponding promarket belief system in the former socialist countries. One may draw the conclusion that countries that have been subject to shock therapy have left a large part of their population in shock, not realizing the beneficial nature of the therapy provided to them. The conclusion is that changes in institutions are not automatically transformed into changes in the "system of beliefs," which, going back to Douglass North's argument, is the most important factor for creating prosperity.

References

Åslund, Anders. 1995. *How Russia Became a Market Economy*. Washington DC: The Brookings Institution.
Bendor, Jonathan and Piotr Swistak. 2000. The Impossibility of a Pure Homo Economicus. Paper presented at the Annual Meeting of the American Political Science Association. Washington DC, August 28–September 1.
Blomkvist, Hans. 2001. Stat och förvaltning i u-länder. In B. Rothstein (ed.), *Politik som organisation*, pp. 216–52. Stockholm: SNS Förlag.
Cawson, Alan. 1986. *Corporatism and Political Theory*. Oxford: Basil Blackwell.
Hedlund, Stefan. 1999. *Russia's "Market" Economy: A Bad Case of Predatory Capitalism*. London: UCL Press.

Hooghe, Marc and Dietlind Stolle (eds.). 2003. *Generating Social Capital: Civil Society and Institutions in a Comparative Perspective*. New York: Palgrave/Macmillan.

Kornai, János. 2000. What the Change of System from Socialism to Capitalism Does and Does Not Mean. *Journal of Economic Perspectives* 14: 27–42.

Lewin, Leif. 1992. The Rise and Decline of Corporatism. *European Journal of Political Research* 26: 59–79.

North, Douglass C. 1990. *Institutions, Institutional Change and Economic Performance*. Cambridge UK: Cambridge University Press.

———. 1998a. Economic Performance Through Time. In M.C. Brinton and V. Nee (eds.). *The New Institutionalism in Sociology*, pp. 247–57. New York: Russell Sage Foundation.

———. 1998b. Where Have We Been and Where Are We Going? In A. Ben-Ner and L. Putterman (eds.). *Economics, Values and Organization*, pp. 491–508. Cambridge: Cambridge University Press.

Olson, Mancur. 1982. *The Rise and Decline of Nations: Economic Growth, Stagflation, and Social Rigidities*. New Haven CT: Yale University Press.

Ostrom, Elinor. 1998. A Behavioral Approach to the Rational Choice Theory of Collective Action. *American Political Science Reveiw* 92: 1–23.

Ostrom, Elinor and James Walker (eds.). 2003. *Trust and Reciprocity: Interdisciplinary Lessons from Experimental Research*. New York: Russell Sage Foundation.

Pejovich, Svetozar (ed.). 1997. *The Economic Foundations of Property Rights*. Cheltenham: Edward Elgar.

Pierson, Paul. 2000. Increasing Returns, Path Dependence, and the Study of Politics. *American Political Science Review* 94: 251–67.

Putnam, Robert D. with Robert Leonardi and Raffaella Nanetti. 1993. *Making Democracy Work: Civic Traditions in Modern Italy*. Princeton NJ: Princeton University Press.

Rodrik, Dani. 1999. Institutions for High-quality Growth: What They Are and How to Acquire Them. Paper presented at the International Monetary Fund Conference on Second Generation Reform. Washington DC, November 8–9. http://www.imf.org/external/pubs/ft/seminar/1999/reforms/rodrik.htm.

Roland, Gerard. 2000. *Transition and Economics: Politics, Markets, and Firms*. Cambridge MA: MIT Press.

Rose-Ackerman, Susan. 2001. Trust, Honesty and Corruption: Reflection on the State-building Process. *Achives Européennes de Sociologie* 42: 526–51.

Rothstein, Bo. 1992. Labor-market Institutions and Working-class Strength. In S. Steinmo, K. Thelen, and F. Longstreth (eds.). *Structuring Politics: Historical Institutionalism in a Comparative Perspective*, pp. 1–27. Cambridge UK: Cambridge University Press.

Rothstein, Bo and Dietlind Stolle. 2003. Social Capital in Scandinavia. *Scandinavian Political Studies* 22: 1–23.

Sally, David. 1995. Conversation and Cooperation in Social Dilemmas—A Metaanalysis of Experiments from 1958 to 1992. *Rationality and Society* 7: 58–92.

Shleifer, Andrei and Robert W. Vishny. 1998. *The Grabbing Hand: Government Pathologies and Their Cures*. Cambridge MA: Harvard University Press.

Soto, Hernando de. 2001. *The Mystery of Capital*. London: Bantam Press.

Tsebelis, George. 1990. *Nested Games: Rational Choice in a Comparative Perspective*. New York: Cambridge University Press.

Uslaner, Eric M. 2002. *The Moral Foundation of Trust*. New York: Cambridge University Press.

Weibull, Lennart. 1995. Det ytliga oförnuftet. *Svenska Dagbladet—Samtider*, November 18.

Weingast, Barry R. 1993. Constitutions as Governance Structures: The Political Foundations of Secure Markets. *Journal of Institutional and Theoretical Economics* 149: 286–311.

———. 1997. The Political Foundations of Democracy and the Rule of Law. *American Political Science Review* 91: 245–63.

PART I

Social Capital and Democratic Transition

CHAPTER ONE

Social Trust and Honesty in Government: A Causal Mechanisms Approach

BO ROTHSTEIN*

A "Most Different" Comparison

Countries in transition from socialism face particular problems in developing habits of trust and honesty. Under Soviet-style socialism, government institutions had become severely discredited among the population. Dishonest behavior toward them was often seen as acceptable and even praiseworthy in the face of their illegitimate power. In general, trusting relationships extended little beyond the circle of family and close friends.

If one looks for cases where the situation is most different from the post-socialist countries, the Scandinavian countries provide instructive examples. First, the Scandinavian countries are at the top when it comes to levels of social trust as measured in the World Values Survey and other similar surveys. Second, confidence in public authorities, especially those implementing public policy, is generally high (Rothstein 2001). Third, corruption as measured by, for example, Transparency International (TI) is very low (cf. Badescu and Uslaner, ch. 2). However, despite these stark differences and the dissimilarities in historical trajectories, the Scandinavian countries do have one thing in common with the former socialist countries. The social democratic welfare states and the socialist systems in the former communist bloc have been (are) systems that provide extended social services or, in other words, they are large states. Even if the situations differ, one thing they had in common was frequent as well as broad-based interactions between government institutions and individual citizens.

My analysis of the Scandinavian countries in this context is not designed to suggest that policies or institutions can be copied to other countries and used as blueprints for social and political reform. There is no easy way for countries to draw lessons from other countries in this area. The rationale for this chapter, instead, is to reach a deeper understanding of how the causal mechanisms between political institutions and social trust operate.

The reason Scandinavians trust their public authorities in general, and their system of social welfare and social insurance in particular, cannot be explained solely by the quality of their representative democratic systems. The reason for this is simple: Trust in politicians, political parties, and their parliaments have gone down quite dramatically since the 1980s (Holmberg 1999). This implies that the high level of social trust in the Scandinavian countries and the high-level confidence Scandinavians have in their public authorities cannot be explained simply by referring to the quality of the representative democratic institutions in these countries. We need to look elsewhere in the political system to find an explanation for how the causality operates.

Social Trust and Civil Society

Robert Putnam's well-known study of Italy (1993) showed that the source of social trust was the density and weight of civil society. The social trust that he and his research team found critical to the democratic project flowered in the context of associativeness. Socialization in the social networks that were the foundation of associations, such as, choral societies, athletic clubs, and local parent–teacher associations, gradually taught individuals the noble art of overcoming the problem of the collective action. The idea that voluntary associations generate social capital has had widespread and rapid impact in research as well as among political practitioners.

The significance of civil society and voluntary associations to social trust has suffered two serious critiques, both conceptual and empirical. On the conceptual level, it has proven impossible to find a working distinction between the kind of organizations that produce social trust and those that produce the opposite. Many voluntary organizations and networks are actually built to instill mistrust of other people in general, and of members of other organizations in particular. This does not apply only to obvious cases, such as the Ku Klux Klan, or the ardent fans of one sports team who are not expected to be particularly fond of the passionate supporters of rival teams. Many voluntary associations are religious-, political-, ethnic-, and gender-based, and their existence is partially based on the logic of separation, that is, establishing distance bordering on mistrust between competing associations or networks. This comprises much of the very nature of human organization. Furthermore, all voluntary associations are not like parent–teacher associations or bird-watching clubs; their raison d'être may be criminality or other forms of deviation that hardly generate interpersonal trust (cf. Arias 2002).

Margaret Levi has aptly distinguished between social versus "antisocial" capital (Levi 1996). Sheri Berman (1997) has underscored that the Nazi takeover of power was considerably eased by the extensive system of voluntary associations in Germany at the time. The Nazis were able to infiltrate many of those associations, but more importantly, many organizations voluntarily affiliated with the Nazis and began quickly to purge the nondesirable element. The spring of 1933 saw a very rapid coordination (*Gleichschaltung*) of voluntary associations from the top down to the grassroots. Ian Kershaw writes that few local associations remained outside the nazification that took place in everything from gardening clubs to choral societies. The result, according to a contemporary witness, was that "there was no more social life; you couldn't even have a bowling club that was not coordinated" (Kershaw 2000: 479). Among the very first voluntary associations that chose to tread the Nazi path were the German student organizations, the culprits behind the infamous book burnings of May 1933 (Friedländer 1999: 322).

Faced with this criticism, Putnam has argued that there is also a dark side to social capital (Putnam and Goss 2002). His defense of the importance of social networks for the creation of social trust and reciprocity is that—like other types of capital—social capital based in the form of associations and networks can be used for both benign and malign purposes. However, if social capital as social trust is to be seen as an asset, Putnam's solution lacks logical consistency. An organization deeply split by factions that mistrust each other cannot be said to possess high social trust. Reasonably, a country in the throes of civil war has low social capital. That members of the contending factions have high trust for others within the same faction does not change this. If social capital is to be defined as an asset, we must be able to establish who owns it. If a society or an organization is torn to pieces by opposing factions, it is the factions that own the social capital, not the society or the organization.

The second problem that Putnam's theory on the origin of social trust has encountered is empirical. It has not been possible to prove any correlation on the individual level between involvement in voluntary associations and high social trust. Although the theory has proven almost amazingly robust at the aggregated level, a correlation at the individual level is nowhere to be found. That is, if one finds a city, country, or region with a vibrant network of voluntary associations and abundant social interaction among citizens, it is highly likely that one will also find a reasonably well-working democracy and a growing economy. The problem, which is common in the social sciences, is that relationships on the aggregated level tell us nothing definitive about causal relationships at the individual level. Statistical associations at the aggregated, or macro, level can only be used as indicators for where on the micro level a further search might be productive. For a causal connection to be considered extant, one must prove that it also holds at the micro level. This requires two things: a theory on how social mechanisms at the individual level should be understood and explained, and empirical indicators that support such a theory (Hedström and Swedberg 1998).

Ascertaining whether such is the case often requires data over time or comparative data. Researchers who have been able to work with such data have determined that the correlation does not exist (Newton 2002; Stolle 2000; Uslaner 2002; Whiteley 1999; Claiborn and Martin 2000;

Wollebeak and Selle 2002). Associativeness and social networks may very well be a good thing for many reasons, but they do not seem to increase interpersonal trust. One example comes from a recent survey in Norway that showed that although it is true that members of voluntary associations state that they have higher social trust than people who are not members, there is no difference at all between active and passive members (Wollebæck et al. 2001).

The connection between high associativeness and high social trust that does exist is probably due to a process of self-selection by which the people who are most likely to join and be active in associations or networks are those who are already high on social trust, often dating back to their childhoods, while associativeness itself does not increase people's inclination to trust others. Eric Uslaner asserts, instead, that trustfulness is instilled through the socialization process in the family that children and adolescents undergo, that is, in plain English, whether or not people are inclined to trust others depends on the image of the surrounding society that parents communicate to their children (Uslaner 2002). However, this is a rather impoverished explanation of how social capital is produced in a society, as those socialization processes do not take place in a social or political void. It is only reasonable to assume that something causes the dissimilarities in views of the surrounding society, its institutions, and its people that parents and others communicate to children.

Why does the social trust produced by socialization differ so markedly between countries?

The argument here is that the main thrust in the causal chain may be precisely the opposite of what Robert Putnam and many in his wake proposed. The most important force in causal connection may not go from the sociological level (civil society—networks) to the political (the state and its institutions), but rather the reverse. It may be that a particular type of state institution produces individuals and organizations with high (or low) social trust. Now that the nearly organic view of the emergence of social capital triggered by Putnam's work is shown to be less plausible, there is reason to think along different lines. It may simply be so that a particular type of political institution produces social capital, rather than that social capital produces a particular type of (working) political institution. It should, in fairness, be added that in his latest publication, Putnam stated that "the myriad ways in which the state encourages or discourages the formation of social capital have been underresearched. Does trustworthy government—that is, a state whose officials are honest and effective in responding to citizens' needs—increase social trust?" (Putnam and Goss 2002: 19). The aim of this chapter is to shed light on this question.

The Godfather and the Question of Trust

In his recently published book on political corruption, Robert Neld (2002) recalls a meeting with the famous Swedish economist and Nobel Laureate

Gunnar Myrdal in the late 1960s. Myrdal's argument was that Western intellectuals often viewed corruption as the exception from normality. But according to Myrdal (1968), this view was a mistake: From a global and historical perspective, noncorruption was to be seen as the exception. Neld follows Myrdal's argument and points out that noncorruption came pretty late in history to a small number of countries in a particular corner of the world. It should be added that Myrdal, in his analysis of poverty in Asia invented the concept of the soft state as early as the 1960s to shed light on the problem nowadays known as quality of government.

From personal experience, I can testify that there is a kind of cultural arrogance among many Scandinavians that can be rather irritating in discussions of the problems of corruption and social trust. The basic premise in such discussions often is that the lack of trust in others and in public political institutions and the occurrence of corruption and abuse of power should be understood as a cultural legacy, or something that is "in the nature" of certain peoples or nations but foreign to Swedes or Scandinavians. I question this line of reasoning for many reasons, including that this kind of primordial or culturally essentialist reasoning often lacks empirical capacity. With respect to the Swedish state administration, we can, for example, go back to political scientist Gunnar Heckscher's classic work about the Swedish civil services, where he wrote that "at the dawn of the 19th century, the Swedish civil service was clearly in a state of decay" (1952: 18). Noteworthy among Heckscher's examples of this "state of decay" were the practice of holding and thus mismanaging multiple offices at the same time and the existence of widespread corruption. Purchase of official posts and circumvention of rules to benefit private interests were common in Swedish state administration at the time when public offices were regarded as a kind of personal reward that office holders could use to feather their own nests to the best of their ability (Rothstein 1998b). As I have suggested elsewhere (2000), from the individual's perspective and under certain circumstances, there is a certain rationality in colluding in the reproduction of corrupt systems that is independent of the individual's social norms and values.

To illustrate the point, we can look at the opening scene of Francis Ford Coppola's cinematic masterpiece, *The Godfather*. In a recent poll, the National Society of Film Critics in the United States ranked it the most important film of the twentieth century, ahead of masterpieces like *Citizen Kane, Gone With the Wind, Schindler's List, Casablanca, The Promised Land*, and *A Clockwork Orange*.

The Godfather can be put in a class of its own for many reasons, one of them certainly being the purely artistic qualities of Coppola's creation. However, this film may also have important things to tell us about what it means to be a human being, about core issues like family loyalty, immigration and social exclusion, multiculturalism, the patriarchy, society, and the eternal questions about the nature of good and evil. The two main characters appear to be at once caring fathers and cold-blooded murderers, absolutely loyal friends and men capable of the most ruthless treachery. "I also made them out to be good guys...except that they committed murder once in a while," said scriptwriter Mario Puzo in a filmed interview shown before the movie in the new widescreen video edition. This film can probably be analyzed in countless ways, but from my perspective, *The Godfather* is first and foremost a saga of trust.

Trust, writes Piotr Sztompka, may be defined as "a bet on the future contingent actions of others" (1998: 20). When we decide to trust an individual or an institution, we are not completely certain what is going to happen, that is, if the person or institution is going to live up to our trust and in fact prove trustworthy. That is why we differentiate between "blind faith" and trust. Even if we do not sit down and perform a probability analysis of the risks that our trust will be abused every time we decide to trust someone, there is usually an element, however small, of uncertainty. If we were entirely sure that someone was trustworthy, we would have no need for a word like confidence, that is, advance belief. Confidence expresses what we believe in advance but do not know for certain.

At any rate, the very first scene in the first film of Coppola's trilogy can illustrate this problem. The first sentence spoken is: "I believe in America," by the pitiful undertaker Amerigo Bonasera, a man who emigrated from Sicily and found fortune and happiness in America, the land of opportunity. But now he has been hit by a great misfortune: His daughter is in hospital recovering from a grievous assault. He relates during his audience in the Godfather's office that a couple of "all-American" boys tried to rape her and when she, to the not inconsiderable pride of her father, defended her "honor," they beat her to a pulp "like an animal." Bonasera says that he wanted to be a real American and had allowed his daughter to socialize with the young men without a chaperon from the family. Between the lines, we understand that the two young men are not from the Italian immigrant community; they are "WASPs."

This kind of situation can be managed in various ways, but since our man, Bonasera believed in America, he went to the police "like a good American" to get justice and not to the local don, as he would have done in his old country. Mario Puzo's novel, on which the film is based, begins like this: "Amerigo Bonasera sat in New York Criminal Court Number 3 and waited for justice; vengeance on the men who had so cruelly hurt his daughter, who had tried to dishonor her." Bonasera believed that, in America, the authorities would help him ensure justice and redress the wrong done to his family and his daughter. So—as he later relates to the Godfather, Don Corleone—he went to the police, who arrested the youths and investigated what had happened in accordance with the law. So far, everything seems to have gone according to the poor man's expectations. However, when the perpetrators are put on trial, it turns out that they are given only suspended sentences due, we understand from the subtext, to their backgrounds and connections. They sneer at the unfortunate Bonasera when they are immediately released and can leave the court with no further consequences. So now, the despairing and deeply offended Bonasera is sitting with Don Corleone and asking him for justice. His trust in the American legal system has been breached.

However, the Godfather is irritated with his old friend: "Why did you go to the police? Why didn't you come to me first?" he asks. The matter would have been dealt with immediately, he assures him. However, he is also displeased because Bonasera has avoided him for many years and rejected his "friendship" because he did not want to be indebted to him. When Bonasera tells him he did that because he didn't want to get into trouble, Don Corleone says he understands. "You found paradise in America, had a good trade, made a good living. The police protected you; and there were courts of law..." and he makes it clear that he wonders how in the world his old friend could have been so incurably gullible that he had trusted in the impartiality and honesty of those institutions. The idea that a Catholic immigrant family from Sicily would be able to have its case fairly tried in a court dominated by White Anglo-Saxon Protestant Americans whose roots probably went all the way back to the Mayflower seems absurd to him, especially because he has a number of judges and politicians on his "payroll" to help with the sundry matters upon which assistance might be needed in the kind of business the Corleone family runs.

Corleone gets even more irritated when Bonasera offers him money to have the two youths murdered. He feels insulted to be seen only as a simple criminal who murders for money. He tells Bonasera it would not be "justice" as the girl is still alive. It emerges that what the Godfather wants in return for delivering his special version of "justice" is not money, but trust and loyalty. "Had you come to me in friendship," he says, "then this scum that ruined your daughter would be suffering this very day. And that by chance if an honest man such as yourself should make enemies, then they would become my enemies. And then they would fear you." It is only when Bonasera bows to him, calls him Godfather, and submissively asks to be allowed to be his "friend" that Corleone "takes on the case" by ordering one of his capos to see to it that both of the youths be crippled as punishment. Corleone then speaks the crucial words of the scene, telling Bonasera that he should regard this as an act of friendship and that some day he may call upon him to do a service for him (and the day, of course, comes, but that is another story).[1] The upshot is that Bonasera and his family stop being generalized trusters and become particularized trusters, to use Eric Uslaner's terms (2002). They will no longer believe that they can "trust people in general," but rather that they can only trust their own small and socially homogeneous ethnic clan. They will no longer look at the future with optimism and believe that they can shape their own lives. They will begin mistrusting most government institutions and believe that those institutions are structured to stack the deck against them.

The logic in this pivotal scene in the film is that the scarcity of social capital that plagues many parts of the world comes about when people do not believe they can trust political institutions, and especially not the ones related to the legal system. As Diego Gambetta, one of the most highly regarded specialists on this problem, writes, it is hardly irrational to acquire protection from the Mafia in a situation like this (1988: 173). In fact, the unfortunate Bonasera does not have much of a choice when the institutions he trusted have betrayed him. One kind of trust is replaced with another, but this should not be seen as some kind of moral defect among the individuals who live in these societies, nor as a defect in their culture. If people cannot trust that public officials will act according to norms like impartiality, objectivity, incorruptibility, and nondiscrimination, they cannot trust "people in general" either.

The Causal Mechanism between Social Trust and Political Institutions

Social capital can thus be both produced and destroyed by the way in which the state organizes the public institutions intended to implement public policy. We need to specify the kind of personal experiences and/or general information that can change how much people trust other people. I propose a three-part causal mechanism:

1. If public officials in a society are known for being partial or corrupt, citizens will believe that even people whom the law requires to act in the service of the public cannot be trusted. They will therefore conclude that most other people cannot be trusted either.
2. If citizens see that most people in a society with partial or corrupt officials take part in corruption, bribery, and various forms of nepotism in order to obtain what they feel is their rightful due, they will conclude that most other people cannot be trusted either.
3. In order to act in such a society, citizens must also begin to take part in bribery, corruption, and nepotism, even though they may consider it morally wrong. They will therefore conclude that since they themselves cannot be trusted, other people cannot generally be trusted either.

The causal mechanisms specified here imply that individuals make an inference from the information they have about how their worlds work. This information need not be correct, of course, but individuals have no choice but to act on the information they have. Individuals think something like this: If I cannot trust the police, judges, teachers, and doctors, then whom can I trust? The ethics of public officials is central here, not only with respect to how they do their jobs, but also as to the signals they send to citizens about what kind of "game" is being played in the society (Levi 1998).

The two following causal mechanisms are logical outcomes of the first. People draw conclusions about themselves from the actions of others—and they also draw conclusions in the other direction: "To know oneself is to know others." The process identified here puts the spotlight on what sociopsychological research calls procedural justice. This research has shown that people not only care about the final result of their personal interactions with public institutions (such as receiving a benefit, being convicted in court, being satisfied with the day-care center). They often are at least equally concerned that the procedures used may be considered fair (Lind and Tyler 1997). There are many aspects of procedural justice: whether one has been treated with respect and dignity, whether one has been able to express one's opinion to the responsible officials throughout the process, and a great deal else (Tyler 1998).

How do people react when they feel they have not been treated equally in personal contacts with the agencies of the state? Naturally, corruption exists to a greater or lesser extent in all countries. What I emphasize here are situations when corruption becomes systematic to the point that it becomes part and parcel of the political and administrative culture. These are situations where all or parts of the public machinery are taken over by severely corrupt networks and where interactions between citizens and civil servants routinely include some form of large scale bribery (Karklins 2002). One example of such a situation is given in a recent report on the current situation in Bosnia Herzegovina. The United Nations Development Program (UNDP) reports the results of a survey study that shows that between 60 and 70 percent of respondents believe that corruption exists in the health care system, justice system, and the media. Slightly more than half believe corruption also exists in the various UN bodies working within the region. The report concludes:

> For the average citizen, therefore, it seems that corruption has broken down all barriers and dictates the rules of life. That is not very different from saying that they interpret life in terms of corruption. As long as bureaucratic practice remains unreformed and there is a lack of transparency and accountability in public business, this will continue to be the case. People will use whatever mechanism they think will bring them an advantage and those in office will take advantage of that in their turn. (UNDP 2002: 17)

The point is that people who "interpret life in terms of corruption" are not only likely to mistrust public authorities; they are also unlikely to trust other people in general. The corruption of the authorities can thus be seen as a main source of social distrust.

The Two Faces of Government

Many survey studies of public trust in political institutions such as the government administration, political parties, and the parliament have been carried out in various countries. The main finding of this research is that there is no strong correlation between political trust, defined as trust in democratic institutions, and social trust. We find a clear example in Sweden, where public trust in the political institutions listed earlier has declined rather dramatically, while social trust remains at a high and stable level (Holmberg 1999). Apparently, people's trust in the parliament, political parties, and the government can decline without affecting their trust in other people. This has led many researchers to conclude that there is no convincing evidence showing that trust in democratic institutions produces social trust and social capital (cf. Newton 1999).

However, we can also, on purely theoretical grounds, ask why such a connection should exist in the first place. Politics in a representative democracy is by nature partisan and interest-driven. Political parties and political majorities believe that promoting their own programs, which often entails supporting the interests of particular groups, is one of their main tasks. If I, as an individual, consider myself a member of the political majority that is currently in control of my city or my country, I have reason to feel confidence in the government administration and parliament (or the city council). But if I belong to the minority, the opposite should occur, that is, I have reason to mistrust the city council, the parliament, or the government (cf. Norén 2002). It is difficult to find any logical reason why these conditions should affect my trust in other people. The causal mechanisms are, to put it delicately, not particularly well specified in this line of research on the meaning of social capital.

The institutions of the democratic state are not limited to the representative side of politics. They are joined by the comprehensive and numerous political institutions whose mandate is to implement public policy, that is, the administrative side of the democratic machinery (cf. Rose-Ackerman 2001). The impact of these institutions on how democracy works and its legitimacy is often gravely underestimated (Lundquist 2000). Administrative institutions encompass everything from law enforcement through courts to unemployment offices, tax-funded health care providers, social services offices, and public schools. These institutions are vital to the legitimacy of the political system for two reasons. First, their actions vis-à-vis citizens can often be of an exceedingly interventional nature and crucial to their welfare. It may be distressing if members of parliament from one's own constituency do not adequately represent one's opinions (or one's gender, ethnicity, social class, sexual orientation, and so on), but nothing that is immediately and palpably deleterious to one's welfare is likely to occur. If, however, judges, doctors, teachers, policemen, and so on, act unethically and/or incompetently, things may occur that are immediately and seriously dangerous to the individual. His or her children may be mercilessly bullied; in case of being ill, he or she may suffer unnecessarily or even die; may be convicted despite being innocent, and so on.

In most societies, the public also has much more frequent contact with the administrative institutions of democracy than with representative institutions. This is especially true in the former socialist countries but also in comprehensive Scandinavian welfare states (Kaase and Newton 1995). We leave our children in state-run day-care centers and hope to get them back relatively unharmed, we entrust large portions of our income to a social insurance system and hope to get the benefits we have been promised when we retire, become ill, or unemployed. The policy implementation side of democracy is thus in many ways more central to the welfare of citizens than the representative side. As Staffan Kumlin (2002) has shown, in Sweden the public's direct experiences of how they have been treated by the public service establishment have a considerable impact on their political views. Thus, the task of administrative institutions is to supply citizens with their democratic and social rights, in concrete terms. Accordingly, these institutions are more closely connected to the preservation of liberty and civil rights than to democracy seen as an aggregation of preferences.

Needs-testing, Universalism, and Social Capital

As corruption is not a prominent feature of Swedish society, it is no simple matter to design an empirical test to identify the linkage between public administrative institutions and social trust. This would be true even if we had empirical material from countries where corruption is rampant, simply because the validity of answers obtained in surveys is probably too low to be useful. By the very nature of the subject, it is impossible to get people honestly to answer questions about whether they usually take or give bribes. However, experiences of bald-faced corruption are not the only reason that citizens may mistrust public agencies. More generally, we can consider how interactions between citizens and public institutions might be designed to uphold the principle of equal treatment and to prevent suspicion of discrimination and cheating.

As one alternative, I will begin with the distinction between selective and universal forms of public service (Rothstein 1998a). Selective public service is allocated to individuals only following individual needs-testing. The citizen must meet a number of more or less specific conditions to gain access to a program. These conditions may be of a financial nature, as with social assistance (cash benefits) and housing subsidies, but may also be related to the individual's health or capacity to care for himself (disability pensions, various forms of care for the elderly, or different types of labor market policy measures).

Needs-testing puts heavy demands on both the public official and the citizen who is applying for financial assistance or other services. The official must interpret general regulations and apply them to the individual who is seeking access to a public service. The difficulty lies in the regulations, which are rarely so precise that they provide clear-cut guidance toward the right decision in an individual case. To manage this difficulty, "street-level bureaucrats" must develop personal interpretive structures, as Michael Lipsky (1980) shows. This interpretive structure is often of an informal and less than explicit nature. As a result, bureaucrats carrying out the needs-testing process can easily be suspected of applying "prejudice, stereotype, and ignorance as a basis for determination" (69). In this situation, the citizen is given the incentives and the opportunity to withhold relevant information from the bureaucrat and to try by various means to persuade him that he should be given access to the program in question (Hermansson 2003).

For these reasons, needs-testing and bureaucratic discretionary power are often more difficult to combine with the principle of equal treatment than in public service programs with universal access. Because selective welfare institutions must examine each case individually, they are more vulnerable to suspicions of cheating, arbitrariness, and discrimination than are universal public programs. Research on public support and the legitimacy of various welfare programs has clearly shown that selective programs fare less well in those respects than universal programs (Svallfors 1996). My argument is based on the premise that selective, needs-tested public programs stimulate suspicions of cheating and arbitrary treatment more readily than do universal programs, and that information about equal treatment and cheating within public agencies affects how citizens estimate the trustworthiness of public workers and other people in general. These assumptions give rise to two hypotheses on needs-testing, universalism, and social trust. First, if the assumptions are true, we suspect that people with many personal experiences of selective, needs-testing welfare institutions will demonstrate lower interpersonal trust than others. Conversely, people with many personal experiences of universal, non-needs-testing institutions will evince higher interpersonal trust than others. As shown in figure 1.1, such

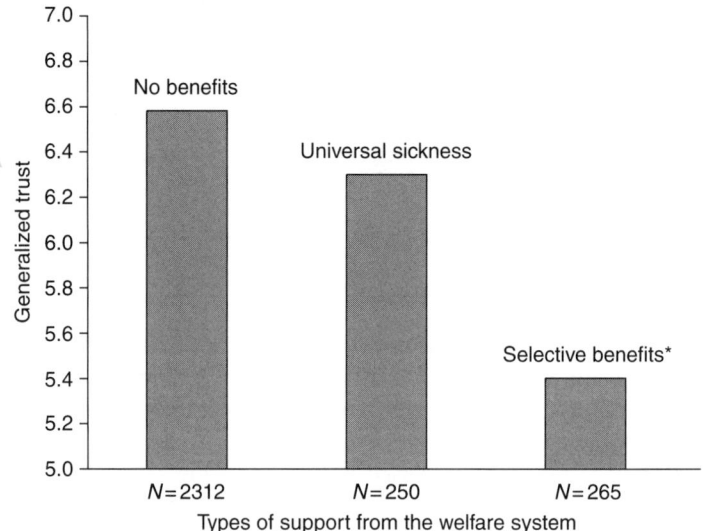

Figure 1.1 Universal and selective benefits and generalized trust, Sweden, 2000
Note: * Significant differences between selective benefits versus others.

an assumption is consistent with the raw survey data from the Swedish Society, Opinion, and Mass Media (SOM) Institute[2].

We see here that people, who are the target of selective measures such as determining eligibility for social assistance and disability pensions, have significantly lower trust in other people than the rest of the population. We also see that having been granted sick pay, which is a general benefit, does not affect trust in other people to any significant extent. Of course, these are just broad correlations that may be caused by other underlying factors. To see if the relationship holds in a more fully specified model, Staffan Kumlin and I used survey data from the SOM Institute (Kumlin and Rothstein 2002). In the survey, respondents were asked to state whether they had dealt with any of the following selective welfare institutions: Housing subsidy, subsidized transportation, disability pension, assistance to people with disabilities, elder care, and the employment office/labor market policy measures. A variable was created to record how many of those institutions each respondent had recently come in contact with. The difference between those who had had no contact with selective institutions and those who had interacted with two or more of them was one step on a scale of 0–10 used to measure interpersonal trust. Initially, this was not particularly surprising, as people who have frequent dealings with selective welfare institutions often also have other characteristics that according to research apply to "low trusters," such as low income and low education. In order to find out whether contact with needs-testing institutions had an independent effect, we used multiple regression analysis in which the effect of these other variables could be controlled. The negative effect on social trust caused by interactions with needs-testing institutions remained (was statistically significant) when the test controlled for the following variables: Age, level of education, class affiliation, income, extent of activity in the civil society, interest in politics, general happiness, political ideology (Left–Right), and job market status (employed or unemployed). In another study based on SOM data as well as data from the World Values Survey, Dietlind Stolle and I were able to confirm the principal findings of this study (Rothstein and Stolle 2003). Thus, we can say that as far as this effect can be tested with survey data, frequent contacts with needs-testing institutions is detrimental to social trust.

The questions asked in the SOM survey also made it possible to test whether citizens' beliefs about how they had been treated by various welfare institutions affected how much they trusted other people. Again, a belief that one had been treated with respect by most of those administrations had significant positive effects on trust in other people (Kumlin and Rothstein 2002).

Conclusions

Social trust and the legitimacy of public authorities are both complex phenomena. There can be no simple, single-factor explanations for variations in any of them. Why individuals differ in their views about the honesty and trustworthiness of their fellow citizens is likely to have several explanations. Nevertheless, there is significant empirical support for the notion that personal experiences of selective, needs-testing welfare institutions undermine interpersonal trust, while experiences of universal institutions tend to increase it. Views on the right to equal and fair treatment by public agencies responsible for the implementation of services seem to be an important factor in explaining variations in social trust. If the theoretical interpretation of the correlations is accurate, we may have stumbled onto one of the explanations for Sweden being a country with a high degree of interpersonal trust: Relatively few Swedes have experienced selectively distributed public welfare and social services, while many encounter universal programs. In a comparative perspective, very few Swedes have encountered corruption in their interactions with public authorities.

Robert Putnam (2001) gives a very different explanation in his comprehensive study of the decline of social capital in the United States. His analysis shows clearly that there are large differences in social capital among various regions in the United States, especially between southern states like Louisiana and Alabama and states in the upper Midwest like Minnesota and Illinois. As in his 1993 book on Italy, Putnam's explanation of these differences is historical and cultural. He writes: "One surprisingly strong predictor of the degree of social capital in any state in the 1990s is, for example, the fraction of the population that is of Scandinavian stock" (2001: 309).

Of course, this is good news for individuals who happen to be of Scandinavian "stock." However, for everyone who does not have such origins, including the author of this chapter, Putnam's conclusion makes for less encouraging reading. We simply cannot do much about our "stock" in cultures with a paucity of social trust, which of course is problematic not only for the post-socialist countries, but also for Latin American and African countries. To take it as an axiom that human norms and beliefs are socially constructed pretty much leaves people high and dry when it comes to their opportunities to change their situations.

Historical determinism was also a prominent feature of Putnam's now famous book on Italy. In one passage, he writes that "the astonishing tensile strength of civic traditions testifies to the power of the past" (1993: 162). He also recounts a conversation with a president in one of the regions with low social trust, who when treated to this historical determinism, exclaims: "this is a counsel of despair! You're telling me that nothing I can do will improve our prospects of success. The fate of the reform was sealed centuries ago" (183).

The discussion of the significance of "history" and "origins" naturally becomes even more problematic in the light of the results of various survey studies in the United States showing that black Americans, that is, people who are mainly of African origin, have considerably lower social trust than people of European origin. This applies even to the trust African

Americans feel in each other and the result holds up even when studies are controlled for factors like income and education (Patterson 1999).

A sociological explanation of this circumstance in the spirit of Putnam builds on the notion that there is something wrong with the inherited cultural tradition (i.e., the stock) that leads to problems in the production of social trust. As shown earlier, support for such a thesis at the individual level is scarcely to be found. A thesis in line with the theory on the significance of public institutions like the one presented here, would provide a completely different explanation for the low level of social trust found among the African American population in the United States. Such an explanation would follow the following logic. African Americans have been, or believe themselves to have been, victims of so much systematic discrimination, special treatment, and other offenses by public agencies that the three causal mechanisms I have specified were triggered and have come to enclose their worldviews and beliefs about the institutions of society and its citizens. According to this explanation, there is nothing wrong with their "stock" when it comes to the creation of social trust. The problem of low interpersonal trust comes from discriminated groups having been forced to live under public institutions that have been, or which they have believed to be, deeply dysfunctional for them.

It has been shown that the collective memory of things like gross police brutality, public lynching, and systematic discrimination has tremendous effects on the belief systems of individuals in groups subject to these indignities. This conclusion also finds support in research that shows that African Americans, to a much greater extent than other Americans, are fascinated by conspiracy theories, most of which are based on the presumption of grossly discriminatory behavior on the part of the authorities. A higher percentage of African American citizens than other Americans believe that AIDS was deliberately spread by the government, that the government spreads drugs to minority groups, and that the FBI murdered Martin Luther King, to give just a few examples (Goertzel 1994).

My institutional theory on how social trust is created may be consistent with Eric Uslaner's (2002) results emphasizing childhood socialization processes. The great variation in social trust between social groups and countries implies that parents' communications cannot be randomly invented by them. If Uslaner is right about the importance of the socialization process, there must be a reason for the systematic variation that exists. If their experiences of the behavior of public institutions leads parents in some countries (or regions) to interpret life in terms of corruption, as stated in the UNDP report cited earlier, they are likely to pass this not so optimistic worldview to their children.

I have added an element of "nondeterminism" to the institutional theory on social trust. Both Putnam's and Uslaner's theories include very little that points toward the possibility of political change. Either you happen to live in a place that, for ancient historical reasons, has too few civil society networks, or you do not. Some people just tend to have a more optimistic worldview than others. The central question is to find a plausible explanation for the sources of this optimism. As argued earlier, it seems not to be grounded in activity in voluntary associations. Instead, the experience, personal or otherwise, gained from interaction with the public authorities seems like a more plausible candidate. Much of the political process in a democracy has to do with how we should design political institutions. Institutional design thus becomes a central element for the creation of honesty and trust (cf. Goodin 1995; 1997). As I have shown in earlier writings (e.g., 1998a) the outcome of such political processes has, in many important cases, been anything but a foregone conclusion. Structural historical factors are not destiny.

Notes

* I would like to thank Staffan Kumlin, Ylva Norén, and Dietlind Stolle for their collaboration in this research. Sören Holmberg, Margaret Levi, and Eric Uslaner gave me lots of good advice. Special thanks to János Kornai and Susan Rose-Ackerman for their comments on earlier drafts and for organizing this project.
1. The quotations are taken from the script by Mario Puzo, *The Godfather*, published by Pan Publishers, London and Signet, New York, 1969.
2. The SOM survey studies are conducted by the SOM Institute, which is operated jointly by the Department of Journalism, the Department of Political Science, and the School of Public Administration at Göteborg University. Each year since 1986, the SOM Institute has conducted a nationally representative questionnaire on the topic of Society, Opinion, and Mass Media (hence the name SOM). The nationwide study, Riks-SOM, has included about 3,000 people since 1999. The study is conducted in the form of a questionnaire distributed by mail. For further information, see the Institute's home page at www.som.gu.se.

References

Arias, Enrique Desmond. 2002. The Trouble with Social Capital: Networks and Criminality in Rio de Janeiro. Paper presented at the Annual Meeting of the American Political Science Association at Boston MA, August 28, 2002.
Berman, Sheri. 1997. Civil Society and the Collapse of the Weimar Republic. *World Politics* 49: 401–29.
Claiborn, Michele P. and Paul S. Martin. 2000. Trusting and Joining? An Empirical Test of the Reciprocal Nature of Social Capital. *Political Behavior* 22: 267–91.
Friedländer, Saul. 1999. *Förföljelsens år 1993–1939. Tredje riket och judarna, första delen*. Stockholm: Natur och Kultur.
Gambetta, Diego (ed.). 1988. *Trust: Making and Breaking Cooperative Relation*. Oxford: Basil Blackwell.
Goertzel, Ted. 1994. Belief in Conspiracy Theories. *Political Psychology* 15: 731–42.
Goodin, Robert (ed.). 1995. *The Theory of Institutional Design*. Cambridge UK: Cambridge Univeristy Press.
———. 1997. *On Constitutional Design*. Oslo: ARENA, Oslo University.
Heckscher, Gunnar. 1952. *Svensk statsförvaltning i arbete*. Stockholm: SNS Förlag.
Hedström, Peter and Richard Swedberg. 1998. Social Mechanisms: An Introductory Essay. In P. Hedström and R. Swedberg (eds.). *Social Mechanisms: An Analytical Approach to Social Theory*, pp. 1–28. New York: Cambridge University Press.
Hermansson, Jörgen. 2003. *Politik på upplysningens grund*. Malmö: Liber Förlag.
Holmberg, Sören. 1999. Down and Down We Go: Political Trust in Sweden. In P. Norris (ed.). *Critical Citizens*, pp. 103–22, Oxford: Oxford University Press.
Kaase, Max and Kenneth Newton. 1995. *Beliefs in Government*. Oxford: Oxford University Press.

Karklins, Rasma. 2002. Typology of Post-Communist Corruption. *Problems of Post-Communism* 49: 22–32.
Kershaw, Ian. 2000. *Hitler. 1889–1936: Hubris*. London: Penguin Books.
Kumlin, Staffan. 2002. Institutions—Experiences—Preferences: How Welfare State Design Affects Political Trust and Ideology. In B. Rothstein and S. Steinmo (eds.). *Restructuring the Welfare State: Political Institutions and Policy Change*, pp. 20–50. New York: Palgrave/Macmillan.
Kumlin, Staffan and Bo Rothstein. 2002. Staten och det sociala kapitalet. In J. Pierre and Bo Rothstein (eds.). *Välfärdsstat i otakt. Om politikens oavsiktliga, uförutsedda och oönskade resultat*, pp. 146–68. Malmö: Liber.
Levi, Margaret. 1996. Social and Unsocial Capital. A Review Essay of Robert Putnam's Making Democracy Work. *Politics and Society* 24: 45–55.
———. 1998. *Consent, Dissent, and Patriotism*. New York: Cambridge University Press.
Lind, Eric A. and Tom R. Tyler. 1997. *The Social Psychology of Procedural Justice*. New York: Plenum.
Lipsky, Michael. 1980. *Street-level Bureaucracy: Dilemmas of the Individual in Public Services*. New York: Russell Sage Foundation.
Lundquist, Lennart. 2000. *Demokratins väktare—ämbetsmännen och vårt offentliga etos*. Lund: Studentlitteratur.
Myrdal, Gunnar. 1968. *Asian Drama: An Enquiry into the Poverty of Nations*. New York: Twentieth Century Fund.
Neld, Robert. 2002. *Public Corruption: The Dark Side of Social Evolution*. London: Anthem.
Newton, Kenneth. 1999. Social and Political Trust in Established Democracies. In P. Norris (ed.). *Critical Citizens: Global Support for Democratic Government*, pp. 169–87. Oxford: Oxford University Press.
———. 2002. *Who Trusts? The Origins of Social Trust in Six European Nations*. Southhampton: Department of Political Science, University of Southhampton.
Norén, Ylva. 2002. *Svenskars politiska förtroende*. Göteborg: Department of Political Science, Göteborg University.
Patterson, Orlando. 1999. Liberty Against the Democratic State. On the Historical and Contemporary Sources of American Distrust. In M.E. Warren (ed.). *Democracy and Trust*, pp. 151–207. Cambridge UK: Cambridge University Press.
Putnam, Robert D. with Robert Leonardi and Raffaella Nanetti. 1993. *Making Democracy Work: Civic Traditions in Modern Italy*. Princeton NJ: Princeton University Press.
———. 2001. *Bowling Alone. The Collapse and Revival of American Community*. London: Simon & Schuster.
Putnam, Robert D. and Kristin A. Goss. 2002. Introduction. In R.D. Putnam (ed.). *Democracies in Flux. The Evolution of Social Capital in Contemporary Society*. New York: Oxford University Press.
Rose-Ackerman, Susan. 2001. Trust, Honesty and Corruption. Reflection on the State-building Process. *Achives Européennes de Sociologie* 42: 526–51.
Rothstein, Bo. 1998a. *Just Institutions Matter: The Moral and Political Logic of the Universal Welfare State*. Cambridge UK: Cambridge University Press.
———. 1998b. State Building and Capitalism: The Rise of the Swedish Bureaucracy. *Scandinavian Political Studies* 21: 287–306.
———. 2000. Trust, Social Dilemmas and Collective Memories. *Journal of Theoretical Politics* 12: 477–503.
———. 2001. Social Capital in the Social Democratic Welfare State. *Politics and Society* 29: 207–41.
Rothstein, Bo and Dietlind Stolle. 2003. Social Capital, Impartiality, and the Welfare State: An Institutional Approach. In M. Hooghe and D. Stolle (eds.). *Generating Social Capital: The Role of Voluntary Associations, Institutions and Government Policy*, pp. 168–89. New York: Palgrave/Macmillan.
Stolle, Dietlind. 2000. Clubs and Congregations: The Benefit of Joining Organizations. In K.S. Cook (ed.). *Trust in Society*, pp. 202–44. New York: Russell Sage Foundation.
Svallfors, Stefan. 1996. *Välfärdsstatens moraliska ekonomi*. Umeå: Borea Förlag.
Sztompka, Piotr. 1998. Trust, Distrust and Two Paradoxes of Democracy. *European Journal of Social Theory* 1: 19–32.
Tyler, Tom R. 1998. Trust and Democratic Governance. In V. Braithwaite and M. Levi (eds.). *Trust and Governance*, pp. 269–314. New York: Russell Sage Foundation.
UNDP. 2002. *Human Development Report 2002. Bosnia and Herzegovina*. New York: United Nation Development Program.

Uslaner, Eric M. 2002. *The Moral Foundation of Trust*. New York: Cambridge University Press.
Whiteley, Paul F. 1999. The Origines of Social Capital. In J.W. van Deth, M. Maraffi, K. Newton, and P.F. Whiteley (eds.). *Social Capital and European Democracy*, pp. 25–45. London: Routledge.
Wollebæck, Dag, Per Selle, and Håkon Lorentzen. 2001. *Frivillig insats: Sosial integrasjon, demokrati og økonomi*. Oslo: Fagbogforlaget.
Wollebeak, Dag and Per Selle. 2002. Does Participation in Voluntary Associations Contribute to Social Capital? The Impact of Intensity, Scope, and Type. *Nonprofit and Voluntary Sector Quarterly* 31: 32–61.

CHAPTER TWO

Honesty, Trust, and Legal Norms in the Transition to Democracy: Why Bo Rothstein is Better Able to Explain Sweden than Romania

ERIC M. USLANER AND GABRIEL BADESCU[*]

Trust is a blessing. As an ideal that leads us to believe that people who are different from us are part of our moral community, trust makes us more willing to deal with people who are different from ourselves and holds us to high standards of honesty and fairness. Trust provides the foundation for a rule of law and for policies that benefit the less fortunate.

Corruption is a curse. It flouts rules of fairness and gives some people advantages that others do not have. Corrupt institutions cause people to lose faith in government.

It should hardly be surprising that where there are high levels of trust, there is less corruption.[1] Across 51 countries, the simple correlation between trust and corruption is .711 (see figure 2.1). The Nordic countries are the most trusting *and* the least corrupt. The countries with the highest levels of corruption—Colombia, the Philippines, Turkey, and Brazil—have the least trusting citizens.

Therefore, it seems that where trust in others is low and corruption is high, as in former communist countries, we can increase the level of trust by reducing corruption. So argues Bo Rothstein (2001: 479, 491). He suggested that Russians could become more like Swedes if they could reduce the level of corruption in their society, creating trust "from above" (see also Cohen 1997: 19-20; Levi 1998: 87; Misztal 1996: 198; Offe 1999). A strong legal system would create a sense of social insurance for ordinary citizens: Neither their fellow citizens nor the government could exploit them if there were an independent and honest judiciary that ensured compliance with the law. Trusting others would be less risky.

In the West, so the argument goes, where there is relatively little corruption, people see their societies as honest and therefore trust each other *and* their governments more than in more corrupt societies. In the formerly

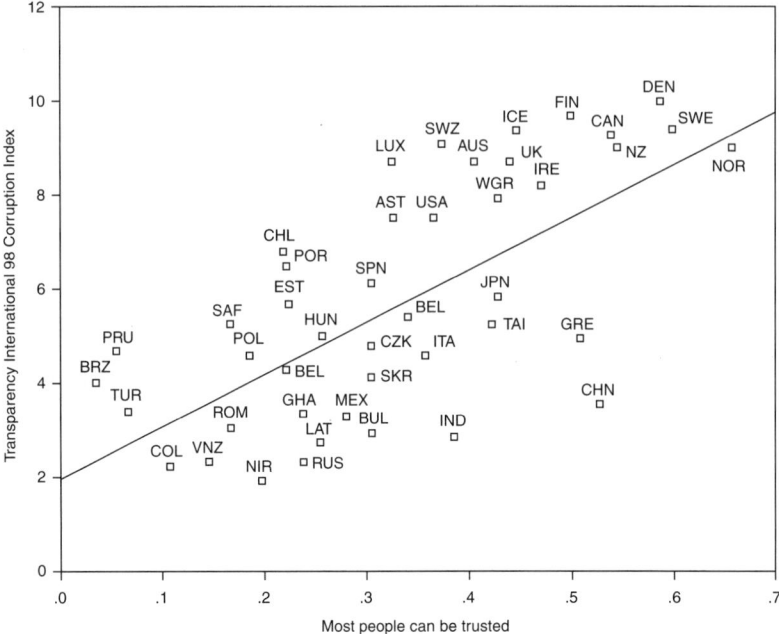

Figure 2.1 Trust and corruption across nations

communist societies, people see corruption all around them and lose faith in others and their system. The communist regimes created much distrust from above (see later), so there is more than a bit of evidence that elite malfeasance sends a powerful signal to the mass public. Crime rates are higher in societies with lower levels of trust (Uslaner 2002: chs. 7, 8). And there is at least a modest correlation between trust in the legal system and faith in other people in Sweden (Rothstein 2001: 492).

As compelling as Rothstein's argument seems, it is misplaced. Rothstein's evidence for a linkage between trust in the legal system and faith in others comes entirely from one rather atypical Western democracy, Sweden. Sweden has the highest level of trust of any country surveyed in the World Values Surveys and is one of the least corrupt countries in the world. The Swedish model may not transfer to formerly communist nations. Even if there *is* a connection between a strong legal system and trust in fellow citizens, the causal direction is more likely to go from faith in others to confidence in the law (Uslaner 2002: 243–5). Swedes and other Westerners can develop strong legal systems *because people trust each other*. Trusting people endorse strong standards of moral behavior and say that it is wrong to take advantage of others, especially those who are more vulnerable (Uslaner 1999a,b). Sweden is, in John Rawls's terminology, a "well-ordered society," where "everyone accepts and knows that the others accept the same principles of justice, and the basic social institutions satisfy and are known to satisfy these principles" (1971: 454). The roots of this moral sentiment rest upon a commitment to social justice and concern for those less well off, hallmarks of the Swedish welfare state (Rawls 1971: 454, 462). A well-ordered society depends upon a shared sense of justice. In Romania and other formerly communist countries, the strong arm of the state and rampant corruption make people skeptical that there is *any equitable system of justice*. Dealing with corruption requires reinventing moral codes on a case-by-case basis—and stands in sharp contrast to the shared values underlying a "well-ordered society."

We shall show, using data across nations and from surveys of Romanians (and Swedes), that the impact of corruption on trust in both other people and government systems is greatest when there is not much dishonesty (as in Sweden). If corruption is rampant, as in Romania, people become inured to it. They do not think worse of their fellow citizens, who must get by in any way they can in a system that seems rigged toward those at the top. People *are* disturbed by corruption in government, but they may feel powerless to do much about it. One government is as corrupt as the next, so getting a regime that performs well on the economy will be more essential than getting one that purports to govern honestly. Rothstein's account works better for (his native) Sweden than for the newer democracies of the former communist nations.

Most of our data analysis focuses on Romania, some on Sweden. However, this is not simply a tale of two nations. Romania and Sweden represent poles of trust and corruption. In addition, the pattern we see for them *is* rather general. We shall show first that people are more likely to link their perceptions of trust and corruption in countries like Sweden (where corruption is low)—and they are less likely to do so when corruption is more prevalent (in Romania). This casts some doubt on the applicability of lessons learned in one context to another, very different one. Those who are too quick to draw lessons for Eastern Europe from Sweden risk committing the fallacy of a Yiddish folk saying: "If my grandmother had wheels, she'd be a bus."

The link between trust and dishonesty is obscured by the different forms of corruption. There is sporadic (at best) evidence that corruption by elites in former communist countries may lead to less trust in others, but there is *less evidence* that petty corruption—payments or "gifts" to service providers—leads people to lose faith in their fellow citizens. Corruption does not rest with ordinary folks striving to get by. As the Chinese say, "The fish rots from the head down." If there is any link from corruption to trust in the former communist societies, it comes from above. This is *not* a new distinction, nor one that emanates from authoritarian societies. The boss of New York City's Tammany Hall Democratic Party machine in the nineteenth century, George Washington Plunkitt, distinguished between "honest" and "dishonest" graft; the former involved rewarding your friends and punishing your enemies. The latter involved theft from the public purse (Riordan 1948).

"Merely" curbing corruption does not provide a quick route to a more trusting society. There is a somewhat stronger linkage between attitudes toward the regime and corruption—not surprisingly, since public officials are the source of most corruption. Yet, even this connection is not terribly strong in the formerly communist states. In that region, corruption has little impact on trust in fellow citizens. Although corruption may have long-term negative consequences, in the short run it solves bureaucratic rigidities. People may thus feel that petty corruption is a decent bargain (Rose-Ackerman 1994: 21). Ordinary citizens are all in pretty much the same boat, so there is little reason for people to let corruption from above shape attitudes toward others. Authoritarian regimes can destroy trust, but democratic reforms will not in and of themselves rebuild it. There is hope for reducing corruption in formerly communist societies, but we should not be too sanguine about the grander implications of cleaner government.

Romania is a particularly good case to examine because it was one of the poorest of the formerly communist countries. Its regime, under Nicolae Ceausescu, maintained a very strong grip on the public. When the communist government fell in 1989, the Romanian public was initially very optimistic about the future. However, more than a decade later, parliamentary regimes of both the (old) left, the (new) right, and the quickly defunct reformist center have failed to gain the public's support. The economy faces severe difficulties, inequality is growing, trust and tolerance are especially low among the young, and corruption still is a continuing problem: Romania ranked sixty-ninth of 91 countries ranked in 2001 by Transparency International (TI), a transnational organization established to fight corruption.

Much of our analysis is cross-national, because we do not want to rest our case on the possibility of Romanian exceptionalism. However, our more detailed information comes from a comparison of Romania with Sweden, a high trusting society with low levels of corruption—and, perhaps not so coincidentally, the source of the most sophisticated version of the received wisdom (Rothstein 2001).

Trust and Honesty: The Received Wisdom and an Alternative

The type of trust we are concerned with is generalized—or moralistic—trust, a faith in strangers, in people we don't know who are likely to be different (and think differently) from ourselves. Moralistic trust is different from strategic trust, faith in people we know well. Strategic trust is based upon experience—with our families, our friends, our coworkers, our business associates, our contractors—people we have faith in and those we do not trust (Hardin 2002). Moralistic (or generalized) trust cannot be based upon experience since it is faith in strangers. But it is the key to acts of generosity such as volunteering and charitable giving, to tolerance, to an endorsement of strong standards of ethics, to better performing governments, and to societies that spend more on the poor (Uslaner 2002).

Moralistic trust is predicated on the notion of a common bond between classes and races and on egalitarian values (Fukayama 1995: 153; Putnam 1993: 88, 174; Seligman 1997: 36–7, 41; Uslaner 2002: ch. 2). Faith in others leads to empathy for those who do not fare well and, ultimately, to a redistribution of resources from the well off to the poor and to more responsive institutions (LaPorta et al. 1997; Uslaner 2002: chs. 7, 8). Faith in others is a moral commitment akin to the Golden Rule, where we treat others as *we would have them treat us* rather than a simple game of tit for tat (Uslaner 2002: chs. 2, 4). Trusters do not need immediate reciprocity: Their faith in others rests on an optimistic worldview and a sense of personal control that gives them a psychological cushion against occasional bad experiences.

Each of these foundations—and effects—of moralistic trust stands in opposition to corruption. Corrupt deals may depend upon trust, but only on trust of people you know well and who are your close confidants (what we call particularized trust). Corruption exploits strangers and, almost always, takes from the poor and gives to those already well off. Generalized trust, in contrast, depends upon an optimistic worldview and an equitable distribution of wealth (Uslaner 2002). Corruption is based on loose standards of ethics and on a legal system that is powerless to stop transactions that let some people exploit others.

Rothstein (2001: 491–2) argues that people are not likely to lose faith in others just because they have venal politicians. However, when the legal system fails to punish transgressors, be they other citizens or political leaders, people will no longer feel quite so warm toward their fellow citizens (cf. Mauro 1995: 12).

In a civilized society, institutions of law and order have one particularly important task: to detect and punish people who are "traitors," that is, those who break contracts, steal, murder, and do other such noncooperative things and, therefore, should not be trusted. Thus, if you think that particular institutions do what they are supposed to do in a fair and efficient manner, then you also have reason to believe that people will refrain from acting in a treacherous manner and you will therefore believe that "most people can be trusted."

Tyler (1990: chs. 4, 5) argues that people respect the law because they believe that the justice system is fair and that they have been treated fairly. If people feel that they have been treated unfairly by the police or in the courts, they are less likely to have faith in the legal system. The key to less corruption—and more trust—then, is an effective system of property rights and the rule of law (Lambsdorff 1999; Leite and Weidemann 1999: 20, 23; Treisman 2000).

There is a better case for linking corruption and trust in government rather than trust in people. People think of government officials when they say that their countries are corrupt. The leap to mistrust of others is not so clear. Across a wide range of countries, there is little link between trust in government and trust in other people (Newton 1999, 2002;

Orren 1997; Uslaner 2002: chs. 5, 8). However, the repressive institutions of the state played a key role in destroying trust under communism (Gibson 2001; Howard 2002), so it makes sense to believe that reformed (and more honest) institutions might help rebuild faith in others. Rothstein's (2001: 477) story begins, after all, with a visit to Russia, where only 26 percent of tax revenue reaches the government, compared to 98 percent in Sweden.

Trust in other people and corruption should be particularly strongly linked in societies where trust was hazardous and corruption was widespread. Creating trust from above is a very enticing prospect for countries in transition: Building confidence in fellow citizens by stronger anticorruption measures might be much easier than reshaping people's attitudes.

In Western societies, strong legal systems *depend upon* trust; they do not produce it. Given the strong role of the state in the former communist countries, we see a greater possibility that *perceptions of procedural fairness*, rather than trust in specific institutions such as the courts, may play a role in shaping interpersonal trust. Generalized trust rests upon the perception of common bonds across different groups within society. If you believe that some people get better breaks from the judicial system than others, you will be less likely to believe that we all have a common fate. Even then, we expect that the fairness of the legal system will not be nearly as important to generalized trust as optimism and control.

Trust, Corruption, and Perceptions of Government

The causal chain from corruption to trust in others can run either directly from perceptions of malfeasance to lack of faith in others or indirectly. Yet, the evidence on *either* linkage ranges from modest (Rothstein 2001: 491) to negligible. Neither trust in government nor confidence in legal systems leads to greater trust in people.

These results stem from research in Western democracies—the United States and Western Europe—where people develop attitudes about trust apart from the strong arm of the state. Authoritarian political systems, especially communist regimes, pit citizens against each other. If people feel compelled to turn on their friends lest the state turn on them, interpersonal trust may become too risky. In such a world, you really cannot be too careful in dealing with people, even if everyone would strongly prefer to treat others as if they were trustworthy. If people are wary of strangers, they will limit their social activities to close friends whom they do see as trustworthy (see Gibson 2001; Hayoz and Sergeyev 2003). In former communist countries, there was little optimism and even less of a sense of personal control; this seems to have changed little in the years since the downfall of the oppressive regimes. Communist societies were also marked by high levels of corruption (see Rose-Ackerman 1994: 21; Trang 1994: 8).

Therefore, it is not unreasonable to presume that (1) trust in others will reflect confidence in the regime more in transitional countries than in other nations; and (2) perceptions of corruption may be stronger determinants of trust in others in formerly communist nations than in other countries. We examine these two linkages in this paper, focusing on Romania in particular. After the fall of Ceausescu in 1989, Romania (like other countries in Central and Eastern Europe) established democratic institutions. However, a parliamentary regime and a system of courts have neither ended corruption nor increased trust. We examine the roots of trust and perceptions of corruption in two surveys: The 1995 World Values Survey (WVS) and our own survey in 2001 that was part of a larger pan-European project on Citizenship Involvement Democracy (CID).[2] We also put Romania and the countries making the transition from communism more generally in context by cross-national aggregate data analysis—and by comparing Romania with the *most* trusting and the *least* corrupt nation, Sweden.

The story we tell is *not* what the literature on trust and corruption might lead us to expect: in Romania and, more generally in the countries making the transition from communism, *the link between trust in people and corruption is weak and inconsistent.* Romanians do not generalize from corruption among the elites to less serious offenses by ordinary citizens. Corruption is something that public officials do. When regular folks skirt the law, they are just getting by. If people need to skirt the law to make do, then flouting standards of moral behavior is not a sign of an intention to exploit others. Elites, however, got benefits unavailable to ordinary citizens under communism, and many Romanians believe that they still have unfair advantages. Small-scale dishonesty is "good corruption"; it is based upon the expectation of reciprocity. As Bertold Brecht wrote in *Mother Courage and Her Children*: "Thank God they're corruptible. They're human and after money like the rest of us. They're not wolves. As long there's corruption, there's hope. Bribes! They're man's best chance. As long as judges go on taking money, then there's some chance of justice" (Scene 3, quoted in Miller et al. 1998: 1).

Large-scale corruption involves misuse of official positions. It makes some people rich at others' expense, giving those at the top extra power and resources over those who struggle to make do (Ledeneva 1998: 42–7). There is a strong disconnect between people's evaluations of other citizens and the people running the country.

There is a roundabout route from corruption to mistrust as well. In both the WVS and CID surveys, we see that Romanians who say that it is acceptable to cheat on taxes are more likely to mistrust their fellow citizens. Although we find either no direct link or at best a very weak connection between trust in governmental institutions (courts, politicians, or legislatures) and faith in people, we do see a connection between views of the procedural fairness of the legal system and trust in people (in the CID surveys). We also see that people who are satisfied with democracy are also more likely to have faith in their fellow citizens.

In the surveys, some people *do* make a strong connection between trust in other people and corruption. However, they are *not* the folks who live day in and day out with corruption. Rather, people are *most* likely to make this connection when there is very little corruption in their polity. We get mad and think the worst of others if we see a little bit of corruption because it is so unusual. If corruption is all around us, we become inured to it and do not let misdeeds bother us so much.

Trust, Corruption, and Transition

Under communism, the state-controlled daily life and neighbors were pitted against each other. Putting trust in strangers must seem a quaint (or even dangerous) idea to people who are afraid to trust all but their closest friends. An oppressive state terrifies all of its citizens. Acting on moral principles makes little sense in a world where even simple reciprocity among strangers is too dangerous to contemplate. Scarcity makes life hard and leads people to seek ways of making their own lives better (Banfield 1958: 110). People have no sense of control and little basis for optimism—so they have little reason not to do whatever they need to do to get by.

If goods and services are in short supply and manipulated by the state, bribery and gift giving seem reasonable ways to obtain routine services. Moreover, state officials will find petty corruption a useful means of getting more resources themselves. Corruption will trickle up throughout the system and at the top will be far from petty. Autocratic societies, with high levels of scarcity and little accountability, are breeding grounds for dishonesty. If people have little reason to trust one another, they will not only engage in corruption but will treat it as just another transaction, marked by no particular moral disapprobation.

Barely more than a third of Hungarians see a moral problem when doctors demand "gratitude payments" for medical services (Kornai 2000: 3, 7, 9). This system of "gift giving" is so widespread that almost all doctors accept "gratitude money"; 62 percent of physicians' total income came off the books. In an economy marked by shortages and arrogant administrators, many people see these payments as a way to ensure supply and to establish longer-term relations with their doctors.

Under communism, people did have social networks of people they could trust. They formed small networks to help them get by in daily life— to stand in line for scarce products, to help out close friends, relatives, and neighbors (Ledeneva 1998). While Putnam (2000: 288) argues that these strong ties are the stepping-stones to trust in strangers, there is little evidence that one form of trust leads to another, either in formerly communist countries or in the United States (Flap and Völker 2003; Gibson 2001; Ledeneva 1998: ch. 5). These informal networks were largely associations of convenience.

An alternative view is that the helping networks, which played such a key role in the communist regimes, were *substitutes* for the wider social networks that were simply not possible under repressive governments (Flap and Völker 2003; Gibson 2001). When communism fell in Central and Eastern

Europe (mostly around 1989) and was replaced by democratic regimes, reformers hoped that the new democratic constitutions would lead to new democracies and market economies. State control of political life would give way to civil society with trusting and tolerant citizenries, and property rights would be respected. The downfall of corrupt dictators would energize people, make them optimistic for the future, and give them the all-important sense of control over their lives and their environment that provides the foundation for trust and the civic culture more generally (Almond and Verba 1963; Lane 1959: 163–6; Rosenberg 1956).

Yet, the transition was not so simple. Communism left a very strong legacy in the political cultures of Central and Eastern Europe. The strong arm of the state was replaced not by a trusting civil society with open markets, but rather by a largely apathetic society where people did not trust their new governments or each other (Badescu and Uslaner 2003; Howard 2002). Many of the owners of the new capitalist businesses were the old communist managers. The boom times that capitalism promised either came and went very quickly or never came at all for most people. Some entrepreneurs got rich, but many ordinary citizens were poorer than ever. The scarcity of the market replaced the scarcity of the state. Economic inequality grew rapidly—and people lost faith with the new institutions that were supposed to make life better. Scarcity, inequality, pessimism, and a distrust of both authorities and other people were a recipe for *more* corruption, not less, in the post-communist transition.

In a world where elites are routinely seen as dishonest—79 percent of WVS respondents from post-communist countries said that either most or all leaders are corrupt (see table 2.1)—people might be unlikely to believe that they live in a trusting (much less trustworthy) society. The end of state control of the economy meant the demise of many of the networks that people used to get by. Yet corruption persisted; a majority of Russians found it necessary to use connections to get clothes and medicine and 10 percent still needed someone's help in getting into a hospital (Ledeneva 1998: 8). With the growth of a very imperfect market, many of these informal networks broke up, leaving no social support system at all in their wake (Howard 2002; Ledeneva 1998: 194–6). The demise of state authority led to more personalized government administration, with more bribery and greater opportunities for personal gain (Miller et al. 2002: 565; Rose-Ackerman 1999: 107).

We see some of the difficulties of transition in table 2.1, where we present measures of trust and corruption. Transition nations rank higher on corruption than other countries (lower TI scores indicate more corruption) and Romania has more corruption than most communist nations. Similarly, trust is higher in nontransition countries, and Romania has the lowest levels of faith in others. In the fight against corruption, the formerly communist countries lag behind two variables that we shall see play a key role in shaping governmental dishonesty: fewer government regulations and governmental stability. The transition economies still control much of business, and

Table 2.1 Trust and corruption across nations[a]

	Other nations	Former communist countries	Romania
Corruption: TI 1998 measure	6.01	3.67	3.00
Perceived corruption (WVS)	.58	.79	.66
Interpersonal trust (WVS)	.31	.25	.16

Note: [a] Corruption as measured by TI ranges from 0 (most corrupt) to 8.3 (least corrupt); perceived corruption is the proportion of respondents saying that most or all officials are corrupted, measured by the WVS surveys from 1981, 1990, 1995–96; trust is measured on a 0–1 scale with one being the highest level of trust.

governments have not achieved political stability. Romania ranks well below the means even for the transition economies.

Trust and Corruption Across Nations

We begin with a cross-national examination of the linkage between trust and *perceptions of corruption* at the individual level. Rothstein's argument would lead us to expect a strong inverse relationship between perceptions of corruption and trust in other people: If people see a lot of corruption, they should be less trusting of fellow citizens. The WVS asked respondents both about generalized trust and about perceptions of corruption. (Happily, the publics have the same perceptions as the elite surveys represented by the TI index; the simple correlation between the two measures is .83.) We calculated correlations between trust and perceptions of corruption for 34 countries in the WVS data set. We also calculated the correlations between confidence in the legal system and perceptions of corruption for 33 countries. These correlations range from the moderately negative (−.2) to the (surprisingly) positive (the coding leads us to expect negative correlations). The mean correlations are not strong. For generalized trust, the mean correlation with perceptions of corruption is −.079. The mean correlation of confidence in the legal system with corruption is −.144. For three countries, the relationship is positive for each trust/confidence measure. The correlations with trust in people are positive in Romania, India, and Taiwan; for confidence in the legal system, they are positive for Romania, Taiwan, and Venezuela.

These correlations would be of modest interest by themselves. However, there is a clear pattern to the correlations that challenges the conventional wisdom of the connection between trust and corruption (see figure 2.2). The correlations between trust and perceptions of corruption are strongest *when corruption is lowest* (as measured by high values of the 1998 TI corruption perceptions index). For example, Swedes who perceive that corruption is high are also likely to state that their country is not run by the will of the people and vice versa for those who perceive low corruption. The correlation

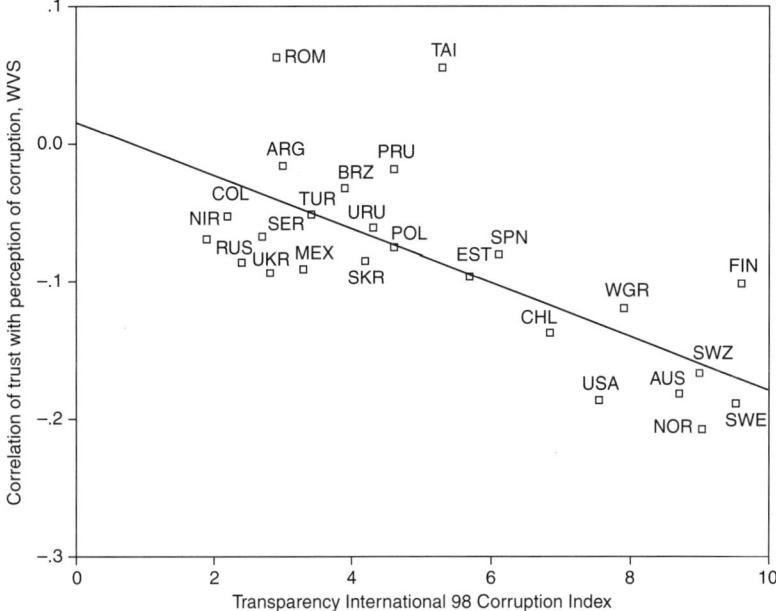

Figure 2.2 Correlation between trust and perceptions of corruption (WVS) and TI estimates of corruption, 1998

between trust in other people and perceived corruption in the WVS for Sweden is −.19, not overwhelmingly strong, but below (in absolute value) only New Zealand and Norway. Romanians do not make a link between corruption and governmental responsiveness. And there is no clear connection between trust and perceived corruption ($r = .05$).

If there is a lot of corruption in a country, people behave pretty much as Romanians do. They do not make a link between corruption (the domain of the elites) and trust in people. If there is little corruption, people are more likely to see venality by the elites as part of a larger cultural problem. Those relatively few individuals who see corruption as a problem extrapolate to the meanness of people in general—and are less likely to trust their fellow citizens. The relationship among these 34 countries is reasonably strong ($r^2 = .480$).

Next, we divided countries into three levels of corruption: least, middle, and most. We calculated simple correlations between perceptions of corruption and trust by levels of corruption for each group using the WVS data. For the *least corrupt* countries, the correlation between aggregated trust and country-level perceptions of corruption was a robust −.754: The greater the perception of corruption, the lesser the trust. For the middle group, the correlation was a respectable −.532. For the *most corrupt countries, the correlation was positive* (.243): The higher the level of perceived corruption, the higher the proportion of trusting citizens—and this relationship is particularly pronounced for the formerly communist countries.[3]

There is no clear relationship between the TI measure of corruption and the correlation between perceived corruption and trust in the legal system ($r^2 = .060$). The average correlation for formerly communist nations is *higher* than for other countries (the average correlations are .190 and .127, respectively). Romania's negative correlation is an exception to this general pattern—and the average correlation for transition countries rises to .204 if we exclude Romania. People in transition countries think less of their legal systems if they believe that the political system is corrupt (see figure 2.3).

This pattern is *not* restricted to the mass public's perceptions of corruption. If we divide the TI measure of corruption at its median (4.70), the powerful aggregate correlation between trust and public perceptions strengthens for the less corrupt countries ($r = -.609$) and actually *reverses in sign* ($r = .179$) for the more corrupt countries. Again, in the most corrupt countries, the more people see corruption in high places, the more trusting they are in fellow citizens (though this result is not significant). In the least corrupt countries, perceptions of corruption lead to much *lower* levels of trust.

There is also clear evidence that when corruption does shape trust, it is the "big" corruption at the top—not the petty payments made in everyday life—that matters. Trust is correlated strongly with the TI index and estimates (for 1997) of bribery by the Global Competitiveness Survey ($r = -.503$) and by Impulse Magazine ($r = -.603$). The correlation is much weaker for

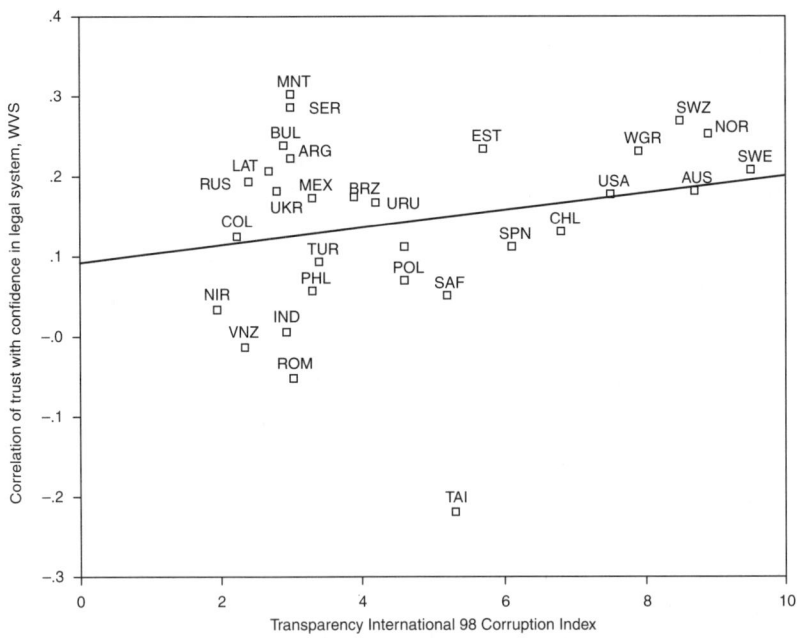

Figure 2.3 Correlation between confidence in legal system and perceptions of corruption (WVS) and TI estimates of corruption, 1998

small-scale corruption, as measured by the currency premium on the black market ($r = -.290$).[4] Again, these correlations are *much* higher when corruption is low. In countries ranking below the median on the 1998 TI index, the Global Competitiveness bribery index is moderately correlated with trust ($r = -.347$), but for the more corrupt countries, the correlation is incorrectly signed ($r = .407$). The black market currency premium is modest when the premium is very low ($r = -.275$), but almost zero ($r = -.009$) for countries above the median premium.

We thus have considerable evidence that the linkage between corruption and trust is highly dependent upon both context and on who benefits from corruption. Ironically, the correlations are strongest when there is the least corruption (and the most trust). Moreover, people are more likely to distrust their fellow citizens when elites, not ordinary citizens, violate the rules.

Romania and Sweden: The Ends of the Rainbow

We shift our focus from comparing nations to a more detailed study of corruption, trust, and confidence in the government in two countries—Romania and Sweden. Romania is not typical. Its government was harsher than most in the former communist bloc. Its public is less trusting, and its government is more corrupt than most in this bloc (the average TI score was 3.6, while Romania's was 3.0). Moreover, both Romanian correlations with perceived corruption—trust in people and confidence in the legal system—are outliers. Therefore, Romania is somewhat exceptional, but overall it is not too much out of line with other former communist nations.

Considering trust in people, we are unable to find strong relationships between perceptions of corruption, informal social networks, and trust in people for Romania. For the three waves of the WVS, the simple correlations between trust in people and confidence in the legal system are .15 in Sweden (close to the .18 reported by Rothstein 2001: 491, for a different survey), .08 in Romania, and .01 in Russia. Perhaps the lessons of Sweden cannot be transferred to Romania because Sweden (or the Nordic nations more generally) is exceptional—high trust, low corruption, and strong state. The state can shape social values from above because it has willing subjects—and not too difficult a task in engineering trust.

We focus first on the 1995 WVS, the only data source with questions on both trust and corruption. Since we wish to examine the reciprocal linkages between trust and perceptions of corruption, we estimate two-stage least squares models.[5]

The trust equation is based upon Uslaner (2002) who posits optimism and control as the key determinants of generalized trust. Trusting strangers is risky. However, the risks seem less consequential for optimists. If people believe that the world is a good place that is going to get better, and that they can make it better, dealing with strangers will seem to offer more opportunities than risks. If people believe that the future looks bleak and that their fate is largely set by others, they will look askance at dealing with strangers.

The corruption equation focuses on general questions of morality, optimism and trust, specific moral dictates, exposure to information (Adsera et al. 2000), and (of course), trust. We present the results in table 2.2.

What stands out most clearly in the WVS data analysis is that there is no reciprocal relationship between trust and corruption: Trust does not affect corruption, nor does corruption shape trust. Both coefficients are

Table 2.2 Trust in other people and perceptions of corruption in Romania, 1995 World Values Survey

	Range		Coefficient	Standard error	t ratio
Corruption equation					
Trust	0 = careful	1 = trust	−.059	.39	−.015
Clear standards good/evil	1 = yes	3 = no	**.150******	**.053**	**2.82**
Hard work vs. luck or connections	1 = work	10 = luck	**−.048*****	**.019**	**−2.57**
Getting rich at the expense of others	1 = expense	0 = all gain	**.052*****	**.020**	**2.66**
Age	18–93		.004	.003	1.27
Left–right placement	1 = left	10 = always	−.022	.022	−1.02
OK to buy stolen goods	10 = right	1 = never	−.034	.029	−1.15
OK to accept bribes	1 = never	10 = always	**.073****	**.030**	**2.44**
Frequency watching TV daily	1 = no TV	4 = 3 + hours	**.152*****	**.055**	**2.75**
Subjective social class	1 = upper	4 = lower	.065	.056	1.15
Constant			**1.623******	**.355**	**4.58**
Trust equation					
Extent of corruption	1 = none	4 = all officials	−.052	.066	−.78
Financial satisfaction	1 = dissatisfied	10 = satisfied	−.008	.011	−.74
Life satisfaction	1 = dissatisfied	10 = satisfied	.001	.011	.09
Clear standards good/evil	1 = yes	3 = no	**−.047****	**.021**	**−2.21**
Religious	1 = religious	3 = atheist	.049	.042	1.16
Age	18–93		−.001	.001	−.52
Education (year ended school)	0–43		.002	.004	.36
Future bright or bleak	0 = bleak	1 = bright	**.084****	**.039**	**2.18**
Democracy is better	1 = strong agree	4 = strong disagree	**.103******	**.023**	**4.45**
Postmaterialism	0 = materialist	8 = post	.024	.012	2.12
Confidence in legal system	1 = none	4 = great deal	**.038****	**.021**	**1.78**
OK to accept bribe	1 = never	10 = always	.011	.014	.79
OK to buy stolen goods	1 = never	10 = always	−.0003	.012	−.02
OK to cheat on taxes	1 = never	10 = always	**−.020****	**.011**	**−1.83**
Less poverty than 10 years ago	1 = more	3 = less	**.058***	**.037**	**1.58**
Constant			.324	.229	1.42

Notes: **** $p < .001$, *** $p < .01$, ** $p < .05$, * $p < .10$. Coefficients significant at $p < .10$ or better are in bold. $N = 463$; RMSE Corruption = 1.019; RMSE Trust = .385; estimation by two-stage least squares. Exogenous variables: OK to avoid paying for transport; OK to claim benefits not entitled to; education; confidence in armed forces; confidence in civil service.

insignificant. Trust is largely shaped by optimism (whether the future is bright or bleak and whether there is less poverty than ten years ago).

People who have confidence in the legal system and people who say that it is wrong to cheat on taxes are (modestly) more likely to trust others, but particular acts of dishonesty do not seem to matter much for either trust or perceptions of corruption: the acceptability of taking bribes and buying stolen goods have no effect on trust. Although the acceptability of taking bribes makes people more likely to say that there is a lot of corruption, buying stolen goods is not related to perceptions of elite honesty.

The Romanian public makes a clear distinction: Bribery is corruption, buying stolen goods (or cheating on taxes, or the other actions in the WVS survey that are not included in this estimation) is not. If people cheat on taxes, it destroys our faith in each other. Cheating on taxes is something ordinary folks do—and unlike claiming benefits you are not entitled to or free riding public transport, people may be more likely to feel that cheating on taxes robs other citizens. There *is* a positive link between confidence in the legal system and trust in other people. However, Romanians do not make a clear link between the legal system and specific norms of moral behavior (the average correlation between trust in the legal system and the five morality questions is .052).

We do see one key exception: People who say that taking bribes is unacceptable are more likely to say that the political system is corrupt. Public officials—the elite—take bribes. Ordinary citizens are not in position to receive favors. Their petty violations (buying stolen goods, claiming government benefits, etc.) do not qualify as corruption for most Romanians. Simply getting by demands working around the system. Everyone bends the rules, some more than others. Equally powerful predictors, however, are measures of optimism and control. Perceptions of corruption are higher among people who believe that some get rich at the expense of others and that some get ahead by luck or connections rather than hard work. Again, what distinguishes corruption is not disrespect for the law, but gain at the expense of ordinary folks.

We briefly summarize the results from the CID survey. There are no questions on corruption in that survey, but we were able to test for institutional effects more clearly and for the possible impact of helping networks on generalized trust. Following Badescu (2003), we substituted trust in people of different ethnic and religious backgrounds for the generalized trust question. These questions are better measures of trust in strangers in a society where there are tensions between ethnic Romanians, Hungarians, and Romani, as well as between Romanian Orthodox adherents and followers of other faiths, but also little contact with people who are different from yourself.

Overall, measures of optimism and control are the strongest predictors of trust in both different ethnic groups and different religions: People who believe that life will be better for the next generation, are satisfied with their lives now, and who believe that hard work (rather than luck) is the key to success are more trusting. However, there is no connection between support networks and generalized trust: How often people borrow from neighbors or relatives or give support to relatives or neighbors does not shape generalized trust.

There are very weak relations between trust in governmental institutions, such as the courts and politicians, and generalized trust (cf. Gibson 2001; Mishler and Rose 2001). However, we do see some greater support than before for Rothstein's argument that institutions matter. People who are satisfied with how democracy works are substantially more trusting in others (though this may also be a measure of optimism). People who feel that the courts treat people fairly are *much more trusting than those who see special favors*. It is not simple faith in the courts but rather perceptions of fairness that matter. How to devise neutral institutions in the absence of generalized trust remains problematic, especially since people who say that it is important for a good citizen to obey the law are significantly *less likely to trust people of different religions*. Trusting people long for a more equitable legal system, but they recognize that people must make do any way they can under the present regime. Ethnic Romanians are far less likely to trust people of different ethnic groups or different religions than either Roma or ethnic Hungarians. Hungarians in particular are more likely to see the legal system as biased against them, so reforming the legal system is far more than a question of institutional design.

Rothstein is correct in forging a link between confidence in the legal system and generalized trust for countries making the transition from communism. In both the WVS and CID data sets, we find significant effects for evaluations of the legal system on generalized trust. In the WVS, the effect of confidence in the law on trust is modest—it is insignificant in the CID estimations, dwarfed by the perceptions that the courts do not treat people equally. However, Romanians do not make Rothstein's hypothesized link between corruption and trust. Romanians *are* disturbed by corruption, but they do not let it dominate their view of fellow citizens. Corrupt government is the scourge of the elite, not the masses.

We find additional support for these arguments in another survey of the Romanian public in 2001.[6] Petty corruption does not shape people's views of others. There is only a minuscule correlation (tau-c = .021) between trust in others and the number of "gifts" people gave during the past year to resolve problems with city hall, the courts, the police, hospitals, or at school. But there is a slightly stronger, though still very modest, correlation (.113) between generalized trust and perceived corruption. Yet, there is only a weak connection between trust and perceptions that the government is fighting corruption (tau-c = .107). The relationships are somewhat stronger for "trust in justice" and perceived corruption (−.188), and the belief that government is fighting corruption (.138). None of these relations is particularly powerful, and they suggest that Romanians are more concerned with the arbitrariness of the court system than they are with putting those who are getting rich at the public trough in jail. Indeed, we see only a moderate correlation between trust in justice and trust in people ($r = .133$).

Fixing Corruption?

People in the formerly communist nations have less confidence in the legal system if they perceive it to be corrupt. Their perceptions of corruption do not affect their trust in strangers (most transition countries are at the corrupt end of the TI scale).

There is both good news and bad news for the transition countries in these findings. The good news is that formerly communist countries can reduce corruption without a change in long-standing values such as trust. We estimated cross-national regressions for corruption for the transition countries and for other nations. The keys to less corruption are more government stability and fewer government regulations on business (cf. Rose-Ackerman 1999: 35, 227).[7] The extent of business regulations *alone* accounts for 57 percent of the variance in corruption in the formerly communist countries. Outside the transition countries, trust is a key determinant of corruption as well.

However, this leads directly to three pieces of bad news. First, if we ease business regulations, this *might* increase economic inequality (though the simple correlation between the two is a mere .044). Moreover, if it does so, it will decrease trust further, because the level of inequality is the single best predictor of trust cross-nationally and in the United States over time.[8] Second, even if we can reduce corruption in the transition nations by economic reform, it will not have the payoff in increasing trust that we might expect elsewhere, because there is no strong relationship between the two. Even if corruption is greatly reduced, to the levels that are similar with the ones in the West, it is not likely that a correlation with trust will emerge (as we have now in the West) because the linkage (if there is one) is from trust to corruption. Third, while confidence in the legal system does seem to lead to more trust in other people, the causal direction of the linkage is far from clear (Rothstein 2001: 491; Uslaner 2002: 243–5). Greater reliance on the legal system in Central and Eastern Europe might be self-defeating if the courts are corrupt or if people settle their disputes outside the legal system (Rose-Ackerman 1999: 152–3). Courts *may* create greater compliance with the law, but coercion is often a poor substitute for trust, leading to asymmetries in power and greater resentment (Baier 1986: 234; Gambetta 1988: 220; Knight 2000: 365). Legal systems that work depend upon a social consensus on what is allowable (Rose-Ackerman 1999: 98; Rothstein 2001: 493; Sitkin and Roth 1993). Putting the old legal norms into new institutions is not likely to reduce corruption or to create trust from above.

Bo Rothstein's Sweden, where the strong underbelly of trust makes for clean government and where honest politicians set a good example for the rest of us, may be too exceptional to serve as an example to countries in transition. It seems like a real-world example of the fictional town of Lake Wobegon, Minnesota (on the public radio program, "A Prairie Home Companion"), where all the men are strong, all the women are good looking, and all the children are above average. Citizens of transition countries are *not* exceptional. Like people elsewhere, their trust depends upon optimism and a sense of control. Their history, which may be exceptional, makes feelings of optimism and control unlikely and the post-transition years have not led people to feel better about the future.[9] A better life, more than new institutions and less corruption, are central to less corruption. Fighting corruption might lead indirectly to more trust, if it results in a fairer legal system and greater income equality. Putting corrupt officials in jail is certainly praiseworthy, but we should be careful of expecting too much from incarceration. We can seek to improve honesty and trust in the transition countries, but we need to work on them separately. Romanians would be pleased to have more of either.

Notes

* We are grateful to the Starr Foundation, through the Institutional Research and Exchanges Board of the United States Department of State for a grant to us, together with in conjunction with Paul Sum of the University of North Dakota and Mihai Pisica and Cosmin Marian of Babes-Bolyai University, Cluj, Romania, under the IREX Caspian and Black Sea Collaborative Program (2001). We are also grateful to Meril James, Secretary-General of Gallup International, for sharing the Gallup Millennium surveys with us. Some of the data come from the InterUniversity Consortium for Political and Social Research (ICPSR). Neither Gallup International nor the ICPSR is responsible for any of the conclusions we reach. Uslaner is also grateful to the Russell Sage Foundation and the Carnegie Foundation for a grant under the Russell Sage program on The Social Dimensions of Inequality (see http://www.russellsage.org/programs/proj_reviews/social-inequality.htm) and to the General Research Board of the Graduate School of the University of Maryland, College Park. Badescu's research for this chapter was supported in part through the Blue Bird Project, which is financed by a consortium of international donors and administered by the Central European University, Budapest. Specifically, contributions from the international donor, Bank of Sweden Tercentenary Foundation, were used to fund his work.

We are particularly grateful for the helpful comments of Mark Lichbach, Marc Morje Howard, János Kornai, Susan Rose-Ackerman, Bo Rothstein, and the participants at the Honesty and Trust workshops, especially Bruce Ackerman.

1. We measure trust by the "standard" interpersonal trust question (here from the World Values Survey [WVS]): "Generally speaking do you believe most people can be trusted or can't you be too careful in dealing with people?" Our measure of corruption is the 1998 estimate by Transparency International (TI). We used the 1995–96 estimates from the WVS when available, but supplemented these data with the 1990–93 estimates when no third wave surveys were available. See Uslaner (2002: ch. 8) for a more detailed discussion of the data sources. The TI estimates of corruption are derived from elite surveys of corruption; they are available at http://www.transparency.de/documents/cpi/index.html. The relationship is weakened somewhat when we control for log GNP per capita and the level of economic inequality (the Gini index), but remains powerfully significant. For the 2001 rankings, see http://www.transparency.org/cpi/2001/cpi2001.html.
2. We also conducted surveys of the mass public in Moldova and of organizational activists in Romania and Moldova using an expanded version of the Citizenship Involvement Democracy (CID) common core questionnaire. See the CID web page at http://www.mzes.uni-mannheim.de/projekte/cid/. See a description of our research project at http://www.irex.org/programs/black-caspian-sea/grantees01-02.htm, and at http://www.policy.ro.
3. At the country level, the correlations between trust and the TI index of corruption are .826 for the least corrupt countries, .251 for the middle group, and $-.098$ for the most corrupt. For the formerly communist countries, the correlation is $-.274$. We also ran a regression of trust on perceived corruption and interactions of perceived corruption for each of the three categories (omitting the constant term, but also including the Gini index of inequality and percent Protestant, as in Uslaner 2002: ch. 8). The main effect was insignificant; the interactions for most and middle levels were marginally significant (at $p < .10$), and the coefficient for least corrupt was significant at ($p < .01$).

4. The black market, or the informal economy, involves a large number of people, at least in comparison to "elite" corruption. The currency premium for the black market thus represents the toll that the informal economy takes on the formal economy. The data from the Global Competitiveness Survey and Impulse Magazine's index come from Friedman et al. (2000) and are available at http://www.worldbank.org/wbi/governance/. The data on the black market premium come from the State Failure Task Force data set, available at http://gking.harvard.edu/data.shtml.
5. Trust is a dichotomy; perceptions of corruption are an ordinal variable. So using two-stage least squares may seem inappropriate. However, it is more important to control for reciprocal causation than to estimate models such as probit or ordered probit and to ignore issues of causal ordering, especially in the absence of routines that would estimate a two-stage ordered probit. The exogenous variables we include in the estimations are listed at the bottom of table 2.2. In the table, we present results that are statistically significant at $p < .10$ or better in bold type.
6. The survey, the November 2001 Romanian Barometer of Public Opinion, was funded by the Open Society Foundation, and conducted by the Research Center for Urban Studies Institute (CURS). Data are posted at http://www.osf.ro.
7. The measure of stability comes from the World Bank governance project. It includes war, social unrest, orderly transfer of power, politically motivated violence, and international disputes. For the details, see Kaufmann et al. (1999: 39). The business regulation measure comes from LaPorta et al. (1997). We estimated a variety of models, including a simultaneous equation model of trust and corruption (see Uslaner 2003). Trust and corruption are clearly interconnected, but the effect of trust on corruption is much stronger than that of malfeasance on faith in people. Our early models included a wide range of factors associated with corruption in the literature—various measures of a country's wealth and well-being, economic inequality, political and social freedoms, institutional factors (including political participation, federalism), the openness of markets, the share of the gross domestic product devoted to government spending, other socioeconomic variables (ethnic heterogeneity, education), media consumption, and other economic policies (including summary indices from the Heritage Foundation, price controls, and the rights of shareholders). None was significant in these estimations.
8. See Uslaner 2002: chs. 7, 8; 2003. These estimates exclude the formerly communist nations.
9. We would expect younger people in Romania to be more optimistic, trusting, and tolerant than people who lived most of their lives under communism. We have about 50 measures of optimism, control, trust, tolerance, support for the polity, and civic engagement in our Romanian CID survey and in each one (save a measure of being able to do what you want to do), the younger cohort was less trusting than any of the older generations.

References

Adsera, Alicia, Carles Boix, and Mark Payne. 2000. *Are You Being Served? Political Accountability and Quality of Government.* Washington DC: Inter-American Development Bank Research Department Working Paper No. 438.

Almond, Gabriel and Sidney Verba. 1963. *The Civic Culture.* Princeton NJ: Princeton University Press.

Badescu, Gabriel. 2003. Social Trust and Democratization in the Post-Communist Societies. In G. Badescu and E.M. Uslaner (eds.). *Social Capital and the Democratic Transition,* pp. 120–39. London: Routledge.

Badescu, Gabriel and Eric M. Uslaner (eds.). 2003. *Social Capital and the Transition to Democracy.* London: Routledge.

Baier, Annette. 1986. Trust and Antitrust. *Ethics* 96: 231–60.

Banfield, Edward. 1958. *The Moral Basis of a Backward Society.* New York: Free Press.

Cohen, Jean L. 1997. *American Civil Society Talk.* National Commission on Civic Renewal Working Paper No. 6. College Park MD.

Flap, Henk and Beate Völker. 2003. Communist Societies, the Velvet Revolution, and Weak Ties: The Case of East Germany. In G. Badescu and E.M. Uslaner (eds.). *Social Capital and the Democratic Transition,* pp. 28–47. London: Routledge.

Friedman, Eric, Simon Johnson, Daniel Kaufmann, and Pablo Zoido-Lobaton. 2000. Dodging the Grabbing Hand: The Determinants of Unofficial Activity in 69 Countries. *Journal of Public Economics* 76: 459–93.

Fukuyama, Francis. 1995. *Trust: The Social Virtues and the Creation of Prosperity*. New York: Free Press.
Gambetta, Diego. 1988. Can We Trust Trust? In D. Gambetta (ed.). *Trust*, pp. 213–37. Oxford: Basil Blackwell.
Gibson, James L. 2001. Social Networks, Civil Society, and the Prospects for Consolidating Russia's Democratic Transition. *American Journal of Political Science* 45: 51–69.
Hardin, Russell. 2002. *Trust and Trustworthiness*. New York: Russell Sage Foundation.
Hayoz, Nicolas and Victor Sergeyev. 2003. Social Networks in Russian Politics. In G. Badescu and E.M. Uslaner (eds.). *Social Capital and the Democratic Transition*, pp. 46–60. London: Routledge.
Howard, Marc Morje. 2002. *The Weakness of Civil Society in Post-Communist Europe*. New York: Cambridge University Press.
Kaufmann, Daniel, Aart Kraay, and Pablo Ziodo-Lobaton. 1999. *Governance Matters*. World Bank Policy Research Paper No. 2196, Washington DC: World Bank.
Knight, Jack. 2000. Social Norms and the Rule of Law: Fostering Trust in a Socially Diverse Society. In K.S. Cook (ed.). *Trust in Society*, pp. 354–73. New York: Russell Sage Foundation.
Kornai, János. 2000. *Hidden in an Envelope: Gratitude Payments to Medical Doctors in Hungary*, at http://www.colbud.hu/honesty-trust/kornai/pub01.
Lambsdorff, Johann Graf. 1999. *Corruption in Empirical Research—A Review*. Transparency International Working Paper, at http://www.transparency.de/working-papers.html/lambsdorff_eresearch.html
Lane, Robert E. 1959. *Political Life*. New York: Free Press.
LaPorta, Rafael, Florencio Lopez-Silanes, Andrei Shleifer, and Robert W. Vishny. 1997. Trust in Large Organizations. *American Economic Review Papers and Proceedings* 87: 333–8.
Ledeneva, Alena V. 1998. *Russia's Economy of Favours: Blat, Networking and Informal Exchange*. Cambridge: Cambridge University Press.
Leite, Carlos and Jens Weidemann. 1999. *Does Mother Nature Corrupt? Natural Resources, Corruption, and Economic Growth?* Washington DC: International Monetary Fund Working Paper No. 85.
Levi, Margaret. 1998. A State of Trust. In V. Braithwaite and M. Levi (eds.). *Trust and Governance*, pp. 77–101. New York: Russell Sage Foundation.
Mauro, Pablo. 1995. Corruption and Growth. *Quarterly Journal of Economics* 110: 681–712.
Miller, William L., Åse B. Grødeland, and Tatyana Y. Koshechkina. 2002. Bribery and Other Ways of Coping with Officialdom in Post-Communist Eastern Europe. In A.J. Heidenheimer and M. Johnston (eds.). *Political Corruption: Concepts and Contexts*, pp. 1–46. New Brunswick NJ: Transaction.
Mishler, William and Richard Rose. 2001. The Origins of Political Trust. *Comparative Political Studies* 34: 30–62.
Misztal, Barbara A. 1996. *Trust in Modern Societies*. Cambridge: Polity Press.
Newton, Kenneth. 1999. Social and Political Trust. In P. Norris (ed.). *Critical Citizens: Global Support for Democratic Government*, pp. 169–87. New York: Oxford University Press.
———. 2002. *Who Trusts?* Manuscript, University of Southampton UK.
Offe, Claus. 1999. Trust and Knowledge, Rules and Decisions: Exploring a Difficult Conceptual Terrain. In M. Warren (ed.). *Democracy and Trust*, pp. 42–87. Cambridge: Cambridge University Press.
Orren, Gary. 1997. Fall from Grace: The Public's Loss of Faith in Government. In J.S. Nye, P.D. Zelikow, and D.C. King (eds.). *Why People Don't Trust Government*, pp. 77–107. Cambridge MA: Harvard University Press.
Putnam, Robert D. 1993. *Making Democracy Work: Civic Traditions in Modern Italy*. Princeton NJ: Princeton University Press.
———. 2000. *Bowling Alone*. New York: Simon and Schuster.
Rawls, John A. 1971. *A Theory of Justice*. Cambridge MA: Harvard University Press.
Riordan, William. 1948. *Plunkitt of Tammany Hall*. New York: Alfred A. Knopf.
Rose-Ackerman, Susan. 1994. Reducing Bribery in the Public Sector. In D.V. Trang (ed.). *Corruption and Democracy. Political Institutions, Processes and Corruption in Transition States in East-Central Europe and in the Former Soviet Union*, pp. 21–8. Budapest: Institute for Constitutional and Legislative Policy.
———. 1999. *Corruption and Government: Causes, Consequences, and Reform*. New York: Cambridge University Press.
Rosenberg, Morris. 1956. Misanthropy and Political Ideology. *American Sociological Review* 21: 690–5.

Rothstein, Bo. 2001. Trust, Social Dilemmas, and Collective Memories: On the Rise and Decline of the Swedish Model. *Journal of Theoretical Politics* 12: 477–501.

Seligman, Adam B. 1997. *The Problem of Trust*. Princeton NJ : Princeton University Press.

Sitkin, Sim B. and Nancy L. Roth. 1993. Explaining the Limited Effectiveness of Legalistic "Remedies" for Trust/Distrust. *Organization Science* 4: 367–92.

Trang, Duc V. 1994. Foreword. In D.V. Trang (ed.). *Corruption and Democracy. Political Institutions, Processes and Corruption in Transition States in East-Central Europe and in the Former Soviet Union*, pp. 1–8. Budapest: Institute for Constitutional and Legislative Policy.

Treisman, Daniel. 2000. The Causes of Corruption: A Cross-National Study. *Journal of Public Economics* 76: 399–457.

Tyler, Tom R. 1990. *Why People Obey the Law*. New Haven CT: Yale University Press.

Uslaner, Eric M. 1999a. Trust but Verify: Social Capital and Moral Behavior. *Social Science Information* 38: 29–56.

———. 1999b. Morality Plays: Social Capital and Moral Behavior in Anglo-American Democracies. In J.V. Deth, M. Maraffi, K. Newton, and P. Whiteley (eds.). *Social Capital and European Democracy*. London: Routledge.

———. 2002. *The Moral Foundations of Trust*. New York: Cambridge University Press.

———. 2003. Trust and Corruption. In L. Robison and M. Siles (eds.), *Capital and Poverty Reduction in Latin America and the Caribbean: Toward a New Paradigm*. Santiago, Chile: United Nations Economic Commission For Latin America and the Caribbean.

PART II

Trust and the Business Environment

CHAPTER THREE

Measuring Trust in Transition: Preliminary Findings from 26 Transition Economies

MARTIN RAISER, ALAN ROUSSO, AND FRANKLIN STEVES

Introduction

Much of the literature on institutions and social capital posits that trust is an important prerequisite to well-functioning markets (Arrow 1972; North 1981; Putnam 1993; Fukuyama 1995; Stiglitz 1999). Trust lowers transaction costs and facilitates cooperation among entities that might otherwise view mutually advantageous exchange as too costly or risky. Especially in places where third-party enforcement—that is, the state and its constituent legal and regulatory institutions—is weak or uncertain, a basic belief in a counterpart's honesty is an "important lubricant" in a social and economic system (Arrow 1974). In these circumstances, trust can be built through repeated interactions, and the creation of a reputation for cooperating, even where incentives for shirking may be strong (Axelrod 1984).

Trust is a commodity in relatively short supply in transition countries, especially in the early stages when institutions are weak and the formal and informal bonds holding the economy together are ruptured. Transition, after all, entails massive transactional upheaval, as markets replace central planning as the main mechanism for matching producers with consumers. In relations among businesses, widespread rematching spells significant social costs, until new relationships have been formed and some degree of durability and predictability has returned (see Blanchard and Kremer 1997). Although costly and complex, the process of breaking up existing ties between firms and allowing for the entry of competitors is necessary and beneficial in the longer term. However, until that point is reached, the experience of transition can be devastating for firms and consumers, a condition that breeds caution and mistrust. Indeed, as Joseph Schumpeter (1934) has written, the process of creative destruction is the essential fact about capitalism, and transition is perhaps the most extreme case of "creative destruction" we know of in recent economic history (see also EBRD 1997). The hope at the beginning was, and remains, that once the cards have been reshuffled, everyone will end up with a better hand.

We are currently in the middle of this process. This paper looks at how enterprises cope with an uncertain contractual environment where trust is lacking. Businesses in this environment face a prisoner's dilemma—they would be best off cooperating with each other in executing a contract, but they each face a powerful incentive to renege on their obligations in the absence of third-party enforcement mechanisms to punish defectors. The literature on repeated games, however, holds that cooperation can be built over time between actors caught in a prisoner's dilemma through strategies of reciprocity—that is, in a strategic interaction, cooperative moves are met with reciprocal cooperation and defections with defection. This has been found to be a robust strategy for building cooperation in the absence of a formal sanctioning mechanism in a variety of settings (Axelrod 1988). The analogy in business transactions is relational contracting—firms building stable business relationships with known partners and resolving disputes through informal rather than formal mechanisms. Even in developed markets, where court systems and other market-supporting institutions are more advanced, firms are more likely to rely on relationships with well-known business partners to resolve disputes than more formal mechanisms (Macauley 1963).

It is not surprising, therefore, that previous research has found a strong correlation between relational contracting and trust at the enterprise level (McMillan and Woodruff 1999; Johnson et al. 1999). Although efficient for the firm, this has social costs, because new entrants are deterred and potentially profitable matches are not made. If courts are perceived to be incapable of enforcing contracts, firms have been able to rely on reputational enforcement mechanisms, by collecting information on new trading partners from other participants in existing business networks and sharing their own information on the business conduct of their trading partners with others. In an economy with high barriers to entry for new firms and dominance by a relatively small number of key players in any specific sector, effective networks may exist to circulate information on business conduct. Under those conditions firms will be disciplined to behave in accordance with relevant commercial norms lest they receive a reputation for unreliability. Recent research has found that third-party enforcement through networks may be a useful complement to enforcement through the court system (see Woodruff, ch. 6).

In this chapter, we employ data from a 2002 survey of firms in transition countries conducted by the European Bank for Reconstruction and Development (EBRD) together with the World Bank, which asked firms specific questions about the contracting environment and the quality of the courts. The Business Environment and Enterprise Performance Survey (BEEPS) is a rich data source for an analysis of the contracting environment for enterprises in transition, both at the firm and at the country level.

In this paper, which we plan to follow up with a series of enterprise-level studies, we investigate the country-level variation in the contracting environment and relate this to other country characteristics, such as progress in economic, legal, and institutional reform. Given the country-level focus, we cannot say much about the importance of relational contracting in building trust among firms and instead emphasize the role of third-party enforcement mechanisms.

In seeking to measure the degree of trust inherent in business relationships, we look at country averages of the demand for prepayment made by suppliers. We find that, when compared with other measures of trust used in the literature, prepayment is the most robust indicator at the country level. We also find that trust increases as reforms progress. Among the various potential determinants of trust, we find that the impartiality and honesty of the courts shows a strong correlation with prepayment, whereas indicators of legal reform or the efficiency (speed and affordability) of courts show weaker results. Social and business networks have a strikingly varied association with trust. In countries where family networks play an important role, trust is significantly higher, whereas the opposite is the case in countries with significant reliance on networks based around government and around enterprise insiders. Finally, we find no association between trust among enterprises as measured by the BEEPS and generalized interpersonal trust as measured in the World Values Survey (WVS).

The remainder of the paper proceeds as follows. In the next section, we briefly describe the data set and how it can be used to test or advance many of the key arguments in the literature on contracting in transition economies. The second section describes how prepayment can be an effective proxy for trust in business relationships. We then investigate the extent to which prepayment is correlated with other factors normally associated with trust: income per capita, governance, and the degree of economic reform. The third section looks at a range of possible candidates for what generates trust in transition economies—legal system reform, experience with the courts, generalized trust in the society, or the formation of business networks. The final section concludes with proposed areas for further research.

The Survey

The BEEPS was conducted with nearly 6,000 firms in 26 transition economies (all of Eastern Europe and the former Soviet Union except Turkmenistan, where implementation was discontinued before the survey was completed).[1] The survey is heavily weighted toward small enterprises and private firms. There are some state-owned firms in the sample, however, and some larger enterprises (with up to 10,000 employees). The sample is stratified to match more or less the productive structure in each country, implying a heavy representation of service firms.

These features distinguish the sample from that used in Johnson et al. (1999), which was based on only private manufacturing firms in five transition economies. Unlike Johnson et al., our survey is not a survey of specific transactions. Our measures of prepayment, trade credit, loyalty, business networks, and so on, are all based on questions relating to the average experience of each firm rather than to a specific transaction. This is a weakness that makes our results far less precise than the transactions-specific survey used by Johnson et al. The advantage of our survey is that it covers more countries, with vastly different contracting environments. One benefit of this larger sample is that we can examine and compare the contracting environment at the country level. It is here that variations in the quality of third-party enforcement through the courts or through reputation networks should be most evident.[2]

Prepayment as a Measure of Trust

We operationalize the notion of trust in business transactions by measuring the level of prepayment demanded by firms from their customers. A firm's willingness to forgo prepayment may be seen as an indication that its directors believe they will be paid fully and on time, either due to trust in the customer's reliability or in the legal system's ability to fairly adjudicate business disputes. High prepayment demands, conversely, can be seen as a measure of distrust in a customer and/or lack of confidence in the contract enforcement regime.

Previously, the literature on trust and contract enforcement used an alternative metric. McMillan and Woodruff (1999) and Johnson et al. (1999; 2002) construct measures of trust and relational contracting at the enterprise level, using the extent to which firms are willing to give trade credit to a customer as a measure of trust. It is assumed that an enterprise will only sell goods to another business on credit if it believes it will be repaid. This belief can be based on the knowledge the enterprise has of its business partner either through repeatedly trading with him, or through a recommendation from a third party. It can also be based on confidence in the efficacy of third-party enforcement—that is, the belief that if repayment is delayed, the creditor firm can go to a court and have its credit rights enforced. Figure 3.1 reports country means for prepayment and trade credit among the firms in the BEEPS.

A priori, both prepayment and trade credit appear to be reasonable proxies for trust in business relationships. We compared trade credit and prepayment as alternative measures of trust between business partners and found prepayment to be the more robust measure at the country level. Using country means for trade credit and prepayment, we ran a number of simple correlations with other factors that are associated with trust in the existing literature—income per capita, good governance, and economic reform. There is a growing body of evidence which suggests that wealthier and better-governed economies are higher trust societies (Fukuyama 1995;

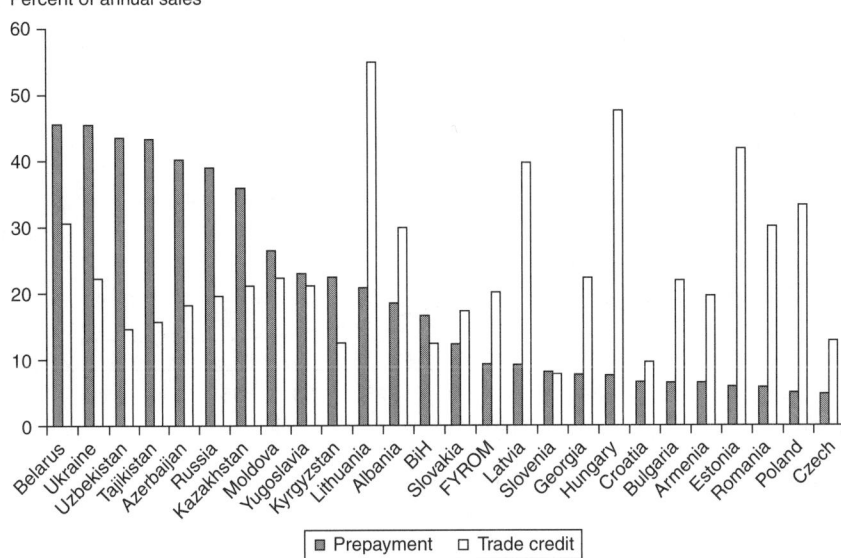

Figure 3.1 Prepayment and trade credit, transition countries, 2002
Source: BEEPS 2002.

Putnam 1993; Rose-Ackerman 2001; Knack and Keefer 1997; Zak and Knack 2001).

We use GDP per capita to measure income, the World Bank's governance indicators to measure good governance, and the EBRD transition indicators to measure market reform. The World Bank governance indicators give scores for voice and accountability, political stability and violence, government effectiveness, regulatory burden, rule of law, and graft. We take the unweighted average across these dimensions as our indicator of governance. The EBRD transition indicators give scores which range from 1 (little reform) to 4 (high level of reform) for small- and large-scale privatization, price liberalization, trade and foreign exchange controls, governance and enterprise restructuring, competition policy, infrastructure (telecommunications, railways, electricity, roads, water), banking reform and interest rate liberalization, and securities markets and nonbank financial institutions. Again, we use the unweighted average of these dimensions as our indicator of reform.

Overall, the correlations between prepayment and these three measures of trust are quite strong: prepayments are significantly lower in countries that are richer and better governed (see figures 3.2 and 3.3).[3] The coefficient of correlation between prepayment and per capita GDP is −.54, significant at the 1 percent level.[4] Similarly, the governance indicator is correlated with prepayment with a coefficient of −0.69, again significant at the 1 percent level.[5]

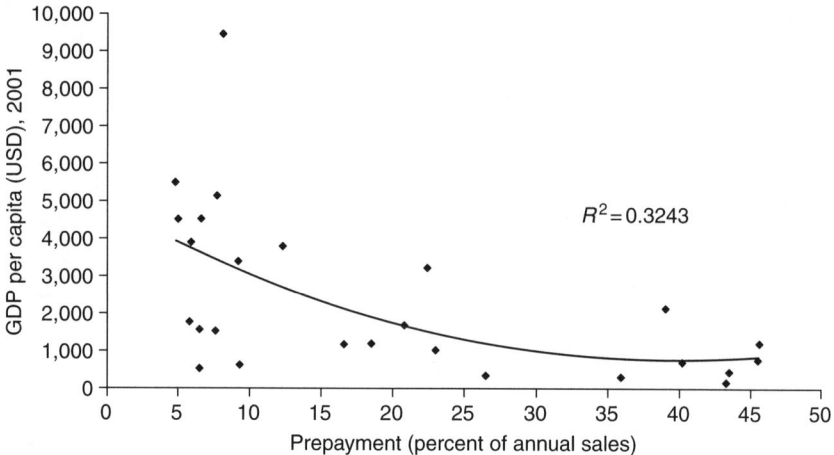

Figure 3.2 Prepayment and GDP per capita, transition countries, 2002
Note: GDP I measured in US dollars at current (2001) exchange rates.
Sources: BEEPS 2002; EBRD database.

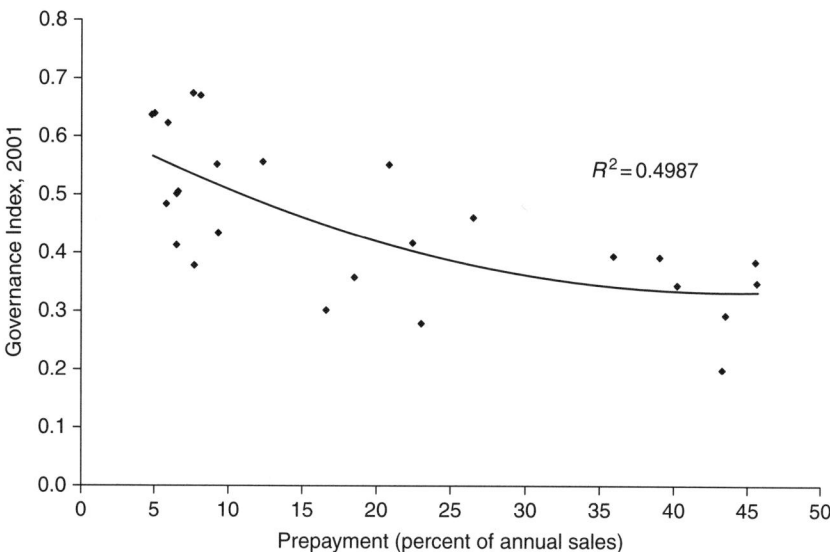

Figure 3.3 Prepayment and governance, transition countries, 2002
Note: The World Bank's Governance Index is composed of scores on six indicators: Voice and accountability; political stability; government effectiveness; regulatory quality; rule-of-law; and control of corruption. For this figure the scale has been normalized to 0–1, with 1 representing better governance.

With respect to reform, figure 3.4 illustrates the close correlation between prepayment and economic reform in the transition countries, as measured by the EBRD transition indicators.[6] The coefficient of correlation between prepayment and the EBRD indictor is −0.70, significant at the 1 percent level.[7]

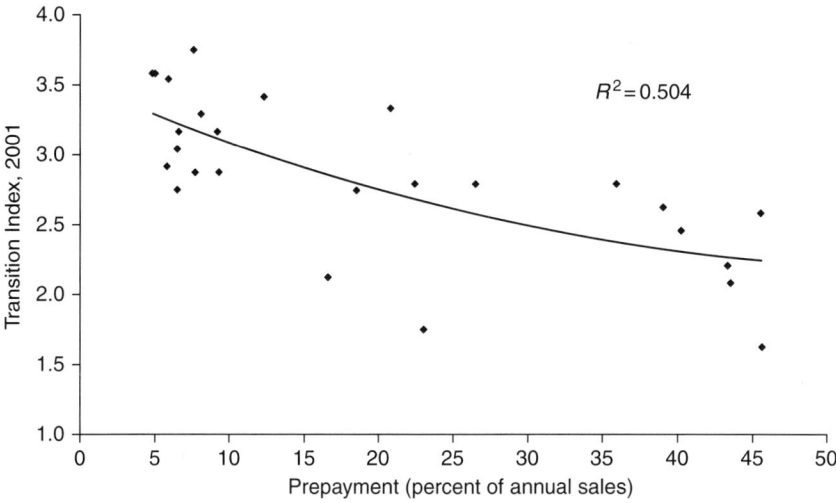

Figure 3.4 Prepayment and economic reform, transition countries, 2002

Note: The EBRD Transition Index is composed of scores on nine indicators: Large-scale privatization; small-scale privatization; governance and enterprise restructuring; price liberalization; trade and forex liberalization; competition policy; banking reform and interest rate liberalization; securities markets and nonbank financial institutions; and infrastructure reform. The scores are scaled on a 1–4 scale, with 4 representing the most reform.

Sources: BEEPS 2002; EBRD.

Why does the level of prepayment demanded by firms provide a better fit with other indicators of trust than trade credit? One answer may be that trade credit works better as a measure of trust at the enterprise level than at the country level. As noted by Johnson et al. (1999), the willingness of an enterprise to extend trade credit to a particular customer increases over time through repeated transactions. A supplier learns over time how good a credit risk his business partner is by examining his record of timely and complete payment in accordance with the terms of the contract. Noncooperative relations would be discontinued. The information on the length of existing business relationships is, however, lost in the aggregation at the country level. It is possible to imagine an economy, where confidence in third-party enforcement is very low and hence businesses trade only within small networks based on relational contracting. Average levels of trade credit in such an economy could be quite high even though we would not regard it as a "high" trust economy. Moreover, in the context of transition it is also possible that some firms would be extending trade credit involuntarily, an aspect that again could be controlled for at the enterprise level but would be lost in the aggregation.

We face fewer such problems with prepayment. If firms demand payment in advance, there is a reduced opportunity to gain information about a business partner's reliability through repeated interaction. The demand for prepayment serves as a substitute for information on the customer's willingness or ability to pay. The amount of prepayment required from a customer is therefore less likely to be strongly influenced by the length of an existing business relationship.[8] The amount of prepayment required is, however, likely to be related directly to a supplier's perception of the quality of the contracting environment. Because prepayment demands impose additional costs on customers, a firm that asks for payment in advance may have to forego potentially profitable business opportunities. If a firm trusts that contracts will be honored it would not choose to demand prepayment. We would therefore expect the amount of prepayment requested on average to fall with improvements in the courts, or with the availability of alternative third-party information and sanctioning mechanisms. In short, prepayment may be a better measure of trust at the country level than trade credit, explaining why it is more closely related to average income levels, the quality of governance, and progress in economic reforms.

What Generates Trust: Reform, Courts, and Networks

The previous section established that reforms seem to be (negatively) correlated with the degree of prepayment (i.e. positively related to the degree of trust). We now investigate how reforms help to build trust. We look at several possibilities in turn: the degree of legal reform on the books, the functioning of the courts and firms' experience with them, increases in generalized trust, and expanding business networks.

Reform of the legal system is often cited as the bedrock of effective transition, as a functioning market system depends first and foremost on a sound legal framework that comprises good laws and consistent enforcement. For legal reform, we rely on data from the EBRD legal transition indicators, which are gathered on the basis of an annual survey in 27 countries by the bank's legal department. The survey asks lawyers working in the field a series of questions regarding the extensiveness (laws on the books) and effectiveness (implementation) of legal reform in areas such as bankruptcy, pledge law, company law, securities markets, and so on.[9] For the purposes of this paper, we ran some simple correlations between legal transition indicators for bankruptcy and pledge law and prepayment, as well as a correlation between prepayment and a general legal system effectiveness rating. The correlations are not very high for any of the legal system variables (except for the effectiveness of bankruptcy legislation), suggesting that trust is not generated through positive signals of government intentions to reform the legal system.[10]

There is more robust evidence of a connection between trust and the functioning of the court system. Enterprises' beliefs about the ability of the courts to enforce their property and contract rights are presumably a crucial determinant of their transactional strategies. Firms that believe they have recourse to a third party which will protect their rights are more likely to take risks with business partners (demand less prepayment), thus making markets function more efficiently (Johnson et al. 1999).

The BEEPS contains a large number of measures of the quality of the courts, as well as the extent to which firms have actually used them. Column 1 in table 3.1 presents the average response to a statement that firms are confident that courts will protect their property and contract rights (responses could range from 1, strongly disagree to 6, strongly agree). The responses show no clear geographical pattern and bear little relationship to priors about the extent of legal reforms in each country. Columns 2–6 report a range of related questions on the quality of the courts, where a higher score indicates higher quality. Countries in Central and Eastern Europe (CEE) generally score higher than countries in Southern and Eastern Europe (SEE) and the Commonwealth of Independent States (CIS) on impartiality, fairness, honesty, and enforceability but less well on speed and affordability. The BEEPS also asks firms directly whether the operation of the courts is an obstacle to the growth of their business (column 7). Courts are viewed as a significant obstacle in all of former Yugoslavia, Albania, Slovakia, and Poland but less so in most CIS countries.

Turning to the correlations between the various measures of the quality of the courts and trust between enterprises, the most straightforward findings at the country level come from the question which asked firms to rank courts in terms of their impartiality, fairness, honesty, enforceability, speed, and affordability. The first four may be thought of as characterizing the level of justice a firm may expect from the court system, and the last two as characterizing the usability of the court system. We find that prepayment is lower where courts are honest and impartial but higher where courts are fast and affordable, suggesting that justice is more important for building trust than usability (see table 3.2). These results are significant, because they suggest that rooting out corruption in the legal system may be more important than actually speeding up its delivery or making it more affordable.

It is, of course, possible that prepayment levels are being driven less by direct positive past experience with business partners or with the courts and more by a more general tendency to trust. We examine this by correlating the extent of prepayment with the average country score for generalized interpersonal trust, obtained from the WVS (for more information on this data, see Raiser 2003). The simple correlation between generalized interpersonal trust and prepayment is positive and not statistically significant (the correlation coefficient is 0.24). This indicates that trust among enterprises, as measured by prepayment, has little to do with interpersonal trust and instead seems to reflect far more directly the quality of the business environment. This result is broadly in line with Frye (2003), who found in a sample of Russian firms that the propensity to extend trade credit was only weakly correlated with generalized trust as expressed by the manager of the firm, and far more closely associated with confidence in the legal system and reliance on business networks.

The final dimension of the contracting environment we examine at the country level is the use of different social and business networks to obtain

Table 3.1 The quality of the courts in transition, 2002

	Security of contract/ property rights	Fair and impartial	Honest/ uncorrupted	Quick	Affordable	Can enforce decisions	Courts are obstacles
Albania	3.3	2.4	2.4	2.4	2.8	3.1	2.9
Armenia	3.5	2.8	2.8	2.7	3.0	3.1	1.7
Azerbaijan	4.0	2.7	2.7	2.8	3.1	3.3	1.2
Belarus	3.4	2.8	2.8	2.7	3.8	4.1	2.0
BiH	3.7	2.8	2.8	2.2	2.8	2.9	2.5
Bulgaria	3.2	2.7	2.7	1.9	3.4	3.7	2.2
Croatia	3.7	2.9	2.9	1.7	2.7	3.3	2.6
Czech Rep.	3.5	2.8	2.8	2.1	2.9	3.2	1.9
Estonia	3.8	3.6	3.6	2.1	3.6	3.5	1.8
Georgia	3.0	2.3	2.3	2.1	2.7	2.5	1.9
Hungary	3.8	3.6	3.6	2.6	3.3	3.4	1.5
Kazakhstan	3.5	2.6	2.6	2.3	2.9	2.9	1.7
Kyrgyzstan	3.1	2.2	2.2	2.0	2.6	2.8	2.0
Latvia	3.5	3.0	3.0	2.2	3.5	3.0	1.6
Lithuania	3.2	2.6	2.6	2.3	2.9	2.9	2.2
FYROM	3.4	2.8	2.8	2.5	3.3	3.0	2.5
Moldova	2.9	2.5	2.5	2.5	3.0	2.9	2.1
Poland	3.5	3.1	3.1	1.9	3.5	3.0	2.5
Romania	3.6	2.9	2.9	2.4	2.8	3.3	2.4
Russia	3.0	2.3	2.3	2.0	2.9	2.7	1.9
Slovakia	3.4	2.9	2.9	1.9	3.2	3.3	2.5
Slovenia	3.5	3.3	3.3	1.9	2.6	3.4	2.0
Tajikistan	3.9	2.6	2.6	2.6	3.0	3.3	1.9
Ukraine	3.4	2.4	2.4	2.3	3.4	3.3	2.1
Uzbekistan	4.4	3.2	3.2	3.0	3.3	3.6	1.7
Yugoslavia	4.0	3.1	3.1	2.3	3.4	3.4	2.1

Notes

On the security of property rights, firms were asked to agree/disagree on a scale of 1–6 rising with the extent of agreement to the statement "I am confident that the legal system will uphold my contract and property rights in business disputes."

On the quality of the courts, respondents were asked to associate descriptions with the courts, ranging from 1 = never to 6 = always.

On business obstacles, firms were asked to rate the severity of different obstacles on a scale of 1 = no obstacle to 4 = major obstacle.

Source: BEEPS 2002.

information on new customers and suppliers. Firms may be more or less inclined to trust their business partners depending on the source of information about them. The measure of business networks follows Johnson et al. (1999). Enterprises are asked to rank the following sources of information from 1 (not important) to 5 (extremely important): family; friends; former employees who now work for a potential supplier–customer; senior manager in firm previously employed by potential supplier–customer; existing suppliers–customers; government agencies; business associations and chambers of commerce; and trade fairs and other public sources of information. In following Johnson et al., we characterize family and friends as social networks; former employees, managers, existing customers and

Table 3.2 Determinants of prepayment in transition countries, 2002: with characteristics of courts; simple correlations

Characteristics of Courts	Prepayment
Fair and impartial	**−0.37**
Honest and uncorrupted	**−0.39**
Quick	**0.51**
Affordable	0.17
Able to enforce	0.16
Uphold contract and property rights	0.18
An obstacle to business	**−0.32**

Notes: Observations: 26. Bold indicates significance at the 5-percent level.

Source: Authors' calculations.

suppliers, and business associations as business networks, and government agencies as government networks. The reliance on trade fairs and other public sources of information reflects a relatively low importance of social or business networks.

Table 3.3 reports the average country scores for each of the eight different networks. There is significant variation across countries in the relative importance of different sources of information, although in general, existing customers and suppliers are the most important source. Looking across countries, the strongest pattern emerging from the data is the higher reliance on government-based networks in the poorer, less advanced transition economies (the correlation coefficients with GDP per capita and average reform are −0.51 and −0.52, respectively). In the more advanced transition economies there is a tendency to rely more on public sources of information and on trade fairs rather than on business networks, but it is not very strong. Membership in business associations is highly variable: between 96 percent of all firms in Ukraine and as few as 10 percent in Kyrgyzstan are members of business associations, but with no clear pattern across regions, income levels, or countries.

Table 3.3 also reports the correlations of the average reliance on each of these different business networks with the degree of prepayment at the country level. The results are striking. We find a significant negative association between prepayment and the reliance on family networks—that is, family networks build trust—and a strong, significant positive association between prepayment and government-based networks, as well as networks based around managers formerly employed by the enterprise. The latter two might be characterized as insider-based networks, and it is highly instructive to find that at the country level these are associated with lower trust. With a serious caveat regarding the aggregation of data on business networks to the country level, our results nonetheless qualify the existing literature in an interesting way. Our results suggest that the type of reputational network matters for trust; Johnson et al. (1999, 2002) found that all

Table 3.3 Determinants of prepayment in transition countries, 2002: social and business networks

	Family	Friends	Former employees	Managers	Customers/ Suppliers	Government	Business associations	Trade fairs/ public sources	Membership in business associations %
Correlation with prepayment	**−.31**	−.13	.17	**.46**	−.19	**−.67**	−.13	−.13	−.25
Albania	1.9	2.5	1.8	2.0	3.2	1.9	2.0	2.8	29
Armenia	2.2	2.7	1.9	2.0	3.1	1.7	1.8	1.9	36
Azerbaijan	1.6	2.4	2.0	2.2	2.9	1.9	1.8	2.1	24
Belarus	1.8	2.2	2.1	2.5	3.3	2.3	1.8	2.7	51
BiH	2.4	2.5	2.2	2.1	3.1	1.8	2.0	3.0	52
Bulgaria	2.0	2.3	1.9	2.1	3.2	1.8	2.0	2.4	77
Croatia	1.9	2.3	2.0	1.9	3.2	1.8	2.2	3.1	19
Czech Rep.	2.3	2.5	2.3	2.5	3.6	1.9	2.3	3.1	40
Estonia	1.5	2.1	2.0	2.1	3.1	1.8	1.9	2.9	32
Georgia	2.1	2.4	2.1	2.1	2.8	1.6	1.7	2.3	39
Hungary	1.8	2.2	2.3	2.4	3.3	1.9	2.2	3.0	17
Kazakhstan	1.8	2.1	2.1	2.3	2.8	2.2	2.1	2.5	55

Kyrgyzstan	1.7	2.1	2.0	2.0	2.9	2.0	1.9	2.4	10
Latvia	1.7	2.1	2.2	2.3	3.3	2.1	2.0	2.9	37
Lithuania	2.8	2.2	2.1	2.3	3.2	2.1	1.0	2.8	24
Macedonia	3.0	3.0	2.5	2.2	3.2	2.1	2.1	2.6	28
Moldova	2.1	2.5	1.9	2.2	3.3	2.8	2.3	3.3	21
Poland	2.0	2.3	2.1	2.2	3.5	1.8	2.4	3.2	25
Romania	2.1	2.3	1.8	2.5	3.2	1.8	2.3	2.9	53
Russia	1.7	2.1	1.9	2.2	3.2	2.1	2.0	2.7	24
Slovakia	2.0	2.3	1.9	2.3	3.3	1.7	1.9	2.8	60
Slovenia	1.9	2.1	1.8	2.0	3.1	1.6	2.2	3.1	85
Tajikistan	1.8	2.4	2.5	2.5	3.3	2.2	2.0	2.5	52
Ukraine	1.7	2.1	2.1	2.8	3.2	1.9	1.9	2.7	96
Uzbekistan	2.2	2.5	2.3	2.5	3.1	2.7	2.5	2.7	48
Yugoslavia	2.5	3.0	2.6	2.8	3.4	2.1	2.5	3.5	30

Notes

Respondents were asked to rate the importance of different sources of information about new customers or suppliers for the firm from 1 (not important) to 4 (extremely important).

Former employees are those that now work for a potential new supplier–customer.

Managers are those that prior to joining the firm worked for potential suppliers–customers.

The question on membership in business associations reports the proportions of firms which are members.

Sources: BEEPS 2002 and authors' calculations.

types of reputational enforcement mechanisms help to build trust. This is clearly an issue that requires further investigation with enterprise-level data. Membership in business associations at the country level is not significantly associated with the level of prepayment, but this result also warrants further enterprise-level investigation, following the finding in Frye (2003), that membership in business associations is a strong predictor of enterprises' willingness to extend trade credit in Russia.

Conclusions

Using country-level averages of results from a large survey of firms across 26 transition economies, this paper has looked at the extent of trust in business relationships by measuring the level of prepayment demanded by suppliers in very different contracting environments. Prepayment is a robust measure of trust that is closely correlated with country characteristics such as higher income per capita, good governance, and reform, which we tend to associate with higher levels of trust.

We have investigated a range of potential determinants of trust, again looking at averages across countries. We have found that, in line with the results of earlier enterprise-level studies, trust is higher where courts are perceived by businesses to be fair and honest, although this positive association with trust does not extend to other dimensions of the legal system, such as speed and affordability. Moreover, legal reforms are not significantly correlated with prepayment at the country level, contrary to what we might have expected. The correlations with different types of business networks suggest that these have a varying impact on the degree of trust between enterprises. Government and insider-based networks, in particular, were positively associated with the average level of prepayment, indicating that these networks are associated with low trust in business dealings.

The country-level analysis lends itself well to a characterization of the contracting environment, as reflected in the degree of confidence in the courts, or in the general level of economic reform. It is encouraging to find that these factors matter for trust as well. Far from destroying social capital, reforms may help to build it. The state can lead by example if its officials act in honest ways. Our analysis also reveals an interesting dichotomy between measures of trust obtained from business surveys and more conventional measures of trust, such as contained in the WVS. As shown by Raiser (2003), the transition economies stand out among other economies around the world for the lack of correlation between measures of income and the level of generalized trust. There is further evidence in this paper that the WVS data on generalized trust may not be a good representation of the existing moral resources in the business sector of transition economies.

However, the country-level analysis is weaker in determining the importance of factors such as relational contracting or reputational enforcement mechanisms for facilitating business transactions in transition economies and how these factors interact with the quality of the courts, for instance. We present some preliminary results on the relative importance of different types of business networks in different countries, and this seems to have some association with the level of trust between enterprises. Future enterprise-level research will, we hope, shed more light on these important issues.

Notes

1. The full BEEPS sample also includes Turkey, which plays no role in our analysis. For a detailed description, see EBRD 2002.
2. The aggregation of enterprise survey data to the country level raises the question of whether country-level results might be driven by differences in sample composition across countries. We checked for this possibility by rerunning all results presented later on country averages corrected for sampling effects. Corrected country means were constructed by regressing individual firm observations on sample characteristics such as size, ownership, industrial sector, and location. The corrected country mean for prepayment—our main metric of trust—has a correlation coefficient with the uncorrected measure of 0.8. All results are unaffected by the correction. We present uncorrected results for ease of interpretation.
3. The correlations with each of the subindicators of the World Bank governance indicator are also positive.
4. By contrast, the correlation coefficient between GDP per capita and trade credit is negative ($-.17$) and is not significant. Moreover, trade credit is comparably low in a sizeable group of countries with higher-than-average GDP per capita.
5. Again, the correlation between trade credit and governance is also weak: the correlation coefficient is .36, significant only at the 10 percent level.
6. The subindicators of the EBRD transition indicator are also positively correlated with prepayment with trade credit and prepayment, albeit with some variation in the strength of the association.
7. Once again the correlation with trade credit is lower, with a coefficient of 0.34, significant only at the 10 percent level. Even when controlling for variables such as liquidity constraints, the development of financial institutions, the extensiveness of the legal system, and firms' belief in the ability of courts to uphold contracts, prepayment is still more closely correlated with the other indicators of trust than is trade credit.
8. Indeed, we find that at the firm level the correlation coefficient of the share of sales going to customers that the firm has had for more than three years and with trade credit is more than twice as high as the correlation coefficient with prepayment. This is obviously no proof of our proposition, which would merit further empirical and theoretical investigation.
9. Pledge law is a synonym for secured transactions law.
10. Extensiveness of legal reform refers to the extent of coverage of the legal system, while effectiveness refers to the implementation and enforcement of the law. The correlation coefficients are: general bankruptcy -0.21; bankruptcy effectiveness -0.38; bankruptcy extensiveness -0.03; general pledge law -0.07; pledge law effectiveness -0.06; pledge law extensiveness -0.08; and general effectiveness -0.30. Of these, only bankruptcy was significantly correlated with prepayment. It should be noted that the legal reform indices are subjective ratings by legal experts and do not always correspond to EBRD views on the status of legal reform in a country.

References

Arrow, Kenneth J. 1972. Gifts and Exchanges. *Philosophy and Public Affairs* 1: 343–67.
———. 1974. *The Limits of Organisation*. New York: WW Norton.
Axelrod, Robert. 1984. *The Evolution of Cooperation*. New York: Basic Books.
———. 1988. The Problem of Cooperation. In T. Cowen (ed.). *The Theory of Market Failure*, pp. 237–54. Fairfax VA: George Mason University Press.

Blanchard, Olivier and Michael Kremer. 1997. Disorganisation. *Quarterly Journal of Economics* 112: 1091–126.
EBRD. 1997. *Transition Report. Growth and Enterprise Performance*. London: EBRD.
——— 2002. *Transition Report. Agriculture and Rural Transition*. London: EBRD.
Frye, Timothy. 2003. Slapping the Grabbing Hand: Credible Commitment and Property Rights in Russia. Mimeo. Ohio State University, Department of Political Science.
Fukuyama, Francis. 1995. *Trust: The Social Virtues and the Creation of Prosperity*. New York: The Free Press.
Johnson, Simon, John McMillan, and Christopher Woodruff. 1999. *Contract Enforcement in Transition*. EBRD Working Paper No. 45, London.
———. 2002. Courts and Relational Contracts. *Journal of Law, Economics and Organisation* 18: 221–77.
Knack, Stephen and Philip Keefer. 1997. Does Social Capital Have an Economic Payoff? A Cross-Country Investigation. *Quarterly Journal of Economics* 112: 1251–88.
Macauley, Stewart. 1963. Non-contractual Relationships in Business: A Preliminary Study. *American Sociological Review* 28: 55–70.
McMillan, John and Christopher Woodruff. 1999. Interfirm Relationships and Informal Credit in Vietnam. *Quarterly Journal of Economics* 114: 1285–320.
North, Douglas C. 1981. *Structure and Change in Economic History*. New York: WW Norton.
Putnam, Robert D. 1993. *Making Democracy Work: Civic Traditions in Modern Italy*. Princeton, NJ: Princeton University Press.
Raiser, Martin. 2003. Social Capital and Economic Performance in Transition. In N. Campos and J. Fidrmuc (eds.). *Political Economy of Transition and Development: Institutions, Politics and Policies*. Boston/Dordrecht/London: Kluwer.
Rose-Ackerman, Susan. 2001. Trust, Honesty and Corruption: Reflection on the State-Building Process, *Archives of European Sociology* 42: 526–70.
Schumpeter, Joseph. 1934. *The Theory of Economic Development*. Cambridge, MA: Harvard University Press.
Stiglitz, Joseph. 1999. Wither Reform. Paper Prepared for the Annual World Bank Conference on Development Economics, Washington DC, April 28–30.
Zak, Paul and Stephen Knack. 2001. Trust and Growth. *The Economic Journal* 111: 295–321.

CHAPTER FOUR

Underground Financing in Russia

ALENA V. LEDENEVA

According to Russian common opinion "Nothing is as strong or as weak in Russia as it seems." This includes the financial system. Few claim to understand fully either the origins of the August 1998 financial crisis or the postcrisis recovery. Post-1998 analyses suggested that reforms did not work as expected because the institutional environment required by market democracies was not in place. This in turn was explained by sociohistorical and cultural factors responsible for the lack of civil society, civic responsibility, and business ethics. As *The Economist* put it, a healthy banking system requires

> honest administrators backed by determined politicians, a legal system in which loans make sense and a financial climate in which people want to lend. All the above are missing in Russia. This is why a whole year since August 1998, not a single significant bank pushed into insolvency has been properly wound up. The World Bank estimated that at the top 18 banks alone, liabilities exceed assets by $9.8 billion. Of the few banks that have lost their licences in 1999, most were those trying to deal honestly with their creditors.... Strangest of all, there has been no official censure of the widespread asset-stripping and book-fiddling which followed the August crisis.
> According to a leaked report from the World Bank, the bad habits in Russian banking are deep-rooted. Apparently, most of the losses incurred by the banks were not on short-term government debt, on which Russia has defaulted to the tune of $40 billion, but on wild loans (presumably to cronies) which were never repaid. The report notes that "the largest banks actually seem to have led the way in developing techniques for concealing basic imprudent conduct."[1]

Lack of transparency, insufficient accountability, and the consequent spread of corruption have often been identified as an important self-reinforcing source of trouble. As a result, Russia's economy continues to be viewed as an economy with nontransparent rules of the game, unattractive for foreign investments.

In order to understand the rules of Russia's economy, one should start by altering the approach. Rather than looking only at what does not work and why, one should concentrate on what firms actually do to run their business. Although one has to agree that fraudulent and largely corrupt practices are one of the main obstacles to economic development, it would be wrong to engage in anticorruption policy making without an in-depth understanding of the genesis of these practices, of their functions in the economy, and of the best ways of affecting them. Many reforms to date were designed to remedy capital flight, tax evasion, and abuses of corporate governance but failed at the stage of implementation following the popular aphorism coined by Yeltsin's long-serving prime minister, Victor Chernomyrdin: "We wanted to make it better, but it turned out as before."

Why? A well-known answer to this question is the lack of an efficient legal framework and other missing elements of working economies, as suggested in the quote earlier. This chapter, in contrast, focuses not so much on what is missing but on what is actually there. I argue that there is a set of extra-legal (or practical, as anthropologists call them [Blundo and de Sardan 2001]) norms and practices in Russia that serve to compensate for the shortcomings of the state and market institutions thus undermining the course of their intended development. Instead of stigmatizing these practices from outside as corrupt, I concentrate on understanding these grassroots practices from the participant's perspective and provide an ethnographic description of what firms do under the specific circumstances deriving from their own "common sense." Respondents in a survey[2] kept referring to such practices as matters of necessity so I start with a note about the nature this self-justification story and offer a historical background of such necessity patterns. I then illustrate how these patterns reproduce themselves in the post-Soviet context with emphasis on the particular role that trust plays in the functioning of the most widespread financial schemes. Finally, I consider the forms of alternative enforcement brought into existence by the distrust of state institutions and used to support the informal workings of these financial schemes. I rely on the opinions of my respondents in offering some conclusions on whether these substitute financial schemes have costs for the present and future development of the economy or whether they represent a genuine long-term substitute for the workings of formal institutions.

Practices "Out of Necessity" and the Use of Trust in a High-Risk Environment

Given the nature and scale of the informal economy in Russia,[3] there is no shortage of examples that illustrate how the weaknesses of the banking system are compensated for and/or used manipulatively at the grassroots level. Although these grassroots practices (use of black cash and various forms of financial fraud) can be perceived as corrupt by the outsiders, they are regarded as a matter of necessity by insiders. "Had to do it in order to survive/to stay in business/to be successful" is the most frequent answer or logic of answers used by respondents in surveys.

Rather than rigid inevitability, however, the notion of necessity in this context implies various strategies of coping with situations involving risk. Historically, practices out of necessity are associated with the need to protect resources from robbery or from excessively strict taxation.[4] It is both intriguing and reassuring that basic models of such protection repeat themselves across time and space under different names. Some of them are shaped by similar risks, comparable economic and legal situations while others are influenced by analogous historical and cultural factors. For example,

> during the T'ang dynasty in China, the growing tea trade between the south and the imperial capital underscored the necessity for a more convenient method of exchange. In response to the need, a medium of transfer poetically named "flying money," or *fei-ch'ien*, evolved. Provincial governors maintained "memorial-offering courts" at the capital. Southern merchants paid the money they made from the sale of goods at the capital to these courts, which then used it to pay tax quotas due from the Southern Provinces to the central government. In return, the courts issued a certificate to the merchants. When the merchant returned home, he presented this certificate to the provincial government and was paid an equivalent sum of money. In this way, both the merchant and the government avoided the risk and inconvenience of carrying quantities of copper and silk.[5]

Another product of necessity is a chit system, considered to be a British colonial invention. The word "chit" itself is the derivative of "chitty," a word of Anglo-Indian origin borrowed from the Hindi *chitthi*, meaning a mark. From the late seventeenth century, the word came into English usage as meaning a note, pass, or certificate given to a servant. The chitty came to China in the nineteenth century by way of British custom. Foreign residents in the treaty ports found handling strings of Chinese cash or silver ingots a major inconvenience. A system was devised to eliminate this inconvenience: "The salary of foreign employees was paid by check drawn on the Chinese compradore, who then held the funds against which the employee wrote chits...memoranda acknowledging debts for retail transactions. These were accepted by the shopkeeper and passed for collection to the firm's compradore" (Lambert 1996).

This scheme also makes use of the offset mechanism and implies trust in the accounting system and/or certificate paper, chits. Both the flying money and chits systems are somewhat similar to the tax and arrears offsets practiced in Russia in the 1990s. Offsets have commonly been used to clear obligations among groups of firms, between firms and tax authorities, and between firms and utilities or government. Multilateral offsets were originally introduced in 1994, primarily in the form of treasury obligations and tax offsets, and were used to clear enterprise tax arrears and budget payment arrears through chains of mutually indebted enterprises (Commander and Mummsen 2000: 115–16).

Despite the linguistic diversity of terms, these schemes are in no way unique. They are based on a triangular model involving a principal, a client, and a third party (an agent) and based on a relationship of trust between them. If the principal and its agents (such as provincial governments, their memorial-offering courts, or the Chinese compradore) are trusted by clients, the schemes work as designed.

A different outcome takes place if the relationship between the principal and its agents is far from transparent, especially if the relationship of trust or personal interest between an agent and a client overweighs the relationship of loyalty between the principal and its agent. This is the classic model of corruption, which we are not going to discuss here.

Finally, if the principal (state) and/or its agents (bureaucracy) are not trusted, horizontal relationships of trust and alliance between clients arise in order to avoid dealing with the principal and its agents or to "beat the system." Such models make use of kinship and personal networks and function to facilitate both legitimate (such as informal exchange, *blat* (Ledeneva 1998) or other forms of petty corruption (Ledeneva 2000a; Varese 2000) and illegitimate activities (such as illicit transactions in black cash, money laundering, or underground banking). A classic scheme of an underground banking transaction is as follows:

> Historically, in China, if you had a quantity of raw opium and I wished to purchase the opium, I would give you a quantity of silver. The silver would become a medium of exchange with which I obtained a commodity. If there was an unsatisfied debt and I had the ability to pay in raw opium, that opium would be a means of payment and a form of money. I accepted the opium from you at the rate of one kilo for each one hundred taels of silver you owed me. I stockpiled silver in anticipation of future purchases, and you did the same with your opium. Suppose I wish to purchase 500 kilos of opium from you. You live in Burma, I live in China. I do not want to transport 50,000 taels of silver, so I tell my cousin in Burma to pay you and I promise to settle with him later. You deliver 250 kilos, but you receive 50,000 taels of silver. I now have a 50,000 tael liability on my cousin's books, a 25,000 tael asset on your books and a commodity worth 25,000 taels on my books. I sell my opium for double its unit cost and have 50,000 taels of silver in my possession. My cousin tells me to pay a 50,000 tael debt he owes in China and thus settle my debt with him in Burma. I have caused the transportation of 250 kilos of opium from Burma to China without moving my silver and have 25,000 taels in Burma which the Chinese authorities will never see. During the course of

this transaction my "money" has taken the form of raw opium; silver taels; notes between my cousin, myself and a third party; and has been alternately (various) mediums of exchange, including a means of payment, a standard of value and a store of value. (Sapra 1996)

Perhaps, the best-known underground banking system is *hawala* which is an Arabic word used in non-Arabic Muslim countries with the spelling *hawallah*, meaning the transfer of money or information between two persons using a third person. It predates Western banking by several centuries. This system also originated as a means of avoiding robbery and repressive tax measures but continues to be used in India by those involved in such illicit activities as tax evasion, drug trafficking, money laundering, political corruption, and arms smuggling.

According to Lambert (1996), the fundamental scheme in Chinese and Indian underground banking, as illustrated earlier, is still working today. Agencies that specialize in gold and precious stones, money exchangers, and import/export businesses form a network that moves cash and commodities with little or no documentation. The system is swift and efficient. Guarantees of payment are assured by relationships between the "bankers" and their clients. Failure to meet obligations has reportedly led to reprisals (possibly by means of alternative enforcement) on the families of bankers. As a result, payments are generally handled with care and dispatch (Sapra 1996).

Hawala is grounded in personal or criminal networks and is associated with local culture. In India, hawala routes are being used to bribe politicians. At the same time, this system can operate globally making it difficult for governments to track illicit funds, halt money laundering and capital flight, and control financial support to subversive organizations. Underground banking has historically proven itself to be one of the safest methods to transfer large sums of money without a trace. Less is known of underground banking in law enforcement circles than any other form of money laundering or cash movement. The lack of understanding is largely due to the lack of understanding of the cultures in which the systems operate and due to the elusive nature of the constituents of the underground schemes (Sapra 1996).

Similar principles of operation can be traced in present-day Russia. Some of them became legalized schemes, such as barter and mutual offsets (*vzaimozachety*) that have been used at every level of national economy in the 1990s. Some of them stay underground, such as black cash movements serving the needs of small and medium size businesses (Yakovlev 1999) or the money-laundering schemes serving large-scale corrupt networks (the Bank of New York international scandal of August 1999[6] is but one example of the latter). The use of the term "underground" is slightly misleading here as the constituent practices of financial scheming make use of the existing legal framework, have a seemingly legal appearance, and can be extremely law-observing. The next section looks at the genesis of the underground financing in Russia, gives basic examples of financial schemes and offers a participant's view on the "common sense" solutions that firms arrive at in order to face uncertainty and high-risk environment, to compete with others, and to "survive" (survival could also mean success).

The Genesis of Underground Financing

There is a certain continuity in financial scheming[7] that originates from Soviet-era mentality and from practices of under and overreporting, backdating, producing fake documentation omnipresent in the planned economy. The practices that are most enduring and not particularly influenced by reforms and legislative changes are those based on false reporting. These are fairly universal around the world, but were also customized by the Soviet past. In the planned economy, false reporting (*pripiski*) was employed to keep plan targets low and secure bonuses for overfulfilling the plans (Shenfield 1983). Now, the comparable practice of not declaring one's profit is a major technique for hiding income and reducing tax liability. Just as pervasive are related practices of multiple bookkeeping (one has to have books for owners, for managers, and for taxation, at least) and falsifying documents (such as counterfeit contracts, fake invoicing, false offsets). Firms and institutions also resort to practices of backdating, often with considerable wit and imagination, in essentially fraudulent activities. For example, a transaction can be deemed void because the signatory to the deal had already been sacked, whereas the dismissal order had actually been backdated. Alternatively, a contract can be judged as counterfeit because an old stamp was used, when in fact the firm wishing to annul the contract has intentionally replaced its stamp.[8]

Some newer practices came into being in response to market reform and are flourishing in the loopholes of the new legal framework. The most damaging for the transparency of the new Russian economy are practices based on the so-called corporate identity split. What this means is that firms insulate themselves by at least two front companies and create various shell firms (*levye firmy*), scam firms (*pustyshki*), or monkey firms (*martyshki*), which are organized in a sophisticated financial network. Specially established offshore companies conduct financial transactions in order to reserve profits for an insiders' club of shareholders or managers. The insiders' club is organized according to another "splitting" principle (*matryoshka*), by which a bigger *matryoshka* is owned by the smaller one inside it, which is in turn owned by a smaller one inside it, and so on—making ownership difficult to trace. The book by Paul Klebnikov, *The Godfather of Kremlin* (2000) claims that such was the organizational principle of the Berezovsky empire. According to Klebnikov's sources, the ownership ties of AvtoVAZ, the giant auto manufacturer that accounted for half the Russian market for passenger cars, are linked to the company, Forus Services S.A. in the town of Lausanne, Switzerland, which was owned by Forus Holding (Luxembourg), which in turn was owned at least partly by a Lausanne shell company named Anros S.A., with Berezovsky behind it.

Together, these Soviet practices and post-Soviet opportunities have produced a hybrid phenomenon—financial scheming. Financial schemes are intricate and convoluted mechanisms, deliberately nontransparent and intended to mislead and misrepresent the true state of affairs. As shown in the examples later, a typical scheme is for managers to divert payment to a shell firm, which serves a variety of functions. From a company's perspective, financial schemes can be divided into two broad classes. Some are designed to organize a company's *internal* finances, that is, to minimize taxes, divert profits, and confuse outsiders. Normally, these involve "satellite" firms that belong to a director either directly or through people he or she trusts or controls, as in the examples earlier. Others are designed to organize *external* deals: outgoing capital flows and payments for the services of important external institutions (the customs, railways, regional administration, private protection companies, etc.). These schemes make use of intermediary firms in order to pay for services, offset taxes, payment for protection, or transfer bribes and political payments.[9] The most elaborate schemes involve multiple stages of transactions between upwards of a dozen ostensibly independent economic agents. Yet, despite their complexity, financial schemes are used almost universally and guided by a simple principle—the diversion of payment, similar to the basic triangular model of underground financing (see figure 4.1).

The diversion of payment implies that somebody, whom you trust and who trusts you, will pay for your purchase in exchange for a similar favor in the future. The principle of financial scheming is to misrepresent the state of affairs: if you have money you should pretend that it does not really belong to you or that you owe it to somebody. This idea transforms every transaction into a circular chain. One example of such a circular chain in

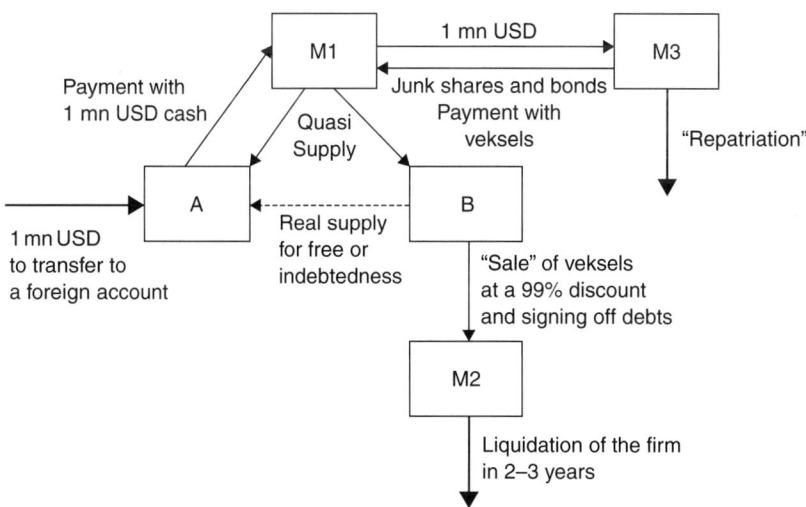

Figure 4.1 The diversion of payment

the banking sphere was a "show" capital, created by a bank giving a loan to one client, who forwards it to another client, who in turn transfers it back to the bank's capital base. Repeating this operation could "enlarge" the capital base as much as desired.

Circular chains or schemes in the 1990s have been associated with barter and mutual offsets, which were used to operate in the "economy of arrears" internally and to export capital. The evolution of these schemes for exporting capital through foreign trade began with barter schemes in 1991–93. These schemes relied on the mispricing of goods in barter exchanges. Exported Russian goods were deliberately priced lower, while imported goods were priced deliberately higher—the exporter usually "received an additional payment from his foreign partner through a money transfer to his private account in a foreign bank or through an unregistered (cash) payment in Russia" (Tikhomirov 1997: 593). Barter trade often involved a sequence of companies in different countries and elaborate financial schemes; this process was facilitated by the absence of proper customs and border controls between former Soviet states (see box 4.1).

Box 4.1 Barter schemes with an intermediary

> The prevalence of barter schemes in the early 1990s can be explained by the following: (1) No need for money to fund the transaction—no need to borrow from banks, which became particularly essential later on in the 1990s when the IMF's tight control on the anti-inflation policies resulted in the acute shortage of money in the Russian economy; (2) The guarantee was provided by a letter of credit from the end-buyer and was used as collateral to fund the entire transaction; (3) Profits could also be made on the contra-goods (consumer goods and foodstuffs) because of the price differential between the world and Russian markets; (4) Under the loose customs control and legal regulation at the time, barter contracts served the purposes of capital flight. The following steps should be undertaken in order to complete a barter transaction (the documents indicated below are prepared as a package, not in chronological order).
>
> Step 1. *Supplier–intermediary contract*: Signing a contract according to which a supplier–seller would provide the product P to the intermediary as a buyer.
>
> Step 2. *Licensing the transaction*: Intermediary, organizing a license for export that should be signed by the ministry of a given industrial branch and approved by the ministry of foreign trade.
>
> Step 3. *Intermediary–end-buyer contract*: Signing a contract between an intermediary as a seller and an end-buyer (one of the major trading companies in the West).
>
> Step 4. *End-buyer's letter of credit*: The end-buyer provides a bank associated with the intermediary with a letter of credit from the bank of the end-buyer. Such a letter would be an irrevocable guarantee to pay an agreed sum within 30 days of the end-buyer taking ownership of the goods, in satisfactory condition and upon receipt of adequate documentation (customs papers, quality certificates). No mutual risk is involved.
>
> Step 5. *Intermediary's letter of credit*: The bank associated with the intermediary issues a letter of credit to the supplier guaranteeing payment for the product P in case the intermediary-buyer for some reason would not. The bank is happy to guarantee this because it is already a holder of the letter from the end-buyer secured at step 4. The bank would be released from the guarantee upon the closing of the contract, whereas the intermediary does not have to invest its own funds in the transaction.
>
> Step 6. *Counter-goods contract*: A contract between supplier and intermediary by which the intermediary provides the supplier (now in the role of the buyer) with counterdeliveries to balance off the supplies of product P. The supplier–seller would normally send people to select contra-goods to

Box 4.1 *Continued*

> import (equipment or consumer goods and foodstuffs that were in acute short supply at a time). It is a "payment in kind" contract with no sums of money changing hands. The intermediary bank controls the intermediary's spending of the funds arriving from the end-buyer of the product P. The funds are used either to pay the supplier directly or through the use of counter-goods (barter transactions allowed flexibility in pricing the exchanged goods and created loopholes for moving capital outside Russia).
>
> In cases of capital flight, the payment is diverted by selling the product to one's intermediary at low prices, who then sells them more expensively and transfers the proceeds to offshore companies or private accounts. Some of these funds can then be used to serve the needs of the supplier (i.e. to import equipment), or they may simply "disappear."

With the further development of the financial sector around 1993, sham credit schemes emerged. Tikhomirov describes sham credit as a "semilegal scheme... [in which] a Russian-based company failed either to receive payment for the commodities supplied to a foreign partner or to receive goods from abroad after making all necessary payments. In both cases the foreign partner (usually a small company established by Russian emigrants or by locals with the help of Russian-connected capital) disappeared leaving the Russian company with 'losses'" (1997: 593).

Later, double invoicing schemes began to take over as a favorite form of capital flight, as the government took steps to regulate barter deals and shady financial and trade deals such as sham credits. According to Tikhomirov, double invoicing requires a close business partnership between Russian and foreign companies and is based on a high level of trust. It essentially involves signing two contracts for the same deal: the "official" contract is used for reporting and taxation, while another, the "unofficial" contract sets out the split of the profit between the two colluding parties. The foreign partners take part of the earnings as payment for their "services," while the larger part is transferred to accounts held by Russians in foreign banks.

The desire to overcome the constraints of having to rely on foreign partners and to produce export production (complications with transportation, customs, licenses, etc.) has produced more sophisticated schemes for exporting capital without foreign trade. Recent schemes (see box 4.2) do not involve any export production and permit rouble income to be transformed into US dollars almost directly, that is, without intermediary transactions involving products or material resources (Aleksashenko et al. 2000: 364–8).

Since 1992, the government has been making efforts to control capital flight in two ways: by attempting to modify Russia's financial system and currency regulations, and by developing state controls over foreign trade. At worst, these measures have been ineffective because they presumed the existence of a system of bureaucratic control, which was not in place. Instead of curtailing capital flight, such measures spread corruption from the foreign trade sector into other areas, such as the bureaucracy and, later,

Box 4.2 Capital flight scheme (simplified)

> Enterprise A wants to transfer some funds to a foreign account. Legally such a transaction is restricted by regulations on currency conversion and bank transfers.
>
> Step 1. *Creating a regional monkey firm*: Enterprise A registers a firm, M1, usually in the corrupt area K. According to the contract signed between A and M1, A pays M1 USD1 million for fuel oil supplies.
>
> Step 2. *Linking the monkey supplier with a real supplier*: The firm M1 is actually an intermediary—it does not produce anything. M1 subcontracts Enterprise B, which is controlled by A, to supply the fuel oil to A. M1 pays B with promissory notes (*veksel'*).
>
> Step 3. *Creating a central monkey firm and setting up the real supplier*: Enterprise B sells the promissory notes at a generous discount to M2, a firm which is created in order to have access to an account with a large commercial bank and to disappear when necessary. M2 will never use those promissory notes, so they are removed from circulation and can be written off as a "little debt" when M2 is liquidated a couple of years later. As a result, enterprise B either has to supply its product for free, or must become indebted to A (which can serve as a basis for launching an insolvency procedure).
>
> Step 4. *Creating an offshore monkey firm*: An offshore firm, M3, is registered in Cyprus. With a minimal sum, M3 opens a special investment account, I, in a large bank in Moscow. There are no limits on the repatriation of capital back to Cyprus with I-type accounts. Money from this account is supposed to be spent for "portfolio investment," which in this scheme means purchasing some "junk" shares in Russian enterprises.
>
> Step 5. *Linking the offshore monkey firm with the regional monkey firm*: Some of the junk purchased by M3 is sold to M1. The latter pays with its USD 1 million, which gets transferred from the regional bank account to account I in the large Moscow bank. In other words, the Cyprus firm made an investment and repatriated the capital gain (capital gains were not adequately taxed until 2000). See the graphic description of the scheme in figure 4.1.

the banks. At best, these measures have prompted financial schemes to become even more intricate, and have thus had only a marginal impact upon capital flight from Russia. Meanwhile, a major contributing factor to the problem of capital flight—the low level of public trust in the government and Russian financial institutions—has not been adequately addressed. Many people think that keeping their money in foreign accounts is safer than investing in their own economy, while managers have their own "commonsensical" reasons to deprive shareholders of their dues.

With the "help" of financial scheming and with the support of a cooperative board of directors, the restrictions on the sales of a company's assets by the director of a company can be circumvented. In October 2000, in the lead up to the Gazprom board of directors meeting, the five government representatives on the board (of 11) were upset by the recent transfers of large chunks of Gazprom shares to other companies. A large contract had been signed with Stroitrangaz, the bulk of whose shares were held by relatives of Gazprom management. According to the 1999 books, approximately 50 percent of Stroitransgaz's shares were held by those close to the upper echelons: 6 percent by Vitaly and Andrei Chernomyrdin (sons), 6.4 percent by Tat'yana Dedikova (daughter of Vyakhirev), 20 percent by Arnold Becker (general director of Stroitransgaz and one of the Gazprom directors), and another 12.3 percent by three of Becker's relatives.[10]

It is important to note that asset stripping can be instrumental for defending a company's assets from a takeover. When somebody tries to gain control over a company through bankruptcy procedures (which will be described later), and it is known that the court's decisions would certainly be prejudiced against the company, the company may opt for stripping its assets. The ownership structure (controlling blocks of shares of this company and controlling blocks of shares in its subsidiaries) can be manipulated. Company buildings and residences will change hands (diversion of ownership). All contracts under which the company should receive payments will be consolidated in a "shift-a-debt" contract (*pereustupka prav trebovaniya*), so that any incoming funds will be transferred to some other firm belonging to the management indirectly (diversion of payment). If the company holds more than a 51 percent share in any of its subsidiaries, this must be reduced to 25 percent minus one share, and so on. In rare cases, the deliberate bankruptcy of company subsidiaries can be undertaken with the subsequent exchange of their devalued shares for shares of holdings belonging to the management and its inner circle.

When asked about the current state of affairs with respect to financial scheming and the prospects for change one of my respondents, a banker, made the following commentary:

> A particularly widespread practice today involving "intermediary" firms is an illegal conversion of roubles into hard currency. In this area, the progress can be seen in the fact that these intermediary firms are not so black or monkey as before. They are registered firms and they pay taxes, though not all of them. They might function for two years or so whereas it used to be three months. The only feature that does persist is that these firms only have "dead souls" for a director or a chief accountant. Because the regulation of conversion is ineffective (i.e. the ban on Latvian banks have brought an extra link to the chain and Belarus' banks into operation), the illegal conversion does take place. However, one should understand that the currency does not stay in the West. It comes back into Russian businesses, serves their needs, and contributes to the economy even if it still goes through gray channels.
>
> Trust in business partners is extremely high. These days one even gets insurance payments for the fire damages even though supplies have being delivered without documents and contracts. One cannot secure the "white" (legal) guarantees when business operates in the "gray" area (extra-legal domain). Offshore business is where the degree of trust is the highest.
>
> An important indicator of progress is the share of offshore companies in business. It is going down but slowly. Most payments for services, supplies, shipment, and storage space are still paid through intermediaries. Even the largest suppliers ask to be paid through their offshore companies, and the financial schemes are organized in the

way that formally everything appears to be lawful whereas intermediaries are created specifically to break the rules.[11]

A general idea behind the financial schemes is to avoid direct connections between a company and its business. Ownership of assets is protected by running business through intermediaries and other companies which are made liable for it but do not have much to lose. Financial schemes are therefore central to understanding how things operate, rather than firms or companies that can be instrumentally used, created, or eliminated for the sake of the scheme.

Decoding Financial Schemes

In order to decode a scheme, one has to establish the true identities of all the agents involved and the connection or relationship of control between them, and to reveal its functions. According to Yulia Latynina's account in *The Moscow Times*,[12] all of Aeroflot's hard-currency turnover passed through two Swiss companies, Andava and Forus, and probably stayed abroad. Nikolai Volkov, the former lead investigator on the case, reported that

> Aeroflot engaged a Russian company called FOK to collect its foreign debts. FOK, in turn, hired an Irish offshore company and that company then collected the money from Andava. Naturally, FOK, the Irish company, and Andava are controlled by the same people (78 percent of shares belonged to Glushkov, one of the heads of Aeroflot, and Berezovsky). In this particular case, FOK and the Irish company collected spectacular fees of $38 million. Basically, it was a scheme by which Aeroflot borrowed its own money and paid a percentage for the privilege.

Did Berezovsky's people do anything illegal? No. There is no law against paying a middleman to perform a service, no matter how ridiculous the service or how high the fee is. Latynina, a journalist and author of a series of fascinating "economic thrillers," argues that this scheme is routinely used. The same pattern applies to Sibneft, Tyumen Oil, or Norilsk Nickel, where Andava is replaced by such companies as Runicom, Crown Trading and Finance, and Norimet.[13]

To establish the identity of offshore companies and other links in a chain is a daunting task. It is normally true that the more successful the enterprise, the more complex its "identity split." In the most elaborate cases, financial flows link the main enterprise with its "pocket bank," its *veksel'* (bill of exchange) center, and more than a dozen firms whose functions are known only by top management. To reveal the functions of financial schemes, however, is even more daunting.

Although the activities described earlier are directly related to tax evasion and capital flight, Latynina's commentary strongly implies that this is what good companies do. First, in order to earn "big money," a company needs skilled and qualified management. Second, the revenues generated must be concentrated in foreign companies, otherwise the efforts of the managers will come to nothing and any revenues will be consumed by Russian taxes.[14] To evade or, rather, to avoid taxes a company has to simulate arrears. Latynina (1999) describes a variety of financial schemes that serve that purpose. For example, firm X sells its product to a Cyprus firm Y at a low price (in order to avoid making any profit) and firm Y pays for the goods in 180 days. Meanwhile, firm X takes a loan from its own "pocket bank" Z, in dollars at an inflated rate of 60 percent per annum. When the money comes from firm Y, it is shifted immediately to repay the loan to bank Z. If the money is kept in the firm's account, it will be levied as tax. However, Latynina argues, taxes will be siphoned by corrupt bureaucrats, as happens with all government funds. However, if the money goes offshore it does not get stolen but comes back to the enterprise.

Latynina also provides fascinating fictional accounts of possible uses for such intermediary structures. She explains how government funds can be diverted in order to finance election campaigns. For example, in her novel the fictional RAO Atomenergo company finances the construction of an Atomic Electric Station (AES) and provides billions of roubles. Atomenergo's subsidiary, AtomStroiFinance, issues promissory notes, which are used by Atomenergo to pay the builders of AES. The builders sell these promissory notes on the market at 18 percent of their nominal value. These are purchased by a number of individuals and organizations. These organizations and individuals bring the promissory notes to Atomenergo, which buys them in cash at their nominal value. As the director of Atomenergo is a member of the Communist Party, the list of individuals includes communist deputies and other "opponents" of Russia's corrupted capitalism. This money serves the needs of the party. In effect, the whole AES project is used to launder money for the elections.

Making the Schemes Work

In the earlier analysis, we focused on financial schemes based on the opportunistic and manipulative use of formal constraints and legislation. What has so far remained unexamined is how these underground schemes are enforced, and how the alternative enforcement itself makes use of formal institutions and informal codes. To understand why matters of enforcement are so crucial, let us begin with a basic scenario—involving an insolvency case—that illustrates the operation of the Russian business environment. Firm C is owed a substantial sum of money by firm X, which cannot or will not pay its debt. Firm C initiates insolvency proceedings against firm X in an arbitration court and has the largest claim among all of firm X's creditors. According to the January 8, 1998 law on insolvency, the arbitration court must appoint an interim manager to oversee firm X's affairs while the case is under review. The interim manager, who watches over firm X's assets, monitors the actions of its management and oversees major transactions, is chosen from among qualified (licensed) managers nominated by firm X's creditors. The appointment of an interim manager is a pivotal decision, yet one which is not transparent: the arbitration court is not obliged to accept the nomination of the main creditor (firm C) and instead appoints an interim manager nominated by a creditor (firm P) with a much smaller claim than firm C.

The management of firm C suspects that the provisions of the insolvency law are being deliberately manipulated—that the appointed interim manager and firm P are controlled by a competing enterprise with links to criminal structures. If the interim manager were to allow firm X's assets to be stripped, for example, and firm C were not to recover its claim, because of its already precarious financial standing it could be ruined. What options does firm C have at its disposal to prevent this from happening?

There are only a few legal defenses open to firm C to prevent the predatory acquisition of firm X and the loss of its claim. Once interim managers are appointed by the arbitration court, they are very difficult to change because the law does not contain any provisions for an appeal. Thus, the stage is set for an informal intervention. Firm P has made the first move, by exploiting the loopholes within the insolvency law in order to file a claim against firm X and to arrange for one of its own to be appointed as interim manager—a move, which it knows, is difficult by law to contest. Because firm C has no legal options open to it, it becomes necessary to resort to extra-legal sanctions to remove the initiator of the problem. Among its extra-legal options, representatives of firm C might arrange to have the license of the interim manager revoked, thereby disqualifying him legally from serving as interim manager. Alternatively, they could threaten to release compromising information about him, or about the relationship between firm P and organized crime groups, in an attempt to pressure him to step down. In particularly high-stakes cases, threats of physical violence could be employed.[15] As one of my respondents put it,

> to bankrupt an enterprise is elementary, only these conflicts do not get settled in the court. And not at the *strelka* (informal negotiations) either. Big things are under control of the *silovye* structures (coercive ministries). Also, much depends on the status of their counterparts. With a medium-size bank, one can rely on just consideration of the case and the comparability of the bribes. With a big bank, a ring from above will induce the arbitration court to make a decision desired by the big bank. An enterprise can win regional arbitration if the governor supports it. But to win the district (*okruzhnoi*) and the Higher Arbitration Court is an entirely different story [in terms of the level of support, influence, or bribe].

The extra-legal sanctions that are used to solve cases such as the one earlier come in diverse guises, but together they comprise a toolbox of techniques for use in enacting justice and enforcing order. The main types of extra-legal sanctions that can be used by agents to enforce the operation of the new Russian economy are summarized in table 4.1.

Let us briefly consider each of these categories in more detail. In today's Russia, as in Soviet times, the ability to solve a problem is dependent not

Table 4.1 Types of extra-legal enforcement in Russia

Type	Action	Institution involved
Provoking administrative actions	Arranging for raids, inspections, and citations for administrative violations; arranging clashes between local/regional/federal levels of administrative control	Administrative institutions
Interference with legal procedures	Opening, suspending, and closing cases and official investigations	Legal institutions, tax police, state security organs
Financial pressure	Freezing assets, demanding repayment of debts, raising the level of kickbacks, and purchasing debts	Financial institutions
Interference in personnel issues	Forced resignations and fixed appointments; staff reorganization	Personal blackmail and blackmail files (*kompromat*) collected by private security services
Informational pressure	Using *kompromat*	Personal blackmail and media institutions
Violence and the threat of violence	Informal negotiations (*razborki*) and violent attacks: contract killing, car bombings, attacks on businesses and property	Security services and agencies

so much upon one's own capacity, as upon the power of the network that one can mobilize.

The first category of sanctions encompasses a set of administrative interventions that can be organized through well-placed links to official structures: regional administrations; tax inspection, tax police, the fire department, departments of sanitation and public health, and so on. It is possible to arrange for a firm's access to water, gas, electricity, and sewers to be cut off by the regional authorities on a pretext of arrears. These techniques have been practiced widely and remain one of the most common ways of neutralizing opponents.

A second area in which sanctions are employed is in influencing the status of official investigations and judicial proceedings. By using connections in various federal and regional authorities, it is possible to arrange for a criminal case to be opened (or closed), for tax evasion charges to be pursued (or conveniently forgotten), and for law enforcement officials to continue an investigation (or to abandon it). Local police and militia can be persuaded to initiate cases against purported suspects by setting them up or by planting falsified evidence. At a higher level, influence with judges and prosecutors can yield desired results in criminal and civil trials, and if unfavorable judgments are handed down there are ways to ensure they are not enforced in practice. In an interview with an ex-judge, Sergei Pashin, he testifies:

> Q: We hear a lot about political pressure put on judges. How does this work?
> A: The mechanism is traditional—distributing favors and privileges. Let's say you are the chairman of a court, and you want to become a member of the Supreme Court. Are you going to refuse to take the advice of the chairman of the Supreme Court? No, you're not. Or for example, the mayor calls you up and says you're really in debt. But I'll pretend not to see it, he says, and, by the way, I have a libel case in your court tomorrow. For some reason, the mayor always wins. (RFL/RL 2000c, 5: 28)

A third way to enforce desired outcomes is to organize changes in key personnel. This can mean forcing someone to resign through public or private channels or arranging for staff reorganization in order to ensure that loyal individuals occupy strategic positions (as in the Aeroflot case described earlier in this chapter).

These first three families of sanctions are similar in the sense that they all involve the manipulation of formal laws, measures, and procedures by individuals with personal links to those who wish to have the sanctions enacted. As a result of a bribe, a long-standing personal relationship, or an exchange of favors, a public official or bureaucrat agrees to use the authority of his or her position in a way not intended by the written rules. Thus, formal procedures and formal justice are substituted by personalized versions that maintain the trappings of legality while the true intentions of the underlying law are subverted.

Financial pressures comprise a fourth type of sanctions that can be levied. Here the permutations are extensive. Examples include arranging for an opponent's shares or assets to be frozen, refusing to renew the terms of a loan and demanding immediate repayment, threatening a firm with insolvency proceedings, and increasing the level of bribes and kickbacks demanded as part of a quasi-legal business deal.

If these four categories of sanctions rely heavily upon administrative and economic methods to get things done, a fifth type is based on the use of information, especially *kompromat* for pressure campaigns.

Under the sixth category, we find a full spectrum of actions ranging from subtle threats of violence (offering a public official the choice between a bribe and a bullet), through violent encounters (physical shakedowns, beatings, and the roughing up of potential witnesses or opponents), to the planning and carrying out of violent attacks and contract killings.

In mid-1998, Russia had 2,500 banks and 72,000 commercial organizations with their own security services.[16] Some of the security services in large banks and financial–industrial groups can rival in size the security apparatus of a small country. They are often headed by high-ranking former officers of the KGB. For example, the head of security at the Stolichnyi

Bank is a former commander of the Alpha Unit, a special force, while the former deputy chief of the KGB, Philip Bobkov, is in charge of security at the Most group. By the end of 1999, there were 4,612 security services of this type in Russia (Volkov 1999, 2002).

Private protection companies, which are used by smaller banks and enterprises, make up the second category of security agencies (Volkov 2000). These firms, which numbered more than 6,700 in Russia by the end of 1999, contract with clients to provide protection and enforcement services. Like the company security services, private firms have often been founded by high-ranking former officers, or groups of individuals from security backgrounds who believe they can market their expertise to clients. Other security firms developed into formalized businesses after beginning as informal security providers for specific commercial deals.

Thus, if taken at face value, it would appear that the private security industry in Russia—as in other societies—performs a relatively standard set of tasks aimed at protecting the rights and interests of clients in market transactions and in interactions with representatives of the state. However, security services in Russia are notoriously associated with the sanctions described earlier, with debt recovery and other "routine" business tasks accomplished in the environment of pervasive corruption and high risk, often requiring extra-legal enforcement. The role of informal contacts and networks of control in this respect should not be underestimated either. One of my respondents explains:

> While trust in the state and in the business community overall is extremely low, trust in those with whom I do business is extremely high, because many deals go through without any documentation whatsoever. I am a banker and my bank gives loans. Of course, I build my relationships with clients on a formal basis as much as I can, but there are no ideal defenses and it's impossible to put every nuance in the contract. You have to trust your clients. The informality comes in when I have to think about the informal leverage I could apply to a client who might chose to ignore my demands. The court system is still useless in many ways, but there are many situations where it takes one call to the right person who would then get in touch with the client advising him to pay.

Such a dissonance between how a market economy is supposed to work and the actual environment means that, in practice, Russia's private security agencies—among other enforcers—fulfill a much broader set of functions than those that are enshrined in law. Such is the necessity. At the same time, this necessity leaves a huge margin for manipulation. This particularly applies to the methods of intelligence gathering by security departments used for compiling *kompromat* on clients, current or potential competitors, civil servants, and elected officials. Although private security services do not have the right to conduct eavesdropping as part of their investigative operations, phone tapping is common, as are other forms of surveillance such as stakeouts, shadowing, and videotaping.[17] This implies that despite all the claims that government monitoring of communications under the SORM system[18] would be undertaken exclusively as part of the fight against crime and espionage, the cyber intelligence by private security departments is under way. The role of the Financial Intelligence Agency created in February 2002 under the aegis of the Ministry of Finance remains to be analyzed in this context.

Conclusion

In conclusion, let us sum up the implications of these practices for the Russian economy and for the fate of reforms that do not consider informal practices. From the participants' point of view, financial scheming is not only a substantial component of the post-Soviet economy in Russia, it is also perceived to be indispensable to the functioning of the economy. Financial schemes enable economic agents to protect their property and business from the exigencies of the market reform, from arbitrary judgments of the tax inspectors, corrupt authorities, and the deformed institutional framework in general. At the level of the firm, financial scheming is presented as a survival strategy. Whether the necessity argument is a genuine one, whether the boundaries between such necessity and manipulation can be defined, and whether the long-term effects of these necessary practices are not more harmful than helpful for the institutions exploiting them, remains unexplored territory. It is likely that the answers will be sector-, size-, and manager-sensitive.

At the same time, the universal principles of false reporting, "corporate identity split," and diversion of payment underpinning financial scheming in the new Russian economy have important implications for the economy's inadequate responses to reforms and the poor investment climate:

- The official documentation that backs up financial scheming does not reflect the real flow of resources; it undermines the basic economic distinction between sellers and buyers (particularly in multi-link chain schemes) and creates statistical problems.
- As a result of the above, changes in economic legislation have little direct influence on real economic processes in the shadow economy. Being protected by nonexistent economic agents (shell firms), real economic agents either avoid appearing on paper altogether, or refrain from showing real transactions or their actual volumes. Thus, changes may considerably influence the "paper" level of transactions, but they may not necessarily reach the level of the real economic agents.
- Apart from the direct detrimental impact on the economy, financial scheming is even more damaging in the long term in that every legal firm or structure is forced (in order to preserve itself) to engage in underground financial scheming, usually to do with its ownership structure, concealed profits, and multiple accounting systems.[19]
- Financial schemes open up numerous opportunities for gain and personal enrichment for a firm's owners and managers by transferring costs to

clients and customers (in particular, through tax evasion, asset-stripping, and mismanaging).
- Moreover, financial scheming on the current scale is indicative of a strong network of vested interests committed to their continued existence, which in turn replicates obscure ownership patterns and insufficiently defined property rights.

The existence of financial schemes thus creates a vicious circle: they compensate for the deficiencies in formal institutions and "help" business activities, but by the same token, they undermine formal institutions and slow down their effective workings.

Notes

1. "The Great Pretenders," *The Economist*, August 21, 1999, p. 69.
2. More than 50 interviews were conducted in the period of 1998–2003 in Moscow, St. Petersburg, the Urals, and Siberia. These include interviews with the elite, narrowly defined as those invited to the World Economic Forum in Davos (over 30 in 2002 and over 50 in 2003) and business practitioners in possession of "know-how" concerning the post-Soviet economy (various sectors and levels); those involved in the technical side of know-how (accountants, auditors, legal experts, law enforcement officers); journalists investigating "how things really are."
3. According to Interfax, Vladimir Makarov, the deputy head of the Interior Ministry's economics crime department, said that up to 45 percent of the country's goods and services are part of the shadow economy. He also said that more than 40 Moscow banks are currently involved in what he called "serious" shady deals. These comments were echoed by Duma Security Committee Chairman Alexander Kulikov, who told the Russian news agency *RIA-Novosti* the same day that the treasury receives only 5 percent of taxes owed because of operations in the shadow economy (RFE/RL 2001, 5: 28).
4. On taxes and regulations being incentives for people to engage in illegal activities, see Benson and Baden 1985.
5. For details see Lambert 1996. Lambert is a California-based specialist on Asian affairs and a consultant on international money laundering issues.
6. For the full coverage, see the September 1999 issues of the *Jamestown Foundation Monitor*, for example, September 23, p. 23.
7. Scheming is used interchangeably with schemes in this paper, both referring to the manipulative use of financial legislation while organizing a firm's finances.
8. See the coverage in the autumn 2002 issues of the newspaper *Vedomosti*. of the Ingosstrakh–Avtobank conflict in which an offshore-based ownership structure was taken over with the help of a fake signature.
9. For the best description of the use of shell firms for tax evasion, see Yakovlev 2000.
10. The assets have been reclaimed by the state since Aleksei Miller became the chairman of Gasprom in 2001; see the article "Gazprom Recovers 'All Core Assets'" by Stefan Wagstyl and Arkady Ostrovsky in *Financial Times*, November 28, 2002, p. 30.
11. The interview was conducted in December 2002.
12. "Persecution: The Price of Achievement," November 15, 2000, p. 8.
13. Ibid.
14. The controversies of tax debtor's accounts are discussed in detail in Tompson 1997.
15. Numerous cases supporting such a scenario can be found in chapter 7 in this volume.
16. *Komsomol'skaya Pravda*, July 14, 1998, p. 3, quoted from Bennett 2000.
17. The Russian Supreme Court declared unconstitutional a directive of the Communications Ministry that allowed the FSB to eavesdrop on the customers of telecommunications companies without informing them or applying for authorization from the Procurator's Office. Quoted from RFL/RL 2000a, 1: 6.
18. SORM (system of technical support for effective investigative activities) would let the FSB monitor electronic mail messages by digitally linking its offices with all Internet service providers throughout Russia. See RFE/RL 2000b, 1: 12, and Ledeneva 2000b: 174.

19. Some respondents from both the banking and industrial sectors suggested that it might be up to 90 percent if calculated in all strictness, that is, if not just the letter of law but the spirit of it is taken into account.

References

Aleksashenko, Sergei V. and the Bureau of Economic Analysis. 2000. *Obzor Ekonomicheskoi Politiki Rossii za 1999 god* (Survey on Economic Policy in Russia in 1999). Moscow: TEIS
Bennett, Gordon. 2000. *The Federal Security Service of the Russian Federation.* Working Paper C102. Surrey: Conflict Studies Research Centre.
Benson, Bruce and John Baden. 1985. The Political Economy of Governmental Corruption: The Logic of Underground Government. *Journal of Legal Studies* 14: 391–410.
Blundo, G. and Jean-Pierre Olivier de Sardan. 2001. La Corruption Quotidienne en Afrique de l'Quest. *Politique Africaine* 83: 8–37.
Commander, Simon and Christian Mummsen. 2000. The Growth of Non-Monetary Transactions in Russia: Causes and Effects. In P. Seabright (ed.). *Vanishing Rouble: Barter Networks and Non-Monetary Exchanges in Post-Soviet Societies*, pp. 114–46. Cambridge, UK: Cambridge University Press.
Klebnikov, Paul. 2000. *Godfather of the Kremlin: The Life and Times of Boris Berezovsky.* Harcourt Paperbacks (Florida, USA).
Lambert, Larry B. 1996. Underground Banking and National Security. In *Sapra India Bulletin*, March, at http://www.subcontinent.com/sapra/bulletin/bulletin.html
Latynina, Yulia, 1999. *Okhota na Izyubrya* (The Deer Hunt). Moskva: Olma-Press.
Ledeneva, Alena V. 1998. *Russia's Economy of Favours.* Cambridge, UK: Cambridge University Press.
———. 2000a. Economic Crime in the New Russian Economy. In A.V. Ledeneva and M. Kurkchyan (eds.). *Economic Crime in Russia*, pp. 1–16. Kluwer Law International.
———. 2000b. Russian Hackers and Virtual Crime. In A.V. Ledeneva and M. Kurkchyan (eds.). *Economic Crime in Russia*, pp. 162–76. Kluwer Law International.
RFE/RL. 2000a. RFE/RL *Security Watch*, August 28, at http://www.rferl.org/securitywatch/
———. 2000b. RFL/RL *Security Watch*, October 9, at http://www.rferl.org/securitywatch/
———. 2000c. RFL/RL *Newsline*, October 17, at http://www.rferl.org/newsline/2000/10/171000.asp
———. 2001. RFL/RL *Newsline*, February 9, at http://www.rferl.org/newsline/2001/02/090201.asp
Sapra. 1996. *Sapra India Bulletin* 1996, February–March at http://www.subcontinent.com/sapra/bulletin/96feb-mar/si960308.html
Shenfield, Stephen. 1983. *Pripiski*: False Statistical Reporting in Soviet-type Economies. In M. Clarke (ed.). *Corruption: Causes, Consequences and Contro*, pp. 239–58. London: Francis Pinter.
Tikhomirov, Vladimir. 1997. Capital Flight from Post-Soviet Russia. *Europe-Asia Studies* 49: 591–615.
Tompson, William. 1997. Old Habits Die Hard: Fiscal Imperatives, State Regulations and the Role of Russia's Banks. *Europe-Asia Studies* 49: 1159–85.
Varese, Federico. 2000. Pervasive Corruption. In A.V. Ledeneva and M. Kurkchyan (eds.). *Economic Crime in Russia*, pp. 99–111. The Hague: Kluwer Law International.
Volkov, Vadim. 1999. Violent Entrepreneurship in Post-Communist Russia. *Europe-Asia Studies* 51: 741–54.
———. 2000. Between Economy and the State: Private Security and Rule Enforcement in Russia. *Politics and Society* 28: 483–501.
———. 2002. *Violent Entrepreneurs: The Use of Force in the Making of Russian Capitalism.* Ithaca, NY: Cornell University Press.
Yakovlev, Andrei. 1999. *Black Cash Tax Evasion in Russia: Its Forms, Incentives and Consequences at Firm Level.* BOFIT Discussion Paper No. 3. Helsinki: Bank of Finland.
Yakovlev, Andrei. 2000. Pochemu v Rossii Vozmozhen Bezriskovyi Ukhod ot Nalogov (Why is Non-Risk Tax Evasion Possible in Russia?). *Voprosy Ekonomiki* No. 11, pp. 134–52.

CHAPTER FIVE

How Trust is Established in Economic Relationships when Institutions and Individuals Are Not Trustworthy: The Case of Russia

VADIM RADAEV

Introductory Remarks

Market relations are not confined to free competition and price-making mechanisms. The market is an instituted process (Polanyi 1992). It is constituted by sets of rules, regulations, and other institutional arrangements, including relations of trust. Starting with this general notion, we define trust as *a belief that other agents will act in a predictable way and fulfill their obligations without special sanctions* (Coleman 1988). Specifying this notion, we differentiate between two levels through which trust relationships can develop. The first level is achieved through the predictability of the behavior of other actors. The second level is reached through mutual obligations to follow accepted conventions, which are voluntarily taken by market actors. We also employ the distinction between one-sided trust in institutions and reciprocal trust among business actors (Rose-Ackerman 2001a,b).

Today Russia demonstrates a prominent example of a *low-trust society*. Formal rules are contradictory and unstable. There is a lack of formal enforcement, which produces a high level of uncertainty. State legislative and regulatory policy is not predictable by the market actors. As a result, one-sided trust in institutions remains low.

One could expect that this deficiency of one-sided trust should be compensated for by reciprocal trust among business partners. However, what makes the situation even more demanding is that reciprocal trust in business-to-business relationships is low because honesty often does not pay. Although business actors put the highest value on honesty in relations, they do not trust each other entirely due to the frequent infringement of business contracts and the nontransparency of business transactions.

Taking this into account, this chapter sets out to investigate the following: How are economic relations established when formal rules are not effectively enforced and both institutions and individuals are untrustworthy? How does trust emerge and develop in these relationships? What role should the state play in developing one-sided trust in institutions and reciprocal trust among business partners?

To study these issues we borrow conceptual tools from two conceptual sources, including works by the representatives of the new institutionalist theory (e.g. Eggertsson 1990; Fligstein 1996; North 1992) and the literature on trust (e.g. Gambetta 1988; Hardin 2002; Rose-Ackerman 2001b; Sztompka 1999). With their help this chapter examines the issues of trust and distrust in Russian business relationships on the empirical level.

The Data

Our empirical evidence is based on data collected from the following two projects: (1) "Transaction Costs in Russian Business," carried out between 1997 and 1998 and funded by the US Center for International Private Enterprise (CIPE) and (2) "The Costs of Legalisation," carried out between 2001 and 2002 and funded by two Russian business associations.

Project 1 included a standardized survey and a set of in-depth interviews with managers of nonstate enterprises and entrepreneurs.

The standardized survey was conducted between November 1997 and January 1998. There were 227 heads of nonstate enterprises in 21 regions (mainly in the European part of Russia) that sent back filled-in questionnaires. All the main areas of economic activity were represented. Selected basic parameters of the surveyed enterprises and entrepreneurs are presented in table 5.1.[1]

Table 5.1 Basic parameters of the sample of Russian firm owners and managers, 1997–98

Parameters	Percent
Privatized state firms	18
Newly established private firms	82
Small firms	79
Large and medium-size firms	21
Male entrepreneurs	75
Female entrepreneurs	25
With university degrees	83
Without university degrees	17
(One of the) owners of the enterprise	79
Managers of the enterprise	21
Members of business associations	28
Nonmembers of business associations	72
Moscow	19
Other regions	81

The in-depth interviews were conducted from May 1997 to April 1998. In total, 96 interviews were recorded. The main focus was on the emerging areas of nonstate businesses. Our sample included 27 follow-up interviews, which were conducted for the second time with the same respondents (the first survey was carried out by the Center for Political Technologies in 1993).[2] The project focused on the issues of corruption, contract enforcement, use of force in business relationships, and problems of entering the market for Russian entrepreneurs.

It is important to point out that both surveys were carried out before the outbreak of the financial crisis in August 1998, which, therefore, could not seriously distort the picture.

Project 2 was initiated by two newly established business associations. The Association of Trade and Production Companies of Electric Durable Goods and Computers (RATEC) includes companies dealing with both the wholesale and retail trade of imported electronic durables and also some home producers of such goods. The Association of Retailing Companies (ACORT) includes companies developing retailing networks dealing in electronics, foodstuffs, clothing, footwear, furniture, construction materials, and stationary.

Thirty-eight in-depth interviews with owners and top managers of Russian companies were conducted in two series. Fourteen interviews were recorded in 2001 and 24 in 2002. The main target of these interviews was the estimation of the transaction costs of different modes of activity including semi-legal (gray) and illegal (black) business schemes with special focus on customs procedures.[3]

Creating Distrust in Business Relations

From the point of view of conventional institutional theory, observers of the transformation of the market in post-communist Russia face the following puzzle: Market relationships should be based on legitimate formal rules and high level of trust. Despite the fact that neither of these conditions exist, new markets keep developing in today's Russia.

In dealing with this institutional controversy the following set of propositions will be examined:

1. Formal rules are contradictory and unstable in the Russian economy. They become subject to informalization. State policy is nontransparent and nonpredictable. This situation produces a high level of uncertainty.
2. Institutional instability undermines one-sided trust in formal institutions. It raises demands for reciprocal trust among business partners.
3. Reciprocal trust in business-to-business relationships is also low due to the frequent infringement of business contracts.

Informalization of Formal Rules

Conventional economic theory is largely based on the assumption that there exist efficient legislation, a relatively cheap state, and arbitration control, which provide enforcement of formal rules (Williamson 1985). This assumption displays its obvious weakness in the case of Russia, where public institutions are not able to impose effective sanctions against opportunism and malfeasance.

A principal reason is that institutional arrangements in Russian businesses are strongly influenced by a developed mechanism of the *informalization of rules*. This means a continuous transformation of institutions, where formal rules are largely substituted for by informal arrangements. The main elements of the informalization of rules can be described as follows.[4]

First, formal rules are imposed by the public officials in a way that leaves room for discretion and creates a high level of uncertainty for market actors.

Second, confronting high costs of compliance with the formal rules, economic agents create specific governance structures to avoid formal rules on a systematic basis.

Third, public officials establish selective control, in which formal rules are used for extortion and selective pressures on economic agents.

Fourth, economic agents, in turn, bargain with the public officials on terms and conditions of the implementation of formal rules.

Fifth, multiple arguments and interpretations are produced to legitimate practices of informalization.

Russian entrepreneurs have proved to be very innovative in inventing informal business schemes to cope with the discrepancies in formal rules without direct confrontation with the state authorities. Normally, it takes less than a week to adjust to a newly adopted formal rule. The best corporate and freelance lawyers and accountants are engaged in elaborating business schemes with various degrees of legality. As a result, Russian business is largely nontransparent. The study of the area of imported electronic goods demonstrates that most of these goods have been brought into the country by using gray (semi-legal) schemes, which do not strictly follow the law. Involvement in such shadow activity leads to the *nontransparency of Russian business*, which prevents the formation of trustworthy relationships.

One of the respondents concluded, "One reason for low trust is that our market is in the shadows and nontransparent. Therefore, everyone is scared to be exposed" (2002, head of a cell-phone selling company).

Lack of One-Sided Trust

Informalization of rules largely originates from common *distrust in the state authorities* as the main provider of formal rules. To illustrate this, we bring in a fragment of survey data collected by the Fund of Public Opinion (FOM) on the level of one-sided trust in Russia's state institutions. Using data from seven nationwide surveys, we compute an index of trust or distrust in institutions. It is the average differences in percentages of the positive and negative answers of the respondents. If this index falls below zero, distrust in the institution prevails among the population. If it is above zero, people are inclined to trust the institution. The outcomes are presented in table 5.2.

It should be added that all attitudes are stable over time and apparently negative with one exception for the attitude to the presidential administration, which is associated with the newly elected President Vladimir Putin. Legislative authorities are trusted even less than executive bodies. Let us add that comparative opinion polls demonstrate relatively low trust in institutions in Russia when compared to other countries (Rose-Ackerman 2001a).

Now let us consider two illustrative examples from our own 1998 data dealing more specifically with business relationships. First, we asked what the entrepreneurs would do if confronting a case of malfeasance among their business partners. It turned out that only 24 percent of Russian entrepreneurs would address the arbitration court when dealing with dispute settlement. The majority (55 percent) would try to negotiate and persuade their partners through informal means, while 11 percent would use force to cover their losses.

Thus, a major part of entrepreneurs prefer *informal means of dispute settlement*. There are several reasons for that. First, arbitration courts have proved to be one of the most corrupt institutions, which are widely used for asset stripping and aggressive mergers. Second, these courts are not independent from the direct influences of government officials and business corporations. Moreover, they are frequently used as instruments of unfair competition to oust rivals. So, the courts are not trusted in Russia at present. Third, arbitration procedures are time consuming and costly. It may cost from 1.5 to 5 percent of the disputed sum (which may be particularly difficult for small firms). Fourth, there is no guarantee that justice will be established due to the many gaps in the existing legislation. Fifth, even in case of success in the court, it does not necessarily mean that the losses will be covered. The court executives are few and not very efficient. They often fail to reach a defector. According to the opinion of a respondent, "It is worthwhile to appeal to the Arbitration Court only if you deal with a reputable business organization" (1998, head of a trading firm). This also reflects a certain paradox: one should trust in other business actors as a precondition for taking them to court.

Table 5.2 Trust in institutions in Russia, 2000–01

Political and governmental institutions	Index (percent)
Presidential administration	+3.6
Regional administration	−8.4
Local administration	−10.7
Federal government	−6.7
Council of the Federation	−11.9
Federal parliament (State Duma)	−29.4
Regional parliament	−15.5

Note: Average of eight nationwide polls.
Source: www.fom.ru/reports/frames/short/d011703.html.

Our second example is about what entrepreneurs would most probably do when confronting the use of force and coercive pressures in relation to their firms and themselves personally. Only 13 percent of them claimed that they would call the police. At the same time, 23 percent would appeal to private (either legal or criminal) protection agencies, and 34 percent would prefer to cope with it on their own. Finally, 30 percent avoided giving a definite answer (Radaev 1998, 2001b). This means that the state has lost a large part of its capacity to impose law and order. Moreover, it is difficult to rely upon state protection agencies when formal rules are violated.

Entrepreneurs presented one more remarkable argument for avoiding formal court and police procedures: "By appealing to the court you can ruin your relationships.... It is not a usual way of doing things. There are two categories—'us' and 'them.' All state authorities involving tax inspections and arbitration courts are viewed as them. It is a mauves ton to address them" (1998, head of a production and trading firm).

Thus, apart from the inefficiency of the state authorities and high transaction costs there exist implicit conventions, which persuade the entrepreneurs to resolve delicate issues among themselves without attracting a third party. This logic of *negative solidarity* dividing "us" (businessmen) and "them" (authorities) is still influential. Moreover, formal appeals to the state are judged frequently on moral grounds as attempts to break somebody down. This is a specific case illustrating how reliance on public institutions could undermine interpersonal trust instead of giving it more strength.

Lack of Reciprocal Trust

When one-sided trust in institutions is low we could expect that it should be compensated for by higher reciprocal trust in kin, friends, and business contractors. Our evidence demonstrates that business-to-business relationships are not subject to such a simple causation.

There is widespread distrust displayed in business relations. First of all, it is reflected in the attitude to newcomers and outsiders. However, even in case of long-term relations with regular partners it presents a serious problem. The low level of reciprocal trust is illustrated by the Business Environment and Enterprise Performance Survey (BEEPS) data comparing 26 post-communist economies. Russia scores very high in terms of prepayment requirements and scores lower than average in terms of commodity credit (see Raiser, Rousso, and Steves in this volume).

The dominant feeling was expressed by one of our respondents in the following way: "I do not trust entirely anyone in business" (1998, head of a real estate firm). It is remarkable that this statement refers not only to rule-based trust but also to *affect-based trust* based on personal ties with family and friends (Rose-Ackerman 2001b). These strong ties are obviously preferred to relations with strangers. Moreover, many entrepreneurs started their businesses by forming teams with their relatives and friends. However, in the course of the 1990s affect-based trust was largely undermined as well.

This is well illustrated by the following statements: "It does not matter if you have very confidential relations with somebody and that somebody loves you tenderly. Payment arrears could happen easily" (1998, head of a firm selling medical equipment). "In those few special cases when I removed the principle of prepayment I was punished severely.... And it was my personal acquaintances who did that to me" (1998, head of an advertising agency).

Are there any differences in relation to Russian and foreign companies? There is a stereotypical vision that Western companies are more transparent and more reliable (which is partially accepted by our respondents). Besides, for many years it was a matter of high prestige for Russians to have business partners in the West. Nevertheless, after having experience with foreign companies, some of the Russian entrepreneurs were fundamentally frustrated, provided their initial expectations were high. In the end, no fundamental difference in attitudes to domestic and foreign business partners is demonstrated. "Unlike five years ago, we check our western partner more thoroughly than the Russian one" (1998, head of a group of companies). "We do not trust western partners because they do not always follow their obligations. We are now used to parting with them in case of failures" (1998, head of a tourist firm).

The main reason for distrust in Western companies was pointed out in our interviews. When perestroika commenced, many swindlers along with quite reliable businessmen from the West were attracted to the emerging Russian markets as a land of new opportunities. Moreover, at the beginning it was difficult to distinguish between swindlers and reputable businessmen by checking their credit history and reputation because information channels were not well developed in Russia. Many Russian entrepreneurs became victims of their initial one-sided trust in the institutions of Western business. Having been cheated, Russian entrepreneurs became more cautious and selective in their relations to Western firms.

Infringement of Business Contracts

Lack of reciprocal trust is closely connected with opportunistic behavior in business relationships. What is the source of this opportunism? It originates from the frequent infringement of business contracts, which leaves a large room for risk and uncertainty in Russian business at present. To measure the level of this sort of opportunism in relationships among business partners we asked the following questions: How often are business contracts violated in Russian business in general today? How often do the entrepreneurs face contract infringement in their own business activity?

Our data confirms the existence of a high level of opportunism. Nearly all the respondents (92 percent) admitted that infringements of business contracts are a matter of fact, with 49 percent claiming it frequent. Only a negligible 8 percent see no problem here at all. These results are supported by previous research findings in the 1996 nationwide survey of entrepreneurs (Radaev 1996: 74–6).

As for the personal experience of entrepreneurs, it strongly correlates with their general attitudes. A vast majority of entrepreneurs (82 percent) reported that they confronted opportunistic behavior in their own day-to-day business activity. One-third faced it on a frequent basis (see table 5.3).

There has been a continuous debate among Russian experts whether the chronic interenterprise payment arrears result from macroeconomic instability and the rigid monetarist policies of the successive Russian governments or if they are largely an outcome of conscious opportunistic strategies of the enterprise managers "seeking their self-interest with guile" (Williamson 1985: ch. 2, 1.2A). In our opinion, both factors contribute to distortions in the payment systems. In any case, these distortions produce serious institutional effects creating *distrust* among business partners.

Request for Honesty

One could ask if low levels of trust are an important problem at all. Our data give a positive answer. In our 1998 standardized survey, we put an open-ended question to Russian entrepreneurs asking them what they considered the most important personal qualities when looking for business partners. The named characteristics totaled almost 40. Having been clustered, they help to display the characteristics most in demand: *business partners must be honest and trustworthy*. Economic and sociological theory claims that it is intuition and intellect, creativity and motivation that are normally imputed to "the real" entrepreneur (Radaev 1997: ch. 6). However, these personal qualities were not frequently mentioned. Honesty and trustworthiness were absolute winners over all other qualities (see table 5.4).

Table 5.3 Contract infringement in Russia (percent)

Contract infringement	Frequently	From time to time	Never
In Russian business in general	49	43	8
In one's personal experience	32	50	18

Note: $N = 227$.

Table 5.4 The most important personal features of business partners in Russia

Features	Percent
Honesty, trustworthiness	79
Responsibility, liability	29
Professional skills, competence	19
Accuracy, precision	12
Initiative	8
Financial sustainability	4
Gender, ethnicity	1
Work experience and other	2

Note: $N = 227$.

Therefore, Russian entrepreneurs are quite conscious about honesty. Moreover, we would argue that their concern is neither about high moral values nor about generalized trust. When laying claims for honesty, entrepreneurs care about very practical rules of business conduct, like payments on time and reliability in payments in general.

Creating Trust in Business Relations

Let us now turn to the main question of our study. How do entrepreneurs cope when their business partners are not entirely reliable and the third parties responsible for dispute settlements are not trusted? The puzzle we face is the following.

Business partners do not trust each other much. However, malfeasance in business relations is decreasing. This is confirmed by one of the respondents: "The problem of reliability of partners always exists in business. However, it is becoming less demanding now" (1998, head of the stock market).

Does this mean that honesty has started to pay off? We would argue that it is not the case or at least not the main reason. Our argument is presented in the following propositions:

1. Formal contractual relations are not sufficient for the enforcement of reciprocal trust. Informal private ordering is widely used.
2. Various precautionary measures are taken and closed business networks are built to raise the predictability of behavior of the other market actors.
3. Business-to-business conventions are built to elaborate common rules of conduct and impose mutual obligations on the market actors.
4. Established conventions of reciprocity stimulate the development of one-sided trust in institutions.

Confronting opportunism and malfeasance, Russian entrepreneurs had to impose methods of private contract enforcement. Business people do not become more trustful. Rather they become more cautious while arranging business deals. This is confirmed by the following statements: "The number of violations has decreased for the number of business ties has diminished. Before one gave money to somebody, and it was not paid back. One was running all around saying that he was cheated. Now he does not give money and nobody lets him down. So there is nothing to complain about. The situation is different" (1998, head of a trading firm). "Everyone is now more cautious than before" (1998, head of a construction firm).

Contractual Forms of Protection

Given that Russian entrepreneurs had to exercise control over transactions at their own risk, they take some precautionary measures. They start with introducing discriminatory elements into business contracts.

The requirement of prepayments could serve as the most prominent example. In case of transactions with new partners, prepayments are considered as a compulsory instrument. As noted by an entrepreneur: "Partial prepayment is the only real guarantee" (1998, head of a trading and production firm).

Another precautionary measure is to start business deals with some small probing contracts and/or divide the transfers into several stages to ensure the outcome. If the probing contracts work successfully, business partners increase the volume of the delivered goods and services step-by-step. "Initially, when we start working with a new company, we get very bad contract conditions, including 100 percent prepayment and other such things. Then in some time normal relationships are established and conditions change for the better" (2002, head of a retailing network).

In spite of these efforts, no formal contract provides perfect protection from the opportunism of market actors. First, the culture of formal business contracting is not yet highly developed in Russia. Second, formal contracts are not able to cover all necessary issues and anticipate all possible intervening factors which means that the parties must rely on various sorts of relational contracting (Williamson 1985). Third, signing a contract by no means protects an entrepreneur. The partner could simply grab the money and disappear. So the status of the firm and the personality of the leaders do play an important role: "No doubt it is necessary to sign contracts in any case. But anyway, implementation of the contract depends on the person" (1998, head of a real estate firm); "The informal word weights much more than any signed contract in our market" (1998, head of an investment company); "You are not able to put everything on paper.... And many decisions are taken across what is written in the contract.... There are certain rules, which could be more powerful than formal papers" (2002, head of a retailing network).

Checking up Business Partners

Because formal contracting is insufficient to secure positive outcomes, entrepreneurs develop the noncontractual elements of business relationships. First of all, they check up on potential partners thoroughly before making business deals. Here are some opinions to illustrate this: "We are used to checking every new partner thoroughly and for a long time. And if we start working with him/her we create the conditions, that provide sufficient guarantees for us" (1998, head of a group of companies); "We do not sign serious contracts before check-ups and do not deal with new partners" (1998, head of a holding company), "It is possible to have a business without check-ups. But in this case, one has to be alert and expect failures. It is necessary to calculate risks and be ready for anything. It takes more energy to make a transaction. One is supposed to ensure each step from a variety of failures" (1998, head of a retailing network).

At the beginning of the 1990s, Russian entrepreneurs took full risks of malfeasance given the lack of reliable and systematic sources of business information. By the end of the 1990s, opportunities for obtaining data on financial sustainability and business reputation of the market actors had considerably improved. The data on potential business partners are collected both from public and commercial registers and databases. Foreign partners are checked through the embassies and trading offices of the large firms in foreign countries. "It was impossible before. Now we are dealing with the Ministry of Home Affairs and banks. They can make inquiries about any client for us" (1998, head of an industrial production firm). "We have got opportunities for checking on firms and their founders. There are long 'black lists' already" (1998, head of the stock market).

Overall, big transactions are ensured by prior checkups. However, even after getting positive information, entrepreneurs are still cautious with newcomers. "A sufficient number of partners have been already checked. It is not a problem to find out anything you like. You are not able to come to the business from nowhere anymore. Nobody would give you anything like before" (1998, head of an investment company). "There are small contracts involving thirty thousand and big contracts involving three hundred thousand [dollars]. No one would make a deal on three hundred thousand with a newcomer right away" (1998, head of an investment company).

Of course, collecting business data costs both time and money. However, not even the most detailed inspection can guarantee positive outcomes. Entrepreneurs have to be wary of outsiders in their business relationships.

Establishing Business Networks

Contracts are largely enforced through personal business networks that also help accumulate social capital (Coleman 1988). A business network is defined here as a stable and relatively closed set of interpersonal links between regular business partners. It is based on a combination of formal control and informal exchange of services. These networks play an increasing part in the Russian business world. Our respondents describe the situation as follows:

"We are giving goods on credit only to permanent clients. We would never do that with others.... If you make purchases you should deal through your own acquaintances. Otherwise, you have no guarantees. They will sell faulty goods to you" (1998, head of a wholesale firm); "It is vitally important to have permanent partners now. They are valuable not because they pay on time but because they pay in principle" (1998, head of a firm selling fuel); "We did not make alliances before. Now we are very active in making alliances with our Russian partners. And we have our joint projects. We did not do that before, and we were cheated, and the work was never done" (1998, head of a computer firm).

Russian businessmen have become more selective, especially when dealing with newcomers and outsiders. Reasonably, they prefer to stay within "their own" exclusive business circles. One of our respondents postulates it very clearly: "We are dealing with a smaller and smaller number of people. Some time ago, one could disseminate a hundred personal cards just to anybody. Now we do not use cards because we do not meet new people. Moreover, even if you are introduced to somebody new it is done by someone with a high reputation. The circle has not closed down completely, but it is extending very slowly" (1998, head of several firms).

Business networks no doubt are established to overcome distrust among business partners. What sort of trust is built through these networks? In the initial stages, many Russian entrepreneurs started up their businesses with their friends and personal contacts. According to our 1993 survey data, 42 percent of the 277 Moscow entrepreneurs started up businesses with personal acquaintances, 23 percent with friends and their relatives, 17 percent with their own relatives, and 11 percent with people unknown to them before (Radaev 1993: 7–8).

Due to the many uncertainties in the business environment, relations were largely built upon affect-based trust. Then a serious shift took place in the 1990s. Initial business teams were often dismantled. Former partners split and started up their own firms. Friendships often became an obstacle to efficient leadership. Overall, business and former friendships started to fall apart. We have several clear statements in support of this observation: "Good acquaintances, as a rule, would let you down in the majority of cases" (1998, head of a law firm); "It is a fundamental truth in business that those will survive who understand that they must end friendships at the right moment" (1998, head of a trading firm).

All this means that affect-based trust is largely replaced by *reputation-based trust*. Strategic alliances are increasingly not built upon personal and long-term friendships and kin relationships but more upon recognition of professional and managerial skills and business reputations. Firms and their leaders are divided into respectable ones ("they will not let you down") and unknown ones ("you should be cautious with them"). Thus, business networks are used to disseminate information on unreliable business agents and to build up reputations. "Nobody would deal with a man who has cheated once.... If the sum is not significant he will be just blacklisted as an unreliable partner" (1998, head of a marketing department); "Information is transferred instantly. And in case of contract infringement you run a risk of losing all your partners.... As soon as you failed to fulfil serious obligations you find yourself cut off from resources. And then your bank goes bankrupt. It is really a closed network" (1998, head of a commercial bank).

By and large, honesty may not pay in free-market relationships while it pays within closed business networks. These networks reduce risks, help to overcome interpersonal distrust, and produce a sort of segmented business ethic. This makes the situation more predictable and creates opportunities for the development of mutual obligations through new business conventions.

Building Conventions Among Business Actors

Established business networks stimulate the process of further institutional change. They present a structural basis for building up new *business conventions* among the market actors. We define these business conventions as shared understandings of the market situation and accepted common rules of business conduct.

Leading market sellers used to monitor closely the actions of their contractors and competitors. However, this monitoring is not enough to cope with market uncertainty. It should be supported by *face-to-face negotiations*. These negotiations are arranged on two interconnected levels. On the *political level*, leading market actors join the ranks of business associations to work on the strategic rules of the game. On the *business level*, they arrange informal roundtable meetings to discuss tactical issues. These business meetings can be carried out both within and beyond the walls of business associations.

Business-to-business negotiations are not easy if participants see each other as direct competitors. Moreover, quite naturally, the initial level of mutual trust is restricted. Even being members of the same business association and exchanging information and ideas, they would never be completely open with regard to their market situation and business strategies. "There are some unreliable managers. When you start sharing with them some of your new ideas... they somehow get silent and in a while you can see them implementing your own plan. I can remember such cases. As a result, you get reserved when discussing issues. First, you would give a small part of the idea and see if the partner is interested. Normally, it becomes a long-term process" (2002, head of a wholesale company in electronics).

However, our study of the electronic durable goods market in 2001–02 demonstrates that in spite of obvious constraints, most of our respondents believe that successful negotiation is possible and does take place. What are the preconditions of success? Many of the leading sellers have known each other on a personal basis for seven or eight years at least. They meet with each other quite often and identify themselves as members of the same business networks. Reputations were built within these networks in the 1990s. Above all, personal contacts are encouraged by the fact that business owners and managers dealing in electronic consumer goods are similar in terms of their age and background. Most of them are between 30 and 40 years of age and have engineering/technical university degrees. They have similar histories of business start-ups and development. Overall, with inevitable reservations, it makes a good ground for confidential relationships. "I think that the level of mutual trust is high enough. We have a unique situation in our business. Nearly everyone graduated from the same universities and entered business at the same time. Almost all top managers are of similar age and background. Exceptions are rare. And they understand each other easily" (2002, head of a retailing network).

Business negotiations and personal contacts are very helpful in raising mutual understanding and formation of the initial level of trust. However, no one could expect that adopted conventions would last for the rest of their lives. Agreements are normally kept within a certain period of time (normally a month). Then these conventions need to be maintained and renegotiated on a periodical basis. "There are wonderful relations in the market. If the folks once a month come to an agreement on a coordinated price policy they would keep it. Approximately in a month somebody starts breaking it, then another.... In a month we should meet again to look into the eyes of each other and make an agreement again" (2002, head of a cell-phone selling company).

Stigmatization of Defectors

Having established conventions, market actors also elaborate special *instruments of demarcation* among those who deserve trust and those who are stigmatized as not to be trusted. Our respondents make an important distinction between three prevalent models of action: acting by laws, acting by rules, and acting by no rules

Acting by laws presumes following the official formal rules (for example, paying the full amount of taxes and duties to the state). In fact, most Russian entrepreneurs are not able to hold this line consistently due to the large number of legal norms in Russia. Large transnational companies with big financial capacities and strict corporate codes may be an exception to this.

The majority of Russian businessmen follow a different line, which is defined as *acting by rules*. These rules differ from laws though they are always related to laws. Existence of this institutional gap does not mean that Russian business is thoroughly criminalized. Rather, firms operate in the so-called gray or semi-legal market segments. Empirically, this prevailing model of acting by rules is not easy to define for many things are not clearly explained on the verbal level. However, the 2001–02 interviews shed some light on this difficult problem. It could be concluded that acting by rules means at least the following: (1) avoiding behavior that "damages the market" (e.g., undermining an existing price level by big and spontaneous clearances); (2) avoiding "black" (illegal and mostly risky) business schemes that could let your contracting partners down in case authorities inspect the business; (3) failing to arrange administrative harassment (*zakaznye proverki*) of ones competitors' businesses, that is, refraining from asking state inspectors to disrupt their activities, an otherwise common activity; (4) settling disputed issues through negotiations.

Leading market actors try to define themselves as ones who act by laws and/or rules, thus distinguishing themselves from *defectors* who do not comply with the rules. The latter are stigmatized as *otmorozki* (following no rules) and *chernushniki* (black dealers) whose actions are damaging for the market. This category of market actors uses drastically reduced prices. They evade tax payments, running a risk beyond an acceptable level. They are reluctant to negotiate and do not follow accepted conventions. Therefore, they are not to be trusted. "We can easily reach an agreement with some companies. And these agreements on the price levels could be kept for months.... But at the same time there are firms that follow no rules. There is no point in talking to them. They would not understand simple words" (2001, head of a cell-phone selling company).

Subordination of market "outcasts" by leading sellers justifies their policy aimed at driving defectors out of the market. In doing so they look at the state as an important instrument, which makes it essential to understand the role the state can play in the formation of relationships based on trust and distrust.

The State as a Source of Trust and Distrust

Any of the conventions among market actors could easily be undermined if they are not backed by a stable state policy. Relations between market actors and state officials present a complex mixture of trust and distrust, in which distrust is dominant. This is reflected to some extent in the following puzzle.

Market actors do not trust the state authorities. However, even more, they do not trust institutions, that are not backed by the state.

We will develop our argument based on the following propositions:

1. The state as a major source of legitimization of rules is expected to take the final responsibility for all serious institutional failures.
2. No strong reciprocal or one-sided trust could be established without reference to the state policies or direct intervention by the state.
3. Predictability of state policies is an important precondition for the formation of trust.

What is Expected of the State?

Market actors' attitudes toward the Russian state contain some elements of almost enigmatic character. Let us illustrate first with two examples, which are beyond the scope of our empirical analysis.

The first one is borrowed from the history of the *Russian financial bubbles in 1994–95*, when a large amount of private savings were grabbed off by teams of swindlers arranging what were called financial pyramids (for details see Radaev 2000). The really striking thing was that the victims turned to the state to reclaim their money. Formally speaking, one can treat that as a clear manifestation of irrational behavior because the firms collecting money were privately owned and the state was not supposed to take responsibility for their actions. However, the state was blamed for the losses in the end.

The second example comes from the history of the *1998 financial crisis*, after which many private savings were lost in the bankrupt commercial banks. Although the crisis was caused by the financial default of state institutions, after the crash there was a massive inflow of private savings to the Sberbank, the largest state-run bank. Thus, the money flowed back to the state, which was a fundamental reason for the market to fail.

Both phenomena can be explained with the help of the concept of *moral economy* (Polanyi 1992), which says the state as the most powerful actor must stand behind public and private economic institutions, especially in case they fail. The state is made responsible for the minimal level of subsistence irrespective of the reasons that lead to the loss. A sort of reciprocity is expected here. As a result, one-sided trust in institutions emerges alongside expecting support from the state. Only institutions that are explicitly backed by the state are considered relatively reliable. These expectations are often not reflexive. However, they are quite persistent whatever people would say about their attitudes to the actual state policy.

Turning back to our empirical observations, leading market actors tend to emphasize their independence from the state—at least at the level of rhetoric. However, in their actual policy claims they largely seek state intervention rather than state withdrawal (Fligstein 2001). Their trust in institutions is also dependent on state policy. Instrumental considerations are also important here. Market actors try to use the state to implement their own concept of control. For instance, they draw a borderline between "bad firms" (i.e. black firms or acting-by-no-rules firms) and "good firms" as a sort of signal to the state authorities. They want to see the "bad firms" ousted from the market. However, they often are reluctant to combat defectors directly through blacklisting and other means leading to an open conflict. They prefer to use the state to legitimize violence against defectors.

Producing these cleavages, leading sellers may also seek some privileged regimes for themselves, which raises concerns in the Russian Federation's AntiTrust Ministry. For instance, the ministry made an attempt to prevent the State Customs Committee from applying a different system of customs value measurements for the official dealers of large international companies in 2002. The latter were allowed not to prove the value of their goods when presenting invoices from the producer. (Let us add that the AntiTrust Ministry lost the case in the Arbitration Court.)

Alongside one-sided trust, reciprocal trust also depends strongly on state activity as it is largely built upon the predictability of actions of other market actors. Predictability makes the first step toward trust in relations, in which distrust still prevails. As far as the state is the main provider of formal and informal rules, no profound reciprocal trust could be established among business actors without predictable state policies. Any business-to-business conventions would be seriously undermined in the case of spontaneous changes in the regulatory framework. Therefore, all these conventions are built upon certain expectations of state actions.

When speaking about the state, we do not see it as a single entity but rather as a set of interrelated administrative bodies represented by public officials. Moreover, to decrease uncertainty market actors have to establish continuous and immediate contacts with these public officials. That is why the success of the business associations' efforts is frequently measured by the density of these contacts. The next question is whether it is easy to build up relationships between leading market actors and state representatives.

Building Conventions with the State

There are several fundamental difficulties in establishing conventions between business and state representatives.

First, there remains much mutual tensions between business leaders and public officials, which prevent successful negotiations. Entrepreneurs tend to see every public official as a bribe-taker predominantly interested in their private gain. At the same time, public officials tend to treat every entrepreneur as a smuggler evading taxes and customs duties. Here are some of the typical complaints: "The main problem concerns how the state treats us. One has the impression that all businessmen are either potential or actual criminals" (2001, head of a wholesale firm dealing in durable consumer goods); "The state authorities treat everyone as if they are engaged in illegal activities and routinely violate the rules" (2001, head of a retailing network).

Second, when negotiations between a business and the state commence, a critical situation of coordination normally takes place because the main parties apply different logics to justify their claims and actions called "different orders of worth" in the French economic theory of conventions (Thevenot 2000). Business leaders operate according to the market logic thinking about how to minimize costs and keep prices at a level attractive to customers. Public officials apply what we would call bureaucratic logic. Their main concern is to fulfill their administrative plans for the collection of the taxes and customs duties and to balance the interests of all political parties involved. This balance of interests includes preservation of their own opportunities for a private gain.

Third, parties in negotiation are far from being equal because power relationships are nearly always asymmetrical. State officials have the upper hand in policy making. State authorities play the role of incumbents imposing their rules while business agents are viewed rather as challengers of these rules (Fligstein 2001). Suggestions by business owners and managers can easily be turned down by the authorities with no plausible explanation. This means that it is difficult to expect that mutual obligations will be accepted and strictly fulfilled. However, the predictability of state policy may contribute to the formation of trust.

Fourth, government actions are nontransparent which produces uncertainty and makes conventions unstable. The point is that public officials are able to change formally adopted or informally accepted rules at any point of time. Moreover, these changes cannot be easily envisaged by the market actors. There were several occasions in 2001 when the State Customs Committee of the Russian Federation issued official orders only to cancel them soon afterwards producing a destabilizing impact on the market. "These companies simply did not join us [the business association] because they do not trust the state. They do not trust the authorities because they suspect a trap. Also, they would let their folks down" (2001, head of a wholesale firm dealing in electronic goods); "In my view relations between businesses and the state authorities are nonexistent. Somehow, the authorities tend to accompany quite positive measures with absolutely inadequate and controversial ones producing a kind of 'equilibrium'" (2002, head of a wholesale firm selling electronic goods).

During 2001 and 2002, there were some positive shifts in these relationships. However, the lack of reciprocal trust among company leaders and public officials still presents one of the major constraints limiting the possibility of building both one-sided trust in institutions and reciprocal trust among businesses.

To conclude, the general logic of building trust in a distrustful environment can be described as follows. On a micro level, there are informal private orders and closed business networks that serve as instruments for creating interpersonal trust. The character of these reciprocal relations is also changing over time. The limits of affect-based trust lead market actors to move toward reputation-based trust. Investment in reputation contributes to the development of one-sided trust in public institutions such as business associations. In turn, these associations become vehicles for establishing trust in the state authorities. Finally, predictability of state policy encourages both one-sided and reciprocal trust.

Conclusion

New Russian markets present a prominent example of a low-trust environment. Formal rules are contradictory and changeable and are often subject to intensive informalization. State policy is often nontransparent and nonpredictable, and, therefore, it becomes a major source of institutional instability. This situation produces uncertainty and undermines one-sided trust in formal institutions.

Reciprocal trust in other market actors is also seriously undermined because being honest often does not pay. Entrepreneurs confront a high level of opportunism and malfeasance in business relationships stemming from the frequent infringement of business contracts.

Capacities of formal litigation in contract enforcement with the assistance of arbitration courts and other third parties are limited. Russian entrepreneurs have to use methods of private contract enforcement including informal ways of settling disputes. Although entrepreneurs do try to protect themselves by introducing discriminatory elements into business contracts, especially when contracting with newcomers and outsiders, noncontractual forms play a major role in preventing malfeasance. To cope with the situation of reciprocal distrust, entrepreneurs collect business information and check up on their potential business partners. They also build up closed business networks. These precautionary measures are necessary to create the first level of reciprocal trust, that is, predictable behavior of the other market actors.

The second level of trust relationships requires firms to fulfill some mutual obligations. This requires a set of conventions among the market actors. To reach shared understandings and elaborate common rules of the game the leading market actors have to go beyond the mere monitoring of the actions of their contractors and competitors and arrange face-to-face negotiations with them. These negotiations are held at the political level of business associations and at the business level of informal roundtable meetings. Through continuous negotiations the market actors (including direct competitors) start to overcome their initial mutual distrust. Leading market actors also elaborate special instruments of demarcation distinguishing those who deserve trust (acting by rules) from those who are stigmatized as untrustworthy (acting by no rules).

Business-to-business conventions would not last long without taking into account the state as the main provider of formal rules. No real reciprocal or one-sided trust could be established without intervention by the state. Although market actors do not trust the state authorities, they trust the institutions that are not backed by the state even less. The state is supposed to take the final responsibility for all market institutions, especially in case of their failure. The state controlling bodies are also used as an instrument to put legal pressures on defectors in the market.

All this means that all conventions in the market are established with explicit or implicit reference to the state. To reduce uncertainty, market actors have to establish some conventions with public officials. Development of mutual obligations between businesses and the representatives of the state as the second level of trust relationships is questionable for the state always has the upper hand in negotiations. However, some predictability of state actions can be achieved.

To sum up, trust formation in a low-trust society starts at the micro level of interpersonal relations in different segments of the market. Then it develops through the mutual trust among members of business networks to one-sided trust in institutions dealing with these networks. As a precondition, the state must back market institutions by being predictable in its policy. In turn, it stimulates further development of reciprocal trust and creates conditions for the continuous self-enforcement of trust.

Notes

1. For a detailed description of the research outcomes, see Radaev 1998 and 2001a.
2. The surveys were conducted by the author and a research team at the Moscow Centre for Political Technologies, headed by Igor Bunin. We would like to thank Igor Bunin, Rostislav Kapelyushnikov, Alexey Zudin, and Natalia Nazarova of the Center and Vladimir Gubernatorov of the Russian Federation Chamber of Commerce and Industry for valuable support in the implementation of the project.
3. The surveys were conducted by the author and a research team of the Moscow State University—Higher School of Economics. We would like to thank the president of RATEC, Alexander Plyatsevoy, the executive director of ACORT, Oleg Sazanov, and the president of INP "Public Agreement," Alexander Auzan for facilitating the project. Svetlana Barsukova, Tatiana Kazantseva (first series of interviews), and Vladimir Karacharovsky (second series of interviews) were extremely helpful in collecting and systematizing important parts of the data. Technical support was provided by Evgenia Nadezhdina.
4. For a detailed description, see Radaev 2001c.

References

Coleman, James. 1988. Social Capital in the Creation of Human Capital. *American Journal of Sociology* 94: 95–120.

Eggertsson, Thrainn. 1990. *Economic Behavior and Institutions*. Cambridge, UK: Cambridge University Press.

Fligstein, Neil. 1996. Markets as Politics: A Political–Cultural Approach to Market Institutions. *American Sociological Review* 61: 656–73.

———. 2001. *Architecture of Markets: An Economic Sociology of Twenty-first-Century Capitalist Societies*. Princeton NJ: Princeton University Press.

Gambetta, Diego (ed.). 1988. *Trust: Making and Breaking Cooperative Relations*. Oxford: Basil Blackwell.

Hardin, Russell. 2002. *Trust and Trustworthiness*. New York: Russell Sage Foundation.

North, Douglas C. 1992. *Institutions, Institutional Change and Economic Performance*. Cambridge UK: Cambridge University Press.

Polanyi, Karl. 1992. The Economy as Instituted Process. In M. Granovetter and R. Swedberg (eds.). *The Sociology of Economic Life*, pp. 29–52. Boulder CO: Westview Press.

Radaev, Vadim. 1993. Rossiiskiye predprinimateli, kto oni? Na primere Moskvy (What are the Russian Entrepreneurs? An Example of Moscow). *Vestnik statistiki* 9: 3–13.

———. 1996. Maly biznes i problemy delovoy etiki: Nadezhdy i realnost (Small Business and Business Ethics: Hopes and Reality). *Voprosy Ekonomiki* No. 7, pp. 72–82.

———. 1997. *Ekonomicheskaya sotsiologiya: Kurs lektsii* (Economic Sociology: A Lecture Course). Moscow: Aspect Press.

———. 1998. *Formirovaniye novykh rossiiskikh rynkov: Transaktsionnye izderzhki, formy kontrolya i delovaya etika* (Formation of New Russian Markets: Transaction Costs, Forms of Control and Business Ethics). Moscow: Center for Political Technologies.

———. 2000. Return of the Crowds and Rationality of Action: A History of Russian "Financial Bubbles" in the mid-1990s, *European Societies* 2: 271–94.

———. 2001a. Entrepreneurial Strategies and the Structure of Transaction Costs in Russian Business. In V. Bonnell and T. Gold (eds.). *The New Entrepreneurs of Europe and Asia: Patterns of Business Development in Russia, Eastern Europe and China*, pp. 191–213. Armonk NY: M.E. Sharpe.

———. 2001b. Entreprise, protection et violence en Russie la fin des annees 1990. *Cultures et Conflits* 42: 47–68.

———. 2001c. Informal Institutional Arrangements and Tax Evasion in the Russian Economy. Paper Presented at the Fifth Annual Meeting of the International Society for New Institutional Economics, Berkeley, USA, September 13–15.

Rose-Ackerman, Susan. 2001a. Trust and Honesty in Post-socialist Societies. *Kyklos* 54: 415–44.

———. 2001b. Trust, Honesty and Corruption: Reflection on the State-building Process. *Archives of European Sociology* 42: 526–70.

Sztompka, Piotr. 1999. *Trust: A Sociological Theory*. Cambridge, UK: Cambridge University Press.

Thevenot, Laurent. 2000. Organized Complexity: Conventions of Coordination and the Composition of Economic Arrangements. Paper Presented at the Conference on New Economic Sociology in Europe 2000, Stockholm University, June 2–3.

Williamson, Oliver E. 1985. *The Economic Institutions of Capitalism: Firms, Markets, Relational Contracting*. New York: The Free Press.

CHAPTER SIX

Establishing Confidence in Business Partners: Courts, Networks, and Relationships as Pillars of Support

CHRISTOPHER WOODRUFF

The ability to trust a trading partner is fundamental to the development of complex economic relationships. Confidence in the actions of a trading partner may be supported in any of three ways. First, firms may use formal contracts, enforced through sanctions administered by courts, to govern trading relationships. Alternatively, confidence in trading partners may be based on knowledge gained through past interactions with the trading partner. The bilateral relationship allows firms to distinguish good and bad "types" (Watson 1999). Cooperation may also evolve in a relationship over time, with the threat of breaking off the relationship serving as a sanction against bad behavior (Lindsey et al. 2001). Finally, firms may rely on a trading partner's reputation, based on information about the trading partner's behavior in other business or social relationships (Granovetter 1986; Greif 1993). As with bilateral relationships, reputation may serve either to identify types or to provide a sanction against improper behavior (McMillan and Woodruff 1999b).

This paper examines the development of both formal and informal enforcement of contracts in the context of the transition to market economies in Eastern Europe. Policy makers and policy advisors in the region have focused their attention on the development of the formal legal system (EBRD 1999). This approach is justified if one believes that bilateral and reputational enforcement act primarily as imperfect substitutes to formal enforcement when the latter is lacking. However, as we demonstrate in this chapter, where courts are imperfect, informal enforcement may complement the formal legal system, allowing courts to function where they would otherwise be ineffective. Using firm level data, we show that the latter circumstances hold in Eastern Europe. Formal and informal enforcement do indeed complement one another in supporting trust among trading partners.

Published work using the same data set utilized here gives an indication of the interaction between bilateral and reputational enforcement (McMillan and Woodruff 1999b; Johnson et al. 2000) and the interaction between courts and bilateral relationships (Johnson et al. 2002). We summarize the findings from this earlier work and provide new evidence on the interaction between reputational networks and formal contracting.

The manner in which various contract enforcement mechanisms interact has important implications for public policy in the transition countries. Establishment of a legal system sufficient to enable firms and individuals to make and enforce written contracts is a worthy goal. The state's role in this is clear. However, if the informal mechanisms complement formal enforcement, then policy should also be directed toward supporting increased flows of information among firms. By establishing credit-reporting bureaus, establishing simple and clear accounting standards and other similar actions, the state can play a role in ensuring that firms are able to learn about the reliability of trading partners more easily, allowing for a freer, more open market to develop.

First, we review the existing literature and the development of a very simple framework to guide the examination of the data. The following section describes the state of legal development in five Eastern European countries for which we have data and describes the data itself. The results from previously published work and new analysis are presented in the next section. The final section offers some concluding remarks.

Supporting Contractual Agreements

The importance of each of the three pillars of contract enforcement has been documented in the literature. Scholars have identified the important role played by informal enforcement from historical times predating the development of formal legal systems and from more contemporaneous times in settings where formal institutions have not yet been developed (Geertz 1978). Bilateral relationships are also important in money lending, particularly in rural settings. The importance of reputational enforcement has also been emphasized, particularly among small, closed groups of trading partners (see, e.g. Clay 1997; Greif 1993; Landa 1994.) The literature also makes clear that the development of formal institutions does not make informal enforcement obsolete. Even where formal legal institutions are well developed, as in the United States, trading relationships continue to be governed by informal enforcement, both bilateral (Macauley 1963) and reputational (Ellickson 1991).

The precise nature of the interaction between either bilateral or reputational enforcement, on the one hand, and formal enforcement, on the other, has been the subject of less discussion. The theoretical literature provides models in which formal and informal enforcement substitute for one another, models in which they complement one another, and models in which they may do either of these, depending on the specific circumstances.[1] Kranton (1996) provides an example of the first type of model; Klein (1996) develops the opposite case, showing that formal and informal contracting may complement one another. More generally, Baker et al. (1994) developed a theoretical model showing that explicit and implicit incentives may be either substitutes or complements.

In contrast to the relatively active theoretical discussion of the interaction between informal and formal enforcement, there is much less empirical evidence on the interaction. Empirical testing depends on finding settings in which the availability of formal or informal enforcement varies in a systematic and exogenous manner. At least in part, the lack of empirical evidence reflects the difficulty in finding such settings. The quality of formal institutions generally changes slowly, making variance across time difficult to measure. One exception to this is Kranton and Swamy's (1999) study of the impact of importing the British legal system to India. They provide data showing a breakdown of cooperation among lenders and borrowers in India's informal rural credit markets. The findings support Kranton's theoretical view that development of a formal contract enforcement mechanism may undermine informal enforcement, suggesting that formal and informal mechanisms are substitutes.

The ability to write and enforce formal contracts may also depend on the characteristics of the goods being traded. This variation leads to the possibility of identifying cross-sectional variance in the degree to which relationships are subject to formal contracting. For example, using cross-sectional data from contracts covering information service outsourcing among manufacturing and service industry firms in the United States, Poppo and Zenger (2002) found evidence that formal and informal contracting complement one another. The depth of the informal relationship is indicated by responses to survey questions on the level of trust, communication cooperation, and related characteristics in those same relationships. They show that there is a positive correlation between contract length and measures of trust, and that both are positively related to the perceived success of the relationship. Under the assumption that written contracts infer formal enforcement,[2] their results suggest that courts and relationships complement one another. Bernstein's (1996) less quantitative study of the US grain and feed industry also suggests complementarity between legal and extra-legal enforcement. Bernstein identifies "relationship preserving norms" (which are self-enforced) and "end game norms" (which are enforced by courts or trade association arbitrators), suggesting that courts and informal arrangements are complementary.

Experimental economics has also provided some evidence on how formal and informal enforcement interacts. Fehr and Falk (1999) find that the availability of formal contracts undermines cooperation, while Lazzarini et al. (2001) find that stricter formal enforcement facilitates informal cooperation.

The Interaction of Information and Institutions

The intuition for the interaction of formal and informal enforcement is straightforward: courts are used when trading partners prove to be unreliable. Courts may be both costly to use and imperfect in their ability to resolve disputes. Informal networks provide information about the expected reliability of a trading partner. The use of informal networks allows firms to avoid at least some unreliable trading partners. Hence, reliance on networks reduces the frequency with which courts will be needed to resolve disputes. Less frequent use allows courts, which are more expensive or less reliable, to play a role in supporting contractual relationships. This intuition is formalized in a simple framework.

There are two firms, a buyer and a seller. The two firms may interact in an instantaneous relationship, in which the buyer pays cash for goods at the instant in which the seller delivers them. We refer to this as a low-risk relationship. Alternatively, the firms may enter into a relationship that involves higher risk for the seller. In this high-risk relationship, the seller moves first, by delivering some goods to the buyer. The buyer then decides whether to pay for the goods or abscond with them. Normalizing the profit from low-risk relationships (e.g. cash sales) to zero, the seller realizes a positive profit $\pi_S > 0$ from high-risk relationships in which the buyer cooperates and negative profits $\pi_L < 0$ from high-risk relationships in which the buyer absconds. The success of the relationship for the seller depends on whether the buyer carries through on the agreement or not.[3] Ex ante, we represent the seller's expectation with respect to the buyer's action with the parameter α. When matched in risky relationships, the seller expects the buyer to cooperate with probability $\alpha \in [0, 1]$. Thus, the seller receives π_S a proportion α of the time and π_L a proportion $1 - \alpha$ of the time.

In the event the buyer fails to cooperate, by, for example, failing to pay after delivery, the seller may resort to courts to resolve the dispute. The seller incurs a cost, C, to use the courts. The reliability of the courts is measured with the parameter $\theta \in [0, 1]$. The courts make the correct decision, and the seller is made whole (except for the court costs), a proportion θ of the time. In expectation, sellers may have different values of θ, representing different views of the effectiveness of courts.

A seller's expected profit from choosing high-risk relationships can be shown to be:

$$\pi = (\pi_S - \pi_L)(\alpha + \theta - \alpha\theta) + \pi_L - (1 - \alpha)C \qquad (1)$$

It is apparent from equation (1) that an increase in either the reliability of the customer (α) or the reliability of the courts (θ) leads to an increase in the expected profit from the risky relationship. Moreover, equation (1) shows that more reliable customers and more reliable courts substitute for one another in producing profits for the seller.[4]

The trade-off is shown in figure 6.1. The figure shows iso-profit lines, or combinations of α and θ which yield the same expected profit. For any belief $\theta^\star$ about the effectiveness of courts, there is some minimum customer reliability which results in expected profits of exactly zero in the high-risk relationships. Call this level of reliability $\alpha^\star$. The dark line shows the combinations of $\alpha^\star$ and $\theta^\star$, those for which risky relationships yield an expected profit of exactly zero. Holding the effectiveness of the courts constant, a movement to the right along the horizontal axis in figure 6.1 represents an increase in the reliability of customers, and an increase in the profitability of the risky relationship. Holding the reliability of customers constant, a movement up represents an increase in the effectiveness of courts and, again, an increase in the profitability of the risky relationship. Hence, the lines to the right (left) of the dark line represent positive (negative) expected profits from the risky relationship. Assuming risk neutrality, sellers prefer the trusting relationship when α and θ lie to the northeast of the dark line and the safe relationship otherwise.[5]

Sellers find buyers in one of two ways. They may select them randomly, which in our survey corresponds to "we advertised," "they contacted us," or similar responses. We assume these are random draws from the population of buyers, so that the expected α is equal to the mean of the distribution, $\bar{\alpha}$. Alternatively, manufacturers may learn about buyers through a business or social network. In our survey, this corresponds to customers who "are managed or owned by a family member," who were identified "through a previous business acquaintance," and so on. The prior information allows the seller to determine the reliability of the buyer with greater

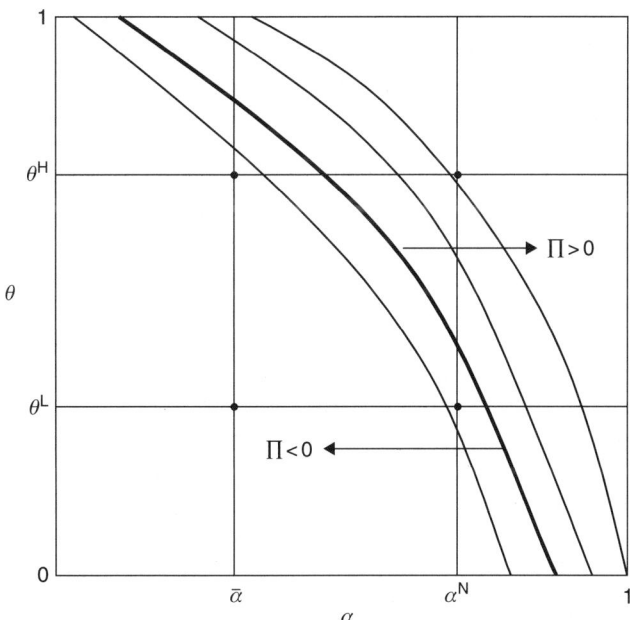

Figure 6.1 Trade-off of reliability of customers and effectiveness of courts

precision, and to avoid (high-risk) relationships with unreliable trading partners. The average reliability of customers found through networks, then, is the average of the (truncated) part of the distribution lying above α^*, a level discretely higher than $\bar{\alpha}$.[6]

From an empirical perspective, our measure of the effectiveness of courts is also discrete. This is an artifact of the wording of the survey question rather than a reflection of reality. Sellers might continuously adjust their estimates of the probability that courts will reach just decisions, as assumed in the model. Our survey asked firms whether courts could enforce a contract with customers or suppliers. A negative response presumably represents a manager with a low value of θ, and a positive response represents a manager with a high value of θ. On average, the estimate of θ given a negative response should be discretely below the estimate of θ given a positive response.

The discrete nature of movements in both α and θ leaves open the possibility shown in figure 6.1.[7] Customers found through networks have reliability denoted α^N; those coming from outside networks have reliability $\bar{\alpha}$. Managers who say that courts are effective have an average $\theta = \theta^H$; those who say that courts are not effective have an average $\theta = \theta^L$. Given θ^L (respectively, $\bar{\alpha}$) a movement from $\bar{\alpha}$ to α^N (respectively, θ^L to θ^H) leaves a firm below the zero profit line and therefore has no effect. Both a belief in courts and prior information from networks are necessary to make risky relationships profitable.[8]

Thus, even a framework in which the reliability of customers and effectiveness of courts are always substitutes at the margin can produce predictions of complementarity in the data. For low levels of α and θ, the profit from the risky relationship is negative. An increase in α (or θ) by itself may result in a smaller loss rather than a larger gain. In such a case, the seller would choose not to enter the risky relationships, regardless of the higher α. Although the model does not tell us on which side of the zero profit line the various combinations of α and θ lie, it does tell us that information networks and courts may appear as either complements or substitutes. Thus, the nature of the interaction between information networks and courts is an empirical question, which we will examine with data from the Eastern European surveys.

Eastern Europe provides an interesting setting to examine these issues because commercial courts have developed quickly in many of the transition countries. By the latter part of the 1990s, nearly ten years after the beginning of the transition, most Eastern European countries had enacted legal reform and created at least modestly effective legal systems. The European Bank for Reconstruction and Development (EBRD) conducts annual surveys of lawyers and legal academics in Eastern Europe. The 1999 survey focused on the effectiveness of commercial courts. The EBRD provides ratings of the legal infrastructure of each country, on a scale of 1 to 4+. A legal system with a 4 rating for effectiveness is one in which laws are "reasonably clear," and enforcement of laws is "reasonably adequate." A 3 rating indicates that laws are clear, but enforcement is "inadequate or inconsistent," and a 2 rating indicates unclear laws and little enforcement. In the 1999 survey, taken about ten years after the transition, the majority of transition countries earned a rating of 3 or better for commercial law. None rated a 4+, and only one (Slovenia) received a 4. However, Bulgaria, Estonia, Macedonia, Hungary, and Romania were rated 4− for effectiveness, and nine countries—including Slovakia and Poland—were rated in the 3 range. Russia and Ukraine were among the eight countries rated 2, indicating an inadequate commercial legal infrastructure.

The Data and Previously Reported Results

The data used here come from surveys conducted among manufacturing firms during 1997 in Poland, Slovakia, Romania, Russia, and Ukraine. All of the surveyed firms had between 10 and 270 employees and were privately owned, though some of them were privatized state-owned enterprises. The survey is described in more detail in Johnson et al. (2000).

We are interested in a measure of the level of trust in buyer–seller relationships, and the characteristics of those relationships that correlate with the level of trust. Surveyed managers were asked a series of questions about their firms' oldest and newest customer relationship. Managers described relationships of varying complexity. Some sales are cash and carry, others involve some delay in payment. Some goods are produced to order, others are produced for inventory. These data form the basis of measuring trust in the relationship. For example, a seller requires a higher degree of confidence in a customer paying with delay than in a customer who pays on delivery.

There is also substantial variation in the information which manufacturers had about their customers, and in the manufacturing manager's belief about the effectiveness of courts. With regard to bilateral enforcement, some of the relationships identified in the survey are new, others are well established. In establishing and monitoring the relationships identified in the survey, firms sometimes use information networks, in other cases they do not.

With regard to courts, the five countries for which we have data have a wide range of scores for the EBRD's commercial law ratings. Romania scores best with a (4−), followed by Poland and Slovakia (3), and finally Russia (2+) and Ukraine (2). Thus, with respect to commercial law, the legal systems in these countries have a presence, but an imperfect one. The firm level survey data used in this paper generally support these views. Firms were asked whether courts can enforce contracts with trading partners. The highest percentage of affirmative answers was in Romania, where 87 percent of firms believe courts can enforce contracts. This compares with positive response rates of 73 percent in Poland, 68 percent in Slovakia, 56 percent in Russia, and 55 percent in Ukraine. The rank ordering of the percentage of affirmative responses aligns with the ordering of the effectiveness of commercial legal infrastructure reported in the EBRD survey.

The rapid development of commercial court systems led to important variance in opinions about the effectiveness of courts even within a given country. In 1997, at the time the surveys used here were administered, only a small percentage of entrepreneurs had actual hands-on experience using the courts. For these entrepreneurs, opinions might be based on first-hand experience. For the majority, they were based on second- or third-hand information involving a relatively small number of cases. The variation in the perceived effectiveness of legal institutions is important because what matters for the structuring of relationships is not the actual effectiveness of the various enforcement mechanisms but the contracting parties' perceptions of their effectiveness. The transition process leads to variance that diminishes over time as entrepreneurs learn when and how the courts are effective.

Before turning to the interaction of formal and reputational means of enforcement, we review evidence on the importance of each of the three pillars of support and on previously reported interactions between them. Analyzing the same data used here, Johnson et al. (2002) show that each of the three pillars discussed earlier plays a significant role in supporting trust in business relationships in Eastern Europe. Johnson et al. measure the manufacturer's trust in its customers with the percentage of the bill that is paid by the buyer some time after delivery of the goods.[9] The greater the percentage of the bill a manufacturer allows the customer to pay with delay, the greater the indicated level of trust in the relationship. On average, about 60 percent of the customer's bill is paid after delivery. The amount of the bill paid after delivery increases by 12 percentage points during the first year of the relationship, indicating that learning about the customer through the bilateral relationship is important. The use of information networks to locate customers is also important, indicating a role for reputational enforcement. Compared to customers who are unknown at the time the relationship was established, customers coming from either social or business networks are allowed to pay just under 15 percentage points more of their bill after delivery.[10] More formal organizations matter as well. Firms which are members of trade associations providing information about the reliability of potential customers and suppliers allow their customers to pay an additional 4 percentage points of their bill with delay. Compared with bilateral and reputational enforcement, formal enforcement appears to play a smaller role. Managers who say that courts can be used to enforce contracts allow their customers to pay, on average, about 5 percentage points more of their bill after delivery.[11]

We are also interested here in how the three pillars interact. On this, the existing work provides some discussion on the interaction between bilateral relationships, on the one hand, and both reputational and formal enforcement, on the other. We review this briefly before turning to the third nexus, the interaction of reputational enforcement and formal enforcement.

The interaction of bilateral and reputational contract enforcement has an interesting interpretation. Social and business networks may serve one or both of two purposes. First, networks provide information that allows the seller to determine whether the buyer is a good or bad "type." Second, they may also provide the ability to sanction a trading partner by reporting deviant behavior to the network. The report limits the deviant's future business prospects. Information about the trading partner's type is also learned through the bilateral relationship. This means that if networks provide only information, their impact on the level of trust in the relationship should diminish as the relationship ages. That is, networks should have a bigger impact early in trading relationships than they do later in trading relationships. If, on the other hand, sanctions are an important part of the use of networks, the effect of networks should endure even as the individual relationship ages. Johnson et al. (2002) find that networks remain an important determinant of trust even after relationships are established, though the networks do have a somewhat larger impact at the start of the relationship. McMillan and Woodruff (1999b) also found support for the role of sanctions in reputational enforcement using data from a similar survey in Vietnam. Relationships established through networks exhibit higher levels of trust even after they have been established for several years. Overall, the evidence suggests that bilateral and reputational enforcement operate independently of one another, rather than substituting for one another.

Johnson et al. (2002) provide results that suggest that courts and bilateral relationships do substitute for one another. They find that belief in the effectiveness of courts has a significantly bigger impact during the first three months of a relationship than later. Sellers who believe courts are effective in enforcing contracts allow new customers to pay 16 percentage points more of their bill after delivery, but courts lose their significance in relationships which are more than three months old.

Finally, we turn to the interaction between reputational enforcement and formal legal enforcement, as yet unexplored in the data. This interaction is particularly important from a policy perspective because policy can affect the development of reputational enforcement. Establishment of credit bureaus and improvements in accounting standards are among the measures that might be expected to produce a freer flow of information and more quickly establish reputations. In the following section, we examine the data from the survey conducted with firms from Eastern Europe in order to understand how formal enforcement and reputational enforcement interact.

Measuring the Interaction Empirically

Following Johnson et al. (2002), we use the percentage of the bill paid after delivery as a measure of the level of trust manufacturers have in customers. We limit the sample to customers that are privately owned and located in the same country as the manufacturer. That is, we exclude transactions with state-owned enterprises and export customers. We also limit the sample to manufacturers that are de novo startups, excluding those that formerly were state owned. The ability to use courts may be different in relationships involving any of these excluded groups. The resulting sample still includes over 1,200 manufacturer–customer relationships.

The right-hand side variables of interest are those that indicate, first, the use of a network in identifying customers and, second, the manager's belief in the effectiveness of the legal system in resolving disputes with trading partners. We asked managers their primary source of information about customers before they started trading. About 18 percent of the time, the customer is managed by a family member or someone who was a friend prior to the start of the relationship. In another 45 percent of the cases, the manager reported that another firm or a business association was the primary source of information about the customer. Other responses indicate a lower level of prior information about the customer.[12] The previously published results reported earlier used separate measures for social and business networks. Because the impact of information from these two sources is very similar, and in the interest of simplicity, we combine these into one variable indicating information from either of these sources. We expect customers coming from these networks to be more reliable on average than those about whom there is no information at the start of the relationship. In other words, we assign a higher value of α to these customers.

In addition to information, we are also interested in the manager's belief about the ability of courts to enforce contracts with customers. The response to this question gives us a value for θ in the framework above. Table 6.1 reports the results of regressions using the percentage of the bill paid with delay as the dependent variable. In the first two columns, the information variable defined earlier and the manager's belief about the effectiveness of courts are included separately. The regressions also include variables indicating other characteristics of the selling firm (e.g. age of firm, number of employees), the buying firm (e.g. the number of employees, whether the firm is a retail, individual, or manufacturing firm), characteristics of the selling firm's manager (age, education, and others), and other variables described in the notes to table 6.1. The first column includes no country or industry controls. The results indicate that customers coming from business or social networks pay about 7 percentage points more of their bill after delivery than those coming from outside these networks. Managers who believe that courts can enforce contracts allow customers to pay almost 10 percentage points more of their bill after delivery.

The second column adds country and industry controls to the regression. These controls have only a modest impact on the measured impact of courts, but result in a higher estimated impact for information networks. The additional percentage of the bill that customers coming from information networks pay after delivery increases from 7 to 12 points.

Table 6.1 Percentage of bill paid with delay (trade credit)[a]

Variables[b]	(1)	(2)	(3)	(4)
Information from social or business network	7.25 (2.84)	12.37 (5.21)	−2.89 (0.59)	5.89 (1.29)
Courts can enforce contracts with trading partners	9.67 (2.99)	8.86 (3.08)	1.01 (0.21)	3.53 (0.82)
Interaction effect Courts × Information network			13.54 (2.40)	8.63 (1.66)
Industry/Country dummies	No	Yes	No	Yes
Observations	1212	1212	1212	1212
R-squared	0.12	0.32	0.13	0.32

Notes

[a] T-statistics in parentheses.

[b] Regressions from random effects regressions, grouped at the level of the manufacturer interviewed. Each regression also includes variables indicating the duration of the relationship with the customer (4 dummy variables), the number of employees in the interviewed firm (3 dummy variables), the age of the firm (3 dummy variables), a variable indicating that the firm received a bank loan in 1996, a variable indicating that the firm was spun off from a state-owned firm, variables indicating that the entrepreneur is younger than 30, between 30 and 40 years old, or between 40 and 50 years old, variables indicating that the manager has between 13 and 16 years of schooling and 17 or more years of schooling, and a variable indicating whether the manager was formerly a high-level manager in a state-owned firm, variables indicating whether the customer is a retailer/wholesaler, the customer is an individual, the customer is foreign-owned, the customer is located in a different city, and variables indicating whether the customer has 16–50 employees, 51–100 employees, or more than 100 employees (15 or fewer employees is the comparison group).

This suggests that information networks are more commonly used in those countries and industries in which trade credit is less common.

To test whether information networks and courts are complements or substitutes, we next add a variable interacting these two variables. The interaction term takes a value of one in relationships which arose from an information network *and* in which the manufacturer's manager believes that courts are effective. Thus, the variable indicates the added value of courts among all those relationships arising from information networks, or the added value of information to those managers who believe that courts are effective in enforcing contracts. A negative sign on the interaction term would indicate that information networks and courts substitute for one another. A positive sign on the interaction term would indicate that the two means of enforcement compliment one another.

The results indicate that the interaction term is positive, and significant at the .05 level when industry/country controls are not included (column 3) and at the .10 level when industry/country controls are included (column 4). Indeed, the results in columns 3 and 4 indicate that courts have no significant impact on the level of trade credit offered customers who do not come from information networks, and that information networks have no significant impact on the level of trade credit offered by managers who do not believe courts are effective. However, the combination of the two is sufficient to support trust in customers' willingness to pay for goods delivered on credit. The situation is similar to that depicted in figure 6.1.

In sum, these regressions suggest that neither courts nor information networks by themselves are sufficient to support trust among startup firms in Eastern Europe. Combined, however, they do support a greater level of trust in customers. Thus, they are complements in production. The use of one raises the marginal value of using the other.

Discussion and Conclusion

Previous research has reached the conclusion that legal systems in Eastern European countries are effective in regulating commercial transactions (Hendley et al. 2001; Johnson et al. 2002). This finding is somewhat surprising given the extent of the reforms made to the legal systems after the transition from a planned to a market economy. The analysis in this paper suggests an important caveat to the existing literature. Courts do have an effect on commercial transactions, but the legal system is not yet efficient enough to support trust between anonymous trading partners. Rather, courts play a role only in conjunction with the use of information networks that help separate reliable trading partners from unreliable ones. The theoretical framework developed in this paper suggests one reason why this might be the case. Information networks reduce the probability of having to use courts, allowing less efficient legal institutions to play a role in contracting.

From a policy perspective, the complementarity suggests that policy should focus not only on legal reform, but also on the development of private sector institutions which promote the flow of information. Credit bureaus and more transparent accounting information are examples of this. Governments can improve the effectiveness of their legal systems by encouraging the development of private institutions such as these. Not all private institutions should be equally encouraged however, as some are more exclusionary than others. McMillan and Woodruff (2000) discuss differences among private order institutions in more detail.

Ultimately, however, the development of legal systems supporting trade between anonymous trading partners is still important. Reliance on information networks, even relatively elastic networks such as those within the business community, leads to some inefficiencies in the way relationships are structured. An example of this is found by examining the flow of trade credit between large and small firms. Economies of scale in formal lending result in larger firms having cheaper and more ready access to finance from banks. However, trade between firms generates information that is relevant to judging the creditworthiness of firms. Compared to banks, then, firms have an informational advantage in monitoring the behavior of smaller customers who borrow from them. Hence, efficiency is served by channeling money from banks through larger firms to smaller firms.

Among firms in Eastern Europe, larger firms receive more trade credit than smaller firms. This makes sense in the context of a contracting system which is still based primarily on informal enforcement. Larger firms have more widely known reputations. However, from the perspective of financial flows, the small-to-large flow of funds is less efficient. A better functioning legal system will allow larger firms to provide trade credit to smaller firms, with the courts providing sufficient incentive for the firms to repay loans. The gains in overall efficiency should benefit all firms, but especially smaller ones lacking direct access to finance through the formal financial markets.

Notes

1. Throughout the paper, the terms complements and substitutes refer to production rather than demand. Klein (1996) points out that formal and informal enforcement can be substitutes in demand—in the sense that an increase in the price of one leads to heavier reliance on the other—at the same time they are complements in production—in the sense that the increased use of one increases the marginal value of using the other.
2. Written agreements do not necessarily imply reliance on formal enforcement. McMillan and Woodruff (1999a) discuss the use of written agreements in Vietnam at a time when formal legal enforcement was nonexistent. Managers reported that written contracts were important in clarifying disputes between trading partners in a purely bilateral setting and in informal, sanction-based enforcement by third parties.
3. The relationship is modeled with one-sided moral hazard. In reality, the buyer may face some risk as well. For example, the seller may deliver defective merchandise. The data do not allow us to examine this side of the transaction. We do not know what information the buyer has about the seller or whether the buyer believes courts are effective.
4. The value to the seller of an increase in α is $\partial\pi/\partial\alpha = (\pi_S - \pi_L)(1 - \theta) + C$. Since $\pi_S - \pi_L > 0$, this is always decreasing in θ. Similarly, the value of an increase in θ is $\partial\pi/\partial\theta = (\pi_S - \pi_L)(1 - \alpha)$, always decreasing in α.
5. Note that the distribution of α may depend on the effectiveness of the courts as perceived by buyers. The models of Kali (1999) and Tirole (1996) presume that there are three types of trading partners: those who are reliable, those who are unreliable, and those who are opportunistic. The latter group behaves reliably when it pays to do so, and unreliably otherwise. As courts become more reliable, the opportunistic buyers behave reliably. In an uncertain legal environment where perceptions about the effectiveness of courts vary across the population, the buyers' behavior will be determined by their own beliefs about the effectiveness of courts, about which our survey provides no information. For simplicity, we presume that the buyer's distribution of α does not depend on the individual seller's perception of the courts' reliability. Given the uncertainty surrounding the effectiveness of legal enforcement in the transition environment, this assumption does not appear excessively unrealistic.
6. Customers identified through networks may also be more reliable because of reputational sanctions enforced by the network. This would reinforce the difference in reliability of customers found through networks and those coming from outside networks. The evidence on the use of networks to sanction trading partners is discussed later. However, network sanctions are not necessary to drive a wedge between the reliability of customers found inside and outside networks.
7. Figure 6.1 is drawn for the case of a very rough partition of α, in which case α^N/θ^L may lie below the zero profit line (as shown). If sellers can identify the reliability of buyers precisely, α^N will always lie on the zero profit line. In such a case, the effect of sellers perceiving that courts are effective will show up as a greater frequency of networked relationships. That is, $\alpha^N/\theta^H < \alpha^N/\theta^L$, so that complex relationships are formed for a larger part of the distribution of α when courts are perceived to be effective.
8. The result is similar to Baker et al. (1994) who conclude that "in some circumstances, neither an implicit nor an explicit contract alone can generate nonnegative profit, but an appropriate combination of the two can" (p. 1128).

9. Sellers allow some customers to pay as many as 30 days after delivery without charging any interest. Given the option, a buyer will always choose to pay with delay. Hence, variation in the proportion of the bill paid with delay reflects variation in the decision of the seller to offer credit rather than variation in the decision of the buyer to accept credit.
10. Social and business networks are identified with reference to the manager interviewed. Social networks include customers managed by a family member, by someone who was a friend before the relationship began, or by someone referred by a family member. Business networks include firms identified through previously existing customers or suppliers, or other firms producing products similar to the respondent's products.
11. Results from a comparable survey in Vietnam, reported in McMillan and Woodruff (1999b), provide estimates of a similar magnitude. Customers in Vietnam pay 7 percent more of their bill one year after the relationship is established. Customers coming from business networks pay around 15 percentage points more of their bill after delivery, compared to customers coming from outside business and social networks. Social networks, however, have no significant effect on payment after delivery among firms in the Vietnam survey. Effective courts were not yet established in Vietnam at the time business managers were surveyed there.
12. The most common source of information for customers outside networks is "he contacted us," followed by "advertisement," and "we met at a fair."

References

Baker, George, Robert Gibbons, and Kevin J. Murphy. 1994. Subjective Performance Measures in Optimal Incentive Contracts. *Quarterly Journal of Economics* 109: 1125–56.

Bernstein, Lisa. 1996. Merchant Law in a Merchant Court: Rethinking the Code's Search for Immanent Business Norms. *University of Pennsylvania Law Review* 144: 1765–821.

Clay, Karen. 1997. Trade Without Law: Private-order Institutions in Mexican California. *Journal of Law, Economics and Organization* 13: 202–31.

Ellickson, Robert C. 1991. *Order without Law*. Cambridge MA: Harvard University Press.

EBRD (European Bank for Reconstruction and Development). 1999. *Transition Report*. London: EBRD.

Fehr, Ernst and Armin Falk. 1999. Wage Rigidity in a Competitive Incomplete Contract Market. *Journal of Political Economy* 107: 106–34.

Geertz, Clifford. 1978. The Bazaar Economy: Information and Search in Peasant Marketing. *American Economic Review* 68: 28–32.

Granovetter, Mark. 1986. Economic Action and Social Structure: The Problem of Embededness. *American Journal of Sociology* 83: 1420–43.

Greif, Avner. 1993. Contract Enforceability and Economic Institutions in Early Trade: The Maghribi Traders Coalition. *American Economic Review* 83: 525–48.

Hendley, Kathryn, Peter Murrell, and Randi Ryterman. 2001. Law Works in Russia: The Role of Legal Institutions in the Transition of Russian Enterprises. In P. Murrell (ed.). *Assessing the Value of Law in Transition Economies*. Ann Arbor MI: University of Michigan Press.

Johnson, Simon, John McMillan, and Christopher Woodruff. 2000. Entrepreneurs and the Ordering of Institutional Reform: Poland, Slovakia, Romania, Russia, and Ukraine Compared. *Economics of Transition* 8: 1–36.

———. 2002. Courts and Relational Contracts. *Journal of Law, Economics and Organization* 18: 221–77.

Kali, Raja. 1999. Endogenous Business Networks. *Journal of Law, Economics and Organization* 15: 615–36.

Klein, Benjamen. 1996. Why Holdups Occur. The Self-enforcing Range of Contractual Relationships. *Economic Inquiry* 34: 444–63.

Kranton, Rachael. 1996. Reciprocal Exchange: A Self-sustaining System. *American Economic Review* 86: 830–51.

Kranton, Rachael and Anand Swamy. 1999. The Hazards of Piecemeal Reform: British Civil Courts and the Credit Market in Colonial India. *Journal of Development Economics* 58: 1–24.

Landa, Janet Tai. 1994. *Trust, Ethnicity, and Identity*. Ann Arbor MI: University of Michigan Press.

Lazzarini, Sergio, Gary Miller, and Todd Zenger. 2001. Order with Some Law: Complementarity vs. Substitution of Formal and Informal Arrangements. Mimeo. Washington University, St. Louis MO.

Lindsey, John, Ben Pollack, and Richard Zeckhauser. 2001. Free Love, Fragile Fidelity, and Forgiveness: Rival Social Conventions under Hidden Information. Mimeo. Yale University, New Haven CT.

Macauley, Stewart. 1963. Non-contractual Relations in Business: A Preliminary Study. *American Sociological Review* 28: 55–69.

McMillan, John and Christopher Woodruff. 1999a. Dispute Prevention without Courts in Vietnam. *Journal of Law, Economics and Organization* 15: 637–58.

———. 1999b. Interfirm Relationships and Informal Credit in Vietnam. *Quarterly Journal of Economics* 114: 1285–320.

———. 2000. Private Ordering under Dysfunctional Public Ordering. *Michigan Law Review* 98: 2421–58.

Poppo, Laura and Todd Zenger. 2002. Substitutes or Complements? Exploring the Relationship between Formal Contracts and Relational Governance. *Strategic Management Journal* 23: 707–25.

Tirole, Jean. 1996. A Theory of Collective Reputations (with Applications to the Persistence of Corruption and to Firm Quality). *Review of Economic Studies* 63: 1–22.

Watson, Joel. 1999. Starting Small and Renegotiation. *Journal of Economic Theory* 85: 52–90.

CHAPTER SEVEN

The Selective Use of State Capacity in Russia's Economy: Property Disputes and Enterprise Takeovers, 1998–2002

VADIM VOLKOV

Students of post-Soviet political economy generally agree that throughout the 1990s exchange relations in emerging markets were made possible by a variety of informal institutions and mechanisms that created a fair degree of predictability for the participants. These mechanisms ranged from soft ones, such as relational contracting and the use of personal networks, to hard ones that depended on organized force (or protection) to promote the survival and expansion of economic enterprises (see Frye 2000; Hertz 1996; Hendley et al. 2000; Pejovich 1997; Radaev 1998; Tambovtsev 1999; Varese 2001). Soft mechanisms involve trust created either by experiences of previous cooperation or social norms governing individuals in a certain milieu. The hard mechanisms that enable sustained exchange are rational and realistic in their nature and derive from perceived levels of relative protection of parties in exchange. They exclude trust although they may be enveloped in the rhetoric of trust. Whatever the means of enforcement, the general feature of both soft and hard mechanisms in Russia is their private and personified character, as contrasted with the formal and impersonal institutions that are normally associated with the state. My research focuses upon the realist mechanisms, that is, those that involve the presence or active use of coercion and which tend to exclude "pure" trust (Volkov 2002). Therefore, the contribution of this chapter to the present volume consists in delineating the realm of trust-based behavior from without—by studying its opposite.

Scholars tend to agree that throughout the 1990s, the role of the Russian state in governing the private economy was rather modest (see Roberts and Sherlock 1999). The central authority had neither the political will nor the instruments for exerting a decisive influence on economic subjects, especially at the regional level. Local ad hoc orders and security arrangements that were created and maintained through interaction among various agencies (some of which were loosely affiliated with the state) made up the initial institutional environment of the emerging markets. Private organizations of various kinds, such as organized criminal groups, private security agencies, informal groups of state police, and security officers were key to resolving property disputes, enforcing contracts, and processing security-related business information. They are frequently referred to as private enforcers. Since 1998 and especially after Vladimir Putin's election to the presidency in 2000, the government declared the reassertion of state capacity as its major concern, simultaneously speeding up liberal economic reforms. How did property transfers and patterns of resolving economic disputes change as the state allegedly became stronger?

Underneath the rhetoric of strengthening the state in 1998–2000, another process was gaining strength in the sphere of property relations commonly referred to as "enterprise takeovers" (*zakhvaty predpriyatii*). This meant a forced change of ownership and management practiced by influential business groups in relation to large- or medium-sized enterprises. The hallmark of enterprise takeovers was the use of state courts, of special police forces, and of regional administrations. The practice reached a nationwide scale by 2001, involving thousands of cases each year. Enterprise takeovers were most frequently framed as either bankruptcy proceedings, involving the use of the 1998 edition of the "Law on Bankruptcy," or as legal actions in defense of the rights of minority shareholders, with reference to the "Law on Joint Stock Companies." The cases in question are frequently referred to as "contract bankruptcies" (*zakaznye bankrotstva*), implying a hidden economic agenda (other than improving economic performance of the enterprise) and the instrumental use of law. According to official estimates, up to 30 percent of bankruptcy cases processed by arbitration courts in the period 2000–01 were contract bankruptcies initiated in order to facilitate hostile enterprise takeovers.[1] In reality, this looked like an iceberg with a small visible and a huge invisible part, the visible tip being 20–30 notorious cases involving the largest industrial enterprises of the post-Soviet economy, featuring violent clashes and receiving extensive coverage by the media, and hundreds of other successful, less violent, and therefore less visible, cases of hostile takeovers.

The scale of open and covert enterprise takeovers of the post-Yeltsin era is comparable to the massive privatization of 1993–94 and represents the most significant redistribution of economic assets since then. If the first wave of privatization gave unconditional advantages to "insiders," that is, former Soviet directors and workers, the new round of struggle for economic assets featured the aggressive advance of "outsiders" who used all available means to change the management and achieve control over major industrial enterprises. This paper is largely about the ends and means of the post-Yeltsin redivision of economic assets. Below I pull together some fragmented data on the practice of enterprise takeovers and reflect on its causes and consequences.[2]

On a more general level, I argue that the actions of economic subjects depend upon the means available to them and that rules (such as the legal framework) also become means rather than constraints if those who are supposed to follow them have a strong influence on their interpretation and enforcement. Thus, if economic subjects can get privileged access to the judicial and coercive capacity of the state and can alter their relative levels of security vis-à-vis their competitors, they will be inclined to use enterprise takeovers as their main source of expansion. Successful defense against takeovers was, to a large extent, also conditional upon access to state capacity. Outside Moscow, state capacity was and largely continues to be in the hands of local and regional governors and administrations that, in their turn, depend upon large business groups and vote-providing enterprises for their reelection. Apart from direct material interests in lending state administrative resources to private groups, local and regional authorities had a political interest in brokering enterprise takeovers, especially in the context of the series of regional elections in 2001–02. This constellation of interests at the regional level determined the way bankruptcy and corporate governance laws were interpreted by powerful actors. This practical interpretation had little to do with the intended purposes of the laws and their respective application procedures. Despite some efforts, until the end of 2002 the central authority was reluctant or incapable of preventing the formation of strong regional politico-economic groups and changing the pattern of hostile redistribution of economic assets—covered up by the veil of legality and relying upon the selective use of state coercive capacity. It was only at the end of 2002, after heated debates and covert struggles, that a new version of bankruptcy law was passed and signed by the president, this time backed up by firmer and more consistent state efforts at governing bankruptcies, mergers, and acquisitions. There were no reports of any major hostile takeovers in the first months of 2003, although hundreds of previous corporate conflicts still await resolution.

The Logic of Enterprise Takeover

Enterprise takeover is a forced change of management of an enterprise achieved by administrative and coercive means. It may or may not lead to the transfer of the controlling interest to the "aggressor," that is, to a change of ownership. This practice may also be viewed as an extreme form of hostile acquisition, one in which administrative and coercive resources are employed to neutralize the resistance of the previous owners or managers and to back up the transfer of the controlling interest. The hallmark of enterprise takeovers is the instrumental use of court decisions, special police forces, and extensive media campaigns to help new management occupy and control the target enterprise. In many cases, in order to suppress resistance, the attacking side initiates criminal prosecution against managers and owners of the target enterprise. Even though court decisions are usually repealed and the criminal charges dropped, once the armed takeover brought new management into the head office, it is very hard and costly to return the enterprise to its previous owners. Another feature of the corporate conflicts explored in this chapter is that they involve a competition for interpreting and enforcing the rules and depend upon privileged access to relevant state organizations. As reported in the Russian press, the new know-how was applied for the very first time on February 16, 1996 by the Metallurgical Investment Company (MIKOM)—that subsequently fell victim of another hostile takeover to achieve control over the Kuznetsk Metallurgical Plant (KMK) in Kemerovo *oblast'* by changing the management with the help of a contingent of armed bailiffs of the regional arbitration court.[3]

The logic of an enterprise takeover is determined by the interrelation of its objective, the size and profile of the target enterprise, and the chosen method ("the scheme"). Since 1998, hostile takeovers have had the following major targets:

- Profitable export-oriented enterprises (e.g. aluminum, steel, or cellulose production; electric machine-building);
- Enterprises of the so-called fuel and energy complex (oil and gas mining facilities, oil-processing plants, electric power plants, etc.);
- Ore-processing plants (vanadium, strontium, etc.) and similar enterprises that supplied vital ingredients to metallurgical enterprises and were therefore vital for creating vertically integrated business groups;
- Enterprises in consumer industries that have a stable market for their products (alcohol, food, cosmetics, and the like);
- Any enterprise possessing valuable assets that could profitably be sold.

The choice of the target enterprise is determined by the objectives of the prospective takeover. However, without a change of management the objectives of the takeover cannot be reached, and the takeover cannot be considered successful. In order to give the change of management a semblance of legality, the aggressor can either use the Law on Bankruptcy and, accordingly, initiate bankruptcy procedure, or frame its assault as a defense of minority shareholders' rights and refer to the Law on Joint Stock Companies. Whatever the strategy, the prearranged and, therefore, quick court decision and the availability of a powerful enforcement agency are vital. The objectives, for which the establishment of managerial control is necessary, can range from a long-term business interest, such as the creation of a vertically integrated holding company or the concentration of assets of a particular industry (the creation of industrial holding), to short-term profiteering, such as speculation, debt recovery, and so on, or securing employees' votes for reelecting the regional governor. The objectives, therefore, largely determine whether the aggressor seeks temporary managerial control or long-term ownership. To obtain the controlling interest (ownership) the aggressor can further use an array of methods, such as amending the register of shareholders, issuance of additional shares, conversion of debts into shares, and so on. Each takeover also relies on a particular combination of all or some of the following actors or agencies: private security agencies, external (crisis) managers, arbitration or general jurisdiction courts, the regional governor or head of local administration, the regional representative of the Federal Agency for Financial Normalization and Bankruptcies, law enforcement (the procuracy, the Ministry of Interior [MVD], or the Ministry of Justice) and their paramilitary units, and media outlets. The logic of enterprise takeover is presented in figure 7.1.

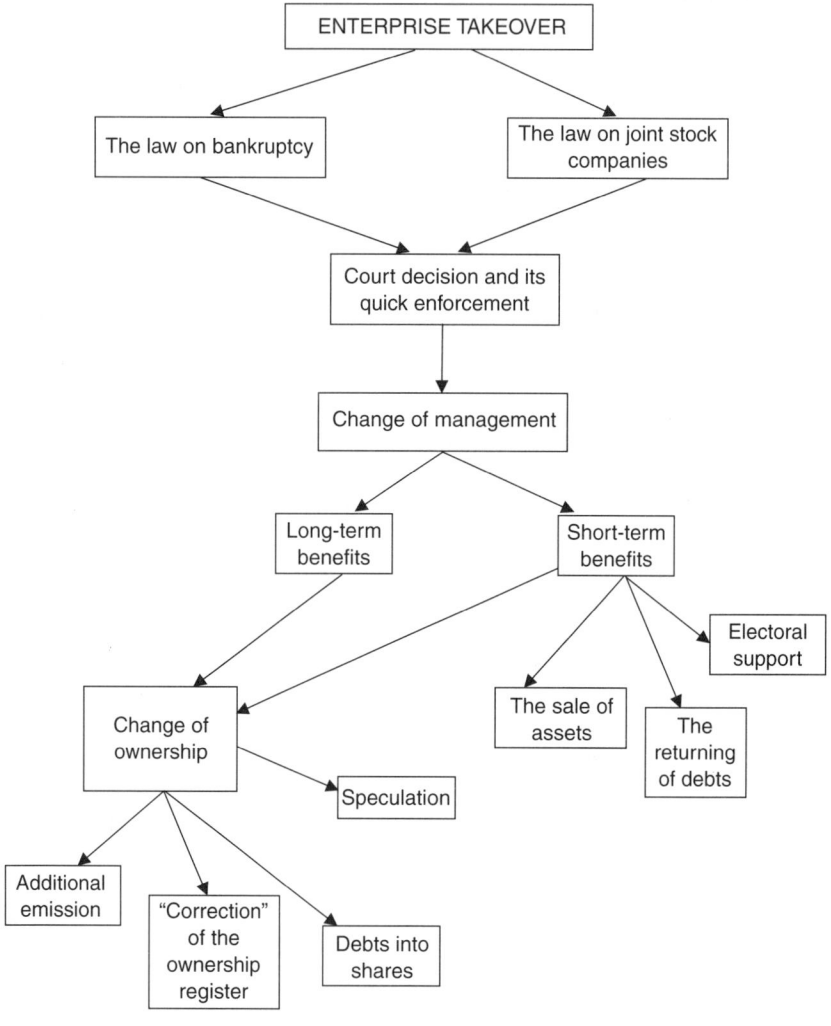

Figure 7.1 The logic of enterprise takeovers

Bankruptcy (Scheme 1)

In theory, the institution of bankruptcy serves to transfer firms from less efficient managers to more efficient and thus to optimize resource allocation (Manne 1965). Liberal reformers in Russia placed high hopes in the invisible hand of the market that would force inefficient Soviet enterprises to restructure or put them out of business through bankruptcy. During the five years between 1993 and 1997 only about 6,000 bankruptcy appeals were submitted to arbitration courts and many fewer were processed. The institution of bankruptcy failed to fulfill its intended function despite the acute problem of insolvency of many industrial enterprises. The first bankruptcy law of 1992 favored debtors and made the bankruptcy procedure rather complex. Furthermore, insider privatizations and the alliance of enterprise directors with regional authorities created a powerful survival mechanism. Barter, subsidies, and nonpayment of taxes allowed industrial enterprises to stay afloat with the complicity of regional authorities who had to ensure social stability and whose political support depended upon large enterprises and their social infrastructure.

After the adoption of the new Law on Bankruptcy in 1998 the situation changed dramatically. The number of court appeals exceeded 12,000 by June 1999. During the first ten months after the adoption of the law, courts initiated 4,573 bankruptcy cases (twice the number of cases in the previous five years), of which 2,006 ended in liquidation procedures.[4] Table 7.1 shows the growth in the number of bankruptcies between 1995 and 2001 (2002 statistics are not yet available).

The data on bankruptcies show the exponential growth of bankruptcy proceedings in the second half of the 1990s (a twofold increase almost every year) and an even more dramatic increase in 2001. What processes and activities are behind these numbers? What is the proportion of contract bankruptcies, which in practice serve as instruments of hostile enterprise takeovers?

First, we should note that the growth of bankruptcy proceedings refers primarily to liquidation without supervision, that is, the liquidation of physically nonexistent, "dummy" firms. These are juridical subjects that have not registered any financial operations (including the payment of taxes) and showed no signs of any entrepreneurial activity during a 12-month period. According to Vassily Vetriansky, deputy chairman of the Higher Arbitration Court of the Russian Federation, state records contain about 2.5 million juridical subjects, of which up to 35 percent are inactive.[5] The increase in bankruptcy cases thus reflects the increasing activity of the state in cleaning its registers of dummy companies and organizations. Therefore, the number of bankruptcy proceedings involving existing and active economic subjects (those in relation to whom either external management or liquidation following supervision was ordered) have grown from about 5,000 in 1998 to about 9,800 in 2001 (see table 7.1).

Table 7.1 Bankruptcy statistics: Russian arbitration courts, 1995–2001

	1995	1996	1997	1998	1999	2000	2001
Claims submitted				12,781	15,583	24,874	55,934
Proceedings initiated	1,108	2,618	4,320	8,337	10,933	19,041	47,762
External management	135	413	850	1,041	1,183	1,089	1,229
Liquidations ordered*	469	500	1,200	2,235	4,094	5,683	7,084
Liquidation of nonexistent firms**				3,444	4,993	11,082	39,214

Notes: * Liquidations ordered after supervision or external management, i.e., of existing and active firms; ** Liquidation without supervision, i.e., of inactive "dummy" firms.
Source: The official site of the Higher Arbitration Court of the Russian Federation, www.arbitr.ru.

Second, a significant proportion of bankruptcy cases were initiated by the state taxation authorities against tax debtors, which reflects the state's effort to improve tax collection. In 1998 their share was under 50 percent of all bankruptcy cases; in 2001 it rose to 67.5 percent. (The overall share of all state organizations among those whose claims resulted in bankruptcy proceedings grew from 53 percent in 1998 to 79 percent in 2001.) In the same year, the share of bankruptcy cases initiated by private organizations and persons was 21 percent, of which only about 10 percent, that is, about 4,700 cases were initiated by private creditors.[6] Thus, if we assume that state organizations did not initiate contract bankruptcies (although they helped at various stages), the potential targets of hostile enterprise takeovers should be sought within this, still quite substantial, number.

Third, consider the widely publicized claim by Tatiana Trefilova, Chairman of the Federal Agency for Financial Restructuring and Bankruptcies (FSFO) made in August 2001 that about 30 percent of bankruptcy cases were related to hostile enterprise takeovers and to the illegitimate redistribution of property.[7] If the claim is correct, this gives us roughly 1,400 dubious bankruptcies for 2001 (30 percent of 4,700). This figure is comparable to the annual number of companies subjected to external management (1,100–1,200), that is, to those that underwent a change of management (temporary or otherwise). The latter figure displays relative stability over the last three years. Of these 1,400 cases, a fair proportion, probably over a half, were connected with hostile takeovers and attempts to avoid repayment of debts to outside investors or taxes to the state while simultaneously preserving ownership and control (the bankruptcy law contained this opportunity as well), because such objectives normally presuppose a change of management and do not involve liquidation. Other cases where external management ended in liquidation may contain takeovers undertaken in order to profit from the selling of assets. In any case, given that the targets of hostile takeovers were mainly medium and large enterprises significant for Russia's economy, the 1,400-range figure for hostile takeovers points to an intense and consequential redistribution of assets.

So what opportunities did the bankruptcy legislation provide for hostile takeovers? Why did the law work the way it did? The 1998 law on bankruptcy provided a relatively easy way of changing the management of an enterprise, the procedure critical for the success of any hostile takeover. The law permitted arbitration courts to initiate bankruptcy procedures against enterprises whose outstanding debts exceeded the equivalent value of 500 monthly minimum wage or about 42,000 rubles in 1999 (about USD15,000) and were not repaid for a period of three months after the due date. One of the major shortcomings of the bankruptcy regulation of 1992 was that it established the debt threshold at the level of the value of enterprise assets, which was found too burdensome to calculate and thus was regarded as an obstacle to the bankruptcy process. It also favored debtors' interests over those of creditors. The new law removed this obstacle. In the aftermath of the barter economy that created large accumulated debts, especially for electricity, and of the August 1998 crisis, the extremely low-debt threshold set by the new law carried enormous potential for another round of struggle for economic assets (Woodruff 2000).

Another weak point and the source of massive abuse was the method of appointing external management. If the court accepts the appeal of a debtor and initiates a bankruptcy case (supervision), it has to appoint a temporary manager whose task is to conduct the meeting of creditors in order to select a candidate for external crisis manager. After the latter is approved by the court, he or she receives extraordinary executive powers over the assets of the bankrupt enterprise. In theory, this manager should act to improve the performance of the enterprise or reach agreements with creditors. The extraordinary powers of crisis managers, however, were not balanced either by strict procedures of selection and appointment of managers or by state control over their activity. So in practice, the law made it relatively easy to initiate bankruptcy even by a minor creditor, to change the management at this creditor's discretion, and then to manipulate the assets and financial flows of the enterprise according to the plan designed by the "aggressor"—given the availability of quick and favorable court decisions and means of enforcing them.

How did takeovers framed as bankruptcies work in practice? First, as soon as a business group singles out an enterprise that it intends to take over, it gives an assignment to its security service (usually headed by a former top officer of the Federal Security Service [FSB] or the MVD) to acquire information on debts, register of shareholders, sales, distribution and procurement partners, and other strategic or compromising data. The extreme case would be deliberate impeding of repayment. Second, the group planning the takeover either forges an alliance with a company to which this given enterprise is indebted or covertly buys off its debts through front companies. The third step is the bankruptcy procedure exercised through the decision of a court that has been prepared (usually through substantial bribes) to quickly issue the required decision. The key point in the court decision is the appointing of an external manager who has already been selected by the aggressor.[8] Having received a formal written decision from the court, the aggressor hastens to take the fourth step—to enforce the decision. The quicker this is done, the greater the chance of success, for at this stage the real intention of the bankruptcy case becomes apparent to the management of the enterprise. This is where the use of state coercive resources becomes vital. In most cases, a special police contingent arrives at the gate of the enterprise just two or three days after the court decision had been issued. Usually, the local Special Police Unit (OMON) or a special force of a local branch of the Ministry of Justice, Typhoon, has been contracted informally beforehand and waits for the formal paper from the court to legitimate the assault. By way of a surprise attack, the armed contingent in camouflage and ski masks arrives at the gate to propel the new management into the head office of the target enterprise and to chuck out the old management. By the same move the enterprise security service is swiftly changed to ensure the old management never returns. In the meantime, the new management takes control of and redirects the sales and financial flows of the enterprise to and through its own trading companies or banks, which becomes the first, soft lever to force the previous stockholders to sell their shares on the conditions set by the aggressor (if the latter wants to achieve legal ownership). In some cases, if the aggressor gets access to the register of shareholders it bluntly amends it, crossing out the old owners and writing in the new ones. In case the previous owners and managers resist, the aggressor has a hard lever to neutralize resistance: criminal prosecution. It mobilizes the local or regional Procuracy or MVD directorate in charge of economic crimes to investigate cases of fraud, tax evasion, or misappropriation of assets in order to initiate a criminal case against the uncooperative owners. The latter face limited mobility, interrogations, arrests, and, possibly, imprisonment. Even though the case has low chances of reaching the court, the investigation could continue for over a year, during which time the Procuracy can keep the defendant in detention or under home arrest. In most cases, the hard levers work, and previous owners agree to part with their shares.[9]

Thus, to proceed with an enterprise takeover the business group has to assemble and coordinate a network of actors that are capable of exercising power or providing protection to enable the property transfer. Most actors in such a network formally belong to the state and are mobilized by the private business group through a combination of formal and informal methods to advance its economic interests. In the contemporary business lexicon this mobilized network is referred to as the "administrative resource" (*administrativnyi resurs*). Its use allows the corporate raider to reach at least three main objectives: to interpret the legislation so as to trigger the takeover and produce the semblance of legality; to ensure one's security while exercising the takeover; and to create insecurity and exercise coercion in relation to the opponent. In the scheme outlined earlier, a successful takeover requires the coordinated effort of the following actors:

1. An intelligence agency or a consulting company gathering and processing information and devising the scenario of the takeover;
2. An allied enterprise or a financial institution to help take control of the debt with the view of initiating the bankruptcy procedure;
3. A court (even a local provincial court would suffice) to initiate the bankruptcy case and order external management;
4. A paramilitary contingent to overpower the security service of the target enterprise and enforce the decision of the court;
5. A state anticriminal agency to put additional pressure or to neutralize resistance of the previous owners and managers by launching criminal prosecutions against them;
6. Cooperative or noninterfering local or regional executive powers.

The mobilization and coordination of such a network is conditional upon the availability of connections or informal representatives in state executive and judicial structures no less than of the regional level and of financial resources to purchase the required services.

According to press reports, the most prominent cases of the application of this scheme took place in the metallurgy, oil, and gas industries as well as in the cellulose and paper industry, all of which involved the largest enterprises of the Soviet and post-Soviet economy. Among them were the acquisition of control over the Novokuznetsk Aluminum Plant (NKAZ) in Kemerovo region by the Siberian Aluminum (Sibal) belonging to the so-called aluminum group of Oleg Deripaska and Mikhail Tchernoi and supported by the head of the copper group, Makhmud Iskanderov;[10] and several takeovers of ore-, gas-, and oil-processing plants by the Alpha-Eko group led by Mikhail Friedman, including the notorious case of the bankruptcy takeover of the oil company Tchernogorneft' in 1999 and the gas-extraction enterprise Rospan, to mention just a few cases.[11] Bankruptcy procedures as part of enterprise takeovers were also used during the violent dispute over the Kachkanar vanadium ore-processing plant in the Urals,[12] over the mineral fertilizers plant Fosforit, and in the struggle for the huge cellulose plant in Bratsk between Sibal and the Ilim Pulp Enterprize (IPE) (see later).

The assault on NKAZ in summer 2000 is a model case of the application of the bankruptcy scheme backed up by coercion, whose many features and techniques appear to figure in many other corporate conflicts in Russia's economy.[13] According to press reports, the energy company Kuzbassenergo (subordinated to the state-owned United Energy System headed by Anatoly Chubais) initiated the bankruptcy procedure against NKAZ, which allowed Sibal to change the management of the enterprise, appointing its representatives. Then the managerial control was used to create levers to influence the owners. The new management swiftly linked the enterprise to their own trading companies and redirected its financial flows, thus acquiring de facto control of its supplies, sales and finance—in order to coerce the brothers Mikhail and Yurii Zhivilo, whose company MIKOM owned the controlling interest of NKAZ, to sell it to Sibal. The Procuracy of Kemerovo *oblast'* initiated a criminal investigation against Mikhail Zhivilo accusing him of planning the assassination of Governor Aman Tuleev. The investigation was conducted by the West-Siberian Antiorganized Crime Directorate (RUBOP). To avoid arrest Zhivilo had to leave the country, while all the assets of MIKOM (NKAZ and a number of coal mines) were transferred to the companies of Deripaska and Makhmudov through additional issuance of shares and other similar techniques.[14] In this case, press reports alleged that the regional governor was directly involved in assisting the takeover supplying local administrative resources and acting as a victim of the alleged assassination as part of the fabrication of the case.[15]

Conflicts Between Shareholders (Scheme 2)

The use of the Law on Joint Stock Companies as the legal framework for mobilizing state agencies is the debut scenario of the second basic option of enterprise takeover. This law is, of course, not the only weapon in corporate conflicts (recent history includes even the use of alimony claims as the legal pretext to put a restriction on shares of a metallurgical plant) but is surely the second most widespread after the use of the bankruptcy law. The tactical objective of this scheme is to put a restriction on the shares belonging to the majority shareholder and thus either to deprive the latter of the right to vote at the shareholders' meeting or to engineer the sale of the shares to the aggressor's front companies. Both moves are designed to change the management of the target company. In the first case, since the shares of the majority or any significant shareholder are restricted by the decision of a state court, this shareholder is temporarily removed from the game, and a minority shareholder can have a majority vote at the general meeting—called for the purpose of changing the management. In the second case, the restricted shares can be purchased by the aggressor as a result of a vote at the general meeting—again, to match ownership with managerial control. In this case, the first task is the acquisition of information concerning corporate policy, meetings of shareholders, payments of dividends, investment policies, and so on, of the target enterprise. In some cases, the key trick is to find or "create" a minority shareholder (one share might be enough) and stimulate him or her to initiate a lawsuit at the court of that person's residence. The appeal by a minority shareholder results in a provincial court annulling decisions taken at previous shareholder' meetings and thereby either allows the raiders to hold a new meeting and appoint new management or to manipulate the stocks of the target enterprise. Once such a decision is produced (the judge would normally resign after delivering the desired verdict), the attacking side would hire bailiffs and special police force to occupy the enterprise headquarters and install the new managerial team. The initial court decision may be disputed and appealed, and the dispute could last for an indefinitely long time, but this will have no effect so long as the new management remains in the head office.

Appeals by minority shareholders were a relatively rare practice before 2001. Since then, they were made popular through attempts to change the ownership of the four major enterprises in the cellulose (pulp and paper) industry: the Ust'-Ilim Wood Processing Complex in August 2001; the Bratsk Wood Processing Complex in December 2001 (both in Irkutsk *oblast'*, Siberia); the Archangelsk Cellulose Plant; and the Kotlass Cellulose Plant (both in Arkhangelsk *oblast'*, Northwestern region) since May 2002 until today. This was probably the largest corporate war thus far, its stake being four large enterprises (with over 10,000 employees in each) together producing 60 percent of the cellulose in Russia, over half for export. The aggressor is Sibal, since 2002 renamed Basic Element (I will use both names depending upon the timing of particular events). The defending side is the cellulose business group IPE that has been consolidating assets in the cellulose industry since 1994. The aluminum group is known to have close connections to the current presidential administration, kinship ties with the family of ex-president Yeltsin, and a long record of using state coercive organizations (and criminal groups in the mid-1990s) to establish control over key enterprises in a number of industries.[16] IPE is a business group with headquarters in St. Petersburg; it did not invest in political protection and had been keeping a low profile in previous oligarchic wars. I will now consider the Bratsk and Kotlass case.[17]

By the end of 2001, the electricity debt of the company Bratsk Complex Holding (BCH) (the subsidiary of IPE and owner of the cellulose giant) to the local energy company Irkutskenergo was 750 million rubles (about USD25 million). In the same year Sibal acquired 30 percent of the shares of Irkutskenergo and appointed its management. Fearing a takeover, BCH came up with a payment scheme and indicated its readiness to repay the debt to avoid bankruptcy. The energy company impeded the repayment of the debt because it anticipated using it as an instrument of pressure. Earlier, as a back-up option, BCH set up a new debt-free company, the Cellulose-Cardboard Plant (CCP) to which it transferred the assets of the wood-processing complex. This is a widespread technique on the fringe of legality designed to avoid repayment of debts. Sibal was quick to react. On December 21, 2001, a group consisting of court bailiffs, armed guards, and managers arrived in Bratsk and presented the decision of the local court of Nizhnii Novgorod of December 18 that annulled the decisions of the previous shareholders' meeting and ordered the dismissal of Sergei Khvostikov, the director of BCH–CCP. Curiously, the court decision was taken as a result of an appeal by a minority shareholder, one Liana Oganesian. (It turned out later that she did not owe any shares of BCH and that the decision, therefore, was entirely ungrounded.) The same day as the new management was introduced at the Bratsk enterprise it cancelled the repayment agreement with Irkutskenergo thus allowing the latter to initiate the bankruptcy procedure. The course of events took a familiar direction: The cellulose plant was overtaken by Sibal managers and set on the bankruptcy course.

However, in about two weeks the lawyers of IPE managed to contest and reverse the Nizhnii Novgorod court decision. By January 16, 2002, it reached a settlement with Sibal and restored control over BCH and the wood-processing plant. On January 21, Irkutskenergo withdrew the bankruptcy case. The managers of Sibal held control over the Bratsk enterprise for about 20 days. What did they achieve and what was the purpose of the takeover? The first obvious achievement was the return of the debt to Irkutskenergo: being on the verge of losing one of its major assets, if only temporarily, IPE repaid its outstanding debt in just a week. From the standpoint of its practical consequences the takeover proved a successful method of debt recovery. The second achievement appears to have been to strip the enterprise of its cash. According to the claims of IPE, the overall damage caused by the takeover was between 24 and 27 million rubles (just under USD1 million) as the alien management manipulated the accounts of the enterprise and sold the plant's product accumulated in stock, appropriating the revenue. It may therefore be assumed that that particular takeover had been either designed for short-term gains from the start or it became such as soon as the aggressor realized that it was likely to fail to achieve longer-term control over the enterprise.

In the case of the Kotlass Cellulose Plant, another key asset of IPE, the takeover had a similar debut scenario. A minority shareholder, one Sergei Mel'kin, filed an appeal in the district court of Kemerovo (a town in western Siberia) to the effect that IPE had failed to observe the privatization agreements of 1994. The complaint stated that the management of IPE did not fulfill the investment plan prescribed by the privatization agreement. The court ruled in favor of the shareholder and ordered compensation from IPE equivalent to 60 percent of the shares of the Kotlass Cellulose Plant. At that moment, the disputed shares were deposited in the Petersburg Central Registration Company affiliated with the Industrial Construction Bank and in the Depository Clearing Company in Moscow.

On May 25, just ten days after the decision of the Kemerovo court, the bailiff service put a hold on the shares. In five days the Petersburg Central Registration Company wrote off 36 percent of the shares of the Kotlass Cellulose Plant and put them up for sale. Then immediately the Baltic Financial Agency bought them for an unknown client. Soon after that, another 25 percent of shares went on sale and were swiftly purchased (the details of this fraud-like operation are beyond the scope of this discussion). In anticipation of attempts to use the shares to change the management, IPE successfully appealed the sale in a Petersburg court. The court ruled that the disputed shares could not be used for voting until the end of the litigation. Nonetheless, undisclosed owners of the newly acquired 60 percent of the shares of the Kotlass Cellulose Plant held a meeting on the premises of a battery farm in Leningrad *oblast'*. The meeting elected a new board of directors that, as it turned out, included, among others, two representatives of Continental Management, a company controlled by Basic Element, formerly Sibal.

By the time the alternative managerial team made a public appearance and claimed to represent the new legitimate owners, it became clear that an armed takeover was imminent. In the case of two conflicting court decisions, it is the enforcement capacity that decides the fate of disputed assets. On June 8, an "enforcement" team of over 90 people arrived in the town of Kotlass. The chief of the security service of Continental Management (the subsidiary of Sibal/Basic Element), the former lieutenant general and chief of Russia's anticriminal police, Viacheslav Trubnikov, demanded that the local Interior Ministry directorate assist the enforcement team in introducing the new management to the plant. By that time, the company town where the disputed plant is located had already been turned into a fortified camp, all roads and railroads leading to the plant being blocked, barricades erected by the factory walls, enterprise security strengthened by the workers' militia on 24-hour alert. The armed stalemate in the best mediaeval tradition continued for two more weeks, the sides exchanging public statements and media accusations. But in the face of a well-organized armed defense of the enterprise, the aggressor did not risk undertaking the seizure. In the meantime, the "workers' collective" of the plant wrote a letter to Putin asking him to interfere. The president ordered the General Procuracy to investigate the case; the latter transferred the order to its regional branch that, after being "neutral" for over two months, interfered to prevent the violent clash. The interference of higher authorities returned the conflict to the legal realm, leaving the old management in the head office of the cellulose plant and its controlling packet of shares in the hands of Basic Element. In the beginning of 2003, the sides still continued the litigation: IPE retained the management of the Kotlass Cellulose Plant; disputed shares stayed with the Continental Management, that is, with Basic Element.

The attempt to change the management of the Taganrog Metallurgical Plant (Tagmet) in Rostov *oblast'* in April 2002 represents another typical corporate conflict: between the management that owns a majority or the controlling shares and an outside investor seeking full ownership and control over the enterprise. In the case of Tagmet, the business group Alfa-Eco attempted to increase its 42 percent share of Tagmet by trying to arrange for the Federal Commission for Securities to annul the previous share issue in order to reduce the share of Sergei Bidash, director of Tagmet from 54 percent to slightly over 40 percent. Bidash disputed the decision in court and refused to hand over control to Alfa-Eco. Then the latter attempted to take the enterprise by force, using OMON force. The enterprise security service and the workers' militia managed to defend the plant in a violent clash. To prevent further violence, the representative of the president in the Southern *okrug*[18] had to interfere and compel the sides to return to court. After several months of litigation and negotiations, Bidash sold his share to the MDM business group, Alfa's major competitor in the metallurgical industry, whose administrative resources match those of Alfa and make the plant less attractive to the latter.[19]

Ownership, Control, and Enforcement After 1998

The account of the legislation on bankruptcies and corporate governance alone is insufficient for understanding the spread of enterprise takeovers and the extreme forms that they often took. One also has to look at the changing property relations as well as at the agencies and mechanisms of their enforcement.

Before 1998, Russia's private economy went through three different phases of privatization and redistribution of economic assets. First, the covert privatization of 1988–91 when state enterprise directors and office holders began capturing private profits by selling the products of state enterprises or siphoning budget funds through affiliated cooperatives. Second, the massive, swift voucher privatization of 1992–94 that turned the majority of managers and employees of formerly state enterprises into legal owners of these enterprises. Third, the loans-for-shares auctions of 1995–96 that transferred a number of large state-owned enterprises to a limited number of business groups in exchange for subsidizing the state budget.

The outcome of the first two rounds of privatization was the domination of insiders (managers and workers) in the structure of ownership in Russia's economy. During the mass privatization of 1993–94, the majority of enterprises (73 percent) chose the so-called second option of privatization that provided for majority employee ownership. It transferred the controlling interest to managers and workers (insiders), leaving the rest either to the state or to potential outside investors. Another sizeable proportion of enterprises followed the first option, whereby insiders acquired no more than 40 percent of shares, leaving the rest in the hands of the state or for later auctioning (Blasi et al. 1997: 50–85). By 1996, about 60 percent of shares in the Russian industry belonged to insiders, about 30 percent to outsiders, and about 10 percent remained with the state. According to different estimates, 12 to 18 percent of insiders' shares belonged to top managers, mainly former Soviet directors, the rest being dispersed among workers (Radygin 1999: 54–76; Shleifer and Vasiliev 1996: 78–108). In conditions of dispersed shares, top managers had a significant priority in realizing their property rights, capturing private benefits from controlling sales and financial flows. For several years, insiders made up a closed and change-resistant group centered around the former Soviet directors most of whom did not want or could not afford a decisive restructuring (often for fear of social instability), shielding their enterprises from market pressure and outside contenders. The loans-for-shares auctions did not significantly affect the overall structure of property, but they increased its concentration in several key industries, strengthening a limited number of business groups and creating the notorious "oligarchs." Of these groups, some would be destroyed by the August 1998 crisis (such as the financial groups SBS-Agro and Incombank), some would fall in the conflict with the government in 2001 (the MOST group and the holding of Boris Berezovsky). The survivors, business groups whose core assets were industrial rather than financial (Gazprom, Interros-ONEKSIM, Yukos, LukOil), consequently grew stronger, as did the new financial–industrial business groups (Sibal, Alfa, MDM) (Pappe 2000a). It is these new groups as well as Vladimir Potanin's Interros of the old cohort that became leaders in the hostile takeovers of 1998–2002.

During the fourth phase of the redistribution of assets through hostile takeovers, several new trends became manifest in the structure of ownership: the redistribution of shares from workers to the top management, the growth of outsiders' share (including changes of managerial teams), and the growth of concentration of ownership. Although existing studies differ in their estimates of the degree to which each of the these three parameters have grown, they all convey a similar story: the arrival of new managers and owners seeking to reduce the ownership stakes of insiders (Kapeliushnikov 2001; Radygin 1999). This trend found its expression either in the gradual increase of outsiders' share at the expense of insiders' and in the increase of top managers' share of enterprise stock. The growth of managers' share was in fact accompanied by the arrival of new managers in place of former Soviet directors, that is, by the replacement of insiders. As was shown earlier, these changes occurred through multiple corporate conflicts and aggressive takeovers.[20]

Why did the redistribution of assets take such extreme forms? The existing legal-procedural explanation emphasizes that the rights of minority shareholders continue to be poorly guaranteed, that is, adequate dividends are rarely paid. Profits are earned in a multitude of ways other than dividends. In reality, therefore, in order to capture benefits from economic activity one has to have control and decision-making powers in the first place. There is little incentive to invest if one does not have adequate control. Hence, outside investors seek controlling shares and attempt a full takeover, otherwise they could themselves be dispossessed through manipulations of the financial flows of the enterprise by its management as well as through the siphoning of assets or bankruptcy (Radygin 2002).

A complementary explanation, I argue, lies in the realm of enforcement, that is, the means by which property relations are being realized. Throughout the 1990s the dominant market ethic was that of self-help. That is, economic subjects had to rely on their own security arrangements for protection and enforcement and expected others to behave accordingly; many simply had no choice but to agree to work with private enforcers on conditions determined by the latter. A great number of different organized groups formed by various violent subcultures (criminal fraternities, sports and marshal art clubs, Cossacks, MVD, KGB and other force-wielding organizations, veterans of local wars, and ethnic minorities) were involved in producing and marketing protection services (Volkov 2002). Some of them set up legal protection enterprises and private security services, some continued as informal and illegal organizations or networks. In general, levels of perceived economic and physical risk were high, and all economic subjects had to invest in security. Relations between economic subjects were mediated (enforced) by their protection agencies through a system of guarantees backed by force. Pure economic relations existed only in theory; in reality, they were closely intertwined with relations of force, as economic enterprises coordinated their activities with their protective agencies, while the latter established safe avenues for future economic transactions between their clients. Organized violence became the key resource throughout the 1990s, as it was widely used to create either competitive advantages (when levels of security among parties involved in exchange were unequal) or conditions for permanent fair exchange (where security levels were equalized). Consequently, any organized group that possessed coercive capacity could successfully engage in violent entrepreneurship, being the source of risk and providing protection at the same time. Understandably, this occurred in the realm of new entrepreneurs in trade and in a few thriving sectors of production rather than in stagnant former socialist enterprises. The peak of anarchic competition passed in 1995–96.

A gradual reconfiguration began sometime in 1998. Its moving springs were the competition between protection agencies and the capitalization of tribute. Initially, the competition was essentially an elimination contest that involved frequent use of force. Those protection agencies, chiefly criminal or private informal groups, that had not been able to grow stronger became weaker and were either exterminated or subsumed by the ones that proved more successful. Besides this, competition favored those protection agencies that adopted a balanced economic policy toward economic subjects, that is, redistributed property rights and provided more efficient security. Thus, legal protection companies and security services as well as informal groups and networks associated with the state gradually gained the upper hand in the competition and came to dominate the security market. Various criminal groups had to either change their policy and legal status or face extinction. Some groups adapted successfully by investing protection tribute into legal businesses and turning themselves into regional business groups. The development of stock markets and new forms of ownership further facilitated investments, that is, the transfer of profits from the illegal protection industry into conventional legal businesses. By the late 1990s, criminal groups increasingly turned to formal ownership, actively accumulating stocks and setting up holding companies. This, in turn, required an army of accountants, managers, and other specialists, as well as new forms of organization geared toward capital accumulation rather than coercion.

When the criminal sector in the security business dwindled and the so-called bandits disappeared from the scene, who occupied the niche? In

1999–2000, state employees actively moved in to substitute for the criminal elements in providing security and governing economic transactions. On the ground level, informal police and FSB protection as well as legal private protection enterprises and security services became the dominant option (Volkov 2002). Apart from that, local and regional interior ministry officials connected with regional governors took a more active stance in administering regional economies, exchanging protection for investments by powerful groups of obscure origins. By the time the so-called strengthening of the state emerged as the new slogan of the post-Yeltsin era, former or acting state security and police employees and administrative officials at various levels had already positioned themselves as key providers of security and legal protection. However, they acted as private or semiprivate groups only loosely affiliated with the state. Their state affiliation did not go further than loyalty to the local chief of the Interior Ministry Directorate or head of the regional administration. Particular segments of the state and some of its regional structures were quite strong in respective domains, yet the overall state capacity remained very low. When in summer 2000 Putin outlined the policy of consolidating the state, some groundwork for that had already been laid, but a decisive effort at uniting disaggregated segments of the state was required in order to create a homogenous rule-governed space for economic exchange. Local administrative orders, and security and justice systems were indispensable for the implementation of the new policy, but they were also its major obstacles because they had long acted as autonomous agencies. The spread of enterprise takeovers and the adventures of the bankruptcy law may be read in the context of the central authority's attempts to strengthen the so-called vertical power, that is, to reassert control over executive branches of state power in Russia's regions.

Conclusion

Although legal codes and their loopholes and omissions are important, a full account of enterprise takeovers compels one to look at extra-legal realities to explain the way laws work in post-Soviet Russia. No law contains the rules of its application. No law defines the legal facts that it is supposed to regulate. It would be an oversimplification to assume that the legal "rules of the game" determine and therefore contain exhaustive explanations of the practices to which they refer. A reference to some "informal rules" or "informal culture" responsible for the discordance between the written laws and their working in practice only obscures reality and explains little, for it leads to a multiplication ad infinitum of various tacit rules allegedly governing the application of formal rules.

To avoid both legal and cultural fetishism, one has to take a closer look at the particular extra-legal reality that, for each law in question, constitutes the practical context that determines its application and therefore its current meaning. The extra-legal reality consists of a variety of players having diverse interests, possessing certain resources, and acting in the context of previous institutional arrangements that already exist before a new law comes into being. Moreover, new laws in post-Soviet Russia have often been designed under the influence of the liberal ideology of the day (i.e. out of abstract principles), as was the case with such key laws as those regulating free elections or the activity of the mass media (Gel'man 2003). As soon as such laws get in contact with the extra-legal reality, they acquire a new meaning determined by the practical usage of these laws by a variety of actors operating in their respective realms.

Understandably, unless there is monopoly control over interpretation and enforcement of a particular law or a consensus of powerful actors over its current practical interpretation, such a situation would not allow sufficient predictability. So before a law and its application take final shape and become effective elements of the institutional environment, they go through multiple practical tests in which they are put to instrumental use by powerful actors in the given sociopolitical context. The final shape of a particular law crystallizes through multiple struggles and requires a consolidated effort of the central authority at supervising its application and enforcement. The case of enterprise takeovers in 1998–2002 provides an illustration of the way the law on bankruptcy played out in the context of extra-legal reality that determined the range of applications of this law. To explain the particular usage of the bankruptcy law we have to account for several extra-legal factors:

- The defects and tensions created by the earlier privatization policies (privileges for insiders and dispersed stock ownership);
- The particular structure of property rights whereby managers have significant privileges in capturing benefits through current financial decision-making;
- The rise of new powerful financial industrial groups seeking to convert financial and political influence into ownership of key industrial assets;
- The availability of cheap and efficient instruments for acquiring corporate control and ownership in the form of state judicial, regulation, and enforcement organs;
- Temporary inability of the central authority (e.g. the MVD, the FSFO, the Higher Arbitration Court) to control the activity of its regional branches.

Furthermore, each group of powerful actors "read" the bankruptcy law of 1998 in the way that best served its interests. The powerful corporate raiders sought to acquire and concentrate economic assets at a relatively low price; the regional state agencies sought to convert their coercive and administrative capacity into private revenue, pursuing further the strategy of violent entrepreneurship; the state taxation organs found in this law a powerful lever to put pressure on tax debtors and thus to improve tax collection; in facilitating or blocking enterprise takeovers the regional governors found yet another opportunity for rent seeking as well as for securing votes of employees in regional elections; and media outlets earned their share of profits making their capacity to shape public opinion available for corporate wars.

The absence of reliable data on the costs of enterprise takeovers[21] and on the performance of the enterprises after the change of management and ownership precludes an objective evaluation of the economic consequences of the fourth redistribution of assets in post-Soviet Russia. It may well be, as some researchers were led to conclude, that enterprise takeovers reflect the coming of more efficient owners and managers who by virtue of their financial power and political connections are capable of delivering decisive benefits to large enterprises necessary for their survival and expansion (Pappe 2000b: 110–19). In this case, the logical assumption would be that the period of hostile takeovers ended with a new equilibrium whereby economically justifiable ends were achieved by legally and morally dubious means. At the same time, however, the bankruptcy law went through a practical test that revealed its meaning in the given extra-legal context, which resulted in the adoption of a new law at the end of 2002. This time, the central authority had a decisive voice in shaping the law. To have better control over its application, the Kremlin used the institution of its representatives in the federal districts to oversee the activities of regional FSFOs and arbitration courts and to prevent the abuse of bankruptcy procedures. It is premature to judge the success or failure of the new law, but one can convincingly argue that success depends in a decisive way upon the degree of internal control and coherence of state institutions rather than upon their nominal administrative strength.

Notes

1. Interview with Tatiana Trefilova, chairman of the Federal Service on Financial Normalization and Bankruptcies. *Trud*, August 23, 2001.
2. The paper is descriptive; it presents generalizations from official data, reports of enterprise takeovers available in secondary sources, and several detailed case studies based on a combination of media reports, private interviews with experts, and unpublished reports of journalistic investigations.
3. *Vlast'*, September 18, 2001, p. 63.
4. *BDI*, 1999, November, No. 1, pp.15–19; *Den'gi*, August 16, 2000.
5. The speech of Vassily Vetriansky on March 14, 2002; at www.bankr.ru.
6. Ibid.
7. *Trud*, August 23, 2001.
8. In many cases, the debtor enterprise would not even be notified about the meeting of creditors that has to elect the external manager. A widespread trick is sending an empty envelope by recorded delivery mail service, which is subsequently used in court as evidence that the debtor has been notified by mail. For more details, see Semenov and Sizov 2002 as well as the internet project "Bankruptcy in Russia" and the analytical material provided by *Ekspert* at www.bankr.ru.
9. For reviews of various "contract" bankruptcy schemes, see *Ekspert*, 1999, No. 8, pp. 19–26; *Kompaniya*, 2002, No. 2, pp. 18–20; *Rossiiskaya gazeta*, December 27, 2002.
10. *Kompaniya*, August 21, 2000.
11. *Vremia MN*, September 16, 2000; *Vedomosti*, January 15, 2003.
12. See *Ekspert*, February 7, 2000; *Ekspert-Ural*, August 28, 2000 (available at www.expert.ru).
13. *Kompaniya*, August, 14, 2000.

14. *Kompaniya*, August, 21, 2000.
15. Having fled abroad, Zhivilo appealed to a federal district court in New York that accepted the case, setting the claim amount at USD2.7 billion. In April 2003, the court refused to process the case further, arguing that the case should be considered in Russia, *Films by Jove, Inc. v. Berov*, 250 F. Supp. 2d 156 (US Eastern District of NY, April 16, 2003).
16. Oleg Deripaska is reported to have married the daughter of the former chief of Yeltsin's administration, Valentin Yumashev who, in turn, married Yeltsin's daughter Tatiana Diachenko. Valerii Pechenkin, the head of the security service of Basic Element (a private protection company called Vympel) is the former deputy director of FSB.
17. The account of the corporate conflict is based on the following sources: *Sibal-Les-230702*; *IPE-Bratsk-31202*; *IPE-Kotlass-31202*; unpublished reports by The Agency of Journalistic Investigations, St. Petersburg, 2002 and the Analytical Reports on Corporate Conflicts by Rosbalt News Agency at www.conflict.rosbalt.ru.
18. *Okrug* is a federal district, seven of which were introduced in 2001 by President Putin in order to oversee the activities of the governors of Russia's 89 so-called Subjects of Federation. Each federal district is headed by the representative of the president, directly appointed by Putin.
19. *Kommersant*, April 8, 2002; *Kompaniya*, April 24, 2003 (www.ko.ru); *Kommersant-Den'gi*, April 24, 2002.
20. For an assessment of the efficiency of redistributing of assets through hostile takeovers, see Radygin and Arkhipov 2000.
21. Experts estimate the cost of an enterprise takeover at two to three times the annual profit of the target enterprise. See *Kommersant*, May 17, 2002.

References

Blasi, Joseph, Maya Kroumova, and Douglas Kruse. 1997. *Kremlin Capitalism: Privatizing the Russian Economy*. Ithaca NY: Cornell University Press.
Frye, Timothy. 2000. *Brokers and Bureaucrats: Building Market Institutions in Russia*. Ann Arbor MI: The University of Michigan Press.
Gel'man, Vladimir. 2003. Institutsional'noe stroitel'stvo i neformal'nye instituty v sovremennoi rossiiskoi politike (Institution-building and Informal Institutions in Contemporary Russian Politics). The European University at St. Petersburg. Manuscript.
Hendley, Kathryn, Peter Murrell, and Randi Ryterman. 2000. Law, Relationships and Private Enforcement: Transactional Strategies of Russian Enterprises. *Europe-Asia Studies* 52: 627–56.
Hertz, Noreena. 1996. *Russian Business Relationships in the Wake of Reform*. Oxford: Macmillan.
Kapeliushnikov, Rostislav. 2001. Sobstvennost' i kontrol' v rossiiskoi promyshlennosti (Ownership and Control in the Russian Industry). *Voprosy ekonomiki* 12: 102–23.
Manne, Henry. 1965. Mergers and the Market for Corporate Control. *Journal of Political Economy* 72: 110–20.
Pappe, Yakov. 2000a. *Oligarkhi* (Oligarchs). Moscow: GU-VshE.
———. 2000b. Treugol'nik sobstvennikov v regional'noi promyshlennosti (The Triangle of Owners in the Regional Industry). In V. Klimanova and N. Zubarevitch (eds.). *Politika i ekonomika v regional'nom izmerenii*, pp. 109–20. Moscow: IGPI.
Pejovich, Svetozar. 1997. The Transition Process in an Arbitrary State: The Case for the Mafia. *IB Review* 1: 18–23.
Radaev, Vadim. 1998. *Formirovanie novykh rossiiskikh rynkov: transaktsionnye izderzhki, formy kontrolia i delovaya etika* (The Formation of New Russian Markets: Transaction Costs, Forms of Control, and Business Ethics). Moscow: Tsentr politicheskikh tecknologii.
Radygin, Alexander. 1999. Pereraspredelenie prav sobstvennosti v post-privatizatsionnoi Rossii (The Redistribution of Property Rights in Postprivatization Russia). *Voprosy ekonomiki* 6: 54–76.
———. 2002. Sliyaniya i pogloshcheniya v korporativnom sektore (Mergers and Acquisitions in the Corporate Sector). *Voprosy Ekonomiki* No. 12: 85–109.
Radygin, Alexander and Sergei Arkhipov. 2000. Sobstvennost', korporativnye konflikty i effektivnost' (Ownership, Corporate Conflicts, and Efficiency). *Voprosy Ekonomiki* No. 11: 45–59.

CHAPTER EIGHT

Mafia Transplantation

FEDERICO VARESE*

Can a Mafia group establish a branch organization in a different territory? This question haunts several Central and Western European countries. Lieutenant colonel Zsolt Bodnár, of the antiorganized crime division of the Hungarian police, said in September 2000: "The Russian Mafia is already present in Hungary in a big way. They come here and start legitimate businesses and then just wait, because they know that Hungary will soon be a member of the EU and then their opportunities for expansion will be immense."[1]

Reportedly, the Russian Mafia is operating in Poland, Italy, and Spain (De Gennaro 1997; Goldman 1996; Sands 2002; *Los Angeles Times* October 23, 1998; *The Daily Telegraph* March 4, 1996). Russian authorities claim—possibly with a dose of pride—that the Russian Mafia is active in at least 26 foreign countries (*Itar-TASS* July 21, 1998, quoted in Galeotti 2000: 37 and BBC monitoring service July 22, 1998; see also *Moscow Times* March 25, 1997 and *AFP* August 16, 2002).

The aim of this chapter is to highlight conditions conducive to successful and long-term transplantation outside their territory of origin of established crime groups (Mafias) that specialize in the selling of private criminal protection (Gambetta 1993a: 1). The first section develops hypotheses on the extent to which Mafia groups can migrate. I consider the level of social capital and trust, the supply of Mafiosi, and the emergence of significant market opportunities that are left unprotected by the state. The second section offers a comparison of two attempts of a Russian criminal group, the Solntsevo, to transplant itself in Italy and Hungary. The outcome was dramatically different in each setting, with the Solntsevo becoming entrenched in Hungary while failing to take root in Italy. In both cases, the group engaged in money laundering and the penetration of the legal economy. In the Hungarian case, however, the Russian Mafia was also able to tap into a vast demand for criminal protection that had been created by the Hungarian government's failure promptly to establish an effective system of

Roberts, Cynthia and Thomas Sherlock. 1999. Bringing the Russian State Back: Explanations of the Derailed Transition to Market Democracy. *Comparative Politics* 31: 477–97.

Semenov, A.S. and Yu. S. Sizov (eds.). 2002. *Korporativnye konflikty. Prichiny ikh vozniknoveniya i sposoby preodoleniya* (Corporate Conflicts. Their Orgins and Ways of Overcoming Them). Moscow: URSS.

Shleifer, Andrei and Dmitry Vasiliev. 1996. Management Ownership and Russian Privatization. In R. Frydman, C.W. Gray, and A. Rapaczynski (eds.). *Corporate Governance in Central Europe and Russia*, 2: 78–108. Budapest: Central European University Press.

Tambovtsev, Vladimir. 1999. Ekonomicheskie instituty rossiiskogo kapitalizma (Economic Institutions in Russian Capitalism). In T. Zaslavskaya (ed.). *Kuda idet Rossiyav?Krizis institutsional'nykh system*, pp. 193–201. Moscow: Intertsetr.

Varese, Federico. 2001. *The Russian Mafia*. Oxford: Oxford University Press.

Volkov, Vadim. 2002. *Violent Entrepreneurs: The Use of Force in the Making of Russian Capitalism*. Ithaca NY: Cornell University Press.

Woodruff, David. 2000. *Money Unmade: Barter and the Fate of Russian Capitalism*. Ithaca NY: Cornell University Press.

dispute settlement among new property owners and to the dual price system in the oil sector that led to massive arbitrage opportunities. The chapter concludes that transplantation is likely to be successful when a market emerges and is left unprotected by the state.

Do Mafias Move?

Transplantation is not easy. According to Diego Gambetta, author of *The Sicilian Mafia*, "not only did the [Sicilian] Mafia grow mainly in Western Sicily, but, with the exception of Catania, it has remained there to this very day" (1993a: 249). For instance, over a century, Sicilian Mafia murder rates broken down per area have remained high in Western Sicily and low in the rest of the island. Gambetta maintains that only one significant new Mafia family emerged in the eastern part of the island in Catania in 1925, and it remains a rather weak group. Although the Sicilian Mafia has existed for over a century, only two new Mafia families have formed outside Sicily, one in Tunis and one in Naples, both in the 1930s.

Similarly, Yiu Kong Chu (2000) argues that "Hong Kong Triads are localized, and they are not international illegal entrepreneurs whose wealth and connections may enable them to emigrate to Western countries." Although Hong Kong Triads might be involved in international crime, writes Chu, they "are not likely to be the key organizers." Increasingly, Hong Kong Triad members have been found to be entering the Chinese market—an instance of what could be transplantation—yet, Chu concludes, these are not "organized movements to China." More likely, "individual Triad members take the initiative to enter the Chinese market" (130-1).[2]

Gambetta suggests that the collection of reliable information is a major factor that hinders expansion and transplantation. Enforcing illegal transactions requires information in addition to violence. The organization involved in the protection of the illegal transactions needs to have an idea of what is transacted and its quality, the reliability of what the actors involved claim to have and are able to deliver, and the identity of the people involved. Information costs increase with the number of people, the number of institutional arenas, and the distance and cultural diversity in which the Mafia group operates. The more complex a transaction into which the group is drawn, the harder it will be to gather reliable information on the *what* and the *who*. Put differently, the enforcement of illegal transaction is easier, the smaller the range and complexity of the transactions the group protects (Gambetta 1993a).

In a related work (Varese 2002), I discuss the endemic lack of trust within Mafia organizations and the strategies used by members to minimize hazards deriving from the difficulties of monitoring agents within the organization. The Mafia sells criminal protection to people who should pay for it. To use American Mafia jargon, "made" Mafia members protect "business associates" in return for a portion of their earnings. In turn, members are supposed to share their profits with other members of the Mafia family. Still, business associates would like to pay as little as possible for the service they receive and Mafia members share as little as possible with other Mafiosi, giving rise to a conflict of interest and the potential for cheating. Such a problem has been noticed by several observers. "Everybody's playing the same bullshit game," writes FBI agent Joseph Pistone (Donnie Brasco) who worked undercover for six years with the Bonanno crime family in New York, "trying to keep as much as they can, pass along as little as they can get away with, regardless of what the rules say." He continues: "They always fudge. They figure they're out doing the job, who wants to give up half of what they get to somebody that's not even there? So you never told anybody the whole story with money. . . . That was the standard. It goes way right up the line. That's why nobody totally trusts anybody" (Pistone and Woodley 1997: 79; see also U.S. Senate 1988).

Mafia organizations have tried to minimize the problem identified by Pistone. They have created a pyramid of supervising roles. Members in higher positions ("captains") monitor members in lower positions ("soldiers") and make them pay a portion of their earnings, the recourse to violence being the costly, albeit effective, way to ensure honesty. Soldiers in turn supervise "connected guys" (also known as business associates) and force them to share earnings. In several cases, to further reduce problems of asymmetric information, Mafiosi institute a fixed tax for those they protect.[3]

Any image of the Mafia as just another corporation is misguided, however. Captains and bosses do not just live off the money they receive from their subordinates; that would not be enough to make ends meet. They also make money on their own, by protecting their own business associates and receiving money from them. However, captains and bosses can also steal "good earners" from the soldiers that they themselves supervise. One case narrated by Pistone in his U.S. Senate testimony and later in his book *Donnie Brasco* (1997) is emblematic: when Sonny Black, a captain in the Bonanno family, realized that Donnie Brasco, a business associate of soldier Lefty Ruggiero, was a good earner, he interfered with Lefty and associated himself directly with Donnie. Given that the captain has a higher position in the organization than the soldier, the soldier is left with little he can do, except complain bitterly. This dynamic, I argue, severely reduces trust and information flow within the organization and is far more disruptive than the standard problem of asymmetric information, which is somewhat solved by the institution of supervising roles and fixed rents.

The above dynamic is indeed a *push* factor for Mafia expansion: soldiers are tempted to expand into far away territories precisely because this allows them to escape the supervision of their captains and bosses, as Ruggiero did by moving his operations to Florida (Pistone and Woodley 1997: 247–335). The more distant the transplantation, the harder it is for the original Mafia to exercise control over its members. Hence, one expects the new operation in the foreign territory to develop a rather high degree of autonomy from the original group.

Still, a move to a new territory is fraught with difficulties and uncertainties. Later, I highlight three factors that may foster or hinder successful transplantation.

Social Capital

Social capital is generated by high levels of interpersonal trust among individual actors that allow them to economize on monitoring costs and engage in collective action (Coleman 1990: 302, 304; see also the comprehensive review by Portes 1998). Social capital affects both law abiders and criminals. Because high levels of social capital ease coordination and communication among actors, collective action among law abiders should be easier if social capital is high; hence, we should expect visible opposition to organized crime. The lower the trust and social capital among law abiders, the less likely that "civil society" will organize to oppose the entrenchment of a Mafia group and turn to the police for protection.

Trust and social capital affect underworld exchanges as well. Illegal exchanges are particularly fragile because actors have already crossed the line into illegality. Other things being equal, one expects them to breach promises, to have predatory intentions, and to lie about the quality of their goods to a greater extent than actors in legal markets (they also are more likely to be a transient population). For the exchange to occur, parties must have good reasons to count on the absence of the inclinations just mentioned—a degree of reassurance is therefore necessary. Trust is one such form of reassurance that allows parties to carry out the exchange (Gambetta 1993b; Rose-Ackerman 2001). The lower the trust among lawbreakers, the higher their demand for protection services. A Mafia facilitates exchanges among criminals who distrust each other by offering enforcement of deals and promises. Put the other way around, high levels of trust among lawbreakers reduce the demand for Mafia protection and operate as a barrier against Mafia transplantation.

In sum, other things being equal, Mafias move more easily from a low-trust region to another, equally low or lower-trust region.

Supply of Mafiosi

The presence of Mafiosi in the new territory clearly plays a role in the ability of a Mafia to take roots. The origin of this peculiar type of human supply can be varied. Mafiosi may be outside their own areas due to several factors, such as generalized migration from areas of high Mafia density, attempts to escape Mafia wars,[4] and a perverse state policy that selects for forced migration individuals with specific Mafia skills.[5] Surely, an optimal supply of Mafiosi in the new territory increases the likelihood of Mafia transplantation. The significant question remains the following: Can a Mafia emerge simply because there is a supply of Mafiosi? Several authors postulate that the presence of individuals who force their "protection" on reluctant victims (often coupled with a weak state) is sufficient for a Mafia to emerge or transplant itself (Catanzaro 1992). We may label this view a "supply-side" interpretation of transplantation. An alternative hypothesis is that Mafias emerge due to other factors, such as a genuine demand for criminal services of dispute settlement in the absence of state-supplied forms of protection (see later).

The Emergence of Significant and Unprotected Markets

In the abstract, individuals exchange goods and services only after they are confident the partner will not default on the agreement. One source of such reassurance is state protection of exchanges and contracts: ideally, the state resolves disputes over ownership and failures to fulfill agreements. When states fail to effectively define property rights and protect exchanges, exchange can still take place, but other forms of reassurance come into play, one being protection supplied by criminal organizations specialized in protection, namely Mafias.[6]

As I have argued elsewhere, the emergence of the Russian Mafia is a consequence of an imperfect transition to a market economy.[7] The transition to the market in Russia allowed actors to own property and engage in market transactions. Several decrees passed in the early 1990s liberalized trade and mandated the privatization of small- and medium-size enterprises. Most large enterprises were in private hands by the mid-1990s. The increase in property owners and economic transactions was not matched by clear property rights legislation. Since 1986, the legal situation in Russia developed in a chaotic fashion. Regulations were a mixture of procedures from the previous regime and new regulations. A plethora of often overlapping and conflicting laws and decrees emanated from a variety of jurisdictions. "The same subjects are often covered by many different and mutually contradictory normative pronouncements, and it is difficult to ascertain their ultimate validity" (Frydman et al. 1993, quoted in Varese 1994: 242).

In addition to unclear property rights legislation in Russia, courts that were empowered to settle disputes among businesspeople failed to enforce decisions, as testified by several studies (e.g., Pistor 1996; Kahn 2002; Varese 2001: 37–54). A demand for protection—first and foremost protection of property rights and contracts—followed, but was not met by state institutions. The Russian solution to the lack of state protection was a combination of the internalization of protection and, more worryingly, the hiring of individuals who were trained in the use of violence and had found themselves unemployed at the time of the transition to the market. In time, these individuals created autonomous criminal groups that were called upon to settle disputes among business competitors and partners and to enforce collusive agreements among market operators (Varese 2001).

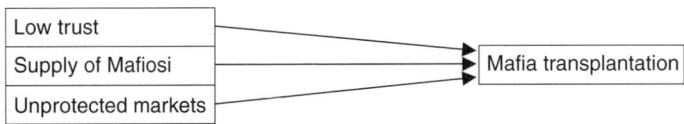

Figure 8.1 Factors that facilitate successful Mafia transplantation

In sum, a demand for protection that was not met by the state at the time of the transition to the market and the presence of people trained in the use of violence who became suddenly unemployed and were ready to sell their services on the market for private protection are the key factors behind the rise of the Russian Mafia. In effect, a vast section of the market economy was left unprotected by the state.

If, instead of Russians or Sicilians, it had been individuals from the outside who had taken advantage of the new opportunities, we might consider this event an instance of transplantation. Foreign Mafiosi perceive the existence of untapped opportunities to offer protection in a new area and migrate there to engage in Mafia activities. In this view, transplantation is then akin to the emergence of a new Mafia due to the existence of favorable local conditions, although the makeup of the group is foreign.[8]

Here, I have singled out three factors that facilitate the successful movement of a Mafia group to a new territory: low trust in the new locale, a supply of Mafiosi, and the presence of significant markets that are unprotected by the state (see figure 8.1).

Is there a factor (or a combination of two factors) that is more significant than another for Mafia transplantation, or must all three factors be present at the same time? In the next section I discuss two instances of the Russian Mafia's attempts at transplanting itself outside its original area, namely the efforts of the Solntsevo crime group to set up branches in Italy and in Hungary. The aim of the comparison is to evaluate empirically the significance of each factor.

The Russian Mafia in Eastern and Western Europe

The Solntsevo

The Solntsevo crime group takes its name from a Moscow suburb, in the west and southwestern part of the city, where it originated. Throughout the city, it runs a protection racket, which in Russian is called *krysha*.[9] For Iosif Roizis, a former member turned state witness, it consists of roughly 9,000 members (SCO 1997, vol. 1, p. 7). The group comprises no less than ten semiautonomous brigades (*brigady*), which operate under the umbrella name of Solntsevo. According to the Russian police, it is the largest crime group in Moscow and controls various banks and about a hundred small- and medium-sized enterprises (see *Kommersant Daily* August 25, 1995; and

SCO 1997, vol. 1, p. 8). In the 1990s, the leading figures were Sergey Mikhaylov (Mikhas') and Viktor Averin (Avera), both with Israeli passports. Sergey Timofeyev (Sil'vestr), the founder of the group, was murdered in September 1994. Other leading members were Yuriy Yesin (Samosval) and Sergey Kruglov (Boroda). Vyacheslav Ivan'kov (Yaponchik), now in prison in the United States, was regarded as the American link of the Solntsevo. Semën Mogilevich, a close associate of the group's leadership, selected Budapest as his residence and workplace until he was forced to leave in 2002. The organization is governed by a council of 12 individuals, who meet regularly in different parts of the world, often disguising the meetings as festive occasions.

According to various witnesses and police reports, the Solntsevo maintains a common fund (*obshchak*), which is reinvested into the legal economy through a number of banks that work for the organization. Members of the organization's council oversee the investment decisions (SCO 1997, vol. 1, p. 190).

The Solntsevo in Rome: The Supply

The attempt at transplantation from Moscow to Rome began in 1993, and by 1997, it was clear it had failed. In November 1993, at a meeting of the 12 leaders held in Miami, the governing council of the Solntsevo decided to open a branch in Italy. Evidence of this meeting comes both from intercepted phone conversations and the testimony of Yossif Roizis (SCO 1997, vol. 1, p. 77; see also CPA 1997: 19–20). Ivankov, Yesin, Averin, Mikhailov, Timofeyev, and Kruglov attended the Miami meeting.[10] Yuriy Yesin, a *vory-v-zakone* (thief-with-a-code-of-honor) and a high-ranking member of the Solntsevo crime group,[11] was entrusted to open the Italian branch.

In addition to the verdict of the council of 12, other factors affected the decision to move to Rome. Although Italy did not have a significant Russian population, it did have the largest Communist Party in Europe. Some of the party faithful had married Russian citizens and spoke some Russian. Rather significantly, one of Yesin's future accomplices had worked for several years at the party headquarters in Rome and had a Russian wife (SCO 1997, vol. 1, pp. 47–75). This background factor eventually facilitated Yesin's work in Rome. Second, Yesin already knew a Russian criminal who happened to be in Italy, Monya El'son, who had been forced to move there by Ivan'kov (Friedman 2000: 238). According to what El'son told Yesin, Italy was a country where it was easy to settle. "Here [in Italy] you can do whatever you want, it is not Europe" (SCO 1997, vol. 1, p. 90; see also CPA 1997, vol. 1, pp. 18–19). Furthermore, Rome was a better choice than other parts of Italy where Italian Mafia organizations were operating: The Russians openly state that they chose Rome as their base precisely because there were no major criminal organizations in the Italian capital, such as the Sicilian Mafia (SCO 1997, vol. 1, p. 20).

To the above reasons, a fourth one must be added: Yesin was afraid of being killed in Russia and, in 1994, was keen to transfer some of his operation abroad (SCO 1997, vol. 1, p. 187). Timofeyev and Kruglov, both his mentors in the group, had just been killed.[12] It is therefore not a coincidence that Yesin moved to Italy just a few months after the murder of Timofeyev; it appears that he was escaping death by accepting his migration to Italy, with the blessing of the leadership (SCO 1997, vol. 1, p. 21). The Italian police have named some 167 people as being part of the Yesin's Italian–Russian crew operating in Rome.

Social Capital

Italy and its capital, Rome have a comparably low level of trust and social capital. Only 34 percent of Italians interviewed in the World Values Survey (WVS) 1990–93 answered "most people can be trusted" to the question "Generally speaking, would you say that most people can be trusted or that you can't be too careful in dealing with people?" Levels of interpersonal trust are higher in Britain (44 percent), West Germany (38 percent), Poland (35 percent), and most of Western Europe. Belgium and Spain are comparable to Italy, scoring, respectively, 33 and 32 percent. Sweden (66 percent), Norway (65 percent), and Finland (63 percent) top the list (Inglehart et al. 1998: V94). As it is well known, Northern Italians have a higher level of interpersonal trust than Italians living in Central and Southern Italy. Putnam found that Lazio (Rome's region) has an "average" degree of civicness, above the low points of Calabria and Campania but well below the high points of Tuscany and Emilia Romagna (1994: 97).

The Activities in Rome and the Absence of Significant and Unprotected Markets

The activities of the Solntsevo group in Italy included resource acquisition, money laundering, investments in the legal economy, and the supply of some basic criminal services. Extensive corruption of officials was undertaken in order to obtain resources to establish the group in Italy. As far as resource acquisition, Yesin and his accomplices arranged fictitious marriages, faked drivers' licenses, and smuggled guns into the country. They illegally introduced into Italy millions of U.S. dollars. Nobody else in the group except Yesin and Dmitriy Naumov (a close collaborator of Yesin who tried to set up an alternative group and was killed on September 23, 1996 in Moscow) was entrusted with financial matters. Numerous wire transfers of funds from banks elsewhere in Europe and in the United States were made. Another money-laundering technique was to ask individuals to carry illegally obtained cash from Russia to Italy, and to use it to buy goods in Italy—such as clothes, jewelry, and watches—which were then brought back to Russia and sold there (SCO 1997, vol. 1, p. 93). The Italian police point out that, although the system may appear rudimentary and of little consequence, it is in fact used by various Russian criminal organizations and may involve thousands of people and millions of dollars (SCO 1997, vol. 1, p. 93, 120; CPA 1997: 19).

Various companies—all based at the same address in Rome—were set up by Yesin's associates in Italy. Their most basic functions were to issue invitations and to justify bank transfers. Some of these companies grew in size and significance. One, Acquarium Ltd. (name changed) was supposed to import fish and even set up a fishery in Italy (SCO 1997, vol. 1, p. 85), but the subsequent behavior of the man in charge of this operation, Igor Rumiantsev (later killed), made Yesin close it down (SCO 1997, vol. 1, p. 88). Yesin then decided to invest more money and energy in another company, World Export (name changed).

World Export was the most high-profile company set up in Italy. Yesin himself had a 30 percent stake in it. Riccardo Brenno (name changed), the most high-profile Italian involved with the Solntsevo, ran the company. Brenno was securing oil and gas contracts with Russia for World Export and Yesin. Most of these contracts were illegal. In one instance, Russian officials in the state oil agency were selling oil to Brenno coming from Iran, which Brenno in turn sold to South Africa. Such oil was not supposed to be sold to a third country according to the Iranian–Russian agreement. In a second deal, Brenno negotiated a contract for 240,000 tons of oil for a value of 300 million U.S. dollars (SCO 1997, vol. 1, p. 211; see also CPA 1997: 21).

World Export could count on significant connections in the Russian oil and gas industry and the energy ministry. Moreover, through corruption of a Ukrainian politician, Brenno secured an exclusive contract for the import of caviar into Italy from the city of Astrakhan. Brenno also negotiated the export of a 300,000-dollar Armani collection, a contract between Olivetti and a Russian firm worth 150 to 200 million dollars, and a contract for the export of Italian sparkling wine between the Soprani (name changed) wine maker and the city Alma-Ata, in Kazakhstan. At the time of Yesin's arrest, Russian partners of World Export were interested in buying furniture. It seems that at least one contract went through and furniture from Pesaro worth 300,000 dollars went to Russia.

The common feature of these ventures was that the money used to pay Italian suppliers was coming from the criminal activities conducted outside Italy, as stated in various conversations (see e.g., SCO 1997, vol. 1, p. 132). In some instances, the group used some reputable banks to transfer the money. In other instances, the payment was made in cash and smuggled through customs. The intermediary—World Export—would not receive any commission for its role, an element that aroused the suspicion of the Italian authorities.

Next to Yesin, the most active member of the group in the sphere of high finance and international deals was Dmitriy Naumov. Among other things, he secured profitable meat export deals to Russia and a shipment of mercury and rubidium from Russia to Taiwan via Italy and the United States. The final destination of the shipment appears to have been North Korea. (Mogilevich told an Austrian journalist that "Naumov is involved in legal deals, import–export of food products, and military products. It is possible that he traded red mercury.")[13]

Compared to the extensive network of financial deals, the amount and the significance of criminal services Yesin's group supplied were minimal: It arranged fictitious invitations to Italy, supplied prostitutes to visiting Russians, and set up fictitious marriages between Italians and Russians. It should be further noted that the customers of such services were only Russians. A member of Yesin's crew was accused—and cleared—of extorting one Russian in 1991, long before Yesin's move to Italy. (The accused was a Russian living in Italy recruited into Yesin's group after 1994.) The time frame suggests that the group as such was not involved in criminal protection rackets.

Further evidence of the fact that the Solntsevo had not been able to penetrate and exercise control over an unprotected market is its lack of the use of violence. Several phone conversations among Yesin's associates and victims show that members of the groups feared punishment if they tried to leave the organization or if they did not follow orders. However, no outsider was ever harmed and severe acts of violence against Russians who operated in Italy were carried out in Russia.

The aim of the Solntsevo hierarchy was to create a subsidiary group in Italy. The evidence presented earlier shows that Yesin was investing the earnings of the Solntsevo and other Russian crime groups in the legal economy, plus offering some basic criminal services to fellow Russians, such as fictitious marriages and invitations to the West. Upon coming to Italy, Yesin changed his role from that of a Mafia boss involved in the day-to-day running of a protection racket to that of a criminal reinvesting illegally obtained capital in the legal economy. In order to carry out this new task, he developed a rational strategy to get the group established, including obtaining passports, collecting information, and bribing local officials.

The group did not take root in Italy because it did not offer criminal services to locals and was not able to identify a significant and unprotected market. Yesin was arrested in Italy in March 1997, and, according to reports by Italian police, subsequent to the arrest of Yesin and his accomplices, this cell of the Solntsevo is effectively "dead."

The Solntsevo in Hungary: Social Capital and the Supply of Mafiosi

Like Italy, Hungary has a comparably low level of trust and social capital. Only 25 percent of Hungarians interviewed in the WVS 1990–93 answered "most people can be trusted" to the question "Generally speaking, would you say that most people can be trusted or that you can't be too careful in dealing with people?" Countries with higher scores include Poland (35 percent), Austria (32 percent), Estonia (28 percent), and East Germany (26 percent) (see Inglehart et al. 1998: V94).

A supply of Russian criminals has been recorded by the Hungarian police since the early 1990s. By 1998, the police estimated that "200 criminal gangs, mostly Russian controlled, have established themselves in the country, with a couple of dozen dominating. Many of the mob bosses, according to U.S. and Hungarian officials, are former Soviet KGB and military officers who created sophisticated and ruthless organizations" (*The Washington Post* December 21, 1998; see also Wright 1997: 70). The story of the Solntsevo penetration of Hungarian society revolves around an Ukranian-born businessman, Semën Yudkovich Mogilevich, who moved to Budapest in 1991 and had solid connections with the Solntsevo's leaders, Mikhailov and Averin (Friedman 2000: 240–1). Both Mikhailov and Averin had also elected Budapest as one of their residences in Eastern Europe (Mikhailov reportedly owns a luxury hotel in Budapest. See Maksimov 1997: 329).

The Transition to the Market in Hungary

Contrary to Rome, at the time of the Solntsevo attempts to move to Budapest, the country was undergoing a transition from a state-planned to a market economy. Hungary had begun restructuring state-owned enterprises before the end of the communist regime, and by 1985, two-thirds of all state enterprises had been granted self-governance through enterprise councils (Urbán 1997: 240). By the end of the 1990s, the proportion of private ownership as a percentage of GDP was between 80 and 85 percent (Csáki and Karsai 2001: 5). The emerging market economy could also rely upon laws and regulations that had been in place even during the communist regime. A Commercial Code, never formally repealed during the communist period, had existed since before World War II and was in turn based on a law passed in 1875. Moreover, reforms began as early as 1968 and continued, with interruptions, up to 1988 had reduced the role of the state in the economy and given greater autonomy to enterprises. The 1988 Act on Business Organizations consolidated previously fragmented corporate law and has been amended throughout the nineties to face the changing commercial environment (Kornai 1996; Sárközy 1993: 243; Csáki and Karsai 2001: 66).

Still, the Hungarian transition has not been entirely problem-free.[14] Hungary underwent what scholars have labeled "spontaneous (or informal) privatization," led by managers who were able to acquire stakes in state companies in the absence of legislation that fully protected shareholders and clearly defined property rights. "Informal privatization ranges on a scale from outright theft of potentially useful physical assets of a SOE [state-owned enterprise] through different forms of simple corruption to more sophisticated appropriation of assets through the creation of new corporations" (Urbán 1997: 243).

Notwithstanding the Hungarian past, a fully developed legal framework was not yet in place by the time the transition got under way. Csáki and

Karsai (2001) point out that "there are several legal and institutional problems that hinder the effective operation of Hungarian enterprises. Certain laws and modifications (for example, the reform of the real-estate law and the contract law) are still lacking. Conceptually, the majority of existing economic regulations is not sufficiently developed and includes a number of internal contradictions as well as contradictions with other laws" (69).

The state apparatus proved slow and ineffective at servicing the new market players. Csáki and Karsai point to the "the inaccurate and out-dated real-estate register [and] the slow process of company registration." In the early 1990s, the poorly computerized Hungarian real-estate registers faced demands for the production and modification of information that were beyond their capacities. Throughout the 1990s boom in company-creation, company registration faced the same challenge. Thus "there is no up-to-date company data with respect to the assets and financial position of market players. The problems caused by overloading, as well as by the widening circle of corruption and other abuses, only make matters worse" (71, 72).

Such inefficiencies decreased public confidence in the legal system and economic crimes increased. In the 1990s, tax avoidance became widespread and the breaching of contracts, VAT fraud, and false bankruptcy petitions were considered minor transgressions (see also Wright 1997: 74; Csáki and Karsai 2001: 71). According to a survey conducted in 1998, some 80 percent of those surveyed agreed that "in order to get by, it was necessary to break the rules" (Csáki and Karsai 2001: 71). As crime against property increased significantly at the time of the transition (Wright 1997: 69), the criminal justice system proved to be, in the view of Csáki and Karsai, "almost entirely powerless in the face of the spread of economic criminality" and the capacity of the civil law courts was "not satisfactory" (2001: 71).

Although Hungary was in 1992 the third largest money launderer in Europe, official statistics up to the end of 1996 record no convictions or completed proceedings for money laundering (Wright 1997: 71). Court proceedings were "lengthy" and delays in the pronouncement of verdicts were "frequent," making the execution of verdicts "often impossible." The introduction in 1994 of an Execution Act has not changed matters significantly according to Csáki and Karsai: "The only substantial change has been the increased costs of, and payments to, private executors who are assigned the task of execution" (2001: 72). Police corruption has also been described as "pervasive" (Pap 2001; see also Mawby and Wright 2001). Not surprisingly, the level of the informal economy is vast and ranges, depending on the estimate between 25 percent of GNI and 31 percentage of GDP.[15]

Géza Katona, former chief of the Investigation Department of the National Police, links the initial shortcomings of the Hungarian transition to the market to the rise of the demand for Mafia-related activities. "It is not surprising that businessmen, some law-abiding and some not, try to defend themselves and find other nonlegal or semilegal ways to defend their interests, without legal support from the state" (1997: 79). Katona concludes by pointing out that organized crime has played a major role in the area of extrajudicial settlement of disputes; indeed, it has virtually "taken over" this sphere.

Katona identifies a second area of opportunity for criminal organizations, namely the oil sector. After 1989, the former state monopoly over the oil trade ceased to exist, while new sector regulations were still absent. Virtually anyone could establish a firm to sell oil because the state failed to screen firms seeking official registration; meanwhile, due to the departure of the Soviet troops, vast storage facilities became available. At the same time, the Hungarian government, in an effort to shield farmers and the very poor from the full impact of growing inflation and rising heating bills, introduced a dual-price system for heating and diesel oil. One side effect was the creation of artificial opportunities for money-making operations.[16]

As compared with the virtual absence of Mafia-related violence in Rome, Mafia-related violence was high in Hungary. *The Washington Post* (December 21, 1998) writes:

> [B]y 1996, violence began to spill onto the streets here. The Hungarian police have recorded 140 mob-related bombings, grenade attacks and killings since 1991, most in recent years. In November 1996, alleged mob leader Jozsef Prisztas was gunned down and killed on a Budapest street. In August 1997, shots were fired into a disco, wounding one woman. Last February [1998], a business magnate with alleged mob ties was assassinated with an automatic weapon as he sat in his car at a traffic light. A grenade was hurled at a bar the following month. And in June, shots were fired into a shop, injuring one person. Mobsters killing mobsters, however, engendered a certain so-what attitude among the public, officials said.[17]

Between 1991 and 1998, there were over 100 gangland murders and 170 explosions in Hungary.[18]

The Activities of the Solntsevo in Hungary

An oblique reference to the Solntsevo appears in *The Boston Globe* (November 29, 1998), which refers to a "Russian-speaking gang believed to be the most powerful and dangerous in Hungary, officials said. This mob, law enforcement sources said, has a presence in the United States" (see also Wright 1997: 72). We now turn more specifically to the activities of this group.

Through Mogilevich, the Solntsevo created an intricate network of companies and factories, laundering and investing a significant amount of money into the legal economy, mainly in arms production and the oil business. In 1995, Mogilevich bought Magnex 2000, a magnet manufacturer in Budapest; Army Co-op, a mortar and antiaircraft gun factory;[19]

Balchug, a firm that produces and sells office furniture; and Digep General Machine Works, an artillery shell, mortar, and fire equipment manufacturer.[20] Mogilevich has been involved in the oil business since the 1980s, creating Arbat International, a petroleum export–import company of which he owned 50 percent (the other shareholders were Ivan'kov, Mikhailov, and Averin; see *The Times* [London] August 20, 1999), and Arigon Ltd., which sold oil products to the Ukrainian railway administration and was allegedly managed by Mikhailov's wife.[21] Most recently, he has been connected to Eural Trans Gas, an obscure Hungarian company holding a contract with Gazprom to provide gas from Turkmenistan to Ukraine.[22]

The Solntsevo did not limit itself to investment in the legal economy but, according to a FBI report, it has tried to defraud the Hungarian government and to push competitors out of the oil market (*Moscow Times* February 22, 2000). It is widely believed that the warfare within the Hungarian underworld, which took place in the 1990s and involved both Russian and Hungarian groups, was due to conflict over how to allocate lucrative state oil and gas contracts (Katona 1997; *CTK Czech News Agency* November 8, 1999). According to a BBC documentary on the activities of Mogilevich, Zoltán Seres, one of his Hungarian partners, was "the victim of the Russian–Hungarian turf wars which have followed the oil rackets."[23] A businessman involved in oil frauds, Tamás Boros, said during confessions made to the police in February 1997 and May 1998 that "company owners who had not imported oil through the Russian Mafia boss Semën Mogilevich were threatened and blackmailed" (*CTK* November 8, 1999; *Index* [Budapest] June 9, 2000). Tamás Boros was killed, together with three other victims, in a car bomb explosion in central Budapest early July 1998 (*MTI Hungarian News Agency* September 17, 1998).

The same FBI report cited earlier also suggests that the Solntsevo has expanded beyond the oil business, runs protection rackets and prostitution rings in Budapest, and has tortured and murdered local opponents using villas Mogilevich owns in the country as jails. (Viktor Averin is suspected by the Hungarian police of the murder of a man in Budapest, Andrey Mochin. Also, he allegedly acted as an intermediary in the kidnapping of another man, Abner Kandov.) According to police sources cited by *Népszava*, a Hungarian daily, some 800 companies in Hungary have direct links to the underworld (*MTI* November 19, 1998). Although it is hard to discern the exact nature of the relationship between these firms and the underworld, a typical connection is that Mafia groups offer criminal protection to firms that cannot turn to the state. Partial evidence of this has emerged at the "bomb factory" trial of former Stasi agent Clodo.[24] At the trial, several defendants named Leonid Goldstein Steicura as the second-in-command of Mogilevich's operation in Budapest and the real owner of the bomb-making facility run by Clodo. More significantly, a killer for the group, Nándor Erdélyi, claimed that criminals in Budapest had to pay a 50 percent "fee" to Steigura in order to be allowed to operate.[25]

Furthermore, at the same trial, it emerged that Steigura had planned the murder of Mogilevich, possibly in an attempt to increase the autonomy of the group from the original, Moscow-based Mafia.

Although the evidence is sketchy, it appears that the Solntsevo, and Russian criminal groups more generally, have firmly established themselves in Hungary—contrary to the outcome we observed in Rome. The Russian Mafia is simultaneously trying to exert a monopoly over certain sectors of the economy, such as the oil business, and offering criminal protection to both businessmen in the gray economy and criminal entrepreneurs.

Conclusions

The comparison between situations in Rome and Budapest allows us to identify a key factor at work in Mafia transplantation. In the case of Rome, a supply of Mafiosi was coupled with low levels of trust and transplantation was unsuccessful. In the case of Hungary, the same two factors existed, plus the presence of significant and unprotected markets. The presence of unprotected markets is the key variable that leads to successful transplantation (see figures 8.2 and 8.3).

Is a supply of criminals as such a sufficient reason to expect Mafias to establish themselves outside their original territories? In the case of Rome, a deliberate decision to create a supply of criminals in Rome was not sufficient for the Mafia to take root. On the other hand, in Hungary it appears that Russian criminals *followed* the opportunities they had seen emerging in that country and possibly had been told by Russian businessmen who were already operating in the country. A further factor at play might well have been the greater ease of traveling within former East European countries, although we should not overemphasize the "cultural similarities" between Hungary and Russia and the difficulties of moving to Italy from Russia.

The emergence of vast market opportunities unregulated and unprotected by the state offers incentives for Mafiosi from different territories to exploit local opportunities either by moving there or, if already present, by offering criminal protection. This concatenation of factors increases the

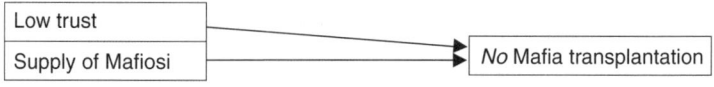

Figure 8.2 Factors present in the unsuccessful Mafia transplantation in Rome

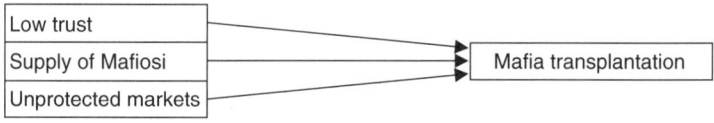

Figure 8.3 Factors present in the successful Mafia transplantation in Hungary

likelihood of Mafia transplantation. Such a conclusion goes against "supply-side" explanations of both the origin and diffusion of Mafias discussed earlier. If Mafiosi exist in an area where no significant unprotected market exists—we contend—they will simply be unemployed Mafia enforcers.[26]

Still, maintaining a subsidiary away from the firm headquarters is not easy, as suggested by Gambetta (1993a). Even when conditions are right, a successful operation in a new territory is hard to sustain over time due to the hard-to-solve problems of asymmetric information and monitoring. Suggestive evidence of a subsidiary's attempts to evolve into an independent organization seems to emerge from the Hungarian case as well, although more work is needed to establish this point conclusively.

The Hungarian case indicates that circumstances conducive to Mafia transplantation can be the product of state failures to equip a country fast enough with the institutional features of a market economy, such as a well-functioning legal system and clearly defined and enforced property rights. The unintended consequences of a well-meaning policy that created easy opportunities to defraud the state and enforce criminal monopolies over supplies of oil constituted a second crucial factor fostering the move of Russian groups to Hungary.

Notes

* I am grateful to the participants of Honesty and Trust workshops for useful responses to my presentation, and to János Kornai, Susan Rose-Ackerman and Bo Rothstein for detailed comments and suggestions that have improved the chapter tremendously. Marshall Goldman and Bernard Tamás have given me most valuable feedbacks on a version of the chapter. Collegium Budapest gave me a grant to support part of this research and was a most generous host in Budapest. György Molnár has drawn my attention to relevant articles in the Hungarian press. Sara Arnold copy-edited a version of the text, while Julianna Parti spotted innumerable inconsistencies and edited the final version of the chapter. I am very grateful to both for their invaluable help.

1. *South China Morning Post* November 7, 2000. The U.S. Federal Bureau of Investigation (FBI) set up a joint task force with the Hungarian police to combat "the growing Russian Mafia influence in the country." *BBC News* February 22, 2002.
2. In spite of Chu's skepticism about its systematic character, transplantation may be occurring in China as well: "It is reported that more than half of the entertainment establishments in Shenzhen are owned by triads, mainly from Hong Kong. It is also said that some Hong Kong triad members collaborate with relatives of prominent Chinese government officials to run entertainment businesses in major cities in China" (Chu 2000: 132).
3. For example, Steve Di Salvo insists with Frank Balestrieri that the best way to go is to "charge all the other bookies in town 1,000 a week just to operate" (Pistone and Woodley 1997: 203). For several instances of Mafias using fixed payment for their clients see Chu 2000: 59; Gambetta 1993a: 181; Varese 2001: 106–7; Jacobs et al. 1999: 34, 43.
4. For instance, members of the Sicilian-based Stidda criminal group escaped to Piedmont in 1986 after losing a confrontation with a Mafia family in Catania (Sciarrone 1998: 247–8). Ciro Mazzarella moved to Switzerland in 1992, after losing a Camorra war in Naples in the early 1990s. In his new motherland, he organized a cigarette and drug smuggling operation between Montenegro and Italy. See Bove and Durante 2000.
5. Since the mid-1950s, the policy of forced resettlement brought hard-nosed lawbreakers to northern regions of Italy, such as Lombardy, Piedmont, and Emilia-Romagna.
6. Trust would be a second form of reassurance of exchanges in the absence of state protection of exchanges.
7. I am drawing below upon Varese 1994.

8. Indeed, this reasoning suggests that a combination of two factors can explain the origin of the Italian-American Mafia. The transplantation of individuals with Mafia skills from Southern Italy and the massive increase in the demand for services of contract enforcement and protection in the underworld at the time of prohibition. Moreover, as we predict later in the chapter, the subsidiary evolved into an autonomous group, with loose links with the original "firm." Put differently, the Italian-American Mafia cannot be considered as a subdivision of the Sicilian Mafia.
9. An FBI report in 1995 described the Solntsevo organization as the most powerful Eurasian organized crime group "in the world in terms of wealth, influence and financial control" (*Moscow Times* February 22, 2000). On the Solntsevo, see also Modestov 1996 and Maksimov 1997. A partly fictional account of the functioning of the group by a Moscow lawyer in Karyshev 2001. For general analyses of organized crime and protection rackets in Russia, see Galeotti 1998; Varese 2001; and Volkov 2002.
10. Apparently, this was just one of the regular meetings of the council that runs the various Solntsevo operations in Russia and abroad. Only made *vory-v-zakone* can participate at these meetings.
11. The *vory* spent most of their lives in the labor camps, consistently refusing to work. They developed an ideology of monastic purity, a ritual for the initiation into the fraternity, and achieved a leading role over the *blatnye*, professional criminals, who aspired to become *vory*, the highest possible honor in the criminal world. The fraternity survived into the post-Soviet period. On the *vory-v-zakone*, see Varese 1998, 2001: 145–66.
12. SCO 1997, vol. 1, pp. I-16–17. The death of Sil'vestr is discussed by several criminals connected to Yesin. A number of supporters of Sil'vestr were killed shortly after the death of Sil'vestr and the "Italians" went to some of the funerals. In their telephone conversations, they show great fears of being associated with what appears a losing faction and being killed as well. Apparently, some people who had little or nothing to do with Sil'vestr were also killed, such as a man nicknamed Drakon. Yesin tells Slava (Vyacheslav Gavrilov, one of his deputies in Italy) that "Drakon had nothing to do with it, and it is not known why they killed him" (SCO 1997, vol. 1, p. 7).
13. *Wirtschafts Woche* April 1993, quoted in SCO 1997, vol. 3, p. 173. The DEA has named a North Korean Army officer based in Florida as being involved in the deal.
14. See Kornai 1990 for pointed criticisms of the early privatization plans and a blueprint for post-socialist transition in Eastern Europe. For a general assessment of the transition in Hungary, see Kornai 1996.
15. The first estimate is by the World Bank (see http://rru.www.worldbank.org). The 31 percent estimate is by Lackó (1997) and is based on electric energy consumption in the year 1994. See also Tóth 1997/1998. According to *Budapest Week* March 23–29, 1995 (quoted in Wright 1997: 74), between 20 and 40 percent of Hungary's half-million unemployed are estimated to be involved in the shadow economy.
16. Furthermore, the international trade embargo against Yugoslavia offered extraordinary profits for smugglers in the southern and eastern cities of the country, in cities such as Miskolc, Kecskemét, and Kiskörös (Katona 1997).
17. Firearms and explosives have also been easily available since the transition to the market. See Wright 1997: 72 and especially Nagy 2000.
18. "The Billion Dollar Don," *BBC1 Panorama* December 6, 1999.
19. Mogilevich bought 95 percent of Army Co-op through Arigon Ltd.
20. *Hetek* August 1999; *Russian Business Monitor* September 1, 1999. A rare but significant confirmation of the fact that Mogilevich used Solntsevo funds for his investments comes from a phone conversation intercepted by the Austrian police and reported in the Italian file on Yesin. The conversation took place in April 1994 between Averin and Mogilevich. The former reminds the latter that he has to return money he obtained from the group's "common fund." The money involved was 5 million U.S. dollars (SCO 1997, vol. 1, p. 79).
21. Most notoriously, Mogilevich infused from Arigon Ltd. 30 million dollars into YBM Magnex International, which merged with Magnex 2000 (Friedman 2000: 249–51).
22. See *RFE/RL Organized Crime and Terrorism Watch* January 16 and March 13, 2003; *Jane's Intelligence Digest* January 31, 2003; *The St. Petersburg Times* February 28, 2003.
23. "The Billion Dollar Don," *BBC1 Panorama* December 6, 1999.
24. Dietmar Clodo created a bomb-making facility in Budapest where bombs later used in the wave of attacks on criminals and businessmen in the period of 1996–98 were produced (*Duna Satellite TV* (BBC Monitoring) November 6, 2000 and December 29, 2001).

25. *Heti Világgazdaság* November 11, 2000. Steigura was also active in the oil market in Budapest. *Világgazdaság* November 22, 2000.
26. A case of a successful Mafia move from Calabria to Piedmont in Northern Italy suggests that *ceteris paribus* high levels of trust and social capital *among law abiders* is insufficient to prevent transplantation (I discussed this case briefly in *Times Literary Supplement* February 23, 2001). A case of unsuccessful transplantation from Calabria to Verona in the 1970s suggests that *ceteris paribus* high levels of trust *among law offenders* can prevent successful transplantation. In Verona, a vast and growing drug market based on trust among dealers was present when would-be Mafiosi from Calabria tried and failed to monopolize the market. Hence, a supply of Mafiosi and even the presence of market opportunities are not sufficient when there is high trust among criminals. In other words, when trust is high among criminals, a Mafia is unwanted.

References

Bove, Antonio and Graziella Durante. 2000. E la Camorra sbarcò in Montenegro. In L. Caracciolo (ed.). *Gli Stati Mafia*, pp. 41–8. Rome: Gruppo Editoriale L'Espresso.
Catanzaro, Raimondo. 1992. *Men of Respect: A Social History of the Sicilian Mafia*. New York: Free Press.
Chu, Yiu Kong. 2000. *The Triads as Business*. London and New York: Routledge.
Coleman, James. 1990. *Foundations of Social Theory*. Cambridge MA: Harvard University Press.
CPA (Commissione Parlamentare AntiMafia). 1997. Audizione del Direttore del Servizio Centrale Operativo della Polizia di Stato, Alessandro Pansa, XIII Legislatura—Disegni di Leggi e Relazioni—Documenti, Rome, April 7.
Csáki, György and Gábor Karsai. 2001. *Evolution of the Hungarian Economy, 1848–2000*. Vol. 3. *Hungary from Transition to Integration*. New York: Columbia University Press.
De Gennaro, Giuseppe. 1997. Statement, US Congressional Committee on International Relations (01/X), Washington. Text at http://pubs.marshallcenter.org/732/lesson5/1924.html.
Friedman, Robert I. 2000. *Red Mafia*. Boston: Little, Brown and Company.
Frydman, Roman, Andrzej Rapaczynski, and John S. Earle. 1993. *The Privatization Process in Russia, Ukraine and the Baltics*. Budapest: Central European University Press.
Galeotti, Mark. 1998. The Mafia and the New Russia. *Australian Journal of Politics and History* 44: 415–29.
———. 2000. The Russian Mafia: Economic Penetration at Home and Abroad. In A. V. Ledeneva and M. Kurkchiyan (eds.). *Economic Crime in Russia*, pp. 31–42. The Hague: Kluwer Law International.
Gambetta, Diego. 1993a. *The Sicilian Mafia*. London: Harvard University Press.
———. 1993b. Trust and Co-operation. In *The Blackwell Dictionary of Twentieth-Century Social Thought*, pp. 678–80. Oxford: Blackwell.
Goldman, Marshall. 1996. Why is the Mafia so Dominant in Russia? *Challenge* January–February, pp. 39–47.
Jacobs, James B., Coleen Friel, and Robert Radick. 1999. *Gotham Unbound. How New York City was Liberated from the Grip of Organized Crime*. New York University Press.
Inglehart, Ronald, Miguel Basanez, and Alejandro Moreno. 1998. *Human Values and Beliefs*. Ann Arbor MI: University of Michigan Press.
Kahn, Peter L. 2002. The Russian Bailiffs Service and the Enforcement of Civil Judgements. *Post-Soviet Affairs* 18: 148–81.
Karyshev, Valery. 2001. *Solntsevskaya Bratva. Istoriya Gruppirovski* (The Solntsevo Brotherhood. History of the Group). Moscow: Izdatel'stvo Eksmo.
Katona, Géza. 1997. Crime and Corruption after Communism. An Interview on Crime Conducted by Andras Mink. *East European Constitutional Review* 6: 78–9.
Kornai, János. 1990. *The Road to a Free Economy. Shifting from a Socialist System: Hungary's Example*. New York: W. W. Norton.
———. 1996. Paying the Bill for Goulach Communism: Hungarian Development and Macro Stabilization in a Political Economy Perspective. *Social Research* 63: 943–1040.
Lackó, Mária. 1997. *The Hidden Economies of Visegrád Countries in International Comparison: A Household Electricity Approach*. Budapest: IEHAS.
Maksimov, Aleksandr. 1997. *Rossiyskaya Prestupnost'. Kto est' Kto?* (Criminal Russia. Who's Who?). Moscow: Izdatel'stvo Eksmo.

Mawby, Robert and Alan Wright. 2001. Police Corruption in Transitional States: The Case of Hungary—"the best police money can buy"? Manuscript.

Modestov, Nikolay. 1996. *Moskva Bandistskaya*. (Bandits' Moscow). Moscow: Tsentrloligrag.

Nagy, László. 2000. Illegal Trade of Arms and Connected Crime. Paper presented at the conference of the Council on Christian Approaches to Defence and Disarmament, Loyola Retreat House, Faulkner MD, September 17–21. Available at http://website.lineone.net/~ccadd/.

Pap, András László. 2001. Street Police Corruption. Paper presented at the Socrates Kokkalis Annual Workshop. J.F. Kennedy School of Government, Cambridge MA, February 9.

Pistone, Joseph D. and Richard Woodley. 1997. *Donnie Brasco: My Undercover Life in the Mafia*. New York: Signet.

Pistor, Katharina. 1996. Supply and Demand for Contract Enforcement in Russia: Courts, Arbitration and Private Enforcement. *Review of Central and Eastern European Law* 1: 55–87.

Portes, Alejandro. 1998. Social Capital: Its Origins and Applications in Modern Sociology. *Annual Review of Sociology* 24: 1–24.

Putnam, Robert D. 1994. *Making Democracy Work: Civic Traditions in Italy*. Princeton NJ: Princeton University Press.

Rose-Ackerman, Susan. 2001. Trust, Honesty and Corruption: Reflection on the State-building Process. *Archives Européennes de Sociologie* 43: 526–70.

Sands, Jennifer. 2002. Exploring Transnational Organized Crime in the Age of Globalization: A Case-Study of the Colombian Cartels and Russian Mafias in Spain. Paper presented at the Italian Political Science Association (IPSA) Meeting. Genoa, September 18–20.

Sárközy, Tamás. 1993. A Legal Framework for the Hungarian Transition, 1989–1991. In I. Szekely and D.M.G. Newbery (eds.). *Hungary: An Economy in Transition*, pp. 239–48. Cambridge: Cambridge University Press.

Sciarrone, Rocco. 1998. *Mafie Vecchie, Mafie Nuove*. Rome: Donzelli.

SCO (Servizio Centrale Operativo).1997. *Rapporto operativo, Yesin et alii*. 3 vols. Rome: Polizia di Stato.

Tóth, István János. 1997/98 The Importance of the Hidden Economy in Hungary in 1995–96. An Estimation on the Basis of the Empirical Analysis of Household Expenses. *Acta Oeconomica* 49: 105–34.

Urbán, László. 1997. Privatisation as Institutional Change in Hungary. In D.L. Weimer (ed.). *The Political Economy of Property Rights*, pp. 239–55. Cambridge: Cambridge University Press.

U.S. Senate Permanent Subcommittee on Investigations of the Committee on Governmental Affairs. 1988. Testimony of Joseph D. Pistone, Former Special Agent, Federal Bureau of Investigation. Text at http://www.americanMafia.com/Pistone_Testimony.html.

Varese, Federico. 1994. Is Sicily the Future of Russia? Private Protection and the Emergence of the Russian Mafia. *Archives Européennes de Sociologie* 35: 224–58.

———. 1998. The Society of the *Vory-v-Zakone*, 1930s–1950s. *Cahiers du Monde Russe* 39: 515–38.

———. 2001. *The Russian Mafia. Private Protection in a New Market Economy*. Oxford: Oxford University Press.

———. 2002. Trust within Mafias. Manuscript.

Volkov, Vadim. 2002. *Violent Entrepreneurs. The Use of Force in the Making of Russian Capitalism*. Ithaca NY: Cornell University Press.

Wright, Alan. 1997. Organized Crime in Hungary: The Transition from State to Civil Society. *Transnational Organized Crime* 3: 68–86.

CHAPTER NINE

Beyond Law Enforcement: Governing Financial Markets in China and Russia

KATHARINA PISTOR AND CHENGGANG XU*

Introduction

This chapter explores the institutional conditions for the development of financial markets in emerging markets and transition economies. We focus on the development of the legal and regulatory framework for stock markets but suggest that our framework would also be applicable to the law governing credit markets and banking institutions. Given the importance of financial markets for economic growth and development (McKinnon 1973), efforts to promote the development of such markets have been a cornerstone of economic policies in transition economies. Not all countries, however, have been equally successful in creating sustainable financial markets. This is true even for countries that have followed blueprints of what are widely regarded as best practices for governing financial markets. This chapter offers an explanation for why this may be the case.

We start from the premise that law is intrinsically incomplete, which implies that it is impossible to write a law that can unambiguously specify all potentially harmful actions. Because law is incomplete, law enforcement by courts may not always effectively deter violations. Rather than attempting the impossible task of completing the law, the effectiveness of law enforcement may be enhanced by reallocating lawmaking and law-enforcement powers (LMLEP). In earlier work, we showed that when law is highly incomplete and violations of the law may result in substantial harm, it is optimal to allocate law enforcement rights to regulators rather than courts (Pistor and Xu 2003; Xu and Pistor 2003).

Similar solutions, which worked reasonably well in developed market economies with a long history of commercial law development, may, however, not work in transition economies. The reason is that transition economies face conditions that render enforcement by courts and regulators both ineffective. We identify two key conditions that undermine classic forms of law enforcement that have been tried and tested in developed market economies: the level of incomplete law and the absence of reliable information. Transition economies have engaged in wholesale reforms of their legal systems. The scope and meaning of newly enacted laws, however, is difficult to discern from statutory law alone. Due to language, cultural, and institutional differences, case law from other countries that may help interpret the law is not easily transferable. Countries that transplant law from elsewhere, therefore, have little or no access to interpretative sources, which makes transplanted laws further incomplete. Only after a substantial body of domestic case law has been developed will individuals as well as law enforcers know the reach and limits of the new law.

The more incomplete the law, the weaker its deterrence effect, as the uncertainties about the scope and meaning of law increase with higher levels of incompleteness. Moreover, courts in transition economies often lack capacity and experience to address new legal problems effectively, which aggravates the problem of incomplete law. Attempts to improve law enforcement by introducing a regulator may not work, primarily because effective regulation depends heavily on reliable information. Companies in transition economies face substantial problems in bringing previous accounting data, which were compiled on the basis of socialist accounting principles, in line with new accounting standards. Even when they do so, substantial concerns remain as to how accurately these new books reflect the intrinsic value of the firm. Moreover, the uncertainties that surround the conversion of accounting data create possibilities for manipulation. As a result, the information that regulators obtain is much noisier than is the case in developed market economies. Over time, information may become more reliable and intermediaries may enter the market that can help verify information—but before then, law enforcement by regulators will be ineffective and may even result in regulatory failure. Transition economies therefore face a fundamental dilemma. They need to develop financial markets, and yet they lack the ingredients it takes to do so. Worst, recipes for law enforcement that have historically worked elsewhere may not help in the short to medium term. Unlike developed economies where extensive commercial law existed at the time financial markets emerged, in transition economies and newly emerging markets, law, legal institutions, and markets need to be created simultaneously.

An alternative strategy for transition economies is to use measures beyond law enforcement to initiate market development. This chapter suggests that an important strategy may be to access insiders' knowledge of a company's potential. This strategy is bound to be less transparent and raises concerns about the accountability of agents charged with selecting companies. Still, these problems can be controlled by ensuring that decisions are taken collectively and by allocating liability for wrongful decisions to those who participate in the selection process. If such checks are in place, measures beyond law enforcement may be less prone to corruption and regulatory capture than standard law enforcement strategies. The reason is that the same factors that render standard law enforcement strategies ineffective in transition economies, that is, highly incomplete law and low-quality information, also give law-enforcement agents ample room for discretion, which can be easily misused. Paradoxically, the appearance of standard law enforcement institutions and practices may disguise the fact that given the underlying problems of incomplete law and information problems, they broaden rather than reduce the scope for corruption. By contrast, processes that may appear to be prone to corrupt practices, may be less vulnerable to misuse as long as other mechanisms, such as multiparty decision-making and competition, are in place to reduce the possible scope of misuse.

We use the experience of China and Russia to exemplify two different strategies in trying to jump-start financial market development. In both countries, the process started in the early 1990s. Russia began the process of financial market development by privatizing thousands of companies and distributing their shares to the public. At the time, courts were the only enforcement agents. By 1994, a securities commission was established. Its powers were limited at the beginning but expanded over time. Available data suggest that both courts and regulators have been quite active in enforcing the law. Financial market development in Russia has, however, been slow. Most of the companies that were privatized in the early 1990s have never been traded. The market is dominated by companies trading in oil, mining, and energy, that is, companies where the underlying assets are sufficiently valuable to balance concerns about lack of information and reliable governance structures. In fact, stocks of listed companies move together, suggesting that investors pay little attention to firm-specific information.

In China, by contrast, virtually all the companies that are listed are partly state-owned. The legal framework developed in the early 1990s established an elaborate merit system for companies wishing to issue shares to the public. This system was, however, replaced by a quota system. Under the quota system, a certain volume of funds to be raised by state-owned enterprises in the form of equity was allotted to regions and/or ministries, which in turn were responsible for selecting the companies for this program. Given the increasing scarcity of bank loans, access to the equity markets was attractive to companies. The risk of bad decisions was borne not only by investors, but also by agents responsible for selecting companies, because they were forced to bail out companies that failed on the market and faced lower quotas in the future. The number of listed companies in China today is much higher than in Russia. Manufacturing companies dominate the market. Most strikingly, increasingly independent stock movements of listed companies suggest that more firm-specific information may be available to investors.

We recognize that incomplete law and information problems may not be the only factors that explain the divergent experiences of Russia and China in developing financial markets. The goal of this chapter is to offer a theory that helps explain why standard enforcement practices work less well in transition economies. We suggest that the evidence we present from Russia and China is consistent with our theory, but we do not claim that we can fully rule out other explanations.

Law Enforcement Under Incomplete Law

In earlier work, we developed the theory of incomplete law (Pistor and Xu 2003). We argued that law is intrinsically incomplete. Even the best, social welfare maximizing, lawmaker cannot write law that is fully complete because lawmakers cannot foresee all future contingencies. A lawmaker (court, legislature, etc.) may choose to write a relatively more or less complete law, but fundamentally cannot escape the problem that even the best efforts will be incomplete. Given that law is incomplete, the power to address future contingencies, that is, the residual LMLEP have to be allocated to maintain effective law enforcement. Although this will not result in full deterrence (after all, law remains incomplete), law enforcement can be enhanced.

If law were complete, that is, if a law could stipulate unambiguously all future contingencies, law could fully deter harmful actions. The key task for such a law would be to stipulate the appropriate level of punishment. Indeed, much of the traditional literature on law enforcement (Becker 1968; Stigler 1970; Polinsky and Shavell 2000) focuses on the appropriate level of punishment and treats law implicitly as complete. By contrast, if law is incomplete, law cannot effectively deter. We argue that in this second best world of incomplete law, legal systems need to allocate LMLEP to deal with future contingencies that were unanticipated at the time the law was made in order to enhance the effectiveness of law enforcement. In the absence of the allocation of LMLEP, many actions will not be sanctioned, even if they result in substantial harm. Legislative change may make law more complete after assembling sufficient expertise, but this will take effect only in the future. Moreover, new actions or factual situations the revised law did not contemplate will undoubtedly arise, leaving it once more incomplete.

Given that law is incomplete, a crucial question is who should hold the power to interpret and/or adapt law in light of new circumstances. We argue that the allocation of LMLEP should be related to the lawmaking and law-enforcement functions that different agents perform. In what follows, we attribute particular functions to different agents, which are admittedly stylized, but closely resemble the functions such agents perform in developed market economies. Legislatures are agents that make law ex ante, but typically do not exercise any law enforcement powers. Courts usually make law ex post, that is, after the critical facts of a case have been revealed. However, case law once made also has ex ante implications for actions taken in the future. Courts also exercise law enforcement powers. More importantly, courts enforce law only after a party other than the court brings an action. This party may be the victim, or it may be a state agent, such as a prosecutor or administrative agency. We therefore call courts reactive as opposed to proactive law enforcers. This design feature is crucial for courts to function as neutral arbiters.

Regulators also combine lawmaking and law-enforcement functions. Just as legislatures, they make law ex ante. Unlike legislatures, regulators are typically vested only with limited lawmaking powers defined by certain activities or sectors, but within the scope of their lawmaking powers, they can change the law more flexibly and with fewer procedural requirements. This allows them to be more responsive to socioeconomic or technological change than legislatures. However, a similar function could be achieved by setting up a special parliamentary committee to deal with a specialized area of the law. The distinctive feature of regulators thus lies not in greater flexibility and/or greater expertise as compared with legislatures, but in combining lawmaking with proactive law enforcement. In contrast to courts, regulators can take the initiative and launch an investigation, enjoin actions, or impose fines and do not have to wait for others to bring such actions. These particular features make regulators potentially very powerful law enforcers. The very same features raise concerns, as regulators may misuse these powers and suppress potentially beneficial actions or even engage in rent-seeking activities. To optimize law enforcement it is therefore important to identify the conditions under which the benefits of regulators outweigh their potential costs.

When law is highly complete, law enforcement by courts in a reactive fashion has sufficient deterrence effect. By contrast, when law is incomplete it may be better to reallocate LMLEP to different agents. The optimal allocation of LMLEP is determined by many factors, including the level of expected harm and the cost of standardizing actions, which is crucial for regulators to enforce law effectively (for details of the analysis see Xu and Pistor 2003).[1] When firms come to the market, investors face a lemons problem (Akerlof 1970). Incidents of misrepresentation of information may seriously discourage investments in shares as is evidenced by market crashes in response to the revelation of stock fraud schemes or systemic misrepresentation in financial statements—as most recently demonstrated by the market response to the discovery of financial misreporting at Enron, Worldcom, and so on. Thus, the expected degree of harm—undermining the functioning of securities markets—is high. Agents that can enjoin actions before harm has been done, are therefore of critical importance. Theoretically, courts may also enjoin actions before harm has been done. They can do this, however, only after an action has been brought by someone else, such as a current shareholder or potential investor, who needs the right incentives to launch a lawsuit at the right time. By contrast, regulators can initiate enforcement procedures on their own and do not need to wait for others to bring action. Disclosure rules for financial markets can be standardized at reasonable costs. Lawmakers can define the type of information that must be disclosed, and adapt these rules over time as market behavior changes or as it becomes apparent that investors require different information. Giving regulators this power ensures that disclosure rules will be adopted faster and more flexibly than leaving this task with legislatures. Moreover, regulators can use their expertise from law enforcement to decide on the need for further lawmaking activities.

In sum, under incomplete law legal systems that rely exclusively on reactive law enforcement by courts may experience deterrence failure and allocating LMLEP to regulators may be superior. The efficacy of regulators, however, hinges on their ability to rely on firm-specific information that can be standardized at relatively low cost. As we will show in the next section, if standardized information is not available or not reliable, legal systems and markets may suffer from regulatory failure. Therefore, alternative governance mechanisms may be needed.

Deterrence and Regulatory Failure in Transition Economies

In transition economies, the incompleteness of law problem and the information problem are both more severe than in developed market economies. Given the scale and scope of economic and legal reforms that are taking place concurrently, law in transition countries is bound to be highly incomplete, that is, its meaning and application to specific cases are largely untested, and the scope of liability is therefore uncertain. As a result, court enforcement cannot effectively deter violations. The intuition for this argument, which we formalize in related work (Xu and Pistor 2003) is the following: Deterrence is said to work effectively if the level of expected punishment is sufficiently high (Becker 1968). The Becker model is based on an implicit assumption that law is complete and that individuals refrain from carrying out harmful actions as long as the expected punishment is sufficiently high, because they know unambiguously the expected punishment for all possible harmful actions. Arguably, the problem of incomplete law is even more severe in transition economies than at the outset of financial market development in the West. When England's stock market soared in the nineteenth century during the railway mania, there were no securities laws or regulators that monitored the amount or type of information companies disclosed when issuing shares to the public. However, a highly developed contract and tort law was at hand. Although the principles of the law had been developed with different cases in mind, a sufficiently large body of case law was available to determine how these principles should be applied to the new securities fraud and misrepresentation of information cases. Moreover, courts had experience with handling matters of a commercial nature and with adapting law over time in response to new fact patterns. Although court enforcement ultimately proved to be insufficient for dealing with the problem of law enforcement in securities matters, courts nevertheless played an important role in advancing legal standards to deal with stock fraud schemes and imposing civil and criminal liability. Moreover, the legislature closely observed case law and readily intervened whenever it saw reasons to fill gaps left by the courts or to correct decisions made by them.

By contrast, Russia or China did not have much of a commercial law system at the outset of transition. China had dismantled its legal system in the late 1950s and virtually started from scratch after 1978 (Zheng 1988). Russia was left with socialist law from the past and basic reform legislation developed during the period of perestroika (Black et al. 1996; Pistor 1997). The entire body not only of corporate and securities, but also of contract, tort, and white-collar criminal law had to be developed anew. The pace of legal reform in transition economies has been remarkable. Most countries put the relevant laws on the books within a decade after the beginning of transition (Pistor et al. 2000).

However, enacting law on the books is only the first step in establishing an effective legal system. The incomplete law theory helps explain why this is the case. Because law is incomplete, its meaning and implication for a particular fact pattern cannot be easily derived from statutory law alone. Even when law is highly specific, new fact patterns raise new questions about how the law should be interpreted. Russian courts, for example, had to determine whether a legal provision that prohibits a director from transacting on behalf of the company he is representing with a company in which he holds a substantial stake, also applies when the director acquired the stake shortly after the transaction had been entered into. It is impossible to stipulate all the possible meanings and applications of the fiduciary duties a director or manager owes to the corporation. Any attempt to do so would leave key aspects unresolved. By using broad, ambiguous terms, lawmakers in essence invite law enforcers to give meaning to this provision when applying it to specific cases, or put differently, they allocate residual lawmaking powers to enforcement agents, that is, courts and/or regulators. Conversely, attempts to clearly articulate actions that are considered violations of the law invite strategies to circumvent the law and require future lawmaking to avoid major gaps in the law from developing. Given the pace of financial market development, the propensity for gaps to develop is high, which results in deterrence failure.

If law is incomplete neither individuals nor law enforcers can stipulate whether a particular action will fall within the scope of a law and will therefore face sanctions. To ensure compliance even with incomplete law, legal systems could increase the level of punishment. However, this might result in excessive punishment of harmless and potentially beneficial actions. Thus, law fails to deter optimally. Moreover, we suggest that the larger a financial market, the more serious the deterrence failure problem.[2] The reason is that for any given punishment level, when market value increases, the issuer's benefits from cheating also increase. To deter cheating the level of punishment would have to be increased. However, for any given incompleteness level of law, this would also increase the expected punishment of harmless actions. To avoid excessive punishment of such actions, the deterrence level is restrained.

The combination of highly incomplete law, low levels of punishment relative to the level of incompleteness, and high market values may result in deterrence failure. The more incomplete the law, the greater the likelihood that deterrence occurs even when financial markets are still small. Given the level of incomplete law in transition economies, they are likely to suffer deterrence failure at an earlier stage of financial market development than did countries with better-developed legal systems.

In order to address the deterrence failure problem it may be advisable to introduce regulators. Regulators can enforce law ex ante by enjoining actions that have the potential of causing harm; they can establish entry barriers and use them to screen companies prior to listing. The efficacy of these regulatory tools, however, depends crucially on the quality of company-specific information.[3] In transition economies, reliable company-specific information is difficult to obtain, and standard practices, such as disclosure of financial information, may be misleading. Financial information was created by translating existing accounts that followed socialist bookkeeping principles with no relation to market prices into accepted market-based accounts. Chinese balance sheets to this day have double entries: one for the value of company assets according to legal accounting principles, which may be legal, but do not present the intrinsic value of the firm and another with reevaluation estimates, which may be closer to the actual market value, but remain guesswork in an environment where markets for many assets remain underdeveloped. Similarly, it has been pointed out that in transition economies financial accounts often do not reflect company practices, in part because of tax avoidance issues, in part because companies are struggling with how to record old debt or barter transactions (Bailey 1995). The information problem is aggravated by the absence of reliable independent sources of information or experts.

In this environment, proactive law enforcement by regulators cannot be effective. Under a disclosure rule, a regulator would require an issuer to reveal a set of standardized information. It would then use this information to perform a "smell test" (Coffee 1999), that is, to determine whether the public issue can go forward, or whether additional information should be requested. Once the additional information is revealed, the regulator decides whether the company may or may not go forward with the issuance. If the information that is submitted is noisy or manipulated, the smell test and the final decision will have a large margin of error. To put it differently, in an environment where information is unreliable, a regulator lacks the necessary ingredient (reliable information) for effective proactive enforcement. The result is regulatory failure. Given the severity of the information problem, regulatory failure is likely to occur at a relatively early stage in financial market development. The result may be either the failure of markets to take off, or the collapse of a market after it has reached a critical threshold where the incentives to cheat outweigh the enforcement ability of existing institutions given the constraints of highly incomplete law and severe information problems.

Governing Financial Markets: The Experience of Russia and China

China and Russia embarked on policies designed to promote the development of financial markets in corporate securities in the early 1990s. There is evidence from China that already in the 1980s companies were searching for new ways to raise funds and many started to issue shares. Markets for shares sprung up spontaneously but were later regulated out of existence (Zhu 2000). In Russia, commodity markets spearheaded the development of financial markets in the late 1980s, but they began in earnest only with the dissemination of privatization vouchers in 1991 and with the trading of corporate shares subsequent to privatization (Frye 1997).

Although we acknowledge that factors other than law enforcement may have an impact on financial market development, research in recent years has pointed out the importance of law as a determinant of financial market development (La Porta et al. 1997). We generate several predictions from our theoretical analysis for the ability of these two transition economies to build effective governance structures for financial markets:

- Given high levels of incomplete law in transition economies, a court regime will not be effective in deterring securities fraud. Courts will therefore play only a minor role in law enforcement, at least during the initial phase of financial market development.
- Law enforcement by regulators is contingent on the quality of information regulators obtain from companies. Given the low quality of company information available from (former) state-owned companies in transition economies and the lack of a well-developed accounting and auditing profession, regulators will not be able to ensure effective law enforcement.
- In the absence of effective law enforcement, financial market development will suffer from deterrence as well as regulatory failure unless countries find ways to overcome the problem of incomplete and/or biased information.

The Case of Russia

We begin by describing Russia's experience with establishing governing structures for financial markets. Russia's experience fits the familiar pattern of law enforcement by courts *cum* regulators. Russia attempted to jump start financial market development by launching a mass privatization program in 1992, which created a nation of shareholders. All Russian citizens were given vouchers, which they could invest either directly or through an intermediary in the company of their choice. Over 15,000 companies were organized as open joint stock companies the shares of which were freely tradable (Boycko et al. 1995). It was hoped that the auction process would reveal company-specific information, as voucher investors could chose among different companies. This proved to be unsuccessful, however, because companies were not put on the auction block simultaneously. Moreover, investors from afar could obtain very little information about companies. Although the government used a standard formula to describe the companies' underlying assets, number of employees, and financial status, the information revealed little about the potential of the company to survive in a competitive market environment. Not surprisingly, most voucher investors invested locally, often in the firms that employed them. Financial intermediaries, such as voucher investment funds, also had little trust in the financial information they obtained from the companies and invested in bribing company officials for better information (Frydman et al. 1996).

Russia completed the mass privatization program in 1994. At that time, the commercial court system—the arbitrazh courts—was already functioning. The courts have handled securities disputes on a regular basis: 1,834 cases in 1997 and as many as 3,483 in 1999, and 2,403 in 2000. To be sure, these numbers include all disputes related to financial instruments and disputes involving corporate stock may only amount for a small fraction of these numbers. Nevertheless, the numbers do suggest that courts were functioning and issuing rulings on a fairly regular basis.

In November 1994, President Yeltsin established the Federal Commission for Securities Market Regulation (FCSM) by presidential decree. It took two more years for a comprehensive securities law to be adopted by the Russian parliament. This new law vested the FCSM with the right to oversee financial markets. Moreover, in 1996, Russia's first comprehensive corporate law was enacted. The corporate law was based on a draft written by leading American scholars in comparative corporate governance and draws heavily, though not exclusively, on US models (Black and Kraakman 1996). The two laws followed somewhat different strategies. The corporate law sought to strengthen shareholder rights but avoided allocating strong lawmaking and law enforcement powers to courts. This was based on the assessment that Russian courts were slow, incompetent, and even corrupt (ibid.). The drafters of the code attempted to circumvent courts by endowing shareholders with extensive self-enforcing rights, including extensive information and voting rights. This strategy was not successful, mostly because the so-called self-enforcing rights proved to be at best "self-help" rights, as shareholders were unable to enforce them against management. The Securities Law, by contrast, vested courts with the ultimate power to enforce the Securities Law. The newly created FCSM had the right to initiate enforcement procedures, but in order to impose fines or delist a company, it had to bring an action in court. This strategy can be interpreted as a response to the legacy of powerful state agents who were feared to undermine rather than support market developments in the post-socialist countries. Alternatively, it may reflect the ongoing power struggle between

President Yeltsin who had established the FCSM by decree and staffed it with his followers, on the one hand, and the Russian parliament (State Duma), which was more skeptical about Yeltsin's economic policies, on the other. In any case, the failure to endow the new regulator with independent enforcement powers undermined its efficacy.

In response to continuing enforcement problems, the law enforcement powers of the FCSM were expanded by a presidential decree in 1996. Finally, an overhaul of the FCSM's powers occurred in 1999 with the adoption of the Investor Protection Law, which took effect at the beginning of 2000.[4] The new law allows the FCSM to fine companies that fail to comply with the provisions of the Securities Law or the Investor Protection Law for an amount of up to 10,000 times the minimum monthly wage without having to go through the courts. Fines may be imposed for violating registration requirements, by, for example, failing to disclose relevant information or disseminating misleading information. The FCSM may delegate enforcement authority to its branch offices in different parts of the country.

As a result of these reforms, Russia today has a legal framework in place that resembles in many aspects US-style securities regulation. Prior to issuing shares to the public, companies need to register with the FCSM and disclose relevant company information. Failure to do so can be punished by a regulator that has the legal power to enjoin actions, to fine, and to initiate court enforcement procedures. In addition, the FCSM makes rules and implements regulations to adapt to a changing market environment. Information on enforcement activities also suggests that Russia has made some headway in establishing a reasonable legal framework for financial market development. In the first year after the enactment of the Investor Protection Law, the FCSM conducted 1,318 enforcement proceedings; in 2001 there were over 6,000.[5]

Still, despite remarkable progress in developing a legal framework that resembles in large parts those in developed market economies, as of now this system has not contributed much to financial market development. Russia's financial market collapsed in August 1998 as a result of the government's default on its loans. In 2002, Russia had once again become a star performer among emerging markets. However, these results can largely be attributed to rising oil prices. Indeed, as of 1999, 73 percent of Russia's total market capitalization was made up of companies in the oil, gas, and mining sectors, followed by utilities and telecommunications companies (IFC 2000). Moreover, there have been few initial public share offerings, suggesting that firms are not using equity markets for external funds, or conversely, that investors have little appetite for parting with their money given the uncertainties they face in obtaining a return on their investment. Finally, the stocks traded on Russian exchanges move overwhelmingly together. Morck et al. (2000) have observed that stocks in emerging markets tend to move together, whereas stocks of different firms in developed market economies move more independently from each other.

They suggest that the reason for this is the lack of firm-specific information. Using the co-movement of stock as an indicator for firm-specific information they find that countries range from co-movement of .03 in the United States to close to .6. In most cases, co-movement declined over time. In Russia, the level of co-movement was .28 in 1995, increased to .46 in 1998, and reached a level of .37 in 2000.[6] This suggests that the legal reforms have not enhanced the level of firm-specific information available to investors. Even leaving aside the data point for 1998, which is affected by the collapse of the financial market in that year, the level of co-movement in 2000 was higher than in 1995.

The Case of China

The Chinese case differs in several important ways from the Russian case. In China, the privatization of state-owned companies did not precede market development but may now come at the end of a ten-year process, which saw state-owned enterprises being listed on stock exchanges and parts of their shares being traded by individual investors. Roughly 60–70 percent of company shares remained in state hands, with only 30–40 percent issued to private investors. In November 2002, the State Council issued regulations that allow foreign investors to acquire stakes held by various state agencies in listed companies. Rather than developing institutions from scratch, China used existing bureaucracies as initial regulators and monitors of financial markets. Only gradually were these institutions replaced with a newly established securities regulator. Although China has also created a remarkably developed legal infrastructure for financial markets over the past ten years, the markets have been governed for most of this period by mechanisms that are not strictly law enforcement mechanisms and that we therefore call "beyond law enforcement." Most importantly, China used a decentralized selection procedure for identifying companies that were to be listed and used a quota system to give incentives to local agents to invest in the selection process.

Regarding the development of the legal infrastructure for financial markets, we observe a proliferation of agencies and rules intercepted by several attempts to streamline and centralize the regulatory infrastructure. The People's Bank of China (PBC) was designated as the key agent for financial market supervision in 1986 and retained this function officially until 1992. There is evidence that to this day, the PBC and its local branches take part in monitoring markets and ensuring law enforcement.[7] In addition, the office of the state auditor has continued to monitor state-owned enterprises, including those whose shares are traded on the exchange. At the regional level, the two major stock exchanges that emerged in 1990, Shanghai and Shenzhen, adopted listing rules and regulations. Over time, their powers were taken over by regulators at the central level. In fact, under the 1999 Securities Law, the stock exchanges seem to serve a function more akin to an agent of China's Securities Regulatory Commission (CSRC), which has emerged as the major financial market regulator.

In 1992, the State Council established the State Council Securities Commission (SCSC). The SCSC became an important body for developing policies for financial markets but did not become a full-blown regulator. This task was taken up by a second body created by the State Council in 1993, the CSRC. In 1998, the two agencies were merged into a single agency, the CSRC. The chairman of the CSRC is an ex officio member of the State Council. Thus, there is no attempt to create an independent regulatory body. The CSRC was given some lawmaking power, and it issued listing requirements as early as 1993. However, until the adoption of the Securities Law in 1999 and the strengthening of the CSRC through its merger with the SCSC, the State Council issued most of the path setting rules and policies that governed financial markets, including the 1993 regulations on the management of stock exchanges and securities fraud and the 1995 adoption of B-share regulations.

In 1994, China adopted the first company law at the national level. The law establishes detailed merit requirements for companies wishing to issue shares and to be listed at a stock exchange. A company must, among other things, show that it has operated profitably for at least three years; that it has issued shares to the public; that at least 25 percent of these are in the hands of the general public; and that its registered capital exceeds RMB 400 million. In addition, the company needs approval from the relevant securities' authority and the stock exchange, must use one of the specially licensed investment banks as an underwriter, and can choose only from among especially licensed law firms to help prepare the relevant work for share issuance and listing. In 1999, China's first comprehensive securities law was enacted. It does not refer directly to the CSRC, but to the State Council's "authorized unit," which is in charge of financial market supervision and which is generally interpreted to be the CSRC. The law vests this unit with primary functions of market regulation, but also allows it to delegate decisions, including admission to trading, to the exchanges. Under the law, the CSRC may issue implementing regulations and has made extensive use of this authority. In February 2000, the CSRC issued new regulations for stock offerings; in March it decreed that for new companies share issuance would be spread over a 24-month period; in the same month it established new guidelines for assessing the creditworthiness of underwriters.

Law enforcement activities by the institutions listed earlier have been rare when compared with Russia and in light of China's much greater financial market development. Administrative sanctions enforced by the CSRC may take several forms, ranging from informal rebukes to a formal ruling. Data are available only for the latter. Between 1997 and the end of 2001, the CSRS published 205 formal rulings, including 15 for market manipulation, 2 for the dissemination of wrongful information, 9 for insider trading, 39 for violation of disclosure rules, 3 for listing on stock exchanges outside the People's Republic of China without relevant approval, as well as for a number of violations related to the management of client accounts and the use of private accounts for speculating in shares (Pissler 2003). During this period there were more than 900 companies listed on Chinese stock exchanges on average, more than four times as many as in Russia.

Until recently, law suits in securities matters have been virtually absent in China. Neither corporate nor the Securities Law gives investors explicit standing in court. Attempts by investors and their lawyers to bring class action suits were frustrated by a Supreme Court Ruling in September 2001.[8] The opinion stated that courts did not have the competence to handle these cases at the time and that they would therefore not accept such cases. In January 2002, this ruling was modified by stating that in cases of companies issuing misleading information in a prospectus, a case may be heard by a court, provided that the CSRC has investigated the matter and effectively penalized the company.[9] Finally, in January 2003, the Supreme Court issued a new guiding opinion, in which it lays down in great detail the conditions for investor suits.[10] This decision has already triggered a new wave of litigation. However, how courts will handle these cases, and whether court enforcement will ultimately enhance the effectiveness of law enforcement remains to be seen. For the past ten years of China's remarkable financial market development, these formal enforcement mechanisms have not played an important role.

Looking only at the familiar framework for financial market regulation outlined earlier would therefore miss much of governance structure for the early period of financial market development in China. For a deeper understanding, one must take a look at measures beyond law enforcement. The most important governance structure for financial markets beyond law enforcement used in China is the decentralized process of selecting companies that could issue shares to the public combined with a quota system that created competition among the regions.[11] We do not claim that the system was designed for the purposes we describe, but we suggest that it has fulfilled important functions where standard law enforcement mechanisms failed as a result of highly incomplete law and lack of reliable standardized information. Under the quota system, Beijing allocated to different provinces and/or ministries a stated amount in renminbi, the country's currency, that companies owned by these agents could use for issuing shares to the public. There is little data available on how this process worked in practice; we rely on a detailed analysis of the early development of the Chinese capital market (Fang 1995) as well as on interviews with knowledgeable insiders. The total amount of capital made available to companies was apparently derived in consultation with the PBC. The bank sought to reduce lending to state-owned enterprises, and the amount by which it cut back its lending was replaced by options to raise equity funds. The distribution of these options—expressed in the value of renminbi allotted to different provinces and ministries—was the result of an intense internal bargaining process. Factors that were beneficial for a region were its size and economic importance, in particular past economic success, as well as the performance of companies that were already traded on the market.

Once the amount was set, it was up to the provincial government, in collaboration with the company's owners, including ministries, local branches of the PBC, and other state agents with a stake in the company, to identify the company for listing and nominate it. In this process, companies were frequently "repackaged." Valuable assets were separated by establishing a subsidiary and this subsidiary rather than the parent company would be nominated for listing (Oi and Walder 1999). Sometimes companies were merged, or assets from different companies were combined in a jointly owned entity that would then be put forward for listing. After the company was nominated by the province, the final decision was left to the CSRC. The CSRC frequently used delaying strategies rather than outright refusal in restricting access to the market. In taking such measures, the CSRC was influenced not only by characteristics of a particular company and/or province but also by concerns about the absorption capacity of the market.

The most important aspect of the quota system in our view is that it triggered a process of decentralized information gathering by knowledgeable agents of the system at a time when it was impossible to standardize the information that might be relevant for investors, and when intermediaries were not available to verify or certify this information. The selection process helped to unearth information about companies. It thereby improved the information basis for those who had to assess the future potential of companies and to give them access to the market. Because the system involved the participation of various state agents, it ensured that it was sufficiently contested to reveal critical information. The relevant company information for making such decisions was not primarily financial reports about past performances, as past performance was at best marginally based on market criteria. Instead, it involved a qualitative assessment of the company's assets and management potential—that is, information that cannot be easily standardized.

This positive interpretation of the quota system is contingent on the notion that provinces and ministries involved in the process of selecting companies had incentives to select better rather than worse companies. There is some evidence that the system worked to create such incentives. Substituting state credits with equity funds was not a guarantee that provinces and ministries would, in fact, invest in selecting viable companies for listing on the market. Indeed, provinces may have hoped to diversify the burden of loss-making companies, and thus may have preferred to bring their lemons to the market (Akerlof and Romer 1993). However, the fact that identifiable state agencies were involved in the process of selecting companies also implied that they could be held responsible for bad decisions. On several occasions, regional governments were pressured to "take care of their children" and bail out loss-making firms. Moreover, regional governors have increasingly come to see the performance of their regions as a stepping-stone in their own political career. This prospect could be seriously harmed, if one of "their" companies went under. Finally, failure by companies from a particular region or ministry could deprive that region or ministry of future allocations of equity quotas. In sum, the quota system instilled some measure of competition into the system, which created incentives for investing in the selection process of companies. We do not suggest that the system ensured that always the best companies were selected, but propose that it created disincentives for bringing the worst companies to the market and thereby considerably reduced the chances of creating a market for lemons.

In 2000, China announced that it would move away from the quota system and that when determining to list a company, the CSRC would rely increasingly on listing requirements established in the company law, its own listing requirements, and information available in financial data that were certified by especially licensed intermediaries. However, because there were still many companies in line, which had been approved but were not able to issue shares, the shadow of the quota system remained for some time after it had been officially abandoned.

The decentralized process of selecting companies without preestablished criteria and transparent sources of information is obviously vulnerable to corruption. The negotiations among various state agencies are nonpublic, and as such nontransparent, making monitoring difficult, if not impossible, and thereby reducing accountability. Apart from the minimum merit requirements established in the 1994 company law, which were effectively overruled by the quota system, clear criteria for selecting companies were absent, creating the appearance that the selection process was a rather murky undertaking. In fact, news reports suggest that the process frequently disfavored companies with less political influence but perhaps higher merits. Still, the sanctions regions or ministries faced for bringing lemons to the market that would soon fail were sufficiently strong to avoid strategies that rested entirely on political bargains and not on economic merits. Moreover, each nomination of a company was the result of a multiparty bargain, which implied that the various parties kept an eye on how many private benefits their counterparts sought to extract from the bargain.

Russia and China Compared

On any standard measure of stock market performance, including the number of listed companies, market capitalization, and market turnover as a measure of liquidity (Levine and Zervos 1998), China outperforms Russia. As of January 2002, there were over 1,131 listed companies in China—up from 10 in 1990, and compared to 245 in Russia. Market capitalization as a percentage of GDP was at USD524 billion, whereas in Russia it stood at USD62.9 billion (Gao 2002). Market capitalization data have to be corrected for the stakes closely held by the state, which amounts to about 60 percent of total company shares. Note, however, that a similar correction would have to be made for Russian firms, as large blockholders, including state agencies or entities controlled by the state, control on average over 50 percent of companies that are listed on the market. Finally, few companies have attempted an initial public offering in Russia or pursued a secondary offering after they were listed. Distortions in both markets may cast doubt on the extent to which these comparisons are meaningful. However, even if we allow for substantial corrections, it is undeniable that in light of China's much lower level of GDP—an indicator that has proved to be a powerful predictor of stock market development (Claessens et al. 2003)—the country's strong financial market performance is quite remarkable.

The most striking feature of China's financial market development in light of the governance system described earlier is that the indicator for co-movements of stock has decreased significantly from .31 in 1993 to .22 in 2001 (Morck et al. 2000). Although this is still far above levels found in developed market economies, it is substantially lower than in Russia. This trend suggests that in China more firm-specific information is available to investors than in Russia.

Beyond Law Enforcement

We argue that China's superior performance in financial market development had taken place not despite, but because of, governance mechanisms beyond law enforcement. In this section, we tie the empirical analysis into our theoretical framework and seek to explain why what may appear to be interventionist measures, including quotas and merit rules, may be beneficial in an environment characterized by highly incomplete law and severe information problems. We use a stylized analysis of quotas, merit rules, and combination of quotas and merit rules to make our point.

In an environment characterized by information problems, too many companies with too little information may be entering the market at the same time. Establishing quotas to control market entry may help to contain that problem. An example of the use of quotas to control a new market is the creation of only 15 investment funds in the Polish privatization program, as compared to the over 400 funds that mushroomed in Russia and the Czech Republic in a market-driven process (Coffee 1999), which made it virtually impossible for regulators to enforce even the little regulation they had.

Simple entry barriers in the form of quotas, however, do not discriminate between viable firms and lemons. This difficulty may be overcome by adding merit requirements, that is, substantive conditions a company must meet to be admitted to the market. Merit rules are based on the presumption that the conditions stipulated are indeed indicative of a company's worth. They have been criticized because lawmakers or regulators may not have sufficient information to identify such indicators. This critique, however, presumes that investors have other sources of information. If they do not, then merit requirements, as crude as they are, may signal that companies are meeting some very basic conditions (such as profit making for the last several years) and thereby enhance investors' confidence.

The Chinese quota system goes substantially beyond a combined quota/merit rule. As discussed earlier, China did not simply impose a nationwide quota, but allocated sub-quotas to different regions. Quotas could remain unused, be reduced, or reallocated to different regions. In order to ensure that a province would have future access to stock markets as a potential source of funds for its companies, it had to be reasonably sure that these companies would perform. This required additional information gathering from company insiders. The process has been less transparent than a pure quota/merit system might have been. However, it fostered the collection of insider information that would have escaped simple merit rules.

The success of this system in China during the early phases of stock market development does not imply that it would be superior to a disclosure system in the long term. Nor does it mean that it should be taken as a simple recipe for developing financial markets elsewhere. The quality of the information in terms of the investment prospects a particular company offered depended heavily on effective checks and balances to guard against misuse. We suggest that competition among regions and ministries and the possible bailout sanction have gone some way in ensuring that relevant state agents invested in the selection of more rather than less viable firms. However, the system has not been flawless, nor is it necessarily sustainable. There is evidence that once companies have made it to the market, the assets they represent are substituted for different assets in takeover transactions that resemble the acquisition of moribund chartered corporations in England at the time of the South Sea Bubble (Davies 1997). This process obviously undermines an elaborate information system that rests heavily on the identity of the corporation that is screened prior to listing with the one that is ultimately traded. Other parts of the system create moral hazard problems. Most importantly, the fact that regions were forced to bail out their companies undermined the incentives for managers to perform at a level that would avoid failure and created disincentives for investors to invest in assets that would generate positive returns. In fact, available evidence suggests that when companies come close to insolvency, their share prices increase. This suggests that the insurance function state ownership provides works fairly well, but also raises the specter of moral hazard problems in hardening the budget constraint for state-owned enterprises.

Yet, the system is not beyond reform. As mentioned, the quota system has already been phased out. Moreover, after several flawed attempts by the state to sell additional shares to the market, which were met by heavy selling and price declines, the latest attempt to reduce state ownership has taken the form of selling blocks to foreign investors. Whether China will successfully manage the transition from a financial market that depends heavily on state agents in selecting and insuring companies to one where market forces will have greater force remains yet to be seen. The comparison with the Russian case, however, suggests that there is no shortcut to complex markets and that law enforcement mechanisms that have become standard in developed market economies may be dysfunctional when the task is to create markets and to govern this initial phase of market creation.

Conclusion and Policy Recommendations

In this chapter, we have analyzed the development of governance structures for financial markets in transition economies, using China and Russia as examples. We argued that even in developed market economies with well-developed legal systems, law enforcement in a sector that is as rapidly changing as financial markets are, is not an easy task. Socioeconomic and technological change renders laws that are designed to deter harmful actions highly incomplete. In order to ensure effective law enforcement, the legal system must allocate the right to adapt, interpret, and enforce the law to agents that are best capable of handling this task. We propose that when law is highly incomplete and harmful actions may cause substantial damages, allocating LMLEP to proactive law enforcers, such as regulators, may be superior to leaving it with courts that enforce the law only reactively. This result is based on the assumption that regulators have access to reliable information about companies, which means that accounting information is meaningful and can be verified by market watchdog institutions as well as law enforcement agents.

In transition economies, law is even more incomplete than in developed market economies, as most laws have only recently been enacted, and law-making and law enforcement agencies lack the experience to apply and interpret this law to a variety of newly emerging cases. Moreover, market watchdog institutions are lacking and reliable information is scarce. We suggest that under those conditions, imitating the practices of developed economies, such as simply shifting law enforcement from courts to regulators, is not sufficient. In the absence of reliable information, a regulatory regime may fail to enhance social welfare, and may instead result in regulatory failure, triggering a collapse of financial markets. We conclude that standard mechanisms of law enforcement may not work effectively during the early period of market development.

The diagnosis of these problems and the acknowledgment of the likely failure of standard recipes do not immediately translate into positive policy recommendations. What should be clear from our analysis, however, is that transition economies cannot simply rely on either courts or regulatory law enforcement. The incentives to cheat are simply too great as highly incomplete law and severe information problems render law enforcement by courts and regulators ineffective. In order to avoid deterrence and regulatory failure, transition economies should move beyond law enforcement. This implies greater involvement of state actors in selecting companies and setting conditions for companies to access the market, which raises concerns about possible misuse of these powers. Any transfer of additional power to government agents should therefore be accompanied by governance mechanisms that minimize the misuse of power and that create incentives for state agents to make decisions that maximize social welfare, not their own personal interests.

We suggest that China has devised a system that accommodates most of these concerns. The decentralized selection process of companies, which relied heavily on state agents with insider information has revealed more critical company information than would otherwise be available. At the same time, the quota system and the likely repercussions state agents faced for making bad decisions created incentives for these agents to invest in the selection process and avoid a race to the bottom. A major drawback of the system is that it relied on continuous state ownership. Only this gave state agents access to company information and ensured that they aligned their interests with those of the companies. Yet, state ownership has created its own moral hazard problems. The ultimate success or failure of the Chinese strategy will therefore depend on whether a transition from dominant state ownership to dominant private ownership can be engineered without major disruptions in financial market development. Yet, the official cancellation of the quota system, the continuous development of merit and disclosure rules, and more recently, the enactment of legislation that allows foreigners to buy shares in companies give hope that the system is already reforming itself.

Whether Russia would have been able to follow a similar strategy is questionable. Certainly after most major companies had been privatized—a measure that was designed to cut the umbilical cord between state agents and enterprises—the China model was no longer an option. Yet, Russia could have used rigid merit requirements to select companies for listing. Instead, Russia based its regulatory system primarily on disclosure. Even the stock exchanges shied away from merit-based listing standards as they feared that companies would move to different exchanges if they introduced entry requirements in the form of merit rules. Given the lack of reliable company information, a disclosure system could not work effectively in Russia. The FCSM has finally realized this and introduced listing requirements, which are applicable to all exchanges in 2002.

A more general lesson of our analysis is that whatever may have emerged as "best practice" in developed market economies, may be dysfunctional in an environment with very different characteristics. Even if the medium to long-term goal is to converge on such practice, at the outset of reforms other means may have to be pursued to initiate market development. This is likely to imply greater involvement by state agents, which in turn requires governance institutions that minimize the abuse of such power. The Chinese example suggests that a combination of collective decision-making and competition between different decision-making units may control these costs to some extent. By contrast, the Western model of powerful state agents with strong decision-making powers subject only to judicial review may be difficult to implement when courts are not very effective and a culture of law abidance has not been developed.

A further policy implication of this analysis is that the success of economic reforms depends on the ability of systems to respond effectively to new challenges that arise and to change and adapt the system over time. In China, this process of experimentation, trial and error, has been the hallmark of economic reforms over the past 30 years. In this process, Chinese state agents have learned the art of adaptation and responsiveness to change. In Russia, by contrast, the attempt to shift the economy and economic institutions rapidly to a market-based economy along Western models has preempted a process of gradual adaptation and change and cut short the learning process that goes along with it. The result has been a system that is dysfunctional because initial conditions in Russia were incompatible with the model chosen for financial market development, and because the process of institution building neglected the need for future self-correction of the system.

Notes

* The authors would like to thank Han Li, Daniel Magida, and Katherine Wilhelm for excellent research assistance. Financial support from the Milton Handler Faculty Research Fellow Fund is greatefully acknowledged by Katharina Pistor.
1. In Xu and Pistor (2003) we develop a formal game theoretical model with four players: a lawmaker, a law enforcer (either a court or regulator), a share issuer, and an investor. The game has two periods and models the impact of lawmaking and law enforcement by courts or regulators on the propensity of share issuers to take actions that may result in damages to investors. There is information asymmetry between the share issuer and the other players. The share issuer has incentives to cheat, which may result in losses suffered by the investor. The law is designed to punish cheating. We show that when law is complete at equilibrium law enforcement by courts achieves the first best, that is, law will effectively deter. This is consistent with the model developed by Becker (1968). However, when law is incomplete, at equilibrium, deterrence failure occurs. The comparative statics of the model shows that the more incomplete the law, the more serious the deterrence failure.
2. In our formal model (Xu and Pistor 2003), we demonstrate the trade-off between courts and regulators using simulation analysis to show that when the market has reached a certain threshold, the incentives of the investor to cheat are sufficiently large to result in deterrence failure. The higher the level of incompleteness of the law, the earlier this threshold is reached, and the earlier a market crash occurs as a result of deterrence failure.
3. In our formal model, a regulator may enjoin an action temporarily and request additional information before making a final decision as to whether the issuing of shares may go forward or not. The information obtained upon request is critical for making the right decision. In the absence of reliable information, a regulator may either enjoin potentially beneficial actions or fail to enjoin those that are likely to cause harm. For details, see Xu and Pistor 2003.
4. Law No. 46 on the Protection of Investors Rights of March 1999.
5. Information published in various issues of the official gazette of the Russian Supreme Arbitrazh Court.
6. These data have been kindly made available by Bernard Yeung.
7. In fact, according to the Law of the People's Republic of China on the People's Bank of China passed on March 18, 1995, one of the functions of the bank is the supervision of financial markets. On several occasions, the PBC has participated in the promulgation of sanctions by the CSRC against violators of financial market regulation.
8. People's Supreme Court Notice on the Temporary Suspension on the Hearing of Securities Related Civil Compensation Cases of September 21, 2001.

9. Decisions of China's Supreme Court of January 15, 2002.
10. Decision of January 10, 2003.
11. Other means, including the retention of large blocks of shares by the state are more problematic for reasons further explained later.

References

Akerlof, George A. 1970. The Market for "Lemons": Quality Uncertainty and the Market Mechanism. *Quarterly Journal of Economics* 84: 488–500.

Akerlof, George A. and Paul M. Romer. 1993. *Looting: The Economic Underworld of Bankruptcy for Profit.* Washington DC: Brookings Papers on Economic Activity No. 2.

Bailey, Michael. 1995. Accounting in Transition in the Transitional Economy. *The European Accounting Review* 4: 595–623.

Becker, Gary S. 1968. Crime and Punishment: An Economic Approach. *Journal of Political Economy* 76: 169–217.

Black, Bernard and Reinier Kraakman. 1996. A Self-enforcing Model of Corporate Law. *Harvard Law Review* 109: 1911–82.

Black, Bernard, Reinier Kraakman, and Jonathan Hay. 1996. Corporate Law from Scratch. In R. Frydman, C.W. Gray, and A. Rapaczynski (eds.). *Corporate Governance in Eastern Europe and Russia*, pp. 245–302. Budapest: Central European University Press.

Boycko, Maxim, Andrei Shleifer, and Robert Vishny. 1995. *Privatizing Russia.* Cambridge MA: MIT Press.

Claessens, Stijn, Daniela Klingebiel, and Sergio L. Schmukler. 2003. The Future of Stock Exchanges: Determinants and Prospects. *European Business Organization Law Review* 3: 403–38.

Coffee, Jack C. Jr. 1999. Privatization and Corporate Governance: The Lessons from Securities Market Failure. *Journal of Corporation Law* 25: 1–39.

Davies, Paul L. 1997. *Gower's Principles of Modern Company Law.* London: Sweet Maxwell.

Fang, Liufang. 1995. China's Corporatization Experiment. *Duke Journal of Comparative and International Law* 5: 149–269.

Frydman, Roman, Katharina Pistor, and Andrzej Rapaczynski. 1996. Investing in Insider-dominated Firms: A Study of Russian Voucher Privatization Funds. In R. Frydman, C.W. Gray, and A. Rapaczynski (eds.). *Corporate Governance in Eastern Europe and Russia*, pp. 182–241. Budapest: Central European University Press.

Frye, Timothy. 1997. Contracting in the Shadow of the State: Private Arbitration Commissions in Russia. In J.D. Sachs and K. Pistor (eds.). *The Rule of Law and Economic Reform in Russia*, pp. 123–38. Boulder CO: Westview Press.

Gao, Sheldon. 2002. *China Stock Market in a Global Perspective.* Dow Jones Indexes.

IFC. 2000. *Emerging Stock Markets Factbook.* Washington DC: IFC.

La Porta, Rafael, Florencio Lopez-de-Silanes, Andrei Shleifer, and Robert W. Vishny. 1997. Legal Determinants of External Finance. *Journal of Finance* 52: 1131–50.

Levine, Ross and Sara Zervos. 1998. Stock Markets, Banks, and Economic Growth. *American Economic Review* 88: 537–58.

McKinnon, Ronald I. 1973. *Money and Capital in Economic Development.* Washington DC: Brookings Institution.

Morck, Randall, Bernard Yeung, and Wayne Yu. 2000. The Information Content of Stock Markets: Why do Emerging Markets Have Synchronous Stock Price Movements? *Journal of Financial Economics* 59: 215–60.

Oi, Jean C. and Andrew G. Walder (eds.). 1999. *Property Rights and Economic Reform in China.* Stanford CA: Stanford University Press.

Pissler, Knut Benjamin. 2003. *Chinesisches Kapitalmarktrecht.* Ph.D. thesis, University of Hamburg.

Pistor, Katharina. 1997. Company Law and Corporate Governance in Russia. In J.D. Sachs and K. Pistor (eds.). *The Rule of Law and Economic Reform in Russia*, pp. 165–87. Boulder CO: Westview Press.

Pistor, Katharina, Martin Raiser, and Stanislav Gelfer. 2000. Law and Finance in Transition Economies. *The Economics of Transition* 8: 325–68.

Pistor, Katharina and Chenggang Xu. 2003. Incomplete Law. *New York University Journal of International Law and Politics* vol. 35.
Polinsky, Mitchell and Steven Shavell. 2000. The Economic Theory of Public Enforcement of Law. *Journal of Economic Literature* 38: 45–76.
Stigler, George J. 1970. The Optimal Enforcement of Laws. *Journal of Political Economy* 78: 526–36.
Xu, Chenggang and Katharina Pistor. 2003. *Law Enforcement under Incomplete Law*. Columbia Law and Economics Working Paper Series 222. Available at ssrn.com (#396141).
Zheng, Henry R. 1988. *China's Civil and Commercial Law*. Singapore and UK: Butterworths.
Zhu, Sanzhu. 2000. *Securities Regulation in China*. Ardsley NY: Transnational Publishers Inc.

PART III

Trust, Cooperation, and Success

CHAPTER TEN

The Emergence of Trust Networks under Uncertainty: The Case of Transitional Economies—Insights from Social Psychological Research

KAREN S. COOK, ERIC R.W. RICE, AND ALEXANDRA GERBASI

Introduction

When uncertainty and risk are associated with economic and social transactions, relatively closed trust networks often emerge to facilitate various types of informal cooperation. In Russia, for example, "blat" is an extensive form of informal exchange that emerged to provide scarce resources and services or favors (Ledeneva 1998; Lomnitz 1988). Moving from a social system in which the dominant mode of interaction is closed groups or networks to more open networks, such as those required to support the transition to a market economy and democratic institutions, is likely to be difficult. Our main claim is that uncertainty and risk (such as that created by corruption and dishonesty) lead to the formation of trust networks that are narrow and closed. One disadvantage of such closed networks of exchange is that they limit access to opportunities outside the network.

Reputation systems and third-party mediators (or guarantors) emerge under certain conditions to facilitate the move from closed trust networks, often involving only family members and close associates, to more open networks such as those required for the operation of market economies[1] involving transactions with strangers, but these systems may also be quite difficult to establish under conditions of corruption and dishonesty. We draw on experimental research on exchange networks to offer insights into these network processes and discuss examples of these processes based on evidence from survey and field research in the context of the transitions that have been occurring in Eastern Europe and Russia. Several traditions of work are relevant including sociological experiments on social exchange relations and networks as well as psychological and, more recently, economic experiments on cooperation and trust.[2]

Under conditions of uncertainty, trust networks emerge to provide a more secure transaction environment, especially when there is no legal enforcement of contracts or when the goods and services exchanged cannot be well handled with explicit contracts. Under high uncertainty and high risk (i.e., risk of loss), transactions are likely to occur primarily among parties who know each other well and form relatively closed associations or groups (e.g., families or informal membership associations), in which the group boundaries are clear and membership is easily determined (e.g., it is easy to detect who is in and who is out of the group). Insiders are included in trades, and outsiders are excluded. Optimum conditions of trade rarely exist under these conditions. Corruption and a high potential for exploitation in the larger society may lead to such closed-association systems of trade. As is well-known in purely economic exchange, a major difficulty with a quasi-closed system of trade is that it restricts the market for both "buyers" and "sellers." Under lower threats of exploitation and levels of corruption, closed-association trade may give way to the formation of rudimentary reputation systems that enable individuals to trade across membership boundaries and to establish indirect network ties to facilitate a broader range of exchanges (cf. Yamagishi 2002). These systems may emerge as transitional phases in the move toward more open networks of exchange.

First, we review the experimental research on commitment between exchange partners under uncertainty. Then we examine the experimental work on the emergence of trust networks.

Commitment in Networks of Exchange

Research on exchange systems in sociology began with the work of George Homans (1974), Peter Blau (1964), and Richard Emerson (1972a,b), among others. It provides insights into the types of economic exchanges that are embedded in social relations and networks. Exchange theory investigates a variety of types of exchange (Molm and Cook 1995). In a dyadic, restricted exchange two parties engage in the exchange of valued goods or services for mutual benefit (see also Blau 1964 and Ekeh 1974). Restricted refers to the fact that the exchange is limited to the dyad. Emerson (1972b) expanded the work on restricted exchange to focus on the linkages between connected sets of exchange relations. Two exchange relations for Emerson were viewed as connected to the extent that exchange in one relation affected the frequency or level of exchange in the other relation. Two exchange relations A:B and B:C are positively connected at B in an A–B–C network if exchange in one relation increases the probability or frequency of exchange in the other relation. The connection is negative if exchange in one relation decreases the frequency or probability of exchange in the other relation. Connected exchange relations form networks of exchange, which may include different types of connections (i.e., mixed networks include both positive and negative connections).

Recent research by Molm et al. (2000) differentiates two forms of exchange: negotiated and reciprocal, dyadic exchange. Classical exchange theorists (such as Blau 1964) proposed that trust is more likely to develop between partners when exchange is "reciprocal," that is, it occurs without explicit negotiations or binding agreements (cf. Macaulay 1963). Under uncertainty and risk, exchange partners have greater opportunity to demonstrate their trustworthiness by acts of reciprocal giving in the absence of negotiated agreements. Molm et al. (2000: 1398) demonstrate that reciprocal exchanges produce higher levels of trust and stronger feelings of affective attachment and/or commitment than do negotiated exchanges. The initial act of giving in a reciprocal exchange acts as a "signal" of the actor's trustworthiness to the recipient and creates the foundation for reciprocity of exchange and eventually trust. The behavioral commitments that form also reduce the inequality in the exchange, and the feelings of commitment that result are dependent upon this reduction in inequality as well as the signaling of trustworthiness. In an interesting paradox, Molm claims that these findings indicate that the mechanisms that were created to reduce risk in transactions (negotiations and strictly binding agreements) have the "unintended consequence of reducing trust in the relationship" because trust is not required if the agreements are binding. This conclusion, however, is based on the fact that in an experimental setting the experimenter serves as the "contract enforcer" and subjects are not allowed to renege on their commitments (but see Rice 2002).

Under environmental uncertainty and conditions of high potential risk (as could be created by corruption and widespread dishonesty) exchange systems are more likely to be set up as negotiated exchanges than as reciprocal exchanges which require more confidence and trust. Molm's findings regarding differences in perceived trustworthiness of one's partners under negotiated and reciprocal exchange regimes, suggest that a "Catch 22" exists. Molm et al. (2000) report that one's most frequent exchange partner is rated as trustworthier under reciprocal exchange than under negotiated exchange. The investigators reason that reciprocal exchange creates more uncertainty (since it is not negotiated), and thus when it is successful and one's initial "gift" of a service or valuable resource (to initiate an exchange) is reciprocated, then a more reliable signal has been offered that one is a trustworthy partner. Negotiated exchange does not provide an opportunity for such a signal—unless the exchange can be reneged on as in Rice's (2002) experimental condition, referred to later as the "nonbinding" exchange condition.

The focus of most recent research within social exchange theory on the concept of commitment has linked commitment to social uncertainty. Cook and Emerson define the degree of uncertainty as "the subjective probability of concluding a satisfactory transaction with any partner" (1984: 13). They found that greater uncertainty led to higher levels of commitment with particular exchange partners. Commitment between exchange partners reduces the uncertainty of finding a partner for trade and insures a higher frequency of exchange. Commitment, as defined by Cook and Emerson (1978), is behavioral. It refers to the decision to continue to exchange with particular partners to the exclusion of alternatives that might be more profitable. Behavioral commitment creates relatively enduring exchange relations (rather than spot markets). Although affective commitment might emerge as a result of such ongoing exchange, it is treated as a separate factor to be explained. Here we use the term commitment to imply behavioral commitment (not affective commitment). Behavioral commitment implies an ongoing exchange relation that typically provides information about the relative trustworthiness of the partners to the exchange. High levels of trustworthiness are assumed to facilitate the emergence of a trust relation. Trust networks are connected exchange relations formed in this manner. Networks of exchange are most likely to become trust networks under conditions of risk.

Social uncertainty can also be created by the risk of suffering from the opportunistic acts of one's exchange partners (Kollock 1994; Rice 2002; Yamagishi et al. 1998). Opportunism can involve the risk of exploitation. (Exploitation is hard to block in networks of exchange unless the networks become closed and those who cheat can be excluded from further interactions with those in the network.) Social uncertainty, created by the risk of exploitation, has also been shown to promote commitment. Kollock (1994), Rice (2002), and Yamagishi et al. (1998) examined behavioral commitments in environments that allow actors to cheat one another in their exchanges. Securing commitments to specific relations is often the most viable solution to the problem of uncertainty in these environments. If actors within a given opportunity structure prove themselves to be trustworthy exchange partners, continued exchange with those partners provides a safe haven from opportunistic exchangers. Such commitments, however, have the drawback of incurring sizeable opportunity costs in the form of exchange opportunities foregone in favor of the relative safety of committed relations (Yamagishi and Yamagishi 1994). This is one of the main dilemmas facing individuals in settings in which untrustworthy behavior is common or where opportunism and corruption of some sort is the norm. Moreover, if the social equilibrium consists of relatively closed trust networks, it may be difficult to break out of this pattern of exchange to generate a more open network of exchange among relative strangers. These trust networks among close kin or ethnic group members may actually serve to reduce trust in outsiders or make it difficult to create since transactions occur rarely across group boundaries (Rose-Ackerman 2001a: 436).

In Kollock's (1994) study connecting opportunistic uncertainty and commitment, actors exchanged in two different environments. In one environment (low uncertainty) the true value of the goods being exchanged was known, while in the other (high uncertainty) environment the true value of goods was withheld until the end of the negotiations. He found that actors had a greater tendency to form commitments in the higher uncertainty environment. Moreover, actors were willing to forgo potentially more profitable exchanges with untested partners in favor of continuing to transact with known partners who have demonstrated their trustworthiness in previous transactions (i.e., they did not misrepresent the value of their goods).

Yamagishi et al. (1998) further explored the connections between uncertainty and commitment. In their experiment, actors are faced with the decision of remaining with a given partner or entering a pool of unknown potential partners. They employed several modifications of this basic design, but in each instance the expected value of exchange outside the existing relation was higher than the returns from the current relation. They found that actors were willing to incur sizeable opportunity costs to reduce the risks associated with opportunism. Moreover, they found that uncertainty in either the form of an uncertain probability of loss or an unknown size of loss was able to promote commitments between exchange partners.

In both the Kollock (1994) and Yamagishi et al. (1998) studies, exchange occurs among actors in environments that allow for opportunism, but in which actors are guaranteed to find an exchange partner on every round. In Rice's (2002) experiment actors exchange in two different environments: one that allows actors to renege on their negotiated exchange rates (high uncertainty) and one where negotiations are binding (low uncertainty). Exchange, however, also occurs within two network structures that vary in the degree of power inequality—a complete network in which all actors can always find a transaction partner, and a T-shaped network, where one actor connecting three others at the center has greater access to alternatives for trade than those on the periphery of the network. Uncertainty promoted commitment in the complete network (power-balanced), but not in the T-shaped network (a monopoly structure with maximum power inequality). Commitments, he argued, are more viable solutions to uncertainty in networks in which power differences are minimal (see also Cook and Emerson 1978; Lawler and Yoon 1998). In networks that include a large power difference among the actors, the structural pull away from commitment to explore alternatives is sufficiently intense as to undermine the propensity to form commitments. Power is determined in such structures by access to alternatives. Giving up alternatives reduces power.

Whereas Kollock and Yamagishi and his collaborators suggested that actors would incur opportunity costs to avoid potentially opportunistic partners, Rice (2002) suggests that such tendencies can be muted by power inequality in the network structure. This finding is consistent with a number of studies in which the effects of power inequalities on the formation of commitments have been investigated (see also Cook and Emerson 1978, 1984; Lawler and Yoon 1996; Molm et al. 2000). It is generally the case that behavioral commitment is inversely related to the level of the power inequality in the network. Thus, commitment is higher among power equals than among power unequals, all other things being equal. Commitment is more common in horizontal than in vertical relationships.

Rice (2002) explores other effects of commitment in exchange networks. In particular, he investigates how commitment affects the distribution of resources across relations and within networks as a whole. He argues that commitments, when they occur, will reduce the use of power in unequal power networks, resulting in a more egalitarian distribution of resources across positions in a network. In networks where power between actors is unequal, power-advantaged actors have relatively better opportunities for exchange than their power-disadvantaged partners. These superior alternatives are the basis of the power-advantaged actor's power. If, as uncertainty increases, power-advantaged actors form commitments with power-disadvantaged actors, they erode the very base of their power. Forming a commitment entails ignoring potential opportunities. Alternative relations are the basis of structural power and as these relations atrophy, the use of power and the unequal distribution of resources will be reduced. For this reason increasing power inequality tends to lower the propensity for commitment even under uncertainty. With increased risk of loss, however, even power-advantaged actors seek committed partners for exchange.

Research results on exchange under uncertainty thus indicate a strong tendency for actors to incur opportunity costs by forming commitments to achieve the relative safety or certainty of ongoing exchange with proven trustworthy partners (Kollock 1994; Rice 2002; Yamagishi et al. 1998). In addition to these opportunity costs, Rice (2002) argues that commitments may also have unintended negative consequences at the macro level of exchange. Actors tend to invest less heavily in their exchange relations under higher levels of uncertainty. Moreover, acts of defection in exchange, although producing individual gain, result in a collective loss, an outcome common in prisoner's dilemma games. Both processes reduce the overall collective gains to exchange in the network as a whole. So although there is a socially positive aspect to uncertainty, in so far as commitments may increase feelings of solidarity (e.g., Lawler and Yoon 1998) and resources are exchanged more equally across relations (Rice 2002), there is the attendant drawback of reduced aggregate levels of exchange, productivity, and efficiency.

As Powell and Smith-Doerr put it, "ties that bind may also turn into ties that blind. When repeat trading becomes extensive it can turn inward, leading to parochialism or inertia" (1994: 392). Marsden (1983) points out that networks may restrict access because they structure the flow of goods, resources, and information, sometimes in less than optimal ways. Two examples provided by Powell and Smith-Doerr (1994: 392) of the potential negative effects of network arrangements involving repeat trading include Powell's (1985) study in which the "ossification of an editor's networks" is defined as the major factor in the decline of the list of products available from the publishing house. The second example they provide concerns the Swiss watch industry that became locked into a particular production network that created inertia and made it vulnerable and unresponsive to the digital technology revolution (Glasmeier 1991, as cited in Powell and Smith-Doerr 1994). Henry Farrell (2004) studied the Italian packaging tool industry, where concentration in the industry limited the contact between suppliers and end-producers in ways that were counterproductive. Concentration limited the alternatives for suppliers, and they become vulnerable to exploitation by end-producers. A committed relation formed between one particular supplier and end-producer further constraining the market and placing the financial security of the supplier under the control of one specific end-producer. In a contrasting case study of French machine producers, Farrell indicates how long-term commitments were avoided as the end-producers strove to keep suppliers from depending too heavily on them. The French producers, though powerful in the network, refrain from long-term commitments and maintain conditions that support market competition for access to suppliers. Hence, they are responsive to changing economic factors.

Commitments can also have unintended consequences. As Mizruchi and Stearns (2001) discovered in their analysis of the use of social networks to complete deals between commercial bankers and their corporate customers. They hypothesize that high uncertainty leads bankers to rely on colleagues with whom they have strong ties for advice and for support of their deals. Their findings reveal that the tendency of bankers to rely on their approval networks and on those they trust leads them to be less successful in closing deals. This lower success rate in closing deals is an unintended consequence of "purposive action." Uncertainty, Mizruchi and Stearns argue, creates "conditions that trigger a desire for the familiar, and bankers respond to this by turning to those with whom they are close" (667). They do this even when seeking advice from a broader range of contacts (perhaps less trusted) might make them more successful in the long run (especially with complex deals).

Under some conditions, then, networks can constrain the ability of the actors involved to adapt to rapid economic or environmental change. We explore some of these conditions in environments that are in flux, politically, socially, and environmentally including the dramatic cases of economic transition in Eastern Europe and elsewhere.

Uncertainty and the Emergence of Trust Networks for Services

During major economic or political transitions, trust networks can emerge as a result of commitment formation between exchange partners under conditions of uncertainty. Uncertainty can result from the general lack of institutional support (and backing) for contracts and for enforcement of the terms of trade, but also from corruption or the potential for exploitation that goes undetected or even unpunished.

Illegal forms of behavior also result in risk and uncertainty and can lead to the formation of similar trust networks. This is the type of trust built up in closed associations such as the Mafia (Gambetta 1993), which are highly exclusionary networks. In the Mafia, the network includes only those who are members of the association, and strong norms exist that determine the nature of acceptable behavior as well as the rules of trade. Only insiders can participate; outsiders are excluded from the perquisites of "membership." Where governments have failed or where general institutions are corrupt, alternative organizations like the Mafia may take over the economic arena and subsequently make it difficult to establish general market mechanisms. In such a situation, risk and uncertainty for those outside the organization may remain high because it is in the interest of the Mafia to mediate economic transactions through its "trust networks." Creating mechanisms to break down the control of the Mafia may be very difficult.

Trust networks can emerge to support corruption as well as to support economic and social exchange under conditions of uncertainty. Corrupt networks are embedded in social structure just as other markets are (Cartier-Bresson 1997). In a discussion of corruption networks and illegal social exchange, Cartier-Bresson argues that in purely economic exchanges corruption arises in the limited dealing of impersonal agents who do not know each other. In such cases, exploitation can occur, and there is uncertainty about the resulting prices and the outcome of the exchange. In social exchanges, corruption can be organized and regular because the parties are likely to have repeat dealings through social networks. It is this organization of corruption by social networks that, Cartier-Bresson argues, enables "a real institutionalization of procedures" and the persistence of this type of "embedded" corruption (466). In his view, the regularization of corruption through networks can lead to its normalization. Illicit activities become commonplace and thus are often left unchallenged.

Networks can promote corruption or they can involve other kinds of illegal activities. In an interesting case study, Carol Heimer (2001) studies the trust network that emerged during the early sixties to help women who needed access to abortion services that were illegal at the time. Before the 1973 US Supreme Court decision that legalized abortion, a Chicago-based feminist abortion service referred to as "Jane" provided help to about 11,000 women. The trust networks built by this informal organization also served to protect the identities of the physicians who provided these services. The risk was high for both parties, because the women's health was at stake and the physicians' license to practice and, much more recently, their lives were at stake. Two features of the situation were critical. First, the clients were vulnerable. The services they needed could not be obtained on the open market (or in appropriate organizations) because the service was not legal and normal information channels did not provide information on the reputations of the medical providers. Second, it was in the interest of the practitioners to establish trust relations with the clients because the stakes were high if they were caught performing illegal abortions. Of course, the network provided information not only on availability of the service, but also on its quality. In this way, one could assume that incompetent practitioners had been eliminated from the network (though this was clearly not always the case because many women died as a result of receiving an abortion during this time period). This reputational information was collected and provided as a critical service to those who needed it by this third party organization, "Jane," committed ideologically to women's rights in the area of fertility decisions.

Under some circumstances, trust networks emerge for the provision of a broad range of services such as health care. These networks often fill the void left by institutions (or simply fill the information void even when institutions work fairly well). In addition to networks used to obtain care, side payments can be required to get high-quality services in certain situations. Hungary is an example (Kornai 1996). Rose-Ackerman (2001a), among others, comments on the medical arena as an area in which corruption exists in some of the post-socialist societies—along with university admissions in Poland and Slovakia and customs officials in a number of countries (see also Miller et al. 2001). Rose-Ackerman examines general issues of trust and honesty in the post-socialist societies. The kinds of benefits that are obtained from contacts and bribes, she suggests, are an important topic for further research given that there are rather large differences across countries in the perceived incidence of corruption. The system of side-payments for medical care, for example, is maintained in some countries both by professionals who seek bribes and by clients who pay them in order to obtain individualized benefits or better service. This leads to what Rose-Ackerman calls a "self-sustaining system of corruption" (2001a: 424). People pay the extra payments because others do. What they continue to do is based to a large extent on what they think others are doing. Public opinion, Rose-Ackerman notes, is against corruption, but the system is maintained at the level of individual behavior because individuals benefit from the system even though it may be collectively irrational (and even against collective opinion).

Commitment and the Formation of Trust Networks under Uncertainty: The Transition in Russia

Exchanges are often "embedded" in networks of ongoing social relations. Uzzi (1996) argues that embeddedness has profound behavioral consequences, affecting the shape of exchange relations and the success of economic ventures. "A key behavioral consequence of embeddedness is that it becomes separate from the narrow economic goals that originally constituted the exchange and generates outcomes that are independent of the narrow economic interest of the relationship" (681). In related experimental research Lawler and Yoon (1996, 1998) and Lawler et al. (2000) discuss experimental results demonstrating that as exchange relations emerge, actors develop feelings of relational cohesion directed toward the ongoing exchange relation. These feelings of cohesion result in behavior which extends beyond the "economic" interests of the relationship, such as gift-giving, forming new joint ventures across old ties, and remaining in a relationship despite the presence of new, potentially more profitable partnerships. Although these are clearly positive aspects of these commitment relations, there is also a downside when these relations become "locked-in" and limit the range of exchange relations or the exploration of new opportunities.

Studies have begun to document the relationship between uncertainty and the emergence of trust-based networks especially in transitional economies. Guseva and Rona-Tas (2001) compare the credit-card markets of post-Soviet Russia and the United States. They are concerned with how credit lenders in each country manage the uncertainties of lending. In the United States, they argue, credit lending is a highly rationalized process that converts the uncertainty of defaulting debtors to manageable risk. Lenders take advantage of highly routinized systems of scoring potential debtors, through the use of credit histories and other easily accessed personal information. This system allows creditors in the United States to be open to any individuals who meet these impersonal criteria.

In Russia, creditors must reduce uncertainties through personal ties and commitments. Defaulting is an enormous problem in Russia, aggravated by the fact that credit information such as that used by American lenders has, until quite recently, been unavailable. To overcome these uncertainties Russian banks seeking to establish credit-card markets must use and stretch existing personal ties. Loan officers make idiosyncratic decisions about potential debtors, based largely on connections to the bank, or known customers of the bank. In this way, defaulting debtors cannot easily disappear, as they can be tracked through these ties.

Viewed through the lens of recent theorizing on the connections between uncertainty and commitments, these different strategies seem quite reasonable. As discussed earlier, exchange theorists have repeatedly shown that as uncertainty increases, commitment to specific relations likewise increases (Kollock 1994; Rice 2002; Cook and Emerson 1984; Yamagishi et al. 1998). In the case of credit-card markets, it is clear that the United States presents an environment of relatively low uncertainty, compared to the high levels of uncertainty present in Russia. Exchange theory argues, therefore, that commitments will be greater in Russia, which is exactly the case. Lending is facilitated by existing commitments to the banks or the bank's known customers.

Rice (2002) argues that network structure will intervene in the process of commitment formation. This insight suggests that sociologists ought to ask how different networks of potential debtors and lenders in Russia affect the use of commitments to procure credit. Rice also argues that uncertainty, while promoting commitment, simultaneously reduces the overall level of exchange in networks. This is another outcome observed in the Russian credit-card market, but one that is largely ignored by Guseva and Rona-Tas (2001). It is this aspect of the problem that is addressed to some extent by Radaev (2002) on the emergence of reputation systems in Russia. Finally, Yamagishi and his collaborators (1998) argue that uncertainty can stem from either the probability of loss or the size of loss. Another question that should be raised in this context is how the size of loss, and not just the potential for loss, relates to the behaviors observed in the Russian versus the American credit-card markets.

Exchange theory tends to focus on commitments as an outcome, not as a social mechanism. In the case of the Russian credit-card market, existing commitments provide a mechanism through which network structures are expanded and changed. This raises the issue of how interpersonal commitments may, in turn, create opportunities for network expansion and/or reduction. Russian banks, for example, expand their trust networks by issuing credit cards to families and friends of top bank executives (see also Ledeneva 1998). As Guseva and Rona-Tas note: "Here the borrower-creditor relationship is intermingled with close social bonds that serve as an additional guarantee and a channel of information" (2001: 638). The social bond serves as a "bond" to reduce the risk of unrepaid credit. Despite the fact that trust networks in which credit can be extended allow economic transactions beyond direct exchanges, there is a limit to the extent to which such networks will allow for movement to free trade. In fact, they may serve to hinder the development of institutions that might serve as the basis for free trade (that is, trade among strangers—what Guseva and Rona-Tas view as the US credit market).

Another way in which trust networks can be expanded to enlarge the number of those in the market, according to Guseva and Rona-Tas, is to stretch the network by extending credit to those indirectly tied to one another. "Trust is transitive," they argue. However, because this extends the risk involved, it is not used as a strategy beyond one-degree of separation. A bank employee reveals the unwritten rule of credit extension: "there should not be more than one person separating a bank official from an applicant" (Guseva and Rona-Tas 2001: 639). In the end, person-to-person interviews are often used in Russia to determine whether to grant credit to an applicant. This requires the interviewer to develop the "art" of assessment of the trustworthiness of the other. These security officers who grant or deny credit are described by Guseva and Rona-Tas as lie detectors: "We have to stare the applicants intently in the eyes, trying to guess whether they are telling the truth and whether they should be issued a card" (p. 639). While applicants may attempt to feign such trustworthiness and honesty, research by Frank et al. (1993) suggests that humans have evolved fairly good mechanisms for detecting signals of cheating and dishonesty. Bacharach and Gambetta (2001) argue that signal detection is the second-order problem of trust: can we trust the signals of trustworthiness? As a kind of insurance against this risk banks often use the networks of trust in which the applicants are embedded for security purposes as well as for contact information should the applicant default. In the United States, this is done through the provision of the names of "credit references" on the application. Applicants usually list a friend, coworker, or family member. In addition to using friends or co-workers for credit references, DiMaggio and Louch (1998) find that consumers most often use their social connections or social networks for particular kinds of consumer transactions such as for service contracts especially when there is greater uncertainty regarding the quality of a product or service.

In his study of emerging markets for nonstate businesses in Russia, Radaev (2002) investigates the mechanisms and institutional arrangements that help actors cope with the uncertainty and opportunism common in such an environment. Two features of the situation are significant. Under uncertainty actors turn to interpersonal ties involving trust and greater certainty to produce some security in the context of high levels of opportunism. In documenting the uncertainty of business relations in Russia, Radaev's surveys indicated how important honesty and trustworthiness were to business partners. This result is driven by the fact that there are frequent infringements of business contracts creating high levels of uncertainty. Half of the respondents admitted that contract infringements were quite frequent in Russian business, in general, and a third of the respondents had had a high level of personal experience with such infringements. This degree of opportunism creates barriers to the formation of reciprocal trust relations. There is widespread distrust of newcomers to the market but established reliable partners are viewed as more trustworthy.

Another reason for the uncertainty is that the existing institutions lack credibility and legitimacy. The courts do not effectively manage dispute resolution, and existing institutions do not secure business contracts. Banks can default, even large ones assumed to be solvent. To cope with this fact the business community creates closed business networks with reputation systems that define insiders and outsiders. This system is based on information obtained from third parties, but more importantly on common face-to-face meetings between potential partners.

In a completely different environment, McMillan and Woodruff (1999b) find a similar process in the transition from a planned economy to a market-based economy in Vietnam. Here the market began as a result of small entrepreneurs using their ongoing relationships to secure agreements. These social relations take the place of the nonexistent contract law in what remains of the planned economy. Cheating is easy in Vietnam because of the lack of contract law and enforcement. According to McMillan and Woodruff, "What is striking about Vietnam is that the entrepreneur's incentive not to cheat a contract partner is not that the partner will sue but that he'll stop dealing altogether" (quoted in Buell 2000: 28). Hardin (2002) identifies this condition as the primary basis for trustworthiness.

Because the courts cannot be trusted to resolve legal disputes (see also Montinola 2004) they create their own reputational system promoted by gossip and meetings in teahouses where information is exchanged about the credibility of various trading partners. "They try to avoid disputes by checking their customers' financial backgrounds and personalities with others who have done business with them" (Buell 2000: 28). These informal exchanges, these investigators argue, create a business ethic that supports a rudimentary market. Here we see the transition between closed trust networks and the beginnings of a market economy through ties that are brokered in teahouses. Reputation systems are essential in the formation of credit information that can be used to extend beyond the reach of personal (and often closed) networks of exchange.

In a 1993 survey conducted by Radaev (2002) the emerging networks of entrepreneurs in Russia primarily included personal acquaintances (42 percent), friends and their relatives (23 percent), and relatives (17 percent). Only a small percentage (11 percent) of the business contacts in 1993 were new or relatively new acquaintances. More recently, however, there is a move away from affect-based relations and trust to reputation-based trust as the networks formed purely on the basis of acquaintance, kin ties, or friendship have tended to fall apart due to their inefficiency. The relatively closed business networks that have emerged to replace the older "familial" and friendship ties provide better information about the trustworthiness of the partners and their competence. Within exchange theory the formation of commitment under uncertainty and trust networks (see Cook and Hardin 2001) in the face of uncertainty provide theoretical support for the evidence provided by Radaev (2002) and others on the recent emergence of business networks in Russia. This argument is also consistent with Rice's (2002) argument that commitments can have negative aggregate level consequences for productivity and efficiency in exchange systems.

Research in the exchange theory tradition on topics such as trust, strategic action, commitment, and reputational networks all have potential applications in the analysis of the emergence of exchange networks in countries with transitional economies. Moving from closed groups to more open networks of trade mirrors some of the processes identified by Emerson (1972b) as important from an exchange perspective—contrasting group-level exchange systems (productive exchange in corporate groups) with network-level exchange. In addition, the return to the study of the significant differences between social processes (e.g., power, justice, and commitment) involved in different types of exchange—negotiated, reciprocal, and generalized exchange (Molm 1988, 1990; Molm et al. 1999) have the potential to provide new insights into a variety of emergent forms of exchange under different circumstances. For example, under uncertainty, negotiated, binding exchange may be more likely to emerge before reciprocal (most often, nonbinding) exchange begins to flourish, in part because it involves greater degrees of uncertainty. Reciprocal exchange, as Molm and her coauthors have documented, generally requires more trust because the terms of exchange are not simultaneously negotiated and opportunism is possible (Molm et al. 1999; 2000).

Transitions from Closed to Open Networks: Possible Solutions and Limitations

We have discussed factors that help explain the emergence of relatively closed trust networks under uncertainty, but the problem for transitional economies is to understand the nature of the changes that occur when societies shift from one type of economy to another (i.e., from a planned economy to a market economy). Relatively closed trade associations or closed trust networks may create problems for the shift to a market economy that requires open networks to facilitate trades among strangers. For example, consumer credit remains limited in the Russian economy primarily because there is no good way to secure these transactions until more general institutions are built up that can provide the kind of "insurance" that will make transactions with strangers involving loans and extensive credit possible. Without these institutions, or in the face of weak and unreliable institutions (not to mention untrustworthy institutions) markets are limited by the reach of actors' ties to one another because trust networks can provide the security for trade that cannot be offered by institutional safeguards. The social embeddedness of these more limited networks for the distribution of goods and services serves to facilitate exchange, but restricts the development of completely open markets of trade. Investment in particular social relations of assurance (as Yamagishi argues) can work to the detriment of the development of "generalized trust." His comparisons between the United States and Japan, in this respect, are telling (see also Cook et al. 2002; Yamagishi et al. 1998).

One key to the problem of trust and the transition from socialism identified by Rose-Ackerman (2001b) is that there may be a contest between the existing trust networks (based on what she terms reciprocal trust) that emerged as a coping mechanism under socialism and the necessary "trust in rules" or confidence in new institutions that will act in a fair and impartial manner. Personal links may undermine reform efforts, she concludes (p. 559). "Russians and Central and Eastern Europeans established dense networks of informal connections to cope with the difficulties of life under socialism and some of these practices have continued as ways of coping with the present (Ledeneva 1998; Rose 1999: 10). One question raised by the transition is whether the legacy of these informal connections is helping or hindering the process of institutionalizing democracy and the market" (Rose-Ackerman 2001a: 427).

In an interesting comparison between Russia and Central and Eastern Europe, Rose-Ackerman (2001b: 565) reports that initial research indicates that in the Central European economies more reliance is placed on the courts as arbiters in the case of contract failures than in the case of Russia.

This makes market deals among strangers possible at an acceptable level of risk. Reciprocal trust can then emerge among initial strangers in repeat transactions. In contrast, where there is less confidence in legal enforcement such as in Russia and in the Ukraine (where the courts are viewed as corrupt and open to bribes) "economic actors are reluctant to deal with outsiders." In this case, as Rose-Ackerman points out, "both buyers and sellers are locked into mutually reinforcing relationships that may limit disputes, but also limit competition and entry." The research question that is posed in this analysis is precisely when and under what conditions does reciprocal trust among close kin and friends undermine or enhance the establishment of "one-sided trust in the reliability of institutions." It requires insiders to interact with outsiders on the basis of standard norms of contractual obligations (ideally backed by law) as if they were members of the same "group." Whether this can be accomplished is an important question and one that goes to the heart of the matter in many countries undergoing a political/economic and major social transition.

The interesting paradox that has been revealed in some of the recent work on different forms of exchange and their implications for commitment and trust under uncertainty is that the very procedures that are put in place to make transactions more reliable and to increase confidence in the market may undermine the basis for trust. As Molm et al. conclude (2000: 1425), when the shadow of the future is short and exploitation is profitable then the risk inherent in reciprocal exchange may outweigh the benefits. In such situations what they call "assurance structures," which are mechanisms for creating negotiations that are binding and enforceable, may actually decrease trust—or at a minimum fail to provide the conditions for building trust.

In contrast, Molm et al. argue, that reciprocal trust relations may have a positive benefit if they lead to generalized trust relations. This is the central dilemma. They may lead to more general trust or may simply reinforce trust for those within the network created by reciprocal exchange relations. They claim that "through numerous experiences with specific others who behave in a trustworthy manner under conditions of risk, we may come to expect that others, with whom we have no direct experience, will also be worthy of our trust" (2000: 1425). However, this is an empirical question and in order to answer it we should vary the level of uncertainty and risk involved in the situation. Only then could we draw inferences about situations like those faced in transitional economies. Although it is agreed that an environment in which generalized trust is high (see Fukuyama 1995; Yamagishi and Yamagishi 1994) may result in advantages—since individuals and firms are able to explore new relations and take advantage of new opportunities in social, business, and political arenas—this depends centrally upon the nature and level of the risks involved. Only under certain conditions is it likely that the kind of particularized trust that emerges in trust networks will lead to trust of those outside one's direct experience (as well as indirect experience through reputations obtained from trustworthy contacts within the network) or to assessments of the generalized trustworthiness of strangers. This move is complex and may rely on the kinds of institutions that arise to manage defaulting.

In an interesting experimental study, Malhotra and Murnighan obtain results that support Molm et al.'s claims about the potential negative effects of the overuse of contracting on the emergence of trust in society. Contracts generally facilitate exchanges by limiting risk and uncertainty, and they make it possible for "risk-averse parties to create mutually beneficial relationships" (2002: 534). Formal structures such as binding contracts may limit the development of trust since the parties involved do not need to attribute trustworthiness to their partners if contracts are binding. Only if exchanges are secured by informal and nonbinding mechanisms of cooperation do they yield attributions of trustworthiness and thus lead to the emergence of trust relations. In this way trust and contracts may be substitutes rather than complementary mechanisms for managing transactions under uncertainty (Zucker 1986). The difficulty is that the fear of exploitation makes parties more comfortable if they have binding contracts. "The bottom line," Malhotra and Murnighan (2002: 556) claim, "is that the creation of confident expectations for the behavior of powerful others (people who are in a position to exploit vulnerability) requires tremendously careful action."

We have focused on uncertainty and its effects on the emergence of trust networks and subsequently the transitions from trust networks to open networks of exchange that move beyond direct personal bonds. We have not dealt explicitly with situations in which the level of distrust is so high that it is difficult to imagine how one would get to real markets. As Rose-Ackerman puts it, widespread distrust in institutions, as exists in Russia and some of the Eastern European countries, leads to a focus on interpersonal distrust. The only "counterweight here," she claims, "is the creation of exclusive trusting networks operating inside or outside the formal institutional framework" (2001a: 436). In situations of high levels of distrust, as we have indicated earlier, the move from these closed trust networks to open networks of trade may be difficult.

The move to reputation systems may be one of the intermediate steps that might work to extend the network. The information provided from the closed trust networks might then be useful in providing reputations that are credible because they could include both positive information about trustworthiness and negative information about defaulting behavior. This step might foster the extension of trade beyond the bounds of direct personal ties. A potential difficulty, however, is that if the distrust of outsiders is intense, the reputational system that evolves may simply reinforce the divide between those in the trust network and those outside of it, making any extension of trade across this divide difficult. This implies that beyond the nature of the reputational system that develops, as Yamagishi (2002) argues, the degree of distrust and its distribution across groups in the society is critical. An interesting aside here is that it may be precisely in this kind of situation that Putnam's panacea might work. Associations that cross-cut the major cleavages in the society, if they exist (perhaps in the form of sports teams or other interest-based clubs not derived from ethnic group identity), may serve to build bridges across this divide.

Another key factor is the proportion of potential cooperators in the society and, as Whitmeyer (2000) demonstrates, when that proportion is low, any reputational system that helps us locate the ones who are cooperative will be useful. Investigating the different paths from closed associations to open networks of trade would be a useful research project in the various countries now undergoing tremendous economic change. From Hungary and Poland to South Africa and Vietnam, the study of uncertainty and the emergence of trust networks as one possible path to open markets (or as a hindrance to the development of open markets) is an important next step in our research agenda. It will also be important to study experimentally the features of reputation systems that may help make open network trading feasible, especially in environments in which some cheating is likely to occur.

Third parties may be important intermediaries in the move from closed to open networks for trade and other business transactions. As in the case of Vietnam, discussed earlier, teahouses link individuals unknown to each other through indirect ties and the transfer of relevant information about trustworthiness. Or, as in the case of Russia, discussed by Radaev, rudimentary credit associations are beginning to emerge that facilitate face-to-face meetings in which reputations for trustworthiness can be transmitted in much the same way as in the Vietnamese teahouses. These informal modes of cooperation may have the externality of extending the credit available in segments of the society by providing information about the trustworthiness of those that can be indirectly linked in networks that extend beyond the trust networks that generally work on the basis of relatively direct ties.

Reputational systems are used to extend credit and make transactions possible that are unlikely without credible information about trustworthiness. In much the same way that rudimentary credit associations are emerging in Russia to "certify" customers as trustworthy, professional associations often emerge to "certify" the competence and trustworthiness of various professionals so that their clients or consumers (often unable to judge for themselves) can be assured that they will be treated appropriately. These associations can do more than certify, they may also regulate those who are members. They can sanction those who do not live up to the reputation of the profession and even exclude from membership those who violate the professional ethics or relevant codes of conduct. The full-fledged emergence of credit associations backed eventually by fiduciary and contract law might take this form in Russia and Eastern Europe. They would involve third-party accreditation and confidence that the information being provided was accurate. Whether any of these reputational mechanisms can work to "guarantee" trustworthiness and under what conditions they can succeed in extending the reach of trust networks to foster markets needs further empirical investigation. Without this step in a climate of dishonesty and exploitation, trust networks are likely to remain the dominant mode of exchange. Restricted network exchange, in this context, is one mechanism for avoiding the risk of entering and reentering the "market for lemons."

Notes

1. See Radaev 2002, on the move from affect-based trust to reputation-based trust networks.
2. Experiments in this tradition are typically conducted in laboratories with participants who are students. More recently, participants in some studies have been drawn from community groups and are randomly assigned to experimental conditions. Experimental research of this type has a long-standing tradition in psychology and social psychology. It has become more important in sociology, political science, and economics in the last two decades. A recent compilation of relevant research is the edited volume on experimental research on reciprocity and trust by Ostrom and Walker (2003). See especially the chapter by Cook and Cooper (2003).

References

Bacharach, Michael and Diego Gambetta. 2001. Trust in Signs. In K. S. Cook (ed.). *Trust in Society*, pp. 148–84. New York: Russell Sage Foundation.
Blau, Peter M. 1964. *Exchange and Power in Social Life*. New Brunswick NJ: Transaction Books.
Buell, Barbara. 2000. Business Deals Rely on Trust, Not Law. *Stanford Business* 68: 27–9.
Cartier-Bresson, Jean. 1997. Corruption Networks, Transaction Security, and Illegal Social Exchange. *Political Studies* 45: 463–76.
Cook, Karen S. and Robin M. Cooper. 2003. Experimental Studies of Cooperation, Trust and Social Exchange. In E. Ostrom and J. Walker (eds.). *Trust and Reciprocity: Interdisciplinary Lessons for Experimental Research*, pp. 209–44. New York: Russell Sage Foundation.
Cook, Karen S. and Richard M. Emerson. 1978. Power, Equity and Commitment in Exchange Networks. *American Sociological Review* 43: 721–39.
———. 1984. Exchange Networks and the Analysis of Complex Organizations. *Research in the Sociology of Organizations* 3: 1–30.
Cook, Karen S. and Russell Hardin. 2001. Norms of Cooperativeness and Networks of Trust. In M. Hechter and K-D. Opp (eds.). *Social Norms*, pp. 327–47. New York: Russell Sage Foundation.
Cook, Karen, Toshio Yamagishi, Coye Cheshire, Robin Cooper, Masafumi Matsuda, and Rie Mashima. 2002. Trust Building via Risk Taking: A Cross-societal Experiment. Manuscript.
DiMaggio, Paul and Hugh Louch. 1998. Socially Embedded Consumer Transactions: For What Kinds of Purchases Do People Most Often Use Networks. *American Sociological Review* 63: 619–37.
Ekeh, Peter. 1974. *Social Exchange Theory: The Two Traditions*. Cambridge MA: Harvard University Press.
Emerson, Richard. 1972a. Exchange Theory Part I: A Psychological Basis for Social Exchange. In J. Berger, M. Zelditch Jr., and B. Anderson (eds.). *Sociological Theories in Progress*, pp. 38–57. Boston: Houghton Mifflin.
———. 1972b. Exchange Theory, Part II: Exchange Relations and Networks. In J. Berger, M. Zelditch Jr., and B. Anderson (eds.). *Sociological Theories in Progress*, pp. 58–87. Boston: Houghton Mifflin.
Farrell, Henry. 2004. Trust, Distrust, and Power. In R. Hardin (ed.). *Distrust*. New York: Russell Sage Foundation.
Frank, Robert H., Thomas Gilovich, and Dennis T. Regan. 1993. The Evolution of One-shot Cooperation: An Experiment. *Ethology and Sociobiology* 14: 247–56.
Fukuyama, Francis. 1995. *Trust: The Social Virtues and the Creation of Prosperity*. New York: Simon and Schuster.
Gambetta, Diego. 1993. *The Sicilian Mafia*. Cambridge MA: Harvard University Press.
Glasmeier, Amy K. 1991. *The High-tech Potential: Economic Development in Rural America*. New Brunswick NJ: Center for Urban Policy Research.

Guseva, Alya and Akos Rona-Tas. 2001. Uncertainty, Risk, and Trust: Russian and American Credit Card Markets Compared. *American Sociological Review* 66: 623–46.
Hardin, Russell. 2002. *Trust and Trustworthiness*. New York: Russell Sage Foundation.
Heimer, Carol. 2001. Trust, Vulnerability, and Uncertainty. In K.S. Cook (ed.). *Trust in Society*, pp. 40–88. New York: Russell Sage Foundation.
Homans, George C. 1974. *Social Behavior and Its Elementary Forms*. New York: Harcourt, Brace and World.
Kollock, Peter. 1994. The Emergence of Exchange Structures: An Experimental Study of Uncertainty, Commitment, and Trust. *American Journal of Sociology* 100: 313–45.
Kornai, János. 1996. Paying the Bill for Goulash Communism: Hungarian Development and Macro Stabilization in a Political-economy Perspective. *Social Research* 63: 943–1040.
Lawler, Edward J. and Yoon, Jeongkoo. 1996. Commitment in Exchange Relations: Test of a Theory of Relational Cohesion. *American Sociological Review* 61: 89–108.
———. 1998. Network Structure and Emotion in Exchange Relations. *American Sociological Review* 63: 71–894.
Lawler, Edward J., Jeongkoo Yoon, and Shane R. Thye. 2000. Emotion and Group Cohesion in Productive Exchange. *American Journal of Sociology* 106: 616–57.
Ledeneva, Alena V. 1998. *Russia's Economy of Favours: Blat, Networking and Informal Exchange*. Cambridge UK: Cambridge University Press.
Lomnitz, Larissa Adler. 1988. Informal Exchange Networks in Formal Systems: A Theoretical Model. *American Anthropologist* 90: 42–55.
Macaulay, Stewart. 1963. Non-contractual Relations in Business: A Preliminary Study. *American Sociological Review* 28: 55–67.
Malhotra, Deepak and J. Keith Murnighan. 2002. The Effects of Contracts on Interpersonal Trust. *Administrative Science Quarterly* 47: 534–59.
Marsden, Peter V. 1983. Restricted Access in Networks and Models of Power. *American Journal of Sociology* 88: 686–717.
McMillan, John and Christopher Woodruff. 1999a. Interfirm Relationships and Informal Credit in Vietnam. *The Quarterly Journal of Economics* 114: 1285–320.
———. 1999b. Dispute Prevention Without Courts in Vietnam. *Journal of Law, Economics and Organizations* 15: 637–58.
Miller, William L., Åse B. Grødeland, and Tatyana Y. Koshechkina. 2001. A Model of Official's Perspectives on Accepting Gifts from Clients in a Post-communist Europe. *Political Studies* 49: 1–29.
Mizruchi, Mark S. and Linda Brewster Stearns. 2001. Getting Deals Done: The Use of Social Networks in Bank Decision-making. *American Sociological Review* 66: 647–71.
Molm, Linda. 1988. The Structure and Use of Power: A Comparison of Reward and Punishment Power. *Social Psychology Quarterly* 51: 108–22.
———. 1990. Structure, Action, and Outcomes: The Dynamics of Power in Social Exchange. *American Sociological Review* 55: 427–47.
Molm, Linda and Karen S. Cook. 1995. Social Exchange and Exchange Networks. In K.S. Cook, G.A. Fine, and J.S. House (eds.). *Sociological Perspectives on Social Psychology*, pp. 209–35. Boston: Allyn and Bacon.
Molm, Linda, Gretchen Peterson, and N. Takahashi. 1999. Power in Negotiated and Reciprocal Exchange. *American Sociological Review* 64: 876–90.
Molm, Linda, N. Takahashi, and Gretchen Peterson. 2000. Risk and Trust in Social Exchange: An Experimental Test of a Classical Proposition. *American Journal of Sociology* 105: 1396–427.
Montinola, Gabrielle. 2004. Corruption, Distrust and the Deterioration of the Rule of Law. In R. Hardin (ed.). *Distrust*. New York: Russell Sage Foundation.
Ostrom, Elinor and James Walker (eds.). 2003. *Trust and Reciprocity: Interdisciplinary Lessons for Experimental Research*. New York: Russell Sage Foundation.
Powell, Walter W. 1985. *Getting into Print: The Decision-making Process in Scholarly Publishing*. Chicago: University of Chicago Press.
Powell, Walter W. and Laurel Smith-Doerr. 1994. The Role of Networks in Economic Life. In N. Smelser and R. Swedberg (eds.). *The Handbook of Economic Sociology*, pp. 368–402. Princeton NJ: Princeton University Press.

Radaev, Vadim. 2002. Entrepreneurial Strategies and the Structure of Transaction Costs in Russian Business. *Problems of Economic Transition* 44: 57–84.

Rice, Eric R.W. 2002. The Effect of Social Uncertainty in Networks of Social Exchange. Ph.D. dissertation. Stanford CA: Stanford University.

Rose, Richard. 1999. *What Does Social Capital Add to Individual Welfare? An Empirical Analysis of Russia.* Studies in Public Policy No. 318. Center for the Study of Public Policy, University of Strathclyde, Glasgow.

Rose-Ackerman, Susan. 2001a. Trust and Honesty in Post-socialist Societies. *Kyklos* 54: 415–44.

———. 2001b. Trust, Honesty, and Corruption: Reflection on the State-building Process. *European Journal of Sociology* 52: 526–70.

Uzzi, Brian. 1996. The Sources and Consequences of Embeddedness for the Economic Performance of Organizations: The Network Effect. *American Sociological Review* 61: 674–98.

Whitmeyer, Joseph. 2000. Effects of Positive Reputation Systems. *Social Science Research* 29: 188–207.

Yamagishi, Toshio. 2002. The Role of Reputation in Open and Closed Societies: An Experimental Study of Internet Trade. Manuscript.

Yamagishi, Toshio, Karen S. Cook, and M. Watabe. 1998. Uncertainty, Trust and Commitment Formation in the United States and Japan. *American Journal of Sociology* 104: 165–94.

Yamagishi, Toshio and Midori Yamagishi. 1994. Trust and Commitment in the United States and Japan. *Motivation and Emotion* 18 (2): 129–66.

Zucker, Lynne G. 1986. Production of Trust: Institutional Sources of Economic Structure. In B.M. Staw and L.L. Cummings (eds.). *Research in Organizational Behavior* 8: 53–111.

CHAPTER ELEVEN

Blindness to Success: Social Psychological Objectives Along the Way to a Market Economy in Eastern Europe

GYÖRGY CSEPELI, ANTAL ÖRKÉNY,
MÁRIA SZÉKELYI, AND ILDIKÓ BARNA[*]

Introduction

This chapter explores moral and sociopsychological objectives important to the functioning of the market system in the new Eastern and Central European democracies. The aim is to analyze the new economic and social relations established by the Eastern European transition, especially how they differ from Western structures and how they have evolved during the transition period.

Understanding the economic and social processes in a developing market system calls for a psychological and value-oriented analysis of the actors in the system. The stability and efficiency of the market system is importantly determined by the legitimacy actors accord to the economic system and the confidence they display in it.

Two opposing concepts are central to our analysis: confidence and suspicion. Confidence means accepting and endorsing the way the social and economic system operates. Confidence is also a sociopsychological mechanism that can positively influence the social behavior of participants in the system and connect personal motives and beliefs with institutional and social goals. The converse of confidence is *suspicion*, where the relationship between individuals and society (or simply other people) is detached and questioned, and belief in the sense and success of their actions undermined (Festinger 1957). Confidence and suspicion appear as social phenomena tied to individuals. Confidence is a type of social capital[1] that is conducive to individual social success,[2] while suspicion hinders the accumulation of such capital. On a society level, confidence in the system is an ingredient of social integration, while lack of system-level confidence leads to social disintegration and delegitimation.

Confidence within society can be measured in relation (a) to the principles that underpin the system (b) to institutions, and (c) to specific actors and groups. If the analysis is focused on the economy, in contrast, confidence can mean acceptance or rejection of market rules, the judgment made of economic institutions, and the positive or negative attitudes displayed toward economic actors. However, it is misleading to separate the economy and society. The guiding principles of the economy also delineate rules of social integration; economic institutions interrelate with political and social ones, and groups of economic actors also represent social differences and inequalities. This definition points to the "embeddedness" of modern economic sociology, emphasizing that the actions of economic actors are influenced by cultural norms and the social capital manifest in network systems (Polanyi 1957; Granovetter and Swedberg 1992). "Modern economic sociology defines separately the cognitive, cultural, structural and political aspects of social embeddedness of social actions" (Zukin and DiMaggio 1990: 14–23), referring to the fact that it depends on the cognitive, cultural, socio-structural, and political factors of economic actions (Szántó 1994).

This study examines attitudes toward economic actors, but the findings are interpretable both at the system level and within wider social relations. Operationalizing attitudes toward economic actors is one way to examine attitudes toward the rich under market circumstances. Wealth is a manifestation of economic success in a market situation and exemplifies the extent of social inequalities. Public attitudes toward the rich are not independent of people's judgments of economic institutions or the guiding principles of the market economy.

The rich are observed keenly all over the world: people want to know who they are and how they came by their wealth. Such curiosity may simply be idle, but the sociological explanation is different. The rich personify success. Attitudes toward them say much about the economy itself and people's judgments of social relations.

Suspicion of the rich and successful belongs within a syndrome of economic and social lack of confidence. Furthermore, such suspicion can degenerate into envy and suspicion of any outstanding achievement. The benefits of undeserved achievement seem unjust. Analysis of envy emerges most strongly in dilemmas of distributive justice. A starting point for discussing the culture of envy in Eastern Europe might be Rawls' definition of it as "the propensity to view with hostility the greater good of others even though their being more fortunate than we are does not detract from our advantages. We envy persons whose situation is superior to ours, and we are willing to deprive them of their greater benefits even if it is necessary to give up something ourselves" (Rawls 1971: 532). Envy, he opines, derives from an experience of failure in competition that erodes self-respect and may engender social animosity.

Examining the role of confidence in the Eastern European transition entails asking whether people identify with the main operating rules of the new economic relations. How far do they accept success as legitimated and delineated by the market economy? How do they view those whose success and enrichment reflect the world of market forces? If suspicion dominates in this context, the legitimation of market rules and principles will be tightly constrained.

The collapse of state-socialist regimes in 1989–90 and the emergence of liberal democracies led to rapid development of a modern market economy in the early 1990s, but this was accompanied by exaggerated expectations. People thought an economic system based on market forces would rapidly improve their living and working conditions, all the more because the Iron Curtain had gone and the ideals embodied by Western countries suddenly seemed widely attainable. But as political, economic, and social reconstruction continued, it emerged that conversion to a market economy was accompanied by a deep, ubiquitous recession costing millions of jobs, cutting real wages, and eroding the purchasing power of pensions, benefits, and allowances. As the trough deepened, people accustomed to full employment and secure livelihoods understandably felt that the economic transition was a zero-sum game, in which enrichment and success for some came at the expense and through the failure of others. This explanatory scheme came at a useful time for losers in the transition, who could cushion their failure by pointing to the undeserved enrichment of others.

If envy is common, delegitimation of market rules and relations sets in, especially in the presence of what Rawls calls *generalized* envy. This differs from *particularized* envy derived from competition and felt by the defeated toward the successful (irrespective of status), for general envy is felt by all those in disadvantageous (low-status) situations. Those of low status envy the successful because they long for their wealth and better opportunities (Rawls 1971: 615). Adam Smith (1993) argues that the main source of envy is wealth manifested in the image of private ownership and inequalities based on it. The market transition in Eastern Europe brought radical privatization that compounded inequalities. The consequent cognitive discordance in the judgment of wealth and success is hardly surprising, especially when stable comparisons going back generations gave way, as judgment criteria for achievements and satisfaction, to comparisons with more fortunate contemporaries.[3] Those who contrast the success of others with their own lack of success easily succumb to envy, usually accompanied by a loss of self-confidence and self-respect and a humiliating feeling of neglect and hopelessness about personal chances.

A modern market economy calls for moral principles in whose absence economic and political institutions lack legitimacy. These may derive from the inner logic of interactions based on market exchanges (trustworthiness, reliability, good reputation, and so on) but they also have significance beyond the economy, in other spheres of society. Morally endorsed economic views rest upon values of justice, equity, and solidarity. Without such positive moral approval, the market economy will be adversely evaluated by many, tainted by assumptions of corruption, unscrupulousness, dishonesty, prodigality, and injustice.

The three dimensions (institutional and legal transformation, restructuring of resources, and cognitive changes) are closely related, but they can function separately as well. Ideally, all three interact harmoniously, so that what is legal is useful, good, and likeable as well, but in times of change, the relations between them are upset and market evaluations discordant.

Eric M. Uslaner distinguishes between strategic trust and moralistic trust. The first refers to mutual transactions and rests on predictions of others' behavior, while "moral trust is a belief that others share your fundamental moral values and therefore should be treated as you would wish to be treated by them" (Uslaner 2002: 18). According to Rawls, individual psychological factors such as envy or jealousy have no moral content, but once they begin to aggregate into collective effects, they can change into envy of a socially dangerous type (Rawls 1971: 615).

None of these dimensions can be neglected in studying the economic and social changes of the 1990s in Eastern Europe. Hitherto, more attention has been paid to the economic dimension and less to the moral and psychological factors affecting the new economic structure. This study goes a little way to redressing the balance. The public, after the collapse of state socialism in 1989–90, was shocked by the abruptness and depth of the transition and took shelter behind moral ideas thought to be safe. However, from that vantage point, the economic transition seemed even more repugnant. Looking at the transition in terms of justice, trustworthiness, and confidence, people discerned corruption, untrustworthiness, injustice, and undeserved enrichment by a new elite, whereas in most cases, nothing had really happened beyond the normal functioning of the market. The adverse feelings arose because the rapid changes had disturbed and confused people's social orientation. The changes were dramatic in quantity and quality. Although external (system-level) value premises and interpretation frames had changed, people's internal value premises did not accommodate this. Many tried to interpret the new reality through their accustomed value preferences. They were overcome by discordance and blindness to success and inadvertently delegitimated and denigrated those who succeeded in the economy, politics, and culture although cultural achievements were viewed with less suspicion than economic success (Csepeli and Örkény 1993). The people who saw themselves as losers by the transition were most incensed by these social differences. Attitudes to success and wealth, as a special case within the transition, were dominated by moral disapproval, so that presumptions of dishonor, dishonesty, and injustice took hold.

Everyday explanations of success and wealth are not value free. New light can be thrown on a phenomenon simply by using different attributions to explain its occurrence (Kelley 1967). One of the two courses open is to fail to acknowledge others' success or to devalue successful people. Observers explain success in terms of external, extra-personal causes that devalue it, or they even dispute that there has been success at all, by dismissing it as luck, connections, or inherited advantages. The other course is to explain success in terms of people's abilities and hard work, so that the successful are at the center of the explanation. This makes the success deserved, legitimate, and concordant with observers' values, even if the latter are not winners by the transition. The choice between the two courses does not depend on caprice. It usually relates to a "dominant ideology" (Abercrombie et al. 1990; Kluegel et al. 1995). Egalitarian, socialist ideologies normally stress external, nonpersonal attributions, while meritocratic, conservative, or liberal ideologies emphasize abilities and virtues.

The implicit ideological direction of the attributions depends on whether they appear as external or internal in relation to the successful (Weiner et al. 1972). With wealth and success, external attributions turn people into beneficiaries of external forces and privileges that put their achievements in a morally, psychologically, or even politically negative light. Such psychological techniques for devaluing the achievements of others can be described as envy (Schoeck 1966). If such "drops" of natural envy for others are aggregated and the same techniques of devaluation used to judge not only successful, wealthy persons, but also members of specific social categories (the nomenclature, the ruling class, the "Jews"), they become organized as identity-constructing factors into *ressentiments* (Szabó 1989).

As the transition progressed, the post-socialist countries became sociologically polarized by the delegitimation of success and wealth, which produced cognitive cleavages between success and failure, rich and poor. While the former moved toward a meritocratic concept of justice, the latter inclined to an egalitarian one.

Judgments of success in general and wealth in particular do not necessarily coincide. Data show that wealth is a greater source of discordance in post-socialist countries than success, because the latter is more elusive and less irritating. The resulting discordance will be referred to here as *social envy* and identified simply in relation to social distrust of wealth. A distinction is drawn between social envy and everyday envy targeted at personal acquaintances.

It is assumed that the efficiency of the transition from state socialism to a market economy depends on the confidence generated in the new economic rules. The stronger this becomes, the faster the counterproductive habits of the redistributive era (egalitarianism, authoritarianism, paternalism, acquired helplessness) can be expected to diminish. Residual suspicion, in contrast, will engender a discordant attitude toward success, upward social mobility, enrichment, and wealth. If it is found that envy has increased considerably in post-socialist countries in recent years, a better understanding of the anomic features of transition and economic change may be obtained by analyzing the culture of envy.

The Research Design

The analysis uses data from cross-national surveys on attitudes taken in 1991 and 1996.[4] These focused on attitudes toward and views about justice, a just society, and the principles of just distribution,[5] and touched, albeit indirectly, on the general lack of confidence and envy described in the previous section.

The 1991 survey used identical questionnaires in 13 countries, including liberal, market societies (the United Kingdom, the Netherlands, the United States, and West Germany just before the unification), and former socialist countries (East Germany, the Czech Republic, Hungary, Bulgaria, and Russia). Because the Eastern European countries were just beginning the process of transition in 1991, the survey was repeated in 1996 and changes in attitudes were examined. This was done in the five Eastern European countries only.

The analysis was done by regions, not countries. Bulgaria, Hungary, Russia, the Czech Republic, and East Germany represented Eastern Europe, while West Germany, the Netherlands, and the United Kingdom represented Western Europe. The United States was examined separately.

The main difficulty with cross-national research is that irrespective of social and cultural differences, identical questions have to be asked, to ensure accurate measurement of differences. This is still more important when measuring acceptance of an economic system. To discover what people think about the rich and the causes of their enrichment involves finding a context in which people's image of their disparate economic systems can be viewed. This common viewpoint was found in the mechanisms of success and judgments made of them. It was assumed that respondents socialized under market systems and under redistributive economic systems would still apply similar criteria to judging success and wealth, but the process of attribution would differ sharply.

Two parts of the questionnaire concerned possible modes of success and enrichment. The question about the mechanism of success was this: "Here are some factors which are sometimes considered important for having a high social standing. Please tell me how important you think each is for success in our society today." Respondents had to judge the importance of the various factors on a five-degree scale.[6] Four attributions were included: talent, hard work, good connections, and greater initial opportunity.

The question about the rich was, "In your view, how often is each of the following factors a reason why there are rich people in your country today?" Respondents could choose again from the alternatives given. The five factors were: talent, hard work, good connections, greater initial opportunity, and dishonesty.

The two groups of questions are closely connected. The means of success refer to mechanisms that allow people to ascend in society. The judgments made of the rich refer to those who have been able to achieve success through those mechanisms. One set of attributions is based on the individual's internal resources and reflects individual efforts, while the other emphasizes the role of external circumstances. These follow the theoretical premises outlined earlier.

Various ideological schemata were constructed to organize typical everyday narratives about success and enrichment in modern market economies and liberal civil societies. Narratives were organized either by an individualistic, meritocratic system of explanation, or by another kind based on external causation, that questioned the value of individual achievements.

The judgments are in themselves examples of different attribution patterns, but aggregating them in a logically consistent way helped produce a complex reconstruction of the everyday system of knowledge. For example, if the answers emphasizing hard work and talent are aggregated,[7] the aggregate measure becomes an index of the extent to which internal meritocratic resources are thought important.

The aggregation produced four new sets of measurements: for success and for wealth, and for the subjective importance of external, social causes and of internal, meritocratic causes. The stock of knowledge of achievement and success marked by these four variables and the combinations of the variables form the focus of this analysis.

Lack of confidence (suspicion) is defined here in terms of four concepts:

1. *General lack of confidence* indicates that external causation of success and enrichment is believed to be more important than internal causes. It is calculated as the sum of the five-point Likert-scale values for the importance of the four external causes, less the sum of the Likert-scale values for the importance of the four internal causes.[8] High index values mean that respondents rejected internal meritocratic attributions and emphasized the importance of external ones. In operationalizing general lack of confidence with variables measuring internal and external causation of success and wealth, the predominance of external over internal causes for both expressed feelings of discordance. Respondents assumed that initial advantages or good connections lay behind wealth and success, rather than hard work or outstanding qualities. The role of personal networks needs considering here. Theoretically, it can also be created by utilizing internal resources. It can be viewed as an indispensable path to achievements and success, in which case it represents a positive resource for individuals. However, connections may mean that people achieved their goals undeservedly and unfairly, which on a macro level translates into corruption, opaque personal interrelations, clientism, and paternalism. This dual meaning of personal network also appears in the judgment of success and riches. However, the findings show that personal connection can be defined here as the opposite of capital based on meritocratic values, because in Eastern Europe, it had a significant *negative* correlation with internal resources,[9] and in Western Europe, it had a closer connection to external causes than to internal resources.[10]
2. *Blindness to success* was measured by the difference between external and internal attributions for success. The variable was constructed by subtracting the variable for internal causation from the variable for external causation. High values mean that respondents explained success by external causes, making them "blind" to individual success.
3. *Suspicion of enrichment* implies animosity toward the rich. The measure is whether the respondent emphasizes the achievements of the rich or external (socioeconomic) circumstances. Again, the variable for internal

causation was subtracted from the variable for external causation of enrichment. High values mean that respondents emphasized external causes of enrichment.

4. Finally, *special envy* involves the assumption that envy is a mental, sociopsychological phenomenon—a latent attitude that can be measured by filtering out attitudes that disguise it. Both general lack of confidence and a negative attitude toward the rich were used. The initial theoretical assumption was that judgments about possible modes of success and about the success of the rich should correlate highly. Those who believe that individual merit and achievements determine success in life should also think they determine success of the rich. But if other factors play a role, the normative aspects of the judgments are replaced (or accompanied) by sociopsychological and psychological phenomena such as envy. Special envy represents the part of the general lack of confidence unexplained by attitude toward success (blindness to success). This residue is independent of normative presumptions. Whatever attitudes or sensations characterized such respondents, the result was a negative judgment of market relations. In the quite complicated method used to measure envy, it is assumed that general lack of confidence has two constituents: lack of confidence in the general rules of the system, and envy. Envy may occur in those with or without confidence in the economic system. (See the typology in figure 11.3). Ordinary Least Squares (OLS) regressions were used to evaluate the envy contained in general lack of confidence. Lack of confidence in the operational rules of the system was filtered out of the general lack of confidence. The residual lack of confidence was taken as a measure of envy that is necessarily independent of confidence in the system.[11]

Research Hypotheses

Our aim is to explore the relationship between the psychological phenomena mentioned, the social position of respondents and the changes in their lives caused by the market transition. To gauge the post-socialist specifics accurately, it is worth examining the different attitudes toward success in Eastern Europe and in the West (Western Europe and the United States). Did the development and consolidation of the market economy raise or lower the general lack of confidence and the envy in the East? To answer these questions we applied the following hypotheses:

Hypothesis 1. Opinions in the West are dominated by internal attributions connected to meritocratic ideologies, while external attributions are more important attributions for success and wealth in the East.

Hypothesis 2. The more market principles and rules for success are accepted, the more probable it will be that respondents would accept wealth (the rich). If a discrepancy could be seen between the explanations for success and for wealth, this implies ambivalence and animosity toward the operation of the market and a kind of legitimation deficit that could produce a sense of injustice, suspicion, and envy on an individual level.

Hypothesis 3. The objective status of individuals would be the most important explanatory dimension for discordance between beliefs in the causes of success and of wealth. It was assumed that the relationship between status and discordance would differ between West and East.

Hypothesis 4. It was assumed that the general lack of confidence and envy would be influenced by subjective status that indicated how respondents saw their position, in general and in relation to others. This could generate either satisfaction or dissatisfaction.

Hypothesis 5. Acceptance of the dominant meritocratic ideology would bring acceptance of the market system and a positive judgment of success and achievements based on it. In the East, where egalitarianism dominated ideologically for decades, this tendency would prevail less than in the West, where meritocratic ideology has been the basis for the evolution of civil society.

Hypothesis 6. As the market economy develops in Eastern Europe, meritocratic value preferences will become stronger and discordance in the judgment of economic success will decrease.

Hypothesis 7. Perceptions of wealth and poverty would reflect people's opinions about the degree of social inequality. Perceiving great inequalities might strengthen the desire for a drastic, aggressively egalitarian redistribution of income. This attitude would relate to the discordant feeling called social envy. However, economic and structural factors would not be the only explanations for support for the redistribution of income, which would also be influenced by sociopsychological factors such as envy.

Analysis

The analysis falls into three main parts. First, using 1991 data, we examine the extent to which people accept or reject various reasons for success and enrichment in Eastern and Western Europe and in the United States. We develop a typology based on these concepts. Next, we apply this logic to study the differences between 1991 and 1996 in Eastern Europe. Finally, models are constructed to explain the general lack of confidence and the persistence of envy. Some people would like to take retributive actions against those who have succeeded or who have become wealth. At the end of the paper we examine the roots of such feelings.

External and Internal Attributions for Success and Wealth in East and West in 1991

The 1991 survey data yielded an overall picture of respondents' opinions on the causes of success and wealth in East and West. Respondents were asked to judge the role of two pairs of attributions. *Talent* and *hard work* are internal causes, able to legitimate success and wealth. More initial opportunity and network connections are external causes that can delegitimate them. With wealth, dishonesty was added. This covers dishonesty of the

Table 11.1 Attributions of success and wealth in 1991 by regions (percentages of "often" and "very often" responses)

	Eastern Europe		Western Europe		USA	
	%	N	%	N	%	N
Attributions of wealth						
Talent	51.9	3,097	59.8	2,955	59.4	840
Hard work	40.2	2,401	56.3	2,783	66.0	933
Network	76.7	4,580	70.7	3,490	74.9	1,059
More opportunity to begin with	59.5	3,551	63.6	3,140	62.3	8,810
Dishonesty	64.8	3,865	30.2	1,494	42.8	605
Attributions of success						
Talent	83.0	4,954	93.2	4,604	92.5	1,308
Hard work	79.0	4,716	89.3	4,409	94.4	1,335
Network	74.5	4,445	85.6	4,228	81.7	1,155
More opportunity to begin with	42.5	2,539	73.3	3,621	72.9	1,031

person concerned or corruption and immorality in the system[12] and greatly contributes to a discordant judgment of market economy. Regional aggregate data appear in table 11.1.

The table shows that attributions for both success and wealth differed between East and West. Eastern respondents seemed more ambivalent about selecting any given explanation and more inclined to think that individual causes played a role in success. There were even bigger differences with wealth, where respondents in the East seemed much less inclined to attribute wealth to internal causes (especially *hard work*) than those in the West. A strikingly high proportion in the East thought that *dishonesty* was at least one cause of wealth.

Figure 11.1 shows the results of aggregating respondents' internal and external attributions, with a theoretical maximum of 5 and a theoretical minimum of 1.[13]

The figure shows that the inclination to give internal attributions increases steadily from East to West, which appears to confirm the first hypothesis. However, data on external causation does not verify the second part of that hypothesis. Success is significantly less frequently attributed to external causes in the East than in the West, while the proportion of "often" and "very often" answers for external attributions of wealth are almost the same. Table 11.1 seems to verify the claims that connections are seen in Western Europe as an external factor behind success and that individual effort played a big role alongside inherited conditions, so that social capital derived from both external and internal resources. This positive value content is apparent in the judgments of success. In the case of wealth, network connections had negative connotations in Western Europe as well, seen in the association between good connections and dishonesty and in the similar weights given to external causation of wealth in the East and the West.

The next stage of aggregation was to create measures of blindness to success and suspicion of wealth, with a theoretical maximum of +4 and a theoretical minimum of −4. Comparing theoretical maxima and minima, the calculated means do not seem very large, but the differences are highly significant (see figure 11.2).

The legitimation potential of success was high in all regions, but there was strong distrust of the rich. This seems to falsify the second hypothesis,

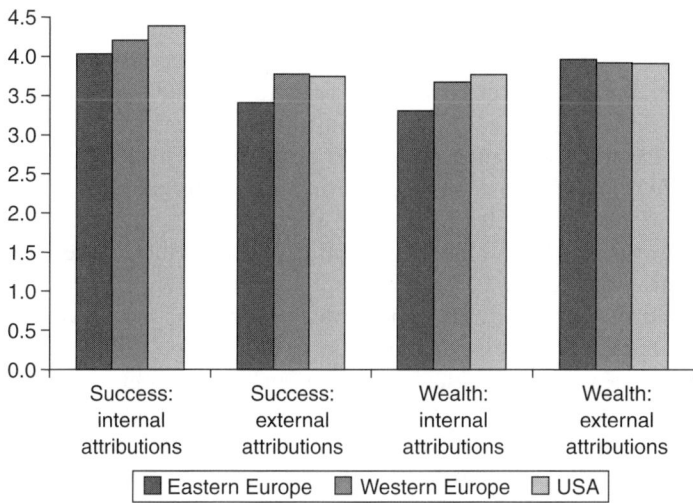

Figure 11.1 Attributions of success and wealth in 1991 (aggregated variables—means of five-degree scales)

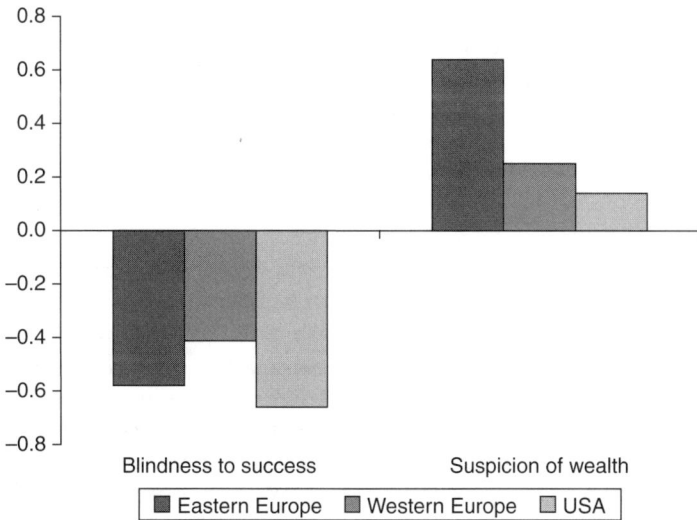

Figure 11.2 Suspicion of success and wealth (aggregated variables—means of scales)

as there was a discrepancy between the explanations of success and wealth, which might imply ambivalence and animosity toward the market. However, the results appear surprising at first sight. Blindness to success was less present in the East than in the West. Success was darkened most by adverse external factors in Western Europe, while in the United States, success-orientated values seemed to prevail. This difference probably derived from a traditionally stronger neoliberal concept of capitalism among Americans. In the East, tolerance of success disappeared when personified in the rich, of whom respondents show deep suspicion.

The analysis so far has explored the inner logic of the concepts, without considering the weights they represent in society. Measuring these requires a typology based on acceptance and rejection of the success and wealth attainable in a market economy. Rejection is defined as the differences between external and internal attributions. High positive values mean rejection, with respondents tending to emphasize external causes. Figure 11.3 shows four possible attitudes toward the market economy. Acceptance means legitimation and refusal rejection of meritocratic market rules.

The fifth hypothesis states that suspicion and envy were pervasive in Eastern Europe at the time of the transition. This conditioning should obviously have been less present among respondents in the West. The hypothesis goes on to say that endorsement of meritocracy, as the direct opposite of envy, should be commoner in the West. Acceptance of wealth accompanied by rejection of success is a deviant attitude that may be present to a moderate extent in East or West. Finally, there is a possible stance of withdrawal and exit from the "game," called here refusal.

Figure 11.4 presents a regional breakdown of the proportions of the four attitude types toward the market economy in 1991. East led West in social envy, while in approval of meritocracy, the case was the reverse. Both these observations support the hypothesis. Frequency of a deviant attitude did not differ significantly between regions. Interestingly, rejection of the market economy was least frequent in the United States and most frequent in Eastern Europe.

		Success	
		Acceptance	Refusal
Wealth	Acceptance	Meritocracy	Deviance
	Refusal	Envy	Rejection

Figure 11.3 Attitudes toward the market economy based on positive internal attribution patterns for success and wealth

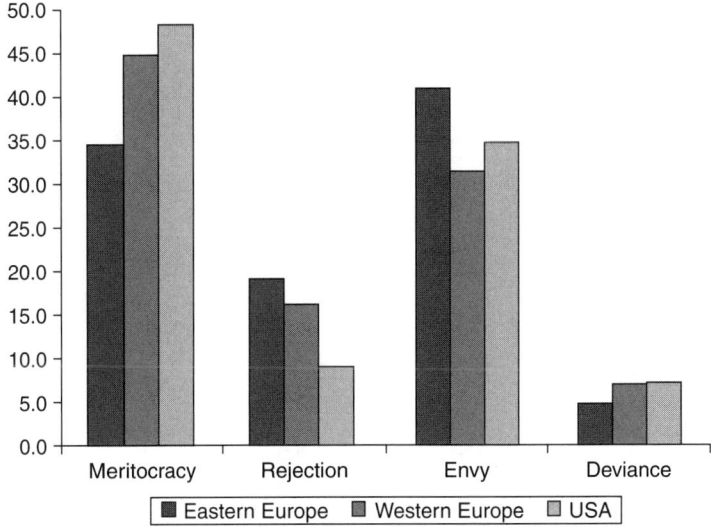

Figure 11.4 Percentages displaying attitude types toward the market economy in 1991, by regions

The Time Factor in Attitude Changes in Eastern Europe

Social judgments on the causes of success and wealth were reexamined in Eastern Europe five years later. Let us look first at changes in the importance attributed to the factors.

Table 11.2 shows that attitudes toward success and wealth were surprisingly stable despite radical changes undergone by the region in 1991-96. However, the importance attached to external factors, such as initial opportunity, dishonesty, and connections, increased in the judgment of success, although hard work also gained importance. In judging the rich, the importance of internal attributions (talent and hard work) remained about the same, but the subjective role of external factors (connections and initial opportunity) significantly strengthened.

Figure 11.5 presents the 1991–96 changes in the attribution of internal and external causes for success and wealth. The figure supports the startling conclusion that over the whole region, blindness to success increased much more than suspicion of wealth. The difference is relative, however, for by 1996, the public evaluation of success and wealth were increasingly adverse, while doubt about the meritocratic rules for individual success and economic success increased. This seems to falsify the sixth hypothesis of a strengthening commitment to meritocratic values in the region. (It does not necessarily mean that people wholly reject the role of internal positive factors or the importance of meritocratic values. The average of the "often" and "very often" answers for internal attributions remained stable.)

This weakening belief in meritocracy appears especially in the judgment of success, which may be because people in 1991 had more illusions and hoped that success was determined by individual abilities, not connections

Table 11.2 Attributions of success and wealth in 1991 and 1996 in Eastern Europe (percentages of "often" and "very often" responses)

	1991		1996	
	%	N	%	N
Attribution of wealth				
Talent	51.9	8,097	46.9	3,141
Hard work	40.2	2,401	45.0	3,013
Network	76.7	4,580	83.4	5,579
More opportunity to begin with	59.5	3,551	68.7	4,598
Dishonesty	64.8	3,865	68.7	4,595
Attribution of success				
Talent	83.0	4,954	81.6	5,463
Hard work	79.0	4,716	77.7	5,202
Network	74.5	4,445	87.4	5,846
More opportunity to begin with	42.5	2,539	53.4	3,573

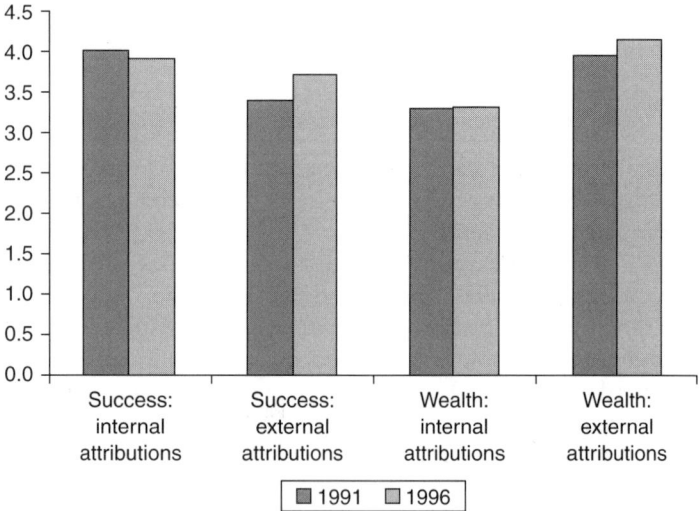

Figure 11.5 Attributions of success and wealth in 1991 and 1996 in Eastern Europe (aggregated variables—means of five-degree scales)

or better initial opportunities. People in the East were skeptical and suspicious of the rich in 1991 as well, but the skepticism and suspicion later increased.

Figure 11.6 presents the temporal changes in suspicion of success and wealth.[14] In the East, belief in a meritocratic evaluation of success wavered, and delegitimation of wealth showed a further increase over the high 1991 value. Six years after the transition, as the market economy consolidated, suspicion and rejection of success and wealth seem to prevail.

Figure 11.7 restructures the typology, based on the four attitude types, toward success and enrichment under a market economy in Eastern Europe. The proportion of respondents endorsing meritocracy decreased modestly (from 35 to 26 percent). Those withdrawing from the world increased (from 19 to 28 percent). The sizes of the deviant and envious groups were stable (5 and 41 percent, respectively). The proportion of those rejecting the market

Figure 11.6 Suspicion of success and wealth in 1991 and 1996 in Eastern Europe (aggregated variables—means of five-degree scales)

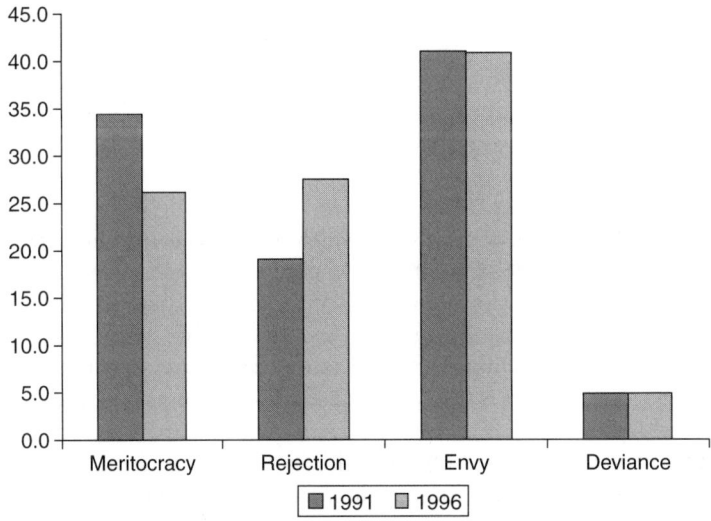

Figure 11.7 Percentages showing attitude types toward the market economy in 1991 and 1996

economy from any point of view increased from 65 to 74 percent,[15] with the deviant and envious groups remaining the same size and the proportion of the passively disappointed increasing. This suggests a remarkable legitimation deficit, at least for acceptance of the market economy.

An Explanatory Model for Discordance over Market Success in 1991

The analysis so far has examined the cognitive structures behind the attributions of success and enrichment in East and West, and how they changed after the transition. The main question that remains is what kinds of factors explain this attitude structure. We constructed explanatory models to elucidate the suspicion and envy phenomena in time and space.

The first question was whether general confidence and social position were related.[16] Social position was gauged through relatively easily measured objective and subjective status attributes. The objective attributes used were education, income, and occupational prestige, measured respectively as number of completed school grades standardized by country, monthly income standardized by country, and Treiman occupational-prestige score. Aggregating these, allowed respondents to be evaluated and ranked simultaneously for all three attributes using principal-component analysis. High values of the principal component indicate high composite objective status.

The other component of social position is self-assessment: subjective status. This principal component is derived from measurements of satisfaction (with income, standard of living, and life as a whole) and of subjective social standing on a ten-degree scale standardized by countries. High values mean high subjective status.

The hypothesis was that objective and subjective status would be strongly related, but this did not prove to be the case. Many people were dissatisfied with their higher social status, while some of those with worse social status were satisfied with it. There was little difference between West and East. Irrespective of the region, it was typical to find correlations between the two indices that were significant, but not very strong (a coefficient of around +0.25).

The next step was to measure the degree to which the objective and subjective status of the respondents influenced the level of confidence in success and the meritocratic rules of success. It was found in all three regions that dissatisfaction with respondents' own status was the main "engine" of discordant feelings toward the success that became attainable in the market economy. Confidence in market rules was dependent on success, but to a far greater extent, perceived situation and satisfaction with it influenced legitimation of meritocratic rules in the market economy. This seems to confirm the fourth hypothesis about the strong connection between subjective status and confidence in market rules.

Nevertheless, the relationship between status and discordance (lack of confidence in meritocratic economic rules) did not differ much between East and West, which seems to disprove the third hypothesis. Objective status had no direct effect on the level of confidence in market rules in either Eastern or Western Europe, other than through respondents' satisfaction or dissatisfaction with their social position.

Objective status showed a significant direct effect on lack of confidence only in the United States. However the direction of the effect was the opposite of what was expected: those with low status were the ones who trusted both in the principles of the system and in those who obtained success and wealth under the constraints of a market economy. This indicated (at least until 1991) that enormous legitimation reserves had been accumulated in American society and the "American dream" had considerable power to motivate those with low status who aspired to rise.

The next step was to use regression path models[17] to explore the cognitive ideology-based explanatory factors behind discordance that were missing from the three variable model. Other variables introduced, besides objective and subjective status, were acceptance or rejection of micro- and macro-level principles of distributive justice (Örkény and Székelyi 2000, 2001). On a micro level, this was measured by summing up the responses to two variables: how much influence respondents thought hard work and education should have in determining pay. High values meant acceptance of micro-level meritocratic values. The variable for acceptance or rejection of ideological, macro-level meritocratic values was created by summing up four variables. The statements were: "The fairest way of distributing wealth and income would be to give everyone equal shares." "It's fair if people have more money or wealth, but only if there are equal opportunities." "People are entitled to keep what they have earned, even if this means that some people will be wealthier than others." "People who work hard deserve to earn more than those who do not." High values for the index denoted acceptance of macro-level meritocratic values.

This aggregated variable consisted of two parts: Rawls-type legitimation of the market economy and acceptance or rejection of a democratic political system. The first dimension, according to Rawls, tests the compatibility of the pure economic rules and laws of market systems with the principle of social justice, so that it also represents a kind of legitimation in terms of social values. This dimension was operationalized by asking if "It is all right if businessmen make good profits because everyone benefits in the end." The second component was the measurement of political legitimation. Respondents were asked about the basic values of modern democratic systems (evaluation of government—government is run for the benefit of all people; trust in government; equality before the law; real voter choice). In the measure aggregated from these two components, high positive values denote delegitimation of the existing political–economic ideologies.

To aggregate the variable measuring acceptance of meritocratic statements and the Rawls thesis, principal component analysis was used. Incidentally, those dissatisfied with their own position and rejecting meritocratic distribution procedures on a micro level also tend to reject meritocratic ideologies. On the one hand, if this general upward mobility increased a person's satisfaction with his or her own position, this brought a rise in confidence as well. On the other hand, we can observe an opposite trend as well. If higher social status did not increase one's personal satisfaction, or if higher social status did not increase one's acceptance of micro-level meritocratic ideologies, then higher objective status could cause a loss of confidence.

Those accepting meritocracy are mildly predisposed to acknowledge the market economy as the optimum system and to accord a higher level of political legitimation to the system in general. Acceptance of meritocratic values in the everyday distribution of income hardly improves confidence in the market economy in itself, but does so significantly if it is accompanied by acceptance of meritocratic ideology and/or the Rawls thesis.

The next step is to present the model explaining the level of confidence (or lack of it) in the rules of the market economy, in terms of respondents' sociological positions and cognitive skills, bearing in mind the different political, economic, and cultural traditions of East and West. Only significant relationships have been shown in figure 11.8, which depicts the path model. The strengths of the connections are shown by beta values along the paths.

The model shows that general confidence in the market economy is stronger in the West than in the East. However, the delegitimation potential is stronger than in the West, which is related to discordant judgments of the economic and political systems. The model reinforces the tendency already mentioned in the case of the United States alone. Higher objective status in the West predisposes respondents to stronger suspicion than lower status does. Moreover, if high objective status is accompanied by satisfaction (high subjective status), the tendency is reversed, and trust becomes stronger.

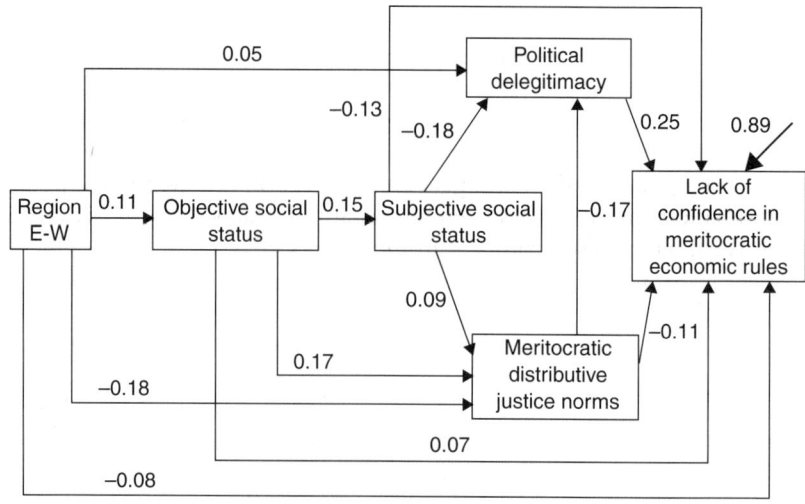

Figure 11.8 Regional embeddedness and lack of confidence in the market economy, 1991

Objective and subjective status also influence discordant judgments of the market economy through dissatisfaction with the political system (Örkény and Liebig 1999). Political dissatisfaction is the main factor in East and West explaining a lack of confidence. The effect described earlier reappears. The main point is that acceptance of the political system is influenced most by high subjective status: the more satisfied people are with their social position, the more satisfied they are with the democratic political system, and thereby, the greater the confidence they have in meritocratic economic rules.

Acceptance of meritocratic value orientations and the market system are not divorced from status or region. Those with higher objective status and higher subjective status are predisposed to accept meritocratic values. Acceptance of meritocratic values is far stronger in the East, due to enhanced expectations from the transition. This improves general confidence in itself and through stronger political-legitimation potential.

To conclude, the lack of confidence measured in 1991 was higher in the East than in the West. In the East, however, political-legitimation potential, not felt for 40 years, was created by the transition. This, along with the new market ideology, created a learned preference for meritocratic values not experienced hitherto, so that the confidence deficit was moderate compared with the Western regions.

Special Envy in East and West in 1991

Rejection of success in general and rejection of wealth are associated with suspicion of the market economy. The next question is whether there is a kind of special envy within general suspicion, separable from the attitudes outlined along the confidence/lack of confidence continuum for the market economy and the democratic system. The next model makes an East–West comparison of this kind of special envy.[18]

It has been seen that wealth is viewed with less envy in the West than in Eastern Europe, where societies have just broken out of a forced egalitarian system. The path model in figure 11.9 shows this. The direction and strength of the path going from region to envy (beta -0.24) indicate that envy has penetrated less in the West. This general trend is lost, however, when political delegitimation appears. It has been seen that political illegitimacy is stronger in the West, which also promotes an increase of envy.

Special envy in Eastern Europe prevails more among those with high status, perhaps due to cutthroat competition in the early transition years. However, it is possible that strong envy of the rich among those with high status derives from the fact that the position of the rich, though visible to them, remains largely unattainable. Those with low status, in contrast, may show weaker envy because they feel so remote from the rich and lead lives burdened by everyday livelihood problems. Satisfaction with social position decreases envy, but high subjective status coupled with acceptance of meritocratic values and political legitimation makes respondents even more resistant to it.

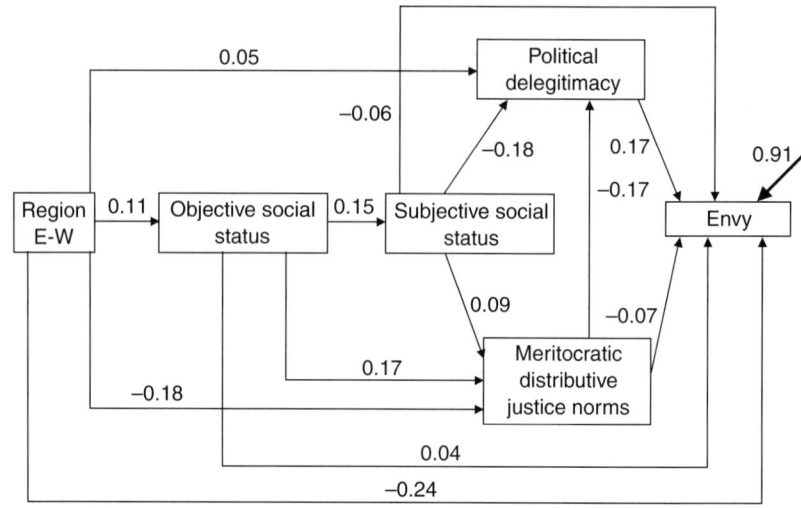

Figure 11.9 Regional embeddedness and special envy

There are no great structural differences between the models for general lack of confidence and for envy, but there are differences in the strengths of the relationships between the dimensions. The general lack of confidence is explained to a great extent by meritocratic values and political legitimation. In contrast, envy is much more determined by personal psychological and moral characteristics of respondents.

Lack of Confidence and Envy in the East over Time, 1991 to 1996

Path analysis was applied again to the causes that lie behind the massive loss of confidence in the rules of the economic system. The structure of the model is the same as for 1991, except that this model measures changes over time only in Eastern European countries: the role of region is replaced by that of time (see figure 11.10).

Disregarding changes in the personal lives of respondents and in their value orientations and attitudes over the five years between 1991 and 1996, it is clear that lack of confidence in the market economy did not increase over time. This means that if people's objective and subjective status and their relation to meritocratic values and the political system did not change in between 1991 and 1996, these changes in themselves could not have caused the loss of confidence.

In fact, most people in Eastern Europe experienced major changes in those five years. The objective status of the economically active population increased on average. In 1991, especially in Eastern Europe, those frustrated with their subjective status also tended to believe that the economic system as a whole was not meritocratic. However, on a micro level, Eastern Europe

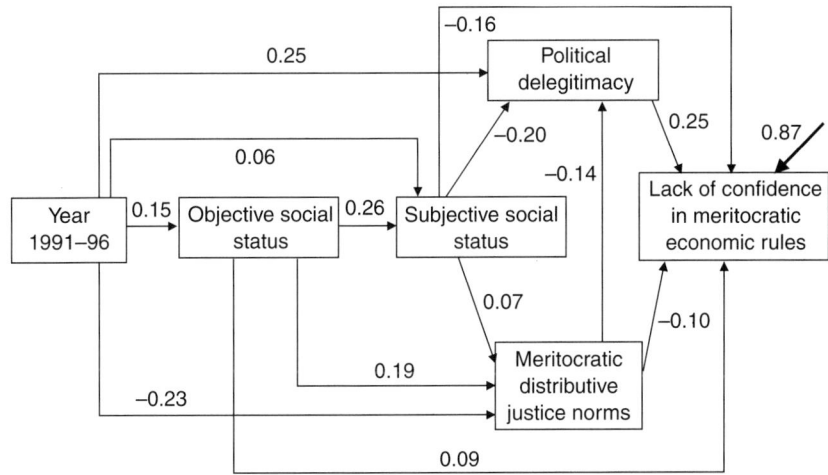

Figure 11.10 Five years of transition and lack of confidence in the market economy

respondents, nevertheless, believed in meritocratic values whatever their social status and level of satisfaction.

Looking at the effect of subjective status irrespective of objective status, dissatisfaction can be said to have increased over those five years and been accompanied, naturally, by a loss of confidence. This otherwise weak relationship may explain the strong "culture of complaint" considered characteristic of the region. Experiences in the early years of the transition turned people away from meritocratic values and decreased political legitimation. At the same time, these effects were softened by the rise in general status and satisfaction with that.

The path model in the post-socialist region shows a split society, in which groups with high and low objective status had grown further apart by 1996. Those with high subjective status looked to the future with an enhanced inclination to political legitimation and increased acceptance of meritocratic values, while those falling behind had decreasing trust in their chances of success because of their rejection of meritocratic values and high political delegitimation potential. This rough picture is made more complex, but not changed by satisfaction with life.

The explanatory path model for special envy (see figure 11.11) shows three important differences from 1991, all three proving that the complex measure really does measure envy and sheds light on the structure of the difference between the symptoms of lack of confidence and special envy.

The first difference is that envy is not directly influenced by acceptance or rejection of meritocratic values; this factor only has an effect if it is accompanied by extreme judgments of the political system. Those who accept meritocratic values in distribution have higher political legitimation potential and are therefore less envious. Albeit to a small extent, the model displays the components that Rawls terms generalized and particularized

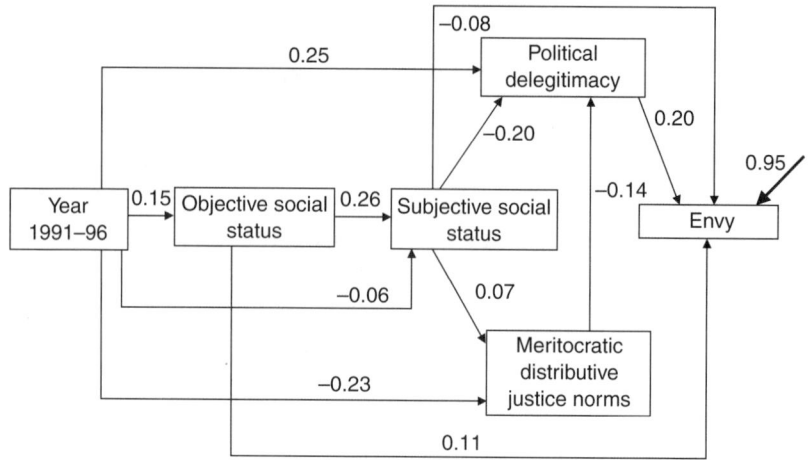

Figure 11.11 Five years of transition and special envy

envy. Where particularized components of envy predominate, meritocratic value orientations and envy should be related. This appears in the path model for 1991, where Eastern and Western countries were included, and envy and normative principles are related because of particularized envy, which is more characteristic of the West. However, in 1996, with analyses confined to the East, where relationships are much more influenced by generalized components of envy, no relationship between meritocratic values and envy was found.

The second difference can be shown by taking objective status as the starting point. It was seen earlier that high social status, in itself, predisposes one toward a general lack of confidence and especially toward envy. This explanatory model of envy shows even more clearly that the higher the position achieved by respondents, the greater the tensions they feel toward groups perceived as successful.

This trend is demonstrated especially well by the third difference, which shows the relation between envy and satisfaction with one's own position. Envy, as lack of confidence, decreases as respondents' satisfaction with their lives increases. Personal satisfaction, however, is much more capable of increasing confidence than it is of decreasing envy.

Should the Rich Pay?

The first decade of the transition to a market economy in Eastern Europe raised the question of whether dissatisfaction and tension over the new distributive rules cause people to engage in political and social activity. The transition to a market economy in the post-socialist societies increased the proportion of those who perceived enrichment as a deviant status achievement. However, envy can be reduced by diminishing the position of those envied or penalizing those at the top. To test this hypothesis, it is worth examining how the motivation to limit incomes changed in Eastern Europe between 1991 and 1996. This concept was operationalized by intentions relating to the desired distribution of incomes. Respondents to both surveys had to estimate the actual and the just income of a managing director. If the quotient of the actual and fair income is taken as a measure, values greater than one indicate an inclination to penalize those on the top. This inclination was already strong in 1991. Those in the East thought that managing directors in a just society should get 69 percent of their actual average income, that is, take a 31 percent pay cut. The inclination had increased by 1996, when respondents in the East thought that the income of top managers should be decreased to 44 percent.

The strange thing here is that the size of the deduction recommended is unconnected with the social status or earnings of respondents. Theoretically, it would be expected that the urge to penalize managers would increase the less respondents were earning themselves. However, respondent status and the income (and status) perceived as just do not explain the increasing punitive intention. This calls for another factor, found in psychological attributes.

The passage of time from 1991 to 1996 did not in itself make people in the East more envious, whereas the inclination to penalize the best paid increased significantly. Something more than envy was at work. The intermediary variable was subjective status. Low subjective-status values point to frustration and so can explain the inclination to aggressive equalization.[19]

The path model depicted in figure 11.12 shows that the inclination to penalize became stronger over time. However, the effect is not wholly direct, but one outcome of increasing subjective dissatisfaction. The most important relationship starts from envy. Stronger envy apparently leads to a wish for drastic curtailment of the income of the rich only if accompanied by dissatisfaction (low subjective social status).[20] This, with certain restrictions, verifies the seventh hypothesis. Where respondents see their own wages as unfairly low and this is accompanied by dissatisfaction and indeed envy, it

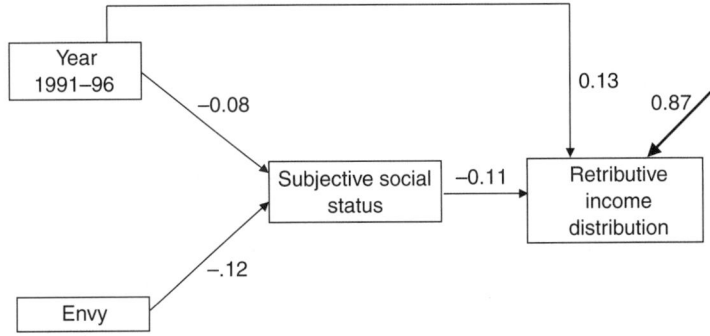

Figure 11.12 Five years of transition and forced egalitarianism

becomes highly probable that they will want to curtail top managers' pay. The tendency, present in both 1991 and 1996, increased over time.

Summary

Social scientists in East and West pay close attention to how quickly and effectively the post-socialist countries have managed to switch from a state-socialist system to a full, modern market economy. The success of these new market economies depends on the formation and characteristics of the new economic and property system, on the privatization process, and on the process by which state-socialist mechanisms give way to market mechanisms. The crucial question is how much the state can limit its interventions in the new economic exchanges. Furthermore, external factors of the transition are as important as internal ones, the two most important being the globalizing economic environment and the transnational political framework. Integration into a unified Western market economy raises the serious question of whether there is a uniform market system that can serve as a pattern for the transition. Perhaps other processes or modified forms would have worked better in Eastern Europe as it emerged from many years in a state-socialist system.

These questions are justifiable if the answer is sought not from instrumental and structural conditions, but through the human resources of the transition and the cognitive characteristics of the transitional societies. This is why the analysis was extended to the sociopsychological inclinations and preferences of the new Eastern European market economies at the time of the transition. Comparing East and West for acceptance and rejection of market rules and the attitudinal background allows testing for embeddedness and legitimation of market systems in the post-socialist societies.

The rule types and behavioral patterns provide information about the quintessence of the political and economic system. Attitudes toward the legitimate rules of success and enrichment model people's attitudes toward the existing economic mechanisms. The findings show that although people's lives are now controlled by market forces, the operation of the market is seen differently in the East. The public there sees the market as a battlefield, with individual effort and personal merit on one side and external factors on the other, so that individuals stand for positive traits against unjust (or at least unfair) external social relations. Thus, the economy and society are penetrated by untrustworthiness, dishonesty, undeserved success, and fraud, while the work and achievements of ordinary people are not recognized or compensated as they deserve. It is perceived that in Eastern Europe, the rich have become wealthy not by hard work or merit, but as an outcome of adverse economic and social conditions.

In the West, success and wealth are viewed not as a struggle between individuals and adverse external conditions, but as the result of successful mobilization of individual resources (internal and external). Thus, internal and external factors are not exclusive, normative attributions. Individuals make the most of opportunities (which may be hard work, talent, network, or better initial opportunities) and both success and wealth depend on mobilizing these resources. People do not select different attributions of success and wealth in the relations of untrustworthiness and dishonesty, so that internal and external factors fall within the same range of values.

The data show, however, that Europe and the United States also differ significantly in their judgments of the normative principles of market relations. In the United States, the most important factor in the case of success and of wealth is the meritocratic commitment of individuals. Compared with this, external causes such as good connections or good social background are secondary and rejection of meritocratic principles (in connection with individual success and with the rich) is negligible. Individuals in the United States are at the core of success, while in Western Europe central stage is taken by the chances offered by the system. All this raises doubts about whether there is a uniform market model at all.

In general, attitudes in the East show opposition between the individual and the system, while in the West they are viewed as providing mutual benefits. The differences strengthen further if the cognitive space of success and wealth judgments is considered along with the sociological and attitudinal background.

The explanation of the Western meritocratic support for market rules follows logically from the fact that legitimation potential is strong among those with high objective and subjective status who are able to mobilize their resources. This also ties closely with acceptance of micro- and macro-level meritocratic ideologies. Political legitimation, along with advantageous personal sociological situations and openness to meritocratic ideologies, leads to normative affirmation of the market economy. Alternatively, low status accompanied by dissatisfaction delegitimates success and wealth in all cases. In the West, respondents imbued with particularized envy may still accept the legitimate rules of success. However, the presence of a stable capitalist system with long historical traditions lessens the chance of generalized envy.

In the East, people who had experienced the market economy only in the last ten years have different values and explanations for success. Meritocratic rules were given surprisingly strong credit in the region in 1991, and the high level of confidence, toward economic transition went with the popularity of meritocratic ideologies (micro- and macro-level) and with strong political legitimation. This belief had weakened by 1996 under the difficulties of the radical changes, which intensified the delegitimation of political and ideological (meritocratic) principles and decreased acceptance of success that was dependent on market forces. Behind this can also be seen a considerable general status decline, paralleled by (or independent of) increasing dissatisfaction. The erosion of market values was not confined to losers in the transition. Those who were winners or whose position was practically unchanged were also imbued with skepticism and suspicion.

The sociopsychological objectives in the acceptance of market relations and new values are most clearly shown by the strength of envy in Eastern

Europe. In 1991, there was a difference from the West not only in the intensity of suspicion of accomplishment and merit, but also in the envy of others' success. Both East and West betrayed envy arising from intensified competition (particularized envy), but generalized envy was present even more strongly. Those imbued with generalized envy are envious of everything and everybody and unconsciously use this mental "resource" to offset feelings of individual loss. Envy is an important psychological trait that increases personal satisfaction (not by increasing personal gains, but by decreasing those of others) and excuses bad performance. The feeling is directed not against real persons, opponents, or achievements, but at the manifestations of personal failure and the general disappointment with the political system, which finally brings total rejection of the existing political and economic system. The psychological associate of envy is fury, which appears in distrust and contempt for the rich, manifested in drastic proposed penalization of the income of those who have prospered.

Although the institutional framework and conditions for market relations developed speedily and successfully in Eastern Europe, the process elicited discordance rather than relief. This contradiction forecasts for the future a physical and mental split within these societies. Our analysis has sought to prove that the success of the economic transition depends at least as much on sociopsychological factors as on the internal and external resources and efficiency of the economy in the new democracies of Eastern Europe.

Notes

* Parts or all of the International Social Justice Project, the collaborative international survey research effort on which this paper draws, received support from the following organizations: The National Council for Soviet and East European Research (USA); the National Science Foundation (USA); the Institute for Social Research, University of Michigan; OTKA (National Scientific Research Fund, Hungary); the Economic and Social Research Council (UK); the Deutsche Forschungsgemeinschaft (Germany); Institute of Social Science, Chuo University (Japan); the Dutch Ministry of Social Affairs; the Bulgarian Academy of Sciences; the Grant Agency of the Czechoslovak Academy of Sciences; Saar Poll Ltd. (Estonia); the Ministry of Science and Technology of the Republic of Slovenia; the State Committee for Scientific Research (Komitet Badan Naukowych, Poland). The principal investigators in the 1996 replication project were Bernd Wegener (Germany), Petr Mateju (Czech Republic), Ludmila Khakhulina and Svetlana Sidorenko-Stephenson (Russia), Andrus Saar (Estonia), Antal Örkény (Hungary), Alexander Stoyanov (Bulgaria), and David Mason and James Kluegel (United States). Further information on the ISJP can be found at the project's web site: www.butler.edu/isjp/

1. Other resources with increasing explanatory importance in economic and social relations, besides capital as defined by Marx in modern social theory, are personal networks (individual social capital), inherited and acquired knowledge (cultural capital and habitus), and influential potential and power position (political capital). These capitals determine separately and together the social position of an individual. They and the conversion mechanisms between them strongly determine the modes and limits of status attainment delineated by society. The autonomy of individuals is constrained by the extent to which they can choose the most profitable mechanism for capital conversion (Bourdieu 1977; Coleman 1989).

2. On the concept of social capital, see Bourdieu 1977; Coleman 1989. Barbara Misztral (1996: 55) views mutual truthworthiness as social capital that benefits the group and frames underlying capitalist relationships.

3. Kant saw envy arising because people compare their goods and resources with those of others instead of seeing them for what they are (Kant 1964: 127).
4. The questionnaire for the survey was developed and written in English. It was then translated into the respective language of each country. The sample design and interviewing were carried out by leading survey research organizations in each country. The target population for each country is all residents 18 years of age or older. In most countries the questionnaire was fielded in face-to-face interviews, the response rate was between 80 and 90 percent.
5. See www.butler.edu/isjp/; Kluegel et al. 1995; and Mason et al. 2000.
6. One means a factor never contributes to a high social standing, five that it very often does so.
7. Averaging the scale-points given to these variables.
8. The Likert Scale is the degree scale 1–5 mentioned earlier.
9. Connection as an attribution of success in Eastern Europe correlates negatively with ability ($r = -0.13$) and hard work ($r = -0.18$) and positively with good starting position ($r = 0.34$). With enrichment, the highest correlations are with dishonesty ($r = +0.35$), inequality of opportunities ($+0.28$) and unequal external economic factors ($+0.31$). The subjective importance of connections correlates negatively with hard work and talent.
10. In the judgment of success in the West, connection has a positive correlation with external starting conditions ($r = +0.36$) and talent ($+0.11$), and a fairly weakly negative correlation with hard work (-0.05). In judging the rich, connection (as in Eastern Europe) correlates positively with external negative factors, but not negatively with hard work or talent.
11. Residuals can be described as differences from the following regression equation:
$\Sigma[\text{general lack of confidence} - (C + B \cdot \text{lack of confidence regarding success})^2] \to \text{minimum}$
where C and B are parameters of the equation minimizing the sum of the squares of these differences.
12. The interpretation of dishonesty differs in East and West. Correlation coefficients between these attributions show that in the transitional East, people think dishonest behavior of the rich correlates strongly with the functioning of the market system ($r = +0.38$) and personal networks ($r = +0.34$). In Western countries, people see dishonesty at a system level. (The correlation coefficient with unfair advantage of the economic system is $+0.40$, and with the role of initial opportunities $+0.12$.) On an individual level, personal networks are apparently viewed as a less negative factor ($r = +0.25$) than in Eastern Europe.
13. Because the attributions for success and wealth were not identical, only those wealth attributions were used in the analysis that had an analogous variant with success.
14. If the view is totally accepted, the value is $+4$, and if totally rejected, -4.
15. The sum of all groups but the meritocratic.
16. The choice of Lenski's complete status model as one of the independent variables inevitably meant that elderly, retired respondents with no present employment or resultant prestige had to be excluded from the model of general confidence. However, the mapping of the sociopsychological background of the post-socialist economic transition is valid primarily among those in the labor market, who became economically active winners or losers by the transition. Originally, age was included to explain lack of confidence, as previous empirical research had shown that winners and losers can be distinguished also by age group and by the age at which they experienced market transition. Age, however, neither alone nor with objective and subjective status, had a significant effect on level of confidence. One probable reason is that the analysis is confined to economically active respondents and cannot reflect the otherwise deep cleavage between economically active and inactive, especially in Eastern Europe.
17. Path analysis is a complex regression model. The outlined models show to what degree various sociological and attitude factors explain the level of distrust. "Explanation" means the strength of the tie between two variables, its degree being indicated by arrows linking boxes. These figures are beta values of regression, a positive sign indicating that the two variables move together, a negative sign that they move in opposite directions. Path analysis shows how independent variables affect the dependent variable directly and through other variables, and the relationship between the independent and dependent variables.
18. The explanatory model of special envy required an envy index operationalized on a high level of measurement. See earlier.
19. Previous path models aimed at presenting the nature of envy. Thus, subjective status was included as one of its sources. However, the relation between subjective status and envy is mutual, which justifies reversing the direction.

20. In Western Europe, the inclination to penalize works differently: neither envy nor subjective status causes an inclination to penalize. On the contrary, those whose pay is unfairly low will probably wish to restore justice by decreasing senior management pay. These relations can be stated only in 1991, but the validity of this model is significantly improved because the model for Eastern Europe in 1991 shows the effect envy has on inclination to penalize through subjective status reflected in the model of figure 11.12, showing changes over time.

References

Abercrombie, Nicholas, Stuart Hill, and Bryan S. Turner. 1990. *The Dominant Ideologies*. London: Allen and Unwin.
Bourdieu, Pierre. 1977. *Reproduction in Education, Society and Culture*. London, Beverly Hills: Sage Publications.
Coleman, James. 1989. *Foundations of Social Theory*. Cambridge MA: Harvard University Press.
Csepeli, György and Antal Örkény. 1993. Az elitpercepció kognitív és társadalmi meghatározói a mai Magyarországon (Cognitive and Social Determinants of Elite Perception in Hungary Today). *Valóság* No. 12: 47–58.
Festinger, Leon. 1957. *A Theory of Cognitive Dissonance*. Evanston: Row, Peterson.
Granovetter, Mark and Richard Swedberg (eds.). 1992. *The Sociology of Economic Life*. Boulder-San Francisco-Oxford: Westview Press.
Kant, Immanuel. 1964. *The Metaphysics of Morals*. New York: Harper and Row.
Kelley, Harold H. 1967. Attribution Theory in Social Psychology. In David Levine (ed.). *Nebraska Symposium on Motivation*, pp. 178–201. Lincoln NB: University of Nebraska Press.
Kluegel, James R., David Mason, and Bernd Wegener (eds.). 1995. *Social Justice and Political Change*. New York: Aldine de Gruyter.
Mason, David and James R. Kluegel, with Ludmilla Khakhulina, Petr Mateju, Antal Örkény, Alexander Stoyanov, and Bernd Wegener. 2000. *Marketing Democracy: Changing Opinion About Inequality and Politics in East Central Europe*. Lanham MD: Rowman and Littlefield.
Misztral, Barbara A. 1996. *Trust in Modern Society*. Cambridge MA: Polity Press.
Örkény, Antal and Stefan Liebig. 1999. Normatív legitimáció és igazságosság (Normative Legitimacy and Social Justice). *Szociológiai Figyelő* Nos. 1–2: 129–40.
Örkény, Antal and Mária Székelyi. 2000. Views on Social Inequality and the Role of State: Post-transformation Trends in Eastern and Central Europe. *Social Justice Research*, special issue on "Social Justice Beliefs in Transition: Eastern and Central Europe 1991–1996," No. 13, pp. 199–218.
Örkény, Antal and Mária Székelyi. 2001. Images of Justice in East Central Europe: During and After the Transition. *East Central Europe* 28: 71–94.
Polanyi, Karl. 1957. The Economy as an Institutionalized Process. In K. Polanyi, C.M. Arensberg, and H.W. Pearson (eds.). *Trade and Market in the Early Empires: Economies in History and Theory*, pp. 243–70. Glencoe IL: Free Press.
Rawls, John. 1971. *Theory of Justice*. Cambridge MA: Harvard University Press.
Schoeck, Helmut. 1966. *Envy*. New York: Helen and Kurt Wolff Books.
Smith, Adam. 1993. *An Inquiry into the Nature and Causes of the Wealth of Nations*. Indianapolis IN: Hackett Pub. Co.
Szabó, Miklós. 1989. *Politikai kultúra Magyarországon 1896–1986* (Political Culture in Hungary 1896–1986). Budapest: Atlantisz Program.
Szántó, Zoltán. 1994. A gazdaság társadalmi beágyazottsága. Megjegyzések a gazdaságszociológia és a szocioökonómia újabb irodalmáról (Social Embeddedness of the Economy. Notes on Recent Literature on Economic Sociology and Socio-economy). *Szociológiai Szemle* No. 3: 141.
Uslaner, Eric M. 2002. *The Moral Foundation of Trust*. Cambridge: Cambridge University Press.
Weiner, Bernard, Irene H. Frieze, Andy Kukla, Linda Reed, Stanley Rest, and Robert M. Rosenbaum. 1972. Perceiving the Causes of Success and Failure. In Edward E. Jones et al. (eds.). *Attribution: Perceiving the Causes of Behavior*, pp. 95–120. Morristown NY: General Learning Press.
Zukin, Sharon and DiMaggio, Paul (eds.). 1990. *Structures of Capital. The Social Organization of the Economy*. Cambridge: Cambridge University Press.

AUTHOR INDEX

Abercrombie, Nicholas, 217
Adsera, Alicia, 44
Akerlof, George A., 171, 181
Aleksashenko, Sergei V., 79
Almond, Gabriel, 39
Arias, Enrique Desmond, 14
Arkhipov, Sergei, 146
Arrow, Kenneth J., 55
Axelrod, Robert, 55, 56

Bacharach, Michael, 203
Baden, John, 89
Badescu, Gabriel, 5, 39, 44
Baier, Annette, 47
Bailey, Michael, 174
Baker, George, 113, 123
Banfield, Edward, 38
Becker, Gary S., 170, 172, 187
Bendor, Jonathan, 5
Bennett, Gordon, 89
Benson, Bruce, 89
Berman, Sheri, 14
Bernstein, Lisa, 113
Black, Bernard, 173, 176
Blanchard, Olivier, 55
Blasi, Joseph, 140
Blau, Peter M., 194, 195
Blomkvist, Hans, 4
Blundo, G., 72
Boix, Carles, 44
Bourdieu, Pierre, 238
Bove Antonio, 163
Boycko, Maxim, 176
Buell, Barbara, 204, 205

Cartier-Bresson, Jean, 200
Catanzaro, Raimondo, 152

Cawson, Alan, 6
Cheshire, Coye, 206
Chu, Yiu Kong, 148, 163
Claessens, Stijn, 183
Claiborn, Michele P., 15
Clay, Karen, 112
Coffee, Jack C. Jr., 174, 183
Cohen, Jean L., 31
Coleman, James, 31, 91, 101, 151, 238
Commander, Simon, 74
Cook, Karen S., 8, 194, 196, 197, 198, 202, 203, 205, 206, 210
Cooper, Robin M., 206, 210
Csáki, György, 158, 159
Csepeli, György, 9, 216

Davies, Paul L., 184
De Gennaro, Giuseppe, 148
DiMaggio, Paul, 204, 214
Durante, Graziella, 163

Earle, John S., 152
Eggertsson, Thrainn, 92
Ekeh, Peter, 194
Ellickson, Robert C., 112
Emerson, Richard M., 194, 196, 197, 202, 205

Falk, Armin, 113
Fang, Liufang, 180
Farrell, Henry, 199
Fehr, Ernst, 113
Festinger, Leon, 213
Flap, Henk, 38
Fligstein, Neil, 92, 106, 107
Frank, Robert H., 203
Friedländer, Saul, 15

Author Index

Friedman, Eric, 49
Friedman, Robert I., 154, 158
Friel, Coleen, 163
Frieze, Irene H., 217
Frydman, Roman, 152, 176
Frye, Timothy, 63, 68, 126
Fukuyama, Francis, 207
Fukuyama, Francis, 35, 55, 58, 207

Gambetta, Diego, 20, 47, 92, 148, 149, 151, 163, 200, 203
Gao, Sheldon, 182
Geertz, Clifford, 112
Gel'man, Vladimir, 144
Gelfer, Stanislav, 173
Gerbasi, Alexandra, 8
Gibbons, Robert, 113, 123
Gibson, James L., 36, 38, 46
Gilovich, Thomas, 203
Glasmeier, Amy K., 199
Goertzel, Ted, 27
Goldman, Marshall, 148
Goodin, Robert, 28
Goss, Kristin A., 15, 16
Granovetter, Mark, 111, 214
Greif, Avner, 111, 112
Grødeland, Åse B., 37, 39, 201
Guseva, Alya, 202, 203

Hardin, Russell, 34, 92, 204, 205
Hay, Jonathan, 173
Hayoz, Nicolas, 36
Heckscher, Gunnar, 17
Hedlund, Stefan, 2
Hedström, Peter, 15
Heimer, Carol, 200
Hendley, Kathryn, 122, 126
Hermansson, Jörgen, 24
Hertz, Noreena, 126
Hill, Stuart, 217
Holmberg, Sören, 14, 22
Homans, George C., 194
Hooghe, Marc, 4, 5
Howard, Marc Morje, 36, 39

Inglehart, Ronald, 155, 157

Jacobs, James B., 163
Johnson, Simon, 49, 56, 58, 61, 62, 64, 65, 112, 117, 118, 119, 122

Kaase, Max, 23
Kahn, Peter L., 152
Kali, Raja, 123
Kant, Immanuel, 239
Kapeliushnikov, Rostislav, 141
Karklins, Rasma, 21
Karsai, Gábor, 158, 159
Karyshev, Valery, 164
Katona, Géza, 159, 160, 161, 164
Kaufmann, Daniel, 49
Keefer, Philip, 59
Kelley, Harold H., 216
Kershaw, Ian, 15
Khakhulina, Ludmilla, 239
Klebnikov, Paul, 76
Klein, Benjamen, 123
Klingebiel, Daniela, 183
Kluegel, James R., 217, 239
Knack, Stephen, 59
Knight, Jack, 47
Kollock, Peter, 196, 197, 198, 202
Kornai, János, 1, 38, 158, 201, 164
Koshechkina, Tatyana Y., 37, 39, 201
Kraakman, Reinier, 173, 176
Kraay, Aart, 49
Kranton, Rachael, 113
Kremer, Michael, 55
Kroumova, Maya, 141
Kruse, Douglas, 141
Kukla, Andy, 217
Kumlin, Staffan, 23, 25

La Porta, Rafael, 35, 49, 175
Lackó, Mária, 164
Lambert, Larry B., 73, 75, 89
Lambsdorff, Johann Graf, 35
Landa, Janet Tai, 112
Lane, Robert E., 39
Latynina, Yulia, 82, 83
Lawler, Edward J., 197, 198, 202
Lazzarini, Sergio, 113
Ledeneva, Alena V., 7, 37, 38, 39, 74, 89, 193, 203, 206
Leite, Carlos, 35
Levi, Margaret, 14, 20, 31
Levine, Ross, 182
Lewin, Leif, 6
Liebig, Stefan, 231
Lind, Eric A., 21
Lindsey, John, 111

Author Index

Lipsky, Michael, 23
Lomnitz, Larissa Adler, 193
Lopez-Silanes, Florencio, 175
Lopez-Silanes, Florencio, 35, 49
Lorentzen, Håkon, 16
Louch, Hugh, 204
Åslund, Anders, 2
Lundquist, Lennart, 22

Macauley, Stewart, 56, 112, 195
Maksimov, Aleksandr, 158, 164
Malhotra, Deepak, 208
Manne, Henry, 131
Marsden, Peter V., 198
Martin, Paul S., 15
Mashima, Rie, 206
Mason, David, 217, 239
Mateju, Petr, 239
Matsuda, Masafumi, 206
Mauro, Pablo, 35
Mawby, Robert, 159
McKinnon, Ronald I., 167
McMillan, John, 56, 58, 61, 62, 64, 65, 111, 112, 117, 118, 119, 122, 123, 124, 204
Miguel, Basanez, 155, 157
Miller, Gary, 113
Miller, William L., 37, 39, 46, 201
Misztral, Barbara A., 31, 238
Mizruchi, Mark S., 199
Modestov, Nikolay, 164
Molm, Linda, 194, 195, 197, 205, 206, 207
Montinola, Gabrielle, 205
Morck, Randall, 177, 183
Moreno, Alejandro, 155, 157
Mummsen, Christian, 74
Murnighan, J. Keith, 208
Murphy, Kevin J., 113, 123
Murrell, Peter, 122, 126
Myrdal, Gunnar, 17

Nagy, László, 164
Neld, Robert, 16
Newton, Kenneth, 15, 22, 23, 35
Norén, Ylva, 22
North, Douglas C., 2, 4, 55, 92

Offe, Claus, 31
Oi, Jean C., 181
Olson, Mancur, 4, 6

Orren, Gary, 36
Ostrom, Elinor, 4, 8, 210
Örkény, Antal, 9, 216, 229, 231, 239

Pap, András László, 159
Pappe, Yakov, 141, 145
Patterson, Orlando, 27
Payne, Mark, 44
Pejovich, Svetozar, 1, 126
Peterson, Gretchen, 195, 197, 205, 206, 207
Pierson, Paul, 4
Pissler, Knut Benjamin, 180
Pistone, Joseph D., 150, 163
Pistor, Katharina, 8, 152, 167, 171, 172, 173, 176, 187
Polanyi, Karl, 91, 105, 214
Polinsky, Mitchell, 170
Pollack, Ben, 111
Poppo, Laura, 113
Portes, Alejandro, 151
Powell, Walter W., 198, 199
Putnam, Robert D., 4, 14, 15, 16, 26, 27, 35, 38, 55, 59, 155, 209

Radaev, Vadim, 6, 96, 97, 98, 102, 105, 109, 126, 203, 204, 205, 209, 210
Radick, Robert, 163
Radygin, Alexander, 140, 141, 146
Raiser, Martin, 5, 63, 68, 96, 173
Rapaczynski, Andrzej, 152, 176
Rawls, John, 32, 214, 215, 216
Reed, Linda, 217
Regan, Dennis T., 203
Rest, Stanley, 217
Rice, Eric R.W., 8, 195, 196, 197, 198, 202, 205
Riordan, William, 33
Roberts, Cynthia, 126
Rodrik, Dani, 3
Roland, Gerard, 1
Romer, Paul M., 181
Rona-Tas, Akos, 202, 203
Rose, Richard, 46, 206
Rose-Ackerman, Susan, 4, 22, 34, 36, 39, 47, 59, 91, 92, 95, 96, 151, 196, 201, 206, 207, 208
Rosenbaum, Robert M., 217
Rosenberg, Morris, 39
Roth, Nancy L., 47

Rothstein, Bo, 4, 5, 13, 17, 23, 25, 28, 31, 32, 33, 34, 35, 36, 46, 47
Rousso, Alan, 5, 96
Ryterman, Randi, 122, 126

Sally, David, 8
Sands, Jennifer, 148
Sardan, Jean-Pierre Olivier de, 72
Sárközy, Tamás, 158
Schmukler, Sergio L., 183
Schoeck, Helmut, 217
Schumpeter, Joseph, 5, 55
Sciarrone, Rocco, 163
Seligman, Adam B., 35
Selle, Per, 16
Semenov, A.S., 145
Sergeyev, Victor, 36
Shavell, Steven, 170
Shenfield, Stephen, 76
Sherlock, Thomas, 126
Shleifer, Andrei, 4, 35, 49, 140, 175, 176
Sitkin, Sim B., 47
Sizov, Yu S., 145
Smith, Adam, 215
Smith-Doerr, Laurel, 198, 199
Soto, Hernando de, 2
Stearns, Brewster Linda, 199
Steves, Franklin, 5, 96
Stigler, George J., 170
Stiglitz, Joseph, 55
Stolle, Dietlind, 4, 5, 15, 25
Stoyanov, Alexander, 239
Svallfors, Stefan, 24
Swamy, Anand, 113
Swedberg, Richard, 15, 214
Swistak, Piotr, 5
Szabó, Miklós, 217
Szántó, Zoltán, 214
Székelyi, Mária, 9, 229
Székelyi, Mária, 9
Sztompka, Piotr, 18, 92

Takahashi, N., 195, 197, 205, 206, 207
Tambovtsev, Vladimir, 126
Thevenot, Laurent, 107
Thye, Shane R., 202
Tikhomirov, Vladimir, 78, 79
Tirole, Jean, 123
Tompson, William, 89

Tóth, István János, 164
Trang, Duc V., 36
Treisman, Daniel, 35
Tsebelis, George, 1
Turner, Bryan S., 217
Tyler, Tom R., 21, 35

Urbán, László, 158
Uslaner, Eric M., 5, 8, 13, 15, 16, 19, 27, 32, 34, 35, 36, 39, 43, 47, 49, 216
Uzzi, Brian, 201

Varese, Federico, 7, 74, 126, 149, 152, 163, 164
Vasiliev, Dmitry, 140
Verba, Sidney, 39
Vishny, Robert W., 4, 35, 49, 175, 176
Volkov, Vadim, 7, 87, 126, 142, 143, 164
Völker, Beate, 38

Walder, Andrew G., 181
Walker, James, 8, 210
Watabe, M., 196, 197, 198, 202, 203, 206
Watson, Joel, 111
Wegener, Bernd, 217, 239
Weibull, Lennart, 3
Weidemann, Jens, 35
Weiner, Bernard, 217
Weingast, Barry R., 1, 4
Whiteley, Paul F., 15
Whitmeyer, Joseph, 209
Williamson, Oliver E., 94, 98, 100
Wollebeak, Dag, 16
Woodley, Richard, 150, 163
Woodruff, Christopher, 6, 56, 58, 61, 62, 64, 65, 111, 112, 117, 118, 119, 122, 123, 124, 204
Woodruff, David, 133
Wright, Alan, 158, 159, 160, 164

Xu, Chenggang, 8, 167, 171, 172, 187

Yakovlev, Andrei, 75, 89
Yamagishi, Midori, 196, 207
Yamagishi, Toshio, 194, 196, 197, 198, 202, 203, 206, 207, 208
Yeung, Bernard, 177, 183

Author Index

Yoon, Jeongkoo, 197, 198, 202
Yu, Wayne, 177, 183

Zak, Paul, 59
Zeckhauser, Richard, 111
Zenger, Todd, 113

Zervos, Sara, 182
Zheng, Henry R., 173
Zhu, Sanzhu, 175
Zoido-Lobaton, Pablo, 49
Zucker, Lynne G., 208
Zukin, Sharon, 214

SUBJECT INDEX

accountability, lack of, 21, 71
administration, state/public
   inefficiency of in Russia, 94, 96
arbitration courts, Russia, 83–4, 95, 131, 133
   Higher Arbitration Court, 131, 144
   see also insolvency law
asset stripping, Russia, 71, 81, 88, 95
attitudes
   changes in, 225–8
   cross national surveys on, 217–18, *n. 4* on p. 239
   reshaping, 36
   toward economic actors, 214
   toward the market economy, 224, 236

banking system
   requirements of a healthy, 71
   underground, 74
   weaknesses of in Russia, 73
   see also underground financing
bankruptcy proceedings/schemes, Russia, 127, 129, 131–6
   1992 Law on Bankruptcy, 127, 131, 133
   1998 Law on Bankruptcy, 128, 131, 133, 145
   2002 Law on Bankruptcy, 145
   contract, 127, 131, 132
   illegitimate redistribution of property through, 132
   initiators of, 131–2
   insolvency law, 84
   liquidation without supervision, 131
   objectives of, 129
   role of temporary/crisis managers in, 133

barter, 75, 78
   schemes with an intermediary, 78–9
bilateral/cooperation-based contract enforcement, 111, 112, 117, 119
   see also contract enforcement, informal
blat, informal exchage, 74, 193
Bosnia Herzegovina, 21
bribery, 4, 20–1, 23, 38, 39, 45, 134, 135, 176, 201
   see also corruption
bureaucratic discretion, 23
business associations, 6, 64, 65, 68, 93, 118
   developing new business conventions, 102–4, 108
Business Environment and Enterprise Performance Survey (BEEPS), 56, 57–8, 63–4, 96
business environment, 194
   high-risk in Russia, 83, 87
   uncertainties in, 102
business relations, 55, 57, 58, 68
   creating distrust in, 93–9
   creating trust in, 99–105
   measuring trust in, 117
   risk in, 114
   role of private protection agencies in, Russia, 141–3
   trust in, 111, 118, 122
   use of force in, 93
business/market actors, Russia, 91
   acting by laws and/or rules, 104
   building conventions with the state/public officials, 107–8, 110
   conventions among, 102–4, 108
   stigmatizing defectors, 104

capital flight, Russia, 78, 82
   schemes to facilitate, 78–80
   schemes to control, 79
China
   China's Securities Regulatory Commission (CSRC), 179, 180, 181
   combined quota/merit rule, 184
   Company Law, 179, 180
   merit rules, 183
   People's Bank of China, 178, 180
   quota system, 180–1
   Securities Law, 178, 179, 180
   selecting companies for listing, 180–1, 184
   State Council Securities Commission, 179
   Supreme Court, 180

citizens, 5, 20
   interactions between civil servants and, 21, 23, 28
Citizenship Involvement Democracy (CID) survey, 37, 45–6
civil society, 39
   lack of, 71
   and social trust, 14–16
cognitive discordance, 215, 229
collective memory, 27
commitment, behavioral, 196
   in exchange networks under uncertainty, 194–9
   and trust under uncertainty, 201–6, 207
confidence, 9, 18, 213–14, 217, 228, 237
   in economic and social system, 213, 220
contract enforcement mechanisms, 58, 93, 112, 118
   formal, 111, 112, 113, 118
   in East European transition countries, 111, 116–17
   informal, 111, 112, 113, 117, 118
   interaction of, 112–13, 114–17, 118–19
   private, 99, 108
   private/informal in Russia, 6, 83
   see also legal enforcement; extra-legal enforcement; third-party enforcement; reputation
contracting environment, 56–8, 63, 68
   see also courts; reform; social and business networks

contracts
   enforcing, 1
   formal, 111, 114
   importance of honesty and trustworthiness in, 98–9
   informal, 94
   infringement of, 91, 97–8, 102, 108
   legal enforcement of, 194, 204
   protective elements of formal, 99–100, 108
   relational, 56, 58, 61, 68
   role of government in enforcing, 5
   see also contract enforcement mechanisms
control, sense of, 36, 38, 43, 48
cooperation, 55, 194
   reciprocal cooperation, 56
corporate identity split, Russia, 76, 82, 88
corruption, 2, 5, 7, 17, 20, 31, 33–4, 71, 79, 93, 155, 168, 182
   and dishonesty, 193
   and trust in others, 36
   by elites, 37
   embedded, 200
   fighting, 47–8
   of Russian firms, 72–6, 87, 88
   petty, 37, 38, 46, 74
   self-sustaining system of, 201
   and trust in government, 35
   see also bribery; trust; Romania; Sweden
courts, 56, 62, 111, 114, 119, 167
   as reactive law-enforcers/makers, 8, 170–1, 172
   effect of on building trust, 62–5, 68
   effectiveness of, 57, 115–16, 117
   firms' perception of the functioning of across countries, 62–5
   impartiality and honesty of, 57
   perception of, 118, 120–1
   see also legal system
criminal protection by the Mafia, 148, 149, 151, 153, 161, 162

democracy
   administrative institutions of, 22–3
   representative, 22
   representative institutions of, 22

deterrence
  failure, 174
  in transitional economies, 172–4, 175, 185
dishonesty, 9, 33, 218, 221, 236
dispute resolution
  informal in Russia, 95
  by the state, 114, 152, 204
  use of force in, 96
distributive justice, 214, 217, 229
distrust, 4, 39, 208–9
  reciprocal, 108
  of Russian businesses in Western companies, 97
  state as a source of, 105–6
diversion of payment, 77, 81, 88
  see also financial scheming

EBRD transition indicators, 59–62, 116–17
economic exchanges/transactions, 193, 200
economic inequality, 34, 39, 47
economic reform, 55, 59, 68
economic systems, 218, 232, 236, 238
enrichment, 215, 218–19, 234, 236
  see also wealth
envy, 216, 217, 232–4, 235, 238
  definition of, 214
  generalized, 215, 233, 237
  the moral content of, 216
  particularized, 215, 233, 237
  social, 217, 221, 224
  special, 220, 231–2, 233
European Bank for Reconstruction and Development (EBRD), 5, 56
exchange relations, 194
  negotiated, 195, 205
  reciprocal, 205, 207
  restricted, 194
exchange schemes
  illegal, 148, 151
  role of trust in, 73
  types of informal, 73
  see also barter, blat, underground banking
exchange theory, 194, 202, 205
extra-legal norms and practices, Russia, 7, 8, 72, 81, 84
  the relation of law and in Russia, 143–5

extra-legal sanctions/enforcement, Russia, 84
  types of, 84, *table 4.1* on p. 85
financial markets
  in China, 169
  in Russia, 169
  in transition economies, 167–70, 185
  regulation of,
    in China, 8, 178–82, 186–7
    in developed market economies, 167, 186
    in Russia, 7, 175–8, 186–7
financial schemes, 75, 76–82, 88
  dealing with internal and external finances, 77
  decoding, 149–52
  false reporting, 76, 161
  as substitute for poorly operating state and market institutions, 72
  types of in Russia, 76, 77–8, 160–2
  undermining formal institutions and hindering reform, 161–2
  see also underground financing; corporate identity split; front companies; asset stripping; capital flight; intermediary firms
firms, 5
  grassroots practices of Russian, 72, 73, 88
  trust between, 6, 56
front companies, 133
  types of, 76
  see also financial schemes; monkey firms

gift-giving, 38, 46
Godfather, The, 17–20
gradualism vs. shock therapy, 1–2

hawala, 74
historical determinism, 26–7
honesty, 28, 34–6, 48
  see also dishonesty

information
  access to realible, 8
  asymmetric, 6, 150, 163
  biased, 175
  cost of, 149
  financial, 174, 176
  firm-specific, 169, 172, 174, 176, 178, 183

Subject Index

imperfect, 6
incomplete, 175
insider, 186
misrepresentation of, 171
reliable, 149, 168–9, 174, 185
reputational, 201
institutions, state, 1
   administrative, 22
   creating credible and efficient for the market to operate, 2–5
   dysfunctional, 2, 4, 5, 27
   legal, 6
   private, 6
   representative, 22
intermediaries, 77, 81–2, 83, 168, 176, 182, 209
International Monetary Fund (IMF), 4

judgments of success and wealth, 219–25
justice, 215, 217
   procedural, 21

kompromat, 85, 86, 87

law
   manipulation of in Russia, 83–4, 86
   the relation of extra-legal reality and in Russia, 143–5
   incomplete, 167–8, 170–2, 173, 185
   case, 168, 170, 172
law enforcement
   by courts, 167, 170, 173, 175, 180
   governance mechanisms beyond, 183–5, 185
   under incomplete law, 170–2
   by regulatory agents, 167, 171, 174, 175
law-making and law-enforcement powers (LMLEP), 167, 170
   allocation of, 171, 185
legal system, 19, 31, 58, 63, 111, 163
   distrust of, 20
   fairness of, 36
   imperfect, 117, 122
   inefficiency of in Hungary, 159
   reform of, 57, 62–3, 68, 122
   trust in, 32, 35, 40, 42, 45
   see also courts
legislatures as proactive law makers, 170, 171

Mafia
   Hong Kong Triads, 149
   Italian–American, 150
   lack of trust within, 149, 150
   Russian Mafia, 148, 152–3
   Sicilian, 149
   see also Solntsevo
Mafia transplantation, 148–50, 151, 162
   factors facilitating, 152–3, 162–3
   in Hungary, 7, 158, 160–62
   in Italy, 7, 154–7
   role of social capital in, 151
   supply of Mafiosi, 148, 151, 154–5, 157–8
   see also Solntsevo
market economy, 213, 215, 220, 224, 236–7
   confidence or lack of confidence in, 228, 230, 236
   legitimation of, 215, 224, 229, 232–3, 236–7, 455
   rejection or suspicion of, 224, 231, 236, 238
   unprotected by state, 148, 149, 152–3, 162
   see also, transition to market economy
meritocracy, 9, 217, 219–21, 224–5, 229–33, 237
minority shareholders' rights, Russia
   legal defense of, 127, 129, 136–40
   Law on Joint Stock Companies, 127, 136
mistrust, 6, 14
money laundering, 74, 148, 155, 159
   for election purposes, 83
monkey firms, 137, 80, 81
   offshore, 144–5
moral behavior, 33, 37, 45

networks
   "to beat the system", 74
   as "administrative resource", 134–5
   business in Russia, 101–2, 103, 108
   corrupt, 21, 200
   criminal, 75
   effect of on building trust, 63–8
   exchange, 193, 195
   illegitimate activities, 74
   informal under communsim, 38, 39
   information, 114–17, 120, 122
   personal, 74, 75, 102, 109, 126, 219

networks—*continued*
    social and business, 15, 56, 57, 63–9, 199, 204
    transition from closed to open, 206–10
    trust-based in transitional economies, 202

offshore companies, 137, 148
oligarchs, 141
opportunism, 196, 204
opportunity costs, 198
optimism, 36, 38, 43–5, 48
organized crime, 7, 151
    see also Mafia; Mafia transplantation

prepayment, 57, 63, 65, 68
    as a measure of trust at the country level, 58–62, 68
    requirements, Russia, 96, 100
private protection agencies, Russia, 86–8, 96, 141–3
privatization, 1, 215, 236
    in China, 178
    in Hungary, 158
    see also Russia
property rights, 1, 35, 39, 163
    disputes, Russia, 127
    inefficient legal protection of in Russia, 152
    securing, 7
public officials, 5, 20, 36, 37, 45, 68
    in Russia, 94, 106, 107, 109
public trust, *see* social trust

regional authorities, Russia, 128
    role of in enterprise takeovers, 128
regulatory agents
    as proactive law enforcers, 8, 167, 171
    as specialized proactive law makers, 171
regulatory failure, 168, 172, 175, 185
rent seeking, 145, 171
reputation
    as enforcement mechanism, 56, 68, 111, 112, 119
    role of in business relations, 55, 56, 97, 101, 103
    reputation systems, 193, 203, 204, 208
    in Vietnam, 204–5, 209
    see also contract enforcement mechanisms, informal

Romania, 5
    corruption, trust and faith in government, 43–6
    perception of trust and corruption, 33–4, 37, 39, 40
rules
    formal, 104, 108
    informalizing formal, 93–4, 108
Russia, 6, 7
    1998 financial crisis, 71, 105, 133, 141, 177
    loans-for-shares auctions, 140
    as a low-trust business environment, 108
    enforcing court decisions, 134
    Federal Commission for Securities Market Regulation (FCSM), 176–7, 186
    inefficiency of court system, 88
    informal/shadow economy, 72, 88, *n. 3* on p. 89
    insiders and outsiders in privatization, 140–1
    Investor Protection Law, 177
    nontransparency of business in, 94
    phases of privatization, 140–1
    reforms in, 72
    role of courts in enterprise takeovers, 128, 136–40
    Securities Law, 176, 177
    tax evasion, 73, 75, 79, 82, 88
    The Costs of Legislation project, 92, 93
    Transaction Costs in Russian Business project, 92–3, 98
    voucher privatization, 140
    see also financial scheming

Scandinavian countries, 5, 13, 17
social capital, 14, 22, 55, 68, 101, 213, 214, 222
    and the Mafia, 148
    antisocial capital, 14
    dark side to, 15
    in Hungary, 157
    in Italy, 155
    in the United States, 26–7
social justice, 33, 229
social norms, 126
social position, 228, 231, 235
sociopsychological factors, 221, 236, 238
Solntsevo, 148, 153–4

Subject Index

state capacity, 127
  reassertion of, 127, 143
  selective use of, 128, 129, 134, 135, 137
state failure, 163, 200
success, 46, 215, 220
  attributions of success, 216, 237
  blindness to, 9, 216, 219, 223, 225
  external, 217, 219, 221–5
  ideological direction of, 217
  internal, 219, 220, 221–5
  and wealth, 216, 217, 221–5, 237
  see also suspicion
suspicion, 9, 213, 237
  residual, 217
  of the rich/wealth and success, 214, 224, 226
Sweden, 5, 22, 26, 47
  corruption, trust and faith in government, 43–6
  perceptions of trust and corruption in, 32–3, 40

takeovers, hostile/agressive, Russia, 7, 95, 127, 141
  actors in, 130, 134
  armed, 139, 142
  logic of, 128–31
  political aspects of, 128
  scheme 1: bankruptcy, 131–6
  scheme 2: conflict between shareholders, 136–40
third party enforcement, 55, 56, 57, 58, 61, 193
  lack of in Russia, 94–6, 99, 108
  through networks, 56, 58
trade credit, 58, 68, 96, 122–3
  as a measure of trust at the firm level, 61–2, 118
transaction costs, 1, 55, 96
  of semi-legal and illegal schemes, 93
transition to market economy, 1, 9, 213, 215, 220, 226, 234, 236
  in Hungary, 158–60
  in Russia, 152
  losers in, 216, 237
  the role of confidence in, 214
  winners in, 217, 237

Transparency International (TI) corruption perceptions index, 34, 39, 40–3
transparency
  lack of, 7, 21, 71, 107
trust, 18, 28, 31, 55, 57, 68, 148, 195
  affect-based, 96–7, 102, 108, 205
  and corruption across nations, 40–3
  and honesty, 34–6, 48
  corruption, and perceptions of government, 36–8
  corruption, and transition, 38–40
  effect of courts on building, 62–5
  generalized (moralistic) trust, 8, 19, 32, 34–5, 43, 46, 62, 133, 206, 207
  in government, 15, 33, 37, 46
  in institutions (one-sided trust), 91–2, 94–6, 105, 106, 108, 207
  interpersonal, 16, 24, 36, 63, 151, 155
  lack of in government institutions, 7
  moral, 216
  particularized, 8, 19, 207, 233
  reciprocal, 91–2, 96–7, 103, 105, 106, 108, 109, 204, 207
  reputation-based, 108, 205
  social, 3–5, 21–7
  strategic, 34, 216
  the state as a source of, 105–6
  under communism, 36, 38
  use of in a high-risk environment, 72–6, 87
  see also Romania; social trust; social capital; Sweden
trustworthiness, 195, 204
  of institutions, 92
  of individuals, 92
  of business partners, 96, 97

uncertainty, 102, 108, 168
  and risk, 193–4, 200, 207
  and trust-based networks in Russia, 202–3, 204
  behavior under risk, 8
  closed networks of trust under, 196, 200
  lack of formal enforcement producing, 91, 93
underground financing, 76–82, 88
  triangular model of, 74, 77
  see also financial scheming
United Nations Developement Program (UNDP), 4, 21, 27

veksel (bill of exchange), 82–3, 150
violence, 84, 86, 149, 152
    mafia-related in Hungary, 160
    use of in business, Russia, 142
voluntary associations, 5, 14–16, 28

wealth, 214, 220
    attributions of wealth
        external, 217, 221–8, 236
        internal, 221–8, 235
    success and, 216, 217, 221–5, 237
    see also attributions of wealth;
        suspicion
welfare/public service
    effect on social trust, 24–5, 26
    needs-testing, 23–5
World Bank, 4, 56, 71
    governance indicators, 59–60
World Values Surveys (WVS), 25, 37, 39,
    40–3, 43–6, 57, 63, 155, 157